Global Perspectives on Global History

In recent years, historians across the world have become increasingly interested in transnational and global approaches to the past. However, the debates surrounding this new border-crossing movement have remained limited in scope as theoretical exchanges on the tasks, responsibilities, and potentials of global history have been largely confined to national or regional academic communities. In this groundbreaking book, Dominic Sachsenmaier sets out to redress this imbalance by offering a series of new perspectives on the global and local flows, sociologies of knowledge, and hierarchies that are an intrinsic part of historical practice. Taking the United States, Germany, and China as his main case studies, he reflects upon the character of different approaches to global history as well as their social, political, and cultural contexts. He argues that this new global trend in historiography needs to be supported by a corresponding increase in transnational dialogue, cooperation, and exchange.

DOMINIC SACHSENMAIER is Assistant Professor of Trans-Cultural and Chinese History at Duke University.

Global Perspectives on Global History

Theories and Approaches in a Connected World

Dominic Sachsenmaier

Duke University

CAMBRIDGE
UNIVERSITY PRESS

CAMBRIDGE
UNIVERSITY PRESS

University Printing House, Cambridge CB2 8BS, United Kingdom

Published in the United States of America by Cambridge University Press, New York

Cambridge University Press is part of the University of Cambridge.

It furthers the University's mission by disseminating knowledge in the pursuit of education, learning and research at the highest international levels of excellence.

www.cambridge.org
Information on this title: www.cambridge.org/9780521173124

© Dominic Sachsenmaier 2011

First published 2011

A catalogue record for this publication is available from the British Library

Library of Congress Cataloguing in Publication data

Sachsenmaier, Dominic.
  Global perspectives on global history : theories and approaches in a connected world / Dominic Sachsenmaier.
     p. cm.
  Includes bibliographical references.
  ISBN 978-1-107-00182-4 (Hardback) – ISBN 978-0-521-17312-4
  (Paperback)   1. World history.   2. Civilization.   3. Globalization.   I. Title.
  D23.S24 2011
  901–dc22

                                                                          2011002694

ISBN 978-1-107-00182-4 Hardback
ISBN 978-0-521-17312-4 Paperback

Contents

Acknowledgments

A book of this kind could not have been written without many conference travels and research stays in different parts of the world, most notably in North America, Europe, and East Asia. Without a comparatively high degree of mobility it would have been hardly possible for me to start reflecting on the status quo of global and transnational historical research in different parts of the world as well as, more generally, on the global landscapes of historical scholarship. Over a period of about five years, my employers, the University of California, Santa Barbara, and subsequently Duke University, were both generous in granting me ample time as well as resources to pursue my studies, often far away from my professional bases. In addition, extramural funding from various institutions allowed me to spend extended periods in different countries, mainly to consult library materials and interview scholars from a wide range of fields. Among the institutions sponsoring single segments of my own research were the University of California's Pacific Rim Program, Humboldt Foundation in Germany, the Academy of Korean Studies Grant funded by the Korean Government (AKS-2010-DZZ-3103), and the German National Research Foundation. In addition, I had both the pleasure and honor to enjoy summer fellowships at the Berlin Social Science Research Center, the Erasmus Mundus Global Studies Program (Leipzig), and the Institute of Advanced Study in Constance/Germany, where I completed the first full version of my manuscript.

Without all this support I would not have been able to gain the professional experience base that I found necessary to tackle a project of this scope. Perhaps more importantly, I would not have had the tranquility required to complete this book in a timely manner. Moreover, at various institutions I enjoyed the help of research assistants who supported me in chores ranging from internet-based research to bibliographic work. This allowed me to focus more on my own research and eventually on conceptualizing and writing this text. While the number of assistants would be too large to be listed, I want to particularly thank my youngest brother, Jan Sachsenmaier, who after his high school classes took much time to edit my footnotes and the bibliography.

Of great significance have been the many stimulating debates and conversations that I was able to lead with scholars around the world. At conferences, workshops as well as in private dialogues I got a chance to present my ideas to such a large number of scholars that trying to list them would be a futile task. Combined, however, all these encounters greatly helped me to critically reconsider some of my assumptions, pay attention to new elements, and adjust my overall methodological framework. A smaller number of scholars actually read parts of my manuscript and provided invaluable feedback on single chapters. Among those are, in the United States, Sven Beckert (Harvard), William Reddy (Duke), Edward Wang (Rowan University and Beijing University), and my grandpaternal friend Bruce Mazlish (MIT). In Germany, Sebastian Conrad (Free University Berlin), Jürgen Osterhammel (Constance), Matthias Middell (Leipzig) as well as Andreas Eckert (Humboldt University Berlin) commented on parts of my text or provided important suggestions, particularly for the third chapter of this book. The same is true for Rainer Hoffmann (Freiburg) with whom I conceptualized parts of this work during a summer hike. In East Asia, it was particularly Jin Yan and Jin Guangyao (Fudan University), Hsiung Ping-Chen and Moo Pu-chou (Chinese University of Hong Kong) as well as Lim Jie-Hyun (Hanyang University/Seoul) with whom I was engaged in particularly close conversations revolving around different themes covered in this book. Needless to say, while this book greatly benefited from the great support of scholars from different parts of the world, I take full responsibility for any potential shortcomings, mistakes, or inaccuracies.

For a long period, my father, Dr. Michael Sachsenmaier, was a lively and engaging dialogue partner on my journey towards the completion of this book. Unfortunately he passed away in the summer of 2009, unexpectedly and far too young, before witnessing its publication. I dedicate it to his memory, with much love and gratitude.

Introduction: Neglected diversities

Landscapes of a field

In recent years, most branches of historiography have witnessed a sharp increase in research operating with border-crossing perspectives. Hitherto unusual spatial concepts, be they transnational, transregional, or transcontinental in nature, have become more clearly visible in very different subfields of historiography, ranging from the complex landscapes of "cultural history" to the equally multifaceted environments of "economic history." Certainly, not all these border-crossing perspectives are "new" in the sense that they were completely unthought-of a generation or more ago. But there has been a decisive change: what were once a few isolated trickles flowing through the landscapes of historiography have now grown into ever more visible currents. Microscopic and macroscopic research interests, which before played only a marginal role in historical scholarship, have now moved closer to the field's centers of attention.

Like many intellectual developments, the growing significance of transnational and global historical approaches did not amount to a radical conceptual break with earlier approaches. As the following chapters will show, it was in incremental steps that research of this kind started becoming further established through the emergence of new research programs, professorships, associations, book series, and conferences dedicated to related themes. From such bases, it has further influenced many areas of research within the study of history, albeit with neither the ambition nor the possibility of monopolizing them. Since the growing presence of border-crossing perspectives occurred in a protracted process, one may find the frequently evoked imagery of academic "turns"[1] slightly inadequate since it suggests a clear, pronounced change

---

[1] Among the many prominent examples are the debates about the cultural turn, the topological turn, and the spatial turn. An overview is provided by Döring and Thielmann (2008).

of direction. It might be more fitting to use the term "trend," which implies the idea of a more gradually changing climate of research interests and academic predilections.[2]

The latter should not suggest that the search for alternative conceptions of space has occurred without clearly visible signs and symbolic indications. In fact, one of them has been the broadening significance of the term "global history," which has spread across many different world regions and languages. In Chinese, for instance, the expression *quanqiu lishi* or *quanqiu shi* has become more common, and the same has been the case with the Japanese *gurobaru reikishi*, or the German *Globalgeschichte*.[3] Yet while field designations, names, and labels play an important role in the spread of an intellectual trend, they should not be confused with these academic transformations as such. As my explorations of very different realms of historical scholarship will reveal, the research commonly subsumed under "global history" is so diverse that it cannot possibly be pinned down through exact definitions and precise categorizations. It is also not feasible to properly separate "global history" from several other terminological options such as "world history" or "transnational history." For this reason, I will mainly use terms such as "global history" as shorthand for many types of research reaching beyond those conceptions of space that have long dominated many, academic and other, ways of conceptualizing the past.

The following chapters, some of which are case studies of global history in single societies, do not altogether ignore many of the great challenges in mapping out translocal historical scholarship now as well as during earlier periods. Yet the primary goal of this book is not to provide a comprehensive bird's eyes view of border-crossing and global historical research in its present state. Rather, my work seeks to make a theoretical intervention based upon the idea that an important facet of global history's intrinsically diverse nature lies in the fact that this trend is currently experiencing surging levels of interest in many parts of the world. At the same time as in the West, an increasing number of scholars in Asia, Africa, Latin America, and elsewhere have become convinced that much of human history is not best understood by containing our investigations within particular national or regional visions. Moreover, in many academic communities, new forms of institutionalization and

[2] See, for example, Veit-Brause (1990).
[3] A special case is the French term "histoire globale," which originally mainly connoted all-encompassing approches to a given theme in history. Yet more recently, the term also started to be used in the sense of "global history." For example: Beaujard, Berger and Norel (2009).

interdisciplinary cooperation have started supporting historical research cutting across national and other boundaries. This wider proliferation of global and transnational historical research, I believe, warrants further reflection, particularly in terms of its conceptual implications and practical consequences.

In that sense, this book is centered on the idea that the debates about the possibilities and dangers of global history cannot just be conceptual in a narrow, methodological sense. They also need to address factors such as the international academic settings underlying the field, for these doubtlessly influence the ideas of historians. As scholars experimenting with hitherto unusual spatial paradigms, historians involved in the global history trend need to become critically aware of the mental, institutional, local, and global spaces within which they operate. Actually, for theories of global history it is important to ask the same sets of questions that historians apply to the study of academic movements and professional networks of the past. If global historians fail to consider their own sociologies of knowledge, as well as the multifarious social, political, and cultural contexts framing their activities, the conceptual debates in the field will only be a pale reflection of what they potentially could be. In other words, the skills of global historians need to include an exceptionally high degree of professional self-reflexivity. Obviously, the theoretical discussions surrounding historical research on human interactions, shared spaces, and encounter zones can only continue proliferating if the relationship between history and historiography becomes more complex.

Thus far, there have been excellent overviews of translocal and world historical scholarship, its path dependencies, and state of the art, but the vast majority of such accounts have primarily focused on academic work in single languages.[4] Some other publications, most notably edited volumes, have provided international perspectives on the field but in most cases they relegate the analysis of different, usually nationally specific world historical traditions to separate chapters.[5] Given these methodological frameworks, the transnational flows, dynamics, and hierarchies that characterize today's global historical scholarship have only been given scant attention. Perhaps surprisingly, also many important theoretical contributions to global and world history have not made explicit efforts to traverse many national or

[4] For example, for the Anglo-American world: Manning (2003); and Bentley (1996b).
[5] Providing essays on the state of the art in several societies: Manning (2008b). About world history in (mostly) Western societies see Stuchtey and Fuchs (2003). See also Loth and Osterhammel (2000); and Middell (2002b).

linguistic boundaries in the body of scholarship they consider. Especially in Western academia, self-reflective walls continue to surround many conceptual exchanges on global history, with voices from other parts of the world often going unnoticed. This is particularly problematic since the reason for these awareness gaps is not a lack of available information about global historical research in other parts of the world. As a matter of fact, overviews of global and world historical research in various countries have been published in English and some other Western languages. But so far there have been only few debates on how contemporary approaches to global history could enrich scholarship in the West. Nor have most Western discussions of global history addressed the question of how research in this area could contribute to an international research environment that needs to become more communicative, cooperative, and dialogical in nature. Polemically speaking, much of global history in Europe and North America remains more characterized by a rising interest in scholarship *about* the world rather than scholarship *in* the world.

Such widespread neglect of recent scholarship produced elsewhere would be at least more explicable if the global trend in historical scholarship had mainly originated in the West. Yet while our global academic system remains characterized by very problematic hierarchies, it would be far too simplistic to treat the Anglo-American academic world or any other part of "the West" as the main originator of the current wave of transnational scholarship. At a closer look it turns out that the main forces behind the growing weight of translocal historical thinking did not emanate from a clearly recognizable epicenter. Instead, the vibrant topographies of the global historical trend need to be envisioned as a complicated interaction between local and global factors. Moreover, there are good reasons to assume that, despite all international entanglements, border-crossing research is not undergoing a process of worldwide convergence. Very specific themes, methodologies, and public issues continue to characterize global and transnational history in various societies. For instance, even the most global of all terms, "globalization," carries very different spectrums of meanings in various languages, and the same is true for other concepts such as "modernity" or "history." Depending on the specific local setting, also the dominant antitheses to "global history" can vary: while in some cases it is mainly the nation, in others it is the region, or some notion of cultural or ethnic belonging.

Paying due attention to local peculiarities in the project of global history, however, requires some caution not to exoticize scholarship in different parts of the world. In today's intellectual and academic landscapes, the global and the local are enmeshed with each other in a wide variety of ways. Historical research at today's academic institutions is to a large degree the result of global transformations, many of which were tied to the worldwide emergence of the nation-state. In addition, since the very beginnings of modern historiography, academic concepts and schools of thought have crossed political, linguistic, and other boundaries. For example, new trends such as the rise of social history or, later, the cultural turn could be felt in many world regions. In many scholarly communities, historiography became quite fragmented in terms of its research approaches, and transnational connections have been an important facet of many methodological schools. Nevertheless, historiography never evolved into an academic discipline that would – analogous to the natural sciences – come to work with a largely identical spectrum of methodological schools all over the globe. Among other forces, also national or regional contingencies keep seasoning the disciplinary fabrics of historiography. This is, for example, the case with specific institutional settings, the availability of funding, political influences, modes of public memory, and the overall intellectual climate. It is thus highly likely that local factors will continue to influence the spectrum of global historical visions even if methodological diversification and international academic connections become more intense.

Considering the complex nature of modern research landscapes makes it almost impossible to reflect upon the trajectories of global historical scholarship without paying due, critical attention to the cultures and structures of modern academic historiography. In that sense, thinking through the current global historical trend leads back *ad fontes* to some very foundational questions surrounding the basic structures and guiding principles of historiography. A move into such directions may seem somewhat unusual – in many countries, among them the United States, fervor for debating the very basic premises of the field seems to have disappeared for decades. In 2002, this situation prompted Lynn Hunt, then president of the American Historical Association, to ask "where have all the theories gone?"[6]

Reflecting upon the nature of the global historical trend in different parts of the world may provide ample opportunities to revisit such crucial themes such as international hierarchies of knowledge or the public roles of historiography. Given the significant intellectual challenges surrounding such problems, it is not only desirable but also necessary to build bridges between the debates on global history and other fields of intellectual activity. This is particularly the case when we

---

[6] Hunt (2002).

reflect upon the implications of the global historical trend for scholarship in different parts of the world and potential modes of cooperation between them. Here the project of global history can gain a wealth of new productive questions from dialogues with various critical positions. For example, it might be fruitful to more systematically take into account at least some aspects of theoretical interventions regarding the relationship between Western-centrism and the cultures of historiography.[7] Similar things could be said about academic fields surrounding more public themes such as the idea of a global civil society, which are usually not centered in history departments.[8]

Needless to say, the pluralistic character of global history and the growing quest for multiperspectivity will hardly allow for a resurgence of monopolizing theories and grand frameworks of explanation, which are supposed to fit all local cases equally and unequivocally. A presumptuous claim of this kind would run directly counter to the program of thinking about global history in a plural world. Instead of developing models that are supposed to be applicable all over the world, it is necessary to reflect upon the challenges and opportunities inherent in the cross-regionally entangled landscapes of global history. This may help to advance dialogues and transnational modes of cooperation in a research field which more than any other branch of historiography is based on the notion of shared spaces.

In other words, while new all-encompassing theories are not suitable for the quest to combine global awareness with local sensitivity, it might be the right time to bring back to the debating table some weighty problems surrounding the nature of historiography as a sociological phenomenon and epistemological endeavor. In such a manner, this book does not search for a new universality but rather for some form of commonality in a very modest sense: it intends to contribute to historical scholarship, finding more common ground where different viewpoints can be negotiated. More concretely, it seeks not only to inject some new perspectives into the theoretical debates on global history as an academic trend, it also strives to help to render the very basic sociologies, institutional structures, disciplinary value systems, and objectives of historiography into the subjects of more sustained discussions. This will surely need to be an aspect of reflecting upon global history in a changing world – a world whose true complexities are often hidden behind the buzzword of "globalization."

---

[7] Theoretical interventions that are particularly relevant for reflections on global history are, for example, Mignolo (2000); and Chakrabarty (2000).
[8] For example, Kaldor (2003); Iriye (2002); and Habermas (2000).

Global perspectives on global history

A book that is both globally interested and locally sensitive cannot possibly set up an Archimedic point around which its entire narrative can be moved. If one takes the claim for local contingency seriously, it is impossible to solely focus on alleged worldwide commonalities that may characterize a growing trend in historiography. At the same time, it would be impracticable to discuss only local theaters of global historical research since this would inevitably overlook the multifarious forms of transnational interconnections and exchanges in the field. It is thus necessary for this book to alternate perspectives between global overviews and local case studies. Yet such a dual approach is not merely a set of methodological crutches but instead reflects the nature of global history as a transnational research environment. Like many academic disciplines in today's world, its contours are constantly evolving along the contact lines of local and translocal dynamics. Yet similarly to Werner Heisenberg's uncertainty principle about the dual nature of position and momentum in a given particle, it will not be possible to conceptualize both the local states and the global waves of an academic field at the same time. For the sake of combining global outlooks with decentered viewpoints, it is therefore methodologically advantageous to adopt rather separate approaches to each aspect.

Epistemological challenges of this kind require *Global Perspectives on Global History* to be composed along two axes. While the first chapter and the epilogue explore general questions and transnational dynamics related to global history, Chapters 2, 3, and 4 focus on single languages and academic communities. Both groups of chapters pursue different lines of inquiry as well as distinct narrative strategies. The globally oriented parts of the book primarily operate from an "outside in"[9] viewpoint. The first chapter mainly illuminates the interplay between global environments, transnational dynamics, and national parameters that need to be understood as frameworks of the global historical trend. Informed by the case studies, the Epilogue returns to the primarily global perspectives of the first chapter. It does so by ruminating on potential intellectual directions and public interventions of future global historical scholarship, particularly if the field comes to be more characterized by transnational academic structures, networks, and interactions. Taking a different approach, the other parts of the book investigate global and transnational history in the United States,

---

[9] My thanks go to Prasenjit Duara for providing me with this metaphor, which he uses in Duara (2009), p. 1.

Germany, and mainland China[10] chiefly from "inside out," which means that they primarily focus on local dynamics in these societies. In addition to developments in academic theory and practice, I also consider relevant factors ranging from social transformations to changing political circumstances. Moreover, I pay attention to important transnational dynamics such as the effects of intellectual migration on US academia or the repercussions of European integration on German scholarship.

Due to the complexity of today's transnational landscapes of scholarship, there were several options for drawing the boundaries of my case studies. It certainly would have been possible to focus on global and transnational trends published in single languages. For example, Anglophone, Francophone, and Sinophone publications are being produced across a wide variety of political boundaries, academic communities, and economic systems. Yet even in the relatively confined public spheres of academia, linguistic realms form such intricate patterns that the task of mapping them out properly would necessitate book-length studies for each case, particularly if one were to pay due attention to their connections, geographical variations, and hierarchies of knowledge. For example, within the English-speaking world there are huge disparities between the conditions and backgrounds of academic production in North America, Europe, India, sub-Saharan Africa, the Caribbean, and Australia. Similar observations could be made about a range of other languages, including some such as French, Spanish, and Portuguese, which like English spread globally under the impact of colonialism. Yet even in the languages central to my second and third case study, Chinese and German, publications are also being produced across a variety of political contexts, academic systems, and topographies of historical memory.[11]

[10] The term "mainland China" (Chinese *zhongguo dalu*) commonly refers to the People's Republic of China, excluding Hong Kong and Macao due to continued differences in political systems and socioeconomic conditions. While in Taiwan and some other regions the term long had rather clear political connotations, the expression has now come to be used across different political and ideological camps. In the following I will mainly use "China" for the mainland and "Greater China" as a marker that includes Hong Kong, Macao, and Taiwan. In some other usages, "Greater China" also refers to overseas Chinese communities in Southeast Asia and other parts of the world.

[11] For a discussion of different global historical approaches in Mainland China, Hong Kong, and Taiwan see Q. Wang (2010a). Compared to these differences in the Chinese-speaking world (which also includes centers of higher learning in Singapore), the differences between the German-speaking countries are rather small.

It is thus not only for reasons of narrative feasibility that, in my locally oriented chapters, I decided to primarily focus on three national academic systems. As these parts of the book show, national parameters continue to be of high importance for historical scholarship, and they are so through many factors ranging from specific funding systems to dominant public discourses. At the same time, it is certainly not the case that research landscapes, publication patterns, and the spread of methodological schools can be clearly divided along national lines. In my case studies, I seek to do justice to an academic environment in which national systems are factors but not firm units in international research. While I mainly focus on structural transformations in single national systems, I do not brush over flows or exchanges of ideas within and across single languages. For example, I certainly do not disregard publications that came to be influential in the United States, Germany, and China even though they have been produced elsewhere.

My attention to interconnections, exchanges, and other dynamics across different academic systems is not the only way in which my methodology departs from the analytical scaffold of a structural comparison. While I investigate the backgrounds and trajectories of global historical scholarship in all three cases, I do not apply exactly the same timelines, categories and questions to each of them. Doing so would mean knitting a systematic straitjacket, depriving my study of the necessary space to remain sensitive to the multifaceted local contingencies and global entanglements, which frame transnational historiography in different parts of the world. Rather, my approach remains largely narrative in character, allowing me to treat global historical scholarship in China, Germany, and the United States as nodes in more complex international nexuses.

To be more precise, Chapters 2 to 4 are not solely meant to identify commonalities and differences across the three case studies, for their respective viewpoints are also meant to complement each other. This is particularly the case since none of the locally oriented chapters aims to provide an exhaustive overview of all world historical traditions as well as recent global and transnational historical research. Rather, each chapter accentuates particular aspects and developments of global and transnational history as a wider trend. These are important for the respective local context but at the same time exemplify problem zones that can also be observed in other academic systems. For example, only the first case study, which focuses on the United States, goes into considerable detail when discussing the problem of how to define the expression "global history," particularly vis-à-vis a wide range of alternative terminological options. The following chapters cover this topic more briefly but put their emphasis on other facets of the global historical trend such as – in the Chinese case – theories of modernity that can hardly be ignored when assessing current developments in global and transnational historical research.

Hence, while the main framework of this book cannot possibly be held together by identical levels of inquiry, the following chapters feed into each other in the sense that they make different characteristics of the same field visible and accessible. In this context, it is important to point out that neither the outlooks of the case studies nor the macroscopic viewpoints taken in the other sections of this book can adequately reflect the entanglements between global and local elements. In fact, none of them should be conceptualized as prior or superordinate to the other. Combined and yet rather separate, however, global perspectives and local viewpoints allow us to navigate the complexities of historical scholarship without getting stranded on either side.

Since this book seeks to make a theoretical intervention, it grants more weight to recent developments within historiography and related fields. While I do not disregard some historical origins and long-term trajectories that are important to understanding global history in its current state, the main emphasis rests on the present. Moreover, within the contemporary body of scholarship, I prioritize the historiography of the nineteenth and twentieth centuries and discuss research on earlier periods only to a lesser extent. I do so because in the study of modern history, the contrast between the national orientations of historiography and the ever-intensifying global interconnections of the same age is particularly stark. Often faced with an uncongenial mainstream, here the rise of global and transnational approaches typically assumes its most revisionist character. Another reason for concentrating on the historiography of the more recent past lies in the archaeologies of the future, the necessary process of introspection that global history will need to experience. The study of global historical topics ranging from the formation of modern academic systems to transnational public spheres can help provide important insights for changes the field may have to face in the future. In that manner, the subjects and objects of global historical study can enter an unusually direct relationship of exchanges.

1 Movements and patterns: environments of global history

The question of traditions

The idea that in the future, global history may experience more sustained dialogues between scholars from different world regions leads to deeper theoretical challenges than may be apparent at first sight. Most importantly, there is the question of how to conceptualize "local" viewpoints in today's complex intellectual and academic landscapes. As I already argued in the introduction, plural approaches to global history cannot be simply based on celebrations of "otherness" or lip service to "authenticity." While searching for greater levels of inclusivity, it is also necessary to consider the global condition of the field with all its networks, flows, and inequalities. After all, all over the world academic historiography has been at least partly the product of international power plays, worldwide transformations, and modern transfers.[1] These translocal entanglements of modern[2] historiography become particularly visible when we look at the field through global lenses and consider the epistemological as well as sociological changes that accompanied its spread to different parts of the world. Nevertheless, the globalization of university-based historiography did not lead to a standardization of scholarship all over the world.

Obviously, the debates on plural approaches to global history can hardly swerve around the question whether or in what regard the

---

[1] A good discussion of this topic is provided by Wallerstein (1996). For the American context see Appleby, Hunt, and Jacob (1995), part 1.

[2] The term "modern" is, of course, highly contested and can hardly be used without further clarification. I choose to apply this term to much of nineteenth- and twentieth-century historiography since the discipline at universities came to be largely characterized by significant breaks from earlier ways of transmitting knowledge about the past. Moreover, the establishment of historiography during the past two centuries was often tied to discourses of political and social modernity. Heading in this direction for example is Iggers (2002). On the plural condition of modernity see Sachsenmaier, Riedel and Eisenstadt (2002).

enunciation of locally specific viewpoints is relatable to the existence of alternative historiographical cultures. The importance of this problem goes far beyond the debates over questions such as whether global history should be primarily seen as a "new" or an "old" academic endeavour.[3] Rather, some important normative and epistemological issues are at stake. For example, if today's border-crossing scholarship could be traced back to culturally specific historiographical conventions of *longue durée*, one would have fewer reasons to be alarmed by world history imposing standards of the West onto the rest.[4] In such a case, global historical thought would be characterized by a diversity of stand-points, each of which would be rooted in a widely independent scholarly tradition and, by implication, provide alternative viewpoints to Western narratives. However, the question of multiperspectivity looks entirely different if we situate the global trend in historiography primarily within the modern academic world, a world that has long been at least partly characterized by Western dominance and concurrent entanglements of historical thought and practice.

In a general sense, it is certainly possible to speak of long "traditions" of global or world historical thought and refer to such renowned figures as Herodotus or Ibn Khaldun as forefathers of the field.[5] In many cultures and world regions there were earlier forms of world historical scholarship, which in some cases reach even back almost to the begin-nings of history writing.[6] However, when referring to "traditions" in a more concrete sense, that is, as trajectories reaching from the past into the present, the problem becomes far more complex. The crux of the matter lies in the mere fact that acknowledging the antecedents of modern border-crossing historiography does not answer questions about conceptual, social, or even institutional continuities. For example, in the Chinese case it would certainly be very problematic to hurriedly construct the idea of a rather timeless scholarly culture that would be characterized by distinct methodological features lasting from the days of Sima Qian up until the present.[7] Blindly assuming such

---

[3] During the 1990s, many debates on globalization (including its historical antecedents) were largely framed around the categories "new" and "old." For more details see Guillén (2001).

[4] For a critical perspective see, for example, Dirlik (2002a); and Mignolo (2000).

[5] For instance, Patrick O'Brien states, "Global Histories have indeed been around since the time of Herodotus." P. O'Brien (2000). See also Hughes-Warrington (2005); Manning (2003), chapters 1 and 2; P. O'Brien (2006); and Crossley (2008).

[6] Generally on the topic: see, for example, Bright and Geyer (2005).

[7] Interpretations of this kind can be found rather frequently in some debates on comparative historiography. See, for example, C. Huang (2007). For a critical response see Q. Wang (2007b).

epistemological permanence from "classical" texts to today's global historical scholarship would, in fact, move us dangerously close to a cascade of problematic intellectual positions ranging from new versions of Orientalism to the belief in pristine national cultures.

Indeed, in almost all world regions university-based historiography is at least partly an outcome of epistemological discontinuities, outside influences, and shared transformations. As I will argue in further detail, these also had an impact on the conceptions of space underlying world historical scholarship in the widest sense. Prior to spread of history as a modern academic field, forms of border-crossing histories were typically written from a clear perspective of cultural, religious, or even ethical centricity, which means that they tended to be tied to distinct value claims. This situation changed decisively during the nineteenth and twentieth centuries, when either colonial rule or nation-building efforts had a profound impact on what elements were selected into the canon of academic historiography and many earlier forms of knowledge were rendered subaltern.[8] Particularly in many countries outside of the West, geopolitical circumstances and domestic transformations no longer allowed for historians to define the cultural self as the center of "world" historical inquiry.[9] This, however, should not make us assume that the dualism of centrity and marginality disappeared from the main currents of world historical thinking. In Dipesh Chakrabarty's words, now a "hyperreal Europe"[10] came to hold a strong position in many scholars' imaginations during and after the global spread of academic historiography. As a general tendency, during the nineteenth and twentieth centuries many scholars from different continents began to share similar mental maps and core assumptions about world historical centers and peripheries. During that time period, significant parts of historical scholarship may have become more globally aware but they did not become more cosmopolitan in the sense of allowing for the idea of multiple, different, and equal centers of enunciation.

A brief look at early forms of historiography reaching across civilizational boundaries will help us fill this rather rough sketch with some more detail and further accentuate the changing conceptions of space that became foundational to modern historiography in many different

---

[8] During that time, local traditions of writing history did not completely disappear, but at least within the confines of modern universities and other state-endorsed institutions their role usually became extremely limited.
[9] As the following sections will demonstrate, this development, which was usually tied to the establishment of modern research universities, did not occur synchronically around the globe but took place in rather complex processes and stages.
[10] Chakrabarty (2000).

parts of the world. This in turn will allow us to reflect upon the specific challenges, dangers, and opportunities that the current institutional and conceptual landscapes of historiography present for today's global historical trend. A well-known European example of early versions of transcultural history writing is the Greek historian Herodotus, who – along with Ephoros (d. 330 BCE), Polybios, and Diodorus – often figures prominently in recent histories of world historical writing.[11] In his account of the Greco-Persian War, Herodotus tried to depict different conditions and traditions from a superordinate perspective, yet at the same time his master narrative was structured around a clear division of the Greek polis as the harbor of freedom, and the Persian Empire as a stronghold of tyranny.[12] An arguably still more centered perspective was taken in the genre of Christian universal histories, which emerged during the later Roman Empire with scholars such as Eusebius (d. 340) or Orosius (d. 417) as leading protagonists. Here important histories of the known world such as the famous works by Otto von Freising[13] (d. 1158) or, centuries later, Jacques Bossuet (d. 1704) were ordered along Christian timelines, and biblical events such as the creation, the deluge, or the incarnation of Christ figured as the main beats in world historical rhythms.

Outside of Europe, world historical outlooks were also usually written from the belief in the normative authority of one's own cultural experience. For example, this was the case with the main works ascribable to the Chinese genre of "universal histories," which dates at least back to the Han dynasty (c. 206–220 BCE). Likewise, the renowned Arabic historian Ibn Al Athir (d. 1233) wrote his "Complete History" covering information about the outside world largely from an Islamic perspective, following a religious chronology.[14] Furthermore, Islamic accounts of the crusades or the Mongol conquests were – like their Christian counterparts – typically not written in the spirit of multiperspectivity.[15] The famed historical work of the Islamic traveler Ibn Khaldun (d. 1406), whose wide range of studies included comparative explorations and was unsurpassed in his time, described the Islamic world as unique and exemplary. Even though he emphasized the rise and fall of civilizations, Ibn Khaldun maintained that only Islam had a universal mission, and according to him one of its great assets was to unite the religious and the secular realms, whereas all other civilizations

---

[11] Manning (2003); and Christian (2005). On the position of these historians in European scholarship see, for example, Momigliano (1990).
[12] For more details see Hartog (1988).   [13] Otto, Bishop of Freysing (1966).
[14] See Hillenbrand (2000).   [15] See Taher (1997).

supposedly separated the two.[16] Similarly, important Ottoman schools that emerged during the expansion of the empire in the sixteenth and seventeenth centuries often included accounts of non-Muslim communities, but did not abandon narratives centered on the primacy of Islam.[17]

Of course, culturally centrist outlooks of world history during the pre-modern period were neither globally uniform nor did they remain completely unchallenged. For example, in the East Asian context Korean and Japanese scholarship often needed to negotiate tropes of cultural belonging and related normative claims with the idea of China's dominant position in the region. However, also here outlooks on the world which acknowledged other but equal cultural centers outside of East Asia were extremely rare. This is not to say that counter-currents of this kind did not exist in premodern Asia. Even in cases like imperial China, challenges to Sinocentric world visions could emerge, particularly during times of political crises.[18] At the same time, throughout Chinese history the main strands of world historical thought had not been written based on the assumption that a distant continent such as, later, "Europe" constituted a key reference culture – a reference culture, which defined many important categories when thinking about history.

Concomitant with the global spread of modern universities and profound changes in historiographical cultures, the belief in Europe as the sole cradle of modern scholarship came to be adopted in many parts of the world. This was certainly less so because European historiography was indeed more advanced or universalizable than other ways of conceptualizing the past. Rather, a complex nexus of global power constellations and rapid transformations led to the emergence of an international academic system that marginalized many local traditions of writing history and privileged "scientific" forms of historical scholarship.[19] The latter were seemingly emanating from long European traditions.[20] The word "seemingly" is important in this context because Western historiography underwent significant transformations at the same time as European academia began to heavily influence historical research elsewhere.[21] Also in Europe the establishment of modern

[16] See, for example, Cheddadi (2005).   [17] See, for example, Robinson (2003).
[18] For more details see Chapter 4.   [19] See Berger (2007b), p. 3.
[20] Excellent examples of the growing global historical literature on historiography are Iggers, Q. Wang and Mukherjee (2008); Raphael (2003); and Woolf (2011). See also Taylor (1989).
[21] See Berger, Donovan and Passmore (1999); and Dussel (1993). See also Bayly (2004a).

academic historiography marginalized other ways of writing history, many of which could look back at long traditions.

Given these massive changes in Europe itself, many globally influential character traits of modern academic historiography need to be seen not as export products of an allegedly pristine European tradition but rather as byproducts of wider, global transformations and entanglements. This is also true for the fundamental conceptions of space, which came to frame much of historical scholarship in many different parts of the world. After all, the idea of the nation as the main container of local history and the notion of West as the source of dynamism in world history had been rather unusual in Europe prior to the late eighteenth century.[22] Such new historical outlooks reflected forms of political order and global power formations during the nineteenth and twentieth centuries. For this reason they became widely influential in conjunction with the global spread of university-based historical scholarship and surrounding sociopolitical transformations.

For these reasons it would be erroneous to treat the global spread of Eurocentric themes in history as the result of diffusion from the West to the rest. Yet even though such outlooks became very influential both in the centers and on the margins of the evolving academic system, their wider implications were rather different inside and outside of the Western world. In Europe it was possible to portray historical scholarship as the outgrowth of a shared Occidental heritage that reached back to the ancient Greeks. On the contrary, the formation of modern academic disciplines in regions such as India, China, or the Middle East was visibly part of changing geopolitical dynamics, despite the fact that many indigenous traditions were being continued at universities and particularly outside of them. In many parts of the emerging Global South and Global East, the reality of imperialism, European intellectual dominance, and the inevitability of understanding nationalization at least partly as Westernization made it impossible to posit the indigenous past and local scholarship as standards for the rest of the world. Rather, familiarity with the West and other supposedly advanced nations came to be regarded as a precondition for new and timely ways of writing history. In many parts of Africa, Latin America, and the Middle East, a highly constructed "West" or "Europe" thus necessarily occupied a large part of the methodologies, concepts, and commonly shared background knowledge of the emerging academic communities.[23]

---

[22] See, for example, K. O'Brien (1997); and Woolf (2005).
[23] About the global spread of "Europe," the "West," and other metageographical concepts see Wigen and Lewis (1997).

By contrast, a majority of scholars in the West were never forced to face the idea that their own conceptual worlds and cultures of rationality were at least partly the products of global interactions and outside influences.

In conclusion, the transformations of nineteenth- and twentieth-century scholarship had great implications for the spatial parameters within which historians in different parts of the world would think about local and translocal history. For example, whereas thinkers ranging from Sima Qian to Ibn Khaldun could still conceive of themselves as rooted in their own cultural universes and regard the outside world accordingly, the situation had been dramatically different for Chinese and Middle Eastern historians during the previous one or two centuries. Even for radically nationalistic or culturally chauvinistic scholarship, it then became impossible to adopt world historical perspectives based on the idea of allegedly unbroken Confucian, Islamic, or other traditions of conceptualizing the past. Local intellectual outlooks as well as the institutional frameworks of universities had too obviously been influenced by exogenous developments. In other words, for many parts of the world, the history of transfers and outside influences has long not constituted an additional perspective that complemented the largely autochthonous tropes of national history; rather, it stood at the very foreground of modern history and historiography.[24]

In that sense, certain hierarchies of knowledge became deeply engrained in the conceptual worlds of modern historiography. Approaching the realities and further possibilities of alternative approaches to global history thus requires us to critically examine changing dynamics and lasting hierarchies which typify historiography as a global professional environment. As a next step, I will first discuss some historical patterns in the emergence of university-based historiography as an almost worldwide phenomenon. I will particularly sketch a few developments leading to some widely shared assumptions about space and historical significance, which came to characterize historiography as an academic field. While the processes behind the spread of modern academic historiography were globally entangled, I will first outline some developments in Europe and then shift the focus to other parts of the world. It will become quite clear that in European societies the question of historiographical traditions tended to be answered in ways that were profoundly different from most academic communities in other parts of the world.

[24] Osterhammel (2003; 2000c).

The formation of a discipline – perspectives on Europe

The spread of historiography at national universities was not a unilinear process originating from a single source.[25] Institutional innovations and facets of scientific-style historiography[26] such as the research seminar, in which professors and doctoral students assembled for academic discussions or critical source work, have often been credited to Rankeanism. But recent case studies have come to challenge the idea of the German or any other academic system exerting massive levels of direct influence on the ways in which history departments were being institutionalized elsewhere.[27] This is not to say that historiography as a professional training and research field with a wider public charter emerged completely independently in parallel national movements. But the pathways of its spread were far more intricate than institutional transmission from one source to a variety of recipients. Since it will not be possible to do full justice to the rich intellectual and regional diversities that characterized the growth of university-based historical scholarship during the 1800s and early 1900s, I will only chart some main patterns which are relevant to situating the recent rise of global historical perspectives within the field's trajectories.

As a general tendency, research conducted at academic history departments in Europe typically did not even come close to mirroring the wide range of historiographical genres co-existing on the eve of the early modern period.[28] This is not to say that academic historiography was isolated from wider intellectual movements. For example, some shifts in intellectual orientations or even public opinion could also be observed within the field's world historical outlooks. Whereas many leading Enlightenment thinkers had at least in principle favored the idea of mutual learning between different civilizations,[29] the European intellectual climate shifted around the time of the industrial revolution increasingly towards the idea that the Occident was advanced beyond any comparison.[30] Certainly, also during the nineteenth and early twentieth

---

[25] In different European countries, the trajectories of historiography pointed in slightly different directions. For example, cultural and social historical aspects were more emphasized in nineteenth-century French historiography. In Great Britain and Italy academic historiography long played only a very marginal role compared to the writing of history produced by other individuals. See Iggers, Q. Wang and Mukherjee (2008), pp. 76ff.

[26] See, for example, Feldner (2003).

[27] See Woolf (2005), p. 60. For the United States see Lingelbach (2003). For Japan see, for example, Mehl (1998).

[28] For insights into the pluralistic world of religious and secular histories in eighteenth- and nineteenth-century Europe see Woolf (2005); and Grafton (2007).

[29] K. O'Brien (1997), Mungello (1977). For a brief overview, see Sachsenmaier (2001).

[30] See Osterhammel (1998a); Mungello (1999); and Lach (1965–1993).

centuries there were remarkable counter-currents to the idea of "the West" as a teaching civilization. Yet in growing opinion camps, the histories of China, India, and many other parts of the world now came to be regarded frequently as monotonous, silent counterparts to the loud tunes of Europe's global concerts. Many renowned intellectual figures were no longer interested in the possibility of taking the present condition of other world regions as a source of inspiration for the future of Western societies or even for world order at large. As part of the same hierarchization of mental maps, parts of Europe, particularly in the South and the East, were also relegated to the periphery in the historical visions of the time.[31]

Such worldviews and, by implication, global power patterns manifested themselves in the division of labor between academic disciplines as they were being institutionalized at European universities.[32] Already at an early stage, fields like Sinology and Indology were philologically oriented and were supposed to focus their attention on premodern time periods, marginalizing the study of more recent developments in these parts of the world. They were not designed as academic disciplines with considerable influence on other disciplines such as historiography or sociology. One did not expect to derive models of universal significance from distant civilizations.[33] In a large number of countries, academic subjects such as "Oriental Studies" were organized according to the visions not of eighteenth-century Enlightenment cosmopolitanism, but of nineteenth-century nationalism and Eurocentrism.[34] Even in terms of their social networks and professional action radiuses, they were kept within these frameworks: exchanges with scholars in Asia and other systematic forms of transcontinental cooperation were not central to their professional charters.

In an unfolding canon of disciplinary tasks and specialized subjects, historiography found itself in the middle between the nomothetic social sciences and the humanities, which were less expected to deduce general

---

[31] See, for example, Todorova (1997).   [32] See Ross (1991); and Pletsch (1981).

[33] A historical analysis of German Indology suggests that the strict distinction between Indo-European and Semitic peoples can be seen in the context of evolving state-endorsed forms of anti-Semitism. See Pollock (2002).

[34] One should be careful not to overemphasize the standing of Enlightenment cosmopolitanism in European societies prior to the age of nationalized academic historiography. Throughout the end of the nineteenth century, Christian universal histories, which measured other civilizations by biblical standards, continued to enjoy a high prominence in some intellectual circles as well as in parts of the wider public sphere. Furthermore, particularly starting from the second half of the eighteenth century, even some acclaimed Enlightenment thinkers in Germany took to rather extreme positions the belief in European civilization as the only universalizable and rational one. For a general overview see Osterhammel (1994a).

laws from social reality.[35] With the latter, historians typically shared a certain aversion to and distrust of universal models, of theories that were being applied to different contexts without corresponding interest in the local specificities. Yet like the social sciences, the great historical schools such as Marxism, positivism, and historicism, which emerged during the nineteenth century, commonly adhered to the notion of scientific progress and objective research standards.[36] Historical truth was deemed to be explorable through auxiliary sciences such as philological studies and textual analysis.[37] Needless to say, historiography was never homogenous, and the belief in supposedly scientific modes of inquiry was being challenged in many societies by such renowned scholars as Wilhelm Dilthey, Karl Lamprecht, Benedetto Croce, or Robin G. Collingwood. Nevertheless, in most Western countries, the swelling mainstream of historiography was flowing towards a disciplinary culture that was driven by faith in universal methodologies. Moreover, the scientism underlying historiography was in several important regards not a universal scientism but a decidedly local one. Its spirit, which "made historical research seem most valid when performed in one's own backyard,"[38] was often strongly inclined to define nations as the primary spatial framework for academic historiography. Moreover, while methodologies and modes of inquiry were often believed to be universal, there was often a great reluctance to fully endorse the idea of a trans-national scholarly guild.

In fact, among the social sciences and the humanities, the origins of no academic field were as closely tied to the concept and the institution of the nation-state as those of historiography.[39] In many regards, the direction of historical research followed new national realities ranging from the availability of funding and other research incentives to the growing importance of national archives. Whereas philosophy and theology had previously figured prominently in European history writing during the eighteenth century, the state now became the field's main reference system. This meant that the history of political elites took the most prominent place in much of historiography. In addition, differing from the ideals and utopias of the eighteenth-century Republic of Letters, the origins and personal backgrounds of historians became an important

---

[35] On the social sciences and humanities see Mazlish (1998b); Heilbron, Magnusson and Wittrock (1998); and Porter and Ross (2003). For more detail about the origins of historiography in Europe see, for example, Berger, Donovan and Passmore (1999).

[36] See, for example, Iggers and Powell (1990). See also Jäger and Rüsen (1992).

[37] See Iggers (1997b).   [38] Wallerstein (1996), p. 16.

[39] On the nation-state framework in historiography and its deconstruction see Palti (2001). See also Hobsbawm (1992).

matter: it was native speakers and national citizens who were increasingly being recruited for faculty positions at the growing universities. At least in this regard, scholarly culture moved closer to the principle of the new national masses, even though academic discourses were certainly not free from feelings of disdain for them.[40] In many cases historians became active advocates of the nation-state by supplying the growing spectrum of national identities with a mythologized past that appeared in the form of objective scholarly research.

Within the realms of universities, the formation of historiography established a dominance of national over transnational assumptions of space, as well as that of secular or at least restrained religious paradigms over confessional and biblical visions. While, generally speaking, notions of progress and development became more important as markers of historical time, space got defined more rigidly, in terms of firm borders.[41] Much of national history was understood as unfolding from a primal core and, for this reason, imperialism tended to be portrayed as an outward projection of European states, with few reverse repercussions for the colonizers. In most cases, the processes of nation formation and imperialism were being historicized as quite clearly separate from one another.[42] This is not to say that imperialism was completely anathema in the nineteenth- and early twentieth-century national historiography, but colonial history often figured primarily as an object of national pride, without being supposed to challenge tropes of national autarky.[43] In that manner, discourses such as Eurocentrism, Social Darwinism, and racism were not only foundational to many world historical perspectives, but could heavily season national historiographies as well.[44]

Given the widespread assumption that the present conditions of societies in other parts of the world had no significance for the West, non-European history usually could only fill the backbenches in the guildhall of European historians.[45] According to the same logic, also world history and transcultural history usually received relatively little academic

---

[40] See Wittrock (2000).   [41] See Calhoun (1999).

[42] Certainly, many theoretical frameworks ranging from Marxist to Weberian approaches emphasized connections between imperialism and processes of nation formation. Yet even in the case of colonial powers such as Great Britain, France, or Belgium these macroscopic approaches failed to influence the main historiographical currents of their time. Interesting ideas on the relationship between imperialism and competitive national capitalisms are offered by Duara (1995), Chapter 3.

[43] See, for example, the excellent study by Hill (2008).

[44] See, for example, Hawkins (1997); and Weitz (2003).

[45] Compare Osterhammel (1997b).

funding, and not much scholarly energy went into studying them.[46] Certainly, academic scholarship did not completely abandon world historical reflections, but in contrast to some important eighteenth-century traditions[47] also in this genre the nation-state often became the key unit of analysis. For example, the *Weltgeschichte* (*World History*) written by the doyen of the field, Ranke, was primarily an accumulative account of different national traditions, which meant that domestic tensions as well as transnational forces were relegated to the very fringes of the historiographical picture.[48] As Ranke and many other influential scholars regarded the nation-state as the most civilized form of political order, their world historical narratives tended to marginalize those parts of the world in which it had not yet been established.[49] In these circles, the logics of power politics and diplomacy were seen as the main frameworks for the international behavior of states.[50] Ranke grounded his distrust of universal narratives in his belief that each and every epoch and locality needed to be understood within its own context and should not be viewed from a superordinate perspective. Yet his world historical reflections were certainly not free from the influence of large-scale, structural interpretations of history and civilizational value judgments. For example, his depiction of China focused on the idea that its entire past had been a regressive movement and was thus characterized by trajectories that ran directly opposite to Europe's development.[51]

Also outside the historicist school, many world historical patterns of thinking took an unabashedly Eurocentric character. For example, in influential Hegelian traditions, history tended to be viewed as the unfolding of the human condition through a dialectic process of material changes and intellectual perceptions of the world ("Weltanschauung"). Hegel himself and many of his followers went as far as to deny other cultures such as China, India, or Persia any kind of history in a progressive sense, since they considered them to be entrapped in endless cycles of dynastic changes without any linear development.[52] A few decades later, the growing genre of left-wing Hegelian, particularly Marxist world historical reflections was also initially premised on the

---

[46] Compare Bentley (1996b). See also Pomper (1995).
[47] Harbsmeier (1991); and van Kley (1971).   [48] See Schulin (1988).
[49] See Mollin (2000).
[50] More generally on the social sciences see, for example, Wagner (1990).
[51] Compare Pigulla (1996), p. 283.
[52] The ideology that Europe had first broken through the shackles of tradition and reached a higher, more dynamic civilization, which gained its strength from the ability of the individual to unfold his or her own potential, also played a major role in colonial rhetoric when it was used to justify European expansionism and imperialism.

assumption that there was no genuine history outside the Western state-building project.[53] At the same time, Marx's overall framework, focusing on the underprivileged, proved fertile for adaptations that granted greater agency to non-Western societies. Particularly influential – and since the founding of the Communist International internationally promoted by a political power – were theories of imperialism, which had been intellectually prepared by individuals like Hilferding and Bukharin and then popularized by Lenin.[54] Yet also in Leninist historiography, the timelines and categories of analysis were almost exclusively derived from the European experience.

Though different in origin, also the widening spectrum of Weberian critiques of the West was mainly characterized by the belief in the order of the nation-state and the universality of European civilization.[55] While Weber's work paid close attention to cultural differences, it remained committed to discourses of European exceptionalism, albeit not in a triumphalist manner. He interpreted Europe as a civilization of reason, and reason as the key to superiority over other parts of the world. Consequently, Weber did not assume the world outside of Europe to be significant for efforts to develop visions for a future world. Weber may have lamented the "iron cage" of modernity, but nevertheless his magnum opus *The Sociology of World Religions* was a set of answers to the overarching questions of what attributes of Europe were "lacking" in other civilizations and why Europe, rather than any other civilization, had managed the "breakthrough" to "modernity."[56] Obviously, such an analytical frame posited European modernity as unique and yet at the same time the only universalizable civilization in the world. According to some historians, this rather teleological outlook and his inclination to see competition as a key principle of history were related to Weber's own nationalist convictions.[57]

Certainly, there also existed important counter-narratives in the West, which viewed world history from the perspectives of rather subaltern groups.[58] Particularly around the time of the First World War, Eurocentric visions of world history became somewhat more subject to criticism.[59] Several prominent scholars and intellectuals in Europe threw doubt on the nimbus of the Western experience as the source of a global standard. For example, historians like Arnold Toynbee and Oswald

---

[53] S. Kim (1993).   [54] See Brewer (1980).   [55] See Schluchter (1981).
[56] Naffrisi (1998).   [57] Mommsen (1984).   [58] See, for example, Kelly (1999).
[59] However, remarkable as they often were, projects of this kind did usually not go far beyond the search for "Oriental" alternatives to modern Western civilization. See, for example, Sachsenmaier (2007a); and Adas (2004).

Spengler, whose works were translated into a wide range of languages, professed to abandon progressivist notions of the past.[60] Instead, they centered their narratives on civilizational frames and paid great attention to what they understood as mechanisms of decay. Spengler operated with a cyclical vision of history, and in his narrative he accentuated the mechanisms for the rise and fall of civilizations.[61] He expressed his effort to decenter the West with the metaphor of shifting from a Ptolemaic to a Copernican system, in which all heavenly bodies are related to each other without assuming a fixed, central point. On the other hand, in his ten-volume *Study of History*, Toynbee identified twenty-one civilizations as well as five "arrested civilizations" that each had specific religious or other "cultural" character traits.[62] However, for the period after the European discoveries, the renowned British historian proposed a "world-encompassing Western civilization" without discussing its relation to other civilizations in due detail.[63]

These brief perspectives of Rankeanism, Marxism, Weberianism, and civilizational analysis show that historiographical Eurocentrism was far from monolithic in character, but instead related to different groups of world historical narratives, which all circulated on an international level.[64] No matter whether the main categories of world historical thinking were defined by nations, classes, or civilizations: Western experiences were often poised as either a supreme or paradigmatic experience against which other cases could be measured. Ironically, the same was also true for many works that either were meant to analyze the decline of the West or were highly doubtful about Western expansionism. In many of these critical works Europe remained very much at the center of the global storyline.[65]

Again it is important to emphasize that the strong influence of Eurocentric tropes was not only a character trait of Western scholarship but an aspect of the evolving worldwide academic system. Even in many

---

[60] For an overview of Spengler's and Toynbee's theories see Manning (2003), pp. 37ff.
[61] Spengler (1918).
[62] Toynbee (1934–1961). In the later volumes Toynbee's work introduced God as a factor in his historical theory and modified his cyclical visions by outlining trajectories of moral development. About discourses of civilization see Wigen and Lewis (1997), pp. 126–35.
[63] This unresolved issue is pointed out by Von Laue (1987). See Chapter 2 for works written in the tradition of civilizational analysis, which were written after the Second World War.
[64] For a different selection and categorization of modern patterns of world historical thought see Osterhammel (1998b). A general overview of world historical writing prior to 1900 is provided by Manning (2003), Chapters 1 and 2.
[65] See, for example, Young (1990); and Dirlik (2002a).

world histories written by academics outside of the West, most narrative compass needles pointed towards Europe, just as other world regions often ended up being categorized as "backward" or "regressive" on new scales of human development. As the previous sections have shown, the Western bias in much historiographical thinking was more closely related to the global triumph of methodological nationalism than it would appear at first sight. Many international hierarchies of knowledge left their marks on the geographical imaginations from which world historical accounts were often written.

Implicit geographies: patterns in the global spread of historiography

In many societies all over the world university-based historiography was established in the context of nation-building efforts.[66] During that time, modern academic disciplines in general and historiography in particular tended to be portrayed as fields that needed to be copied from allegedly successful modernizers, just as national transportation systems or forms of urban planning were to be taken largely from outside examples. Within such a constellation of forces, historical visions often transformed in a pattern that Prasenjit Duara described in the following manner: *nations emerge as the subjects of History just as History emerges as the ground, the mode of being, of the nation.*[67] In many cases, a national past was supposed to imbue the new citizens with a sense of unity, common heritage, and shared historical bonds, which – according to many expectations – would mobilize the masses sufficiently to build a dynamic, coherent country. Since academic historiography was regarded as part of modern education and a necessary precondition for setting up a functional nation-state,[68] there was pressure to restructure historical narratives according to allegedly rational, national, and scientific principles.

Seen from that angle, it is small wonder that – despite all local variations – university-based historiography in many non-western societies came to widely share the dual dominance of nation-centered and Eurocentric perspectives. Yet in contrast to most European cases,

---

[66] Not always was it the nation state that created national history, though. In many cases the beginnings of "modern" history movements already occurred under colonial rule.

[67] The combination of modernization discourses and anti-imperialist outlooks often became, in a very immediate sense, part of national identities and forms of historical consciousness. See, for example, Duara (1995), p. 27.

[68] See, for example, Lönnroth, Molin and Ragnar (1994). See also C. Conrad and S. Conrad (2002a).

nation-building programs in most other world regions were closely tied to discourses of "learning from the world's centers." An important element of such impulses was the notion that Europe in its essence constituted a culture of rationality.[69] In that manner, scientific ways of exploring history were not only seen as active forces in the formation of national societies, but also as ways of understanding other parts of the world, particularly those societies that seemed more advanced and progressive. For these and other reasons, world history tended, from the very beginning of modern academic scholarship, to play a more dominant role in many, albeit not all, countries outside of the West. Examples range from Japan and China in the East to Chile and Mexico in the West. Most commonly, the envisioned role of this field was to explore the allegedly universal forces that made the industrial powers triumphant on the global stage.[70] Such a charter did not leave much room for conceptualizing the new forms of world history primarily as continuations of earlier indigenous traditions.

Similar things were true for a plethora of new national histories that were emerging all over the globe. In most cases, they were at least partly understood as imports from successful modernizers.[71] By mobilizing new forms of national consciousness, the field was typically supposed to contribute to achieving the interlinked objectives of personal sovereignty and national liberation.[72] Elements of "modern" historical scholarship were thus often deemed to have universal implications that would help weave the disjointed elements of the local pasts into pointed national historical narratives.[73] Hence in many countries the spatial assumptions of nation-centered historiography were not only national, but at the same time international and Western-centric. The latter was not necessarily meant to endorse the global roles of the West: for example, in much of Chinese, Indian, and Middle Eastern scholarship, the modernization discourses surrounding the new historiography were intrinsically tied to anti-imperialist outlooks.[74] Moreover, Eurocentric orientations in academic historiography did not necessarily mean that the "West" figured as the sole reference system in world historical thought.[75] For example, Japanese history and historiography were highly influential in China ever since the late nineteenth century. However, the

---

[69] For more details see Wigen and Lewis (1997), pp. 81–92.
[70] Often such tropes were linked with the concept of "civilization." See G. Gong (1984).
[71] For the Indian case see, for example, Lal (2003); for Korea: H. Pai (2000).
[72] An overview is provided by Iggers, Q. Wang and Mukherjee (2008).
[73] For China see, for example, L. Kwong (2001); for Japan see Conrad (1999b).
[74] For the Chinese example see Duara (2009), particularly Chapters 1 and 2.
[75] For more details see Chapter 4.

Japanese experience was usually treated as the successful adaptation of Western elements to an East Asian context.

The changing reference spaces and the importance of progressivist discourses are only a few aspects of the massive epistemological and institutional changes that accompanied the spread of university-based historiography throughout the world. The transformations leading to the establishment of academic history departments were usually paralleled by the marginalization of earlier forms of knowledge, which in some instances was initially driven by direct colonial interference, while in other cases it was mainly conducted by local elites in their efforts to reshape society.[76] The discontinuities and even acts of epistemicide that frequently accompanied the establishment of modern universities and the advent of academic historiography did not necessarily take the form of clear ruptures and decisive breaks. Rather, they were locally specific and typically occurred in protracted processes full of competing visions, hybridizations, and the continuation of parallel historiographical traditions.

For example, in many Islamic societies such as Egypt or Syria, efforts to understand the "West" in its historical and conceptual dimensions went back to the eighteenth and nineteenth centuries, and already during this time period terms such as "nation" or "civilization" began to be used among historians.[77] Later, a lasting tension emerged between the nationalization efforts in single societies and efforts to write the Arab nation into history. In both cases, however, methodologies, institutions, and ways of conceptualizing the past were significantly different from earlier traditions.[78] Also in Meiji Japan, academic historiography was greatly transformed when specialized state offices conducted dramatic institutional and professional reforms that were modeled after Western prototypes.[79] These state bureaus had only a limited influence on the contents of national historical literature in Japan, though they were still essential for the professionalization and scientification of historical scholarship under a national ethos.[80]

Certainly, in many cases the purported nationalization of historical studies was not without opponents. For instance, during the nineteenth and early twentieth centuries Japan, China, and India witnessed significant opposition movements to radical Westernization programs, with

---

[76] Several examples are discussed in Berger (2007c).
[77] See, for example, Haddad (1994); Choueri (2000); and Crabbs (1984).
[78] See, for example, Schaebler (2007).
[79] See Morris-Suzuki (1993). See also the comparative analysis by Hill (2008).
[80] Brownlee (1997); and Mehl (1998).

many groups advocating more restrained forms of transformation.[81]
Yet also here discourses of catching up with selected international
powers remained important in the debates about the future of historiography. For example, direct representatives of the Ranke School in Japan
were a great asset for those reformers who sought to rebuild historical
research by following the example of Germany. Similarly, in nineteenth-
century Russia many important figures within the reform movement of
historiography derived their authority partly from having traveled to
academic centers in Germany and other countries.[82] Taken together,
examples of this kind demonstrate that notions of a hierarchical relationship between the West and the rest underlay many institution-building
efforts in the study of history.

In Latin America, where indigenous historical narratives had been
heavily disrupted as early as the sixteenth century, more concerted
efforts to institutionalize modern academic historiography were taken
from the 1830s onwards in several newly independent countries.[83]
Here the nationalization of historical tropes could take different routes
and accentuate different parts of the population. For example, whereas
in some countries such as Argentina, national history became largely
centered on the former colonizers' struggle for independence, in
Mexico a stronger emphasis was placed on the pre-colonial past.
However, this does not mean that the main currents of Mexican
historiography necessarily sought to continue indigenous historiographical traditions within the new realms of universities.[84] Yet in
many cases such as in Peru for instance, the new conceptions of
national history widely suppressed the diversity of society.[85] Similar
developments can be observed in other former European settler
colonies like Australia.[86]

In India, many institutional facets of modern professional historiography were already established during the late colonial period, particularly in missionary schools as well as in the new vernacular teaching
centers built to train an administrative elite. Nevertheless, these colonial
structures became forums for debating themes related to nationalism

[81] See Sato (1991b). For more details see Gottlob (1997).
[82] This was for example the case with Sergey Solvyov (1820–1879) who traveled through
various European countries as a tutor for the Stroganov family. His main work was
A History of Russia from Earliest Times that emphasized the Christian roots of Russia and
was written in the spirit of national historiography. See Siljak (1999); and Thaden
(1999).
[83] De Freitas Dutra (2007); and Woll (1982).   [84] See Bouchard (2001).
[85] See, for example, Adorno (1986).
[86] See, for example, Hearn (2007); and Haebich (2005).

and national history.[87] Even many anti-colonial movements and post-independence thinkers came to accept the idea that India had no genuine history prior to the arrival of the European powers. Actually some quite outspoken critics of the "Western experience" primarily referred to Europe and the US as contrast foils to support their visions of a new local or national history. For example, India's prime minister Nehru's famed *Glimpses of World History* was certainly far from idealizing Western civilization and even argued for a specifically Indian way of modernization. Yet at the same time his work did not abandon Western theories of history but rather radically applied them as part of a quest for Indian emancipation.[88] Many other world histories written in South Asia and elsewhere also focused their world historical narratives on power centers and their elites, which pushed much of the non-Western world into passive roles. In a wide spectrum of primarily nation-centered visions, nomadic peoples, diasporic formations, and other transnational groups lay outside the narrative scopes.[89]

Among the new national images of history, which emerged in India under colonial rule and continued after independence in 1947, were attempts to center the concept of Indian nationhood primarily on the Hindu heritage. Already early in the twentieth century there had been a strong tendency in Indian scholarship to portray the presence of Islam as an intrusion into an allegedly national culture dominated by Hinduism – which in turn was accompanied by a rising interest in the pre-Islamic or non-Islamic past. Then, after decolonization, the methodologies and scopes of academic historiography grew wider. During the 1960s and 1970s Marxism had a strong presence in the Indian university sector, yet historians operating with Marxist categories of analysis usually remained loyal to the concept of the nation, even though they took a critical stand vis-à-vis the past. In that sense, a growing majority of Indian thinkers still resorted primarily to Western historical categories in their quest to imbue the subcontinent with what they interpreted as the dynamics of the West.[90] The tropes and master narratives of the nation continued to be embattled, however, along such dividing lines as the question whether historic India was primarily a Hindu or a multi-religious society.[91]

---

[87] Chatterjee (1993).
[88] Nehru (1939). Gandhi was one of the few Indian independence leaders who expressed great concern over the new conceptions of history.
[89] See Christian (2005); and P. O'Brien (2006).
[90] For more details see Gottlob (1997).   [91] See Lal (2003).

In some other parts of the world, decisive measures to establish national historiography at modern universities were only taken during the Cold War. For instance, in a number of newly independent Arabic societies, secular historical narratives were heavily promoted from the 1960s onwards, which could cause a strong rivalry between various historical outlooks, especially between nationalistic, Pan-Arabic, and Islamic ones. In several countries in this part of the world, different historiographical currents were centered on questions like why the West had been able to progress while the Islamic world had stagnated.[92] Hence, here too, Eurocentric discourses came to characterize much nationally framed, anti-colonial, and even anti-Western historiography in the region. Similar statements could be made about many sub-Saharan African countries where governments proceeded to nationalize historiography after decolonization, often by openly deciding to follow European examples.[93] As in cases like India, here efforts to institutionalize the study of linear and national forms of historical thinking could also continue some colonial initiatives. Across different academic disciplines, the newly independent national elites tended to endorse discourses of development and progress that were to be anchored in a long, scientifically explored indigenous past. There was a mounting presence of the idea that the same political steps and institutional measures could be applied across cultural boundaries in any newly forming national context.[94]

This brief glance at the growth of university-based historiography in different parts of the world suggests that local experiences were extremely diverse and diachronic in character. At the same time it is possible to identify some general trends that can be observed in societies which were not connected directly through dense networks of exchanges. In a remarkable number of countries all over the world, an initial phase of attempted moderate reforms and a search for syntheses between new and old perspectives was followed by more radical Westernization programs affecting many areas of knowledge, including historiography.

The Turkish case can serve as a further example of this specific pattern. During the Tanzimat Reforms in the late Ottoman Empire, a highly constructed "Europe" became an important reference space for historical scholarship, yet at the same time there was still room for a continuation of earlier forms of scholarship such as the use of the

---

[92] See, for example, Fürtig and Höpp (1998). See also Freitag (1999).
[93] For India see, for example, Chakrabarty (2006); for Africa see Eckert (1999).
[94] See Cooper (1997b).

chronicle.[95] Later, Mustafa Kemal's new secular history was characterized by some iconoclastic elements since it purportedly marginalized
Islamic and Ottoman tropes in favor of decidedly Turkish perspectives
on the past – perspectives which were openly modeled after European
tropes of ethnic national history.[96] Here, just as in other cases, an invention of a "negative" tradition accompanied efforts to put visions of the
past into national frames. Similarly, in nineteenth-century Persia more
customary outlooks on history had remained highly influential in political and intellectual circles, even though at that time nationalist historians had begun to more clearly separate Persian culture and its history
from Islam. After the Great War, however, decidedly nationalist histories
were heavily expanded in conjunction with secular institutions of higher
learning.[97] At Persian universities, historiography as an academic discipline was part of a state-led package, and its scholars were supposed to
play a central role in the creation and dissemination of a new historical
consciousness. While these processes took place within academic environments, Islamic interpretations of history remained quite influential in
other segments of society.[98]

Despite the widespread idea of international forerunners and models,
the critical evaluation of sources, the backbone of modern scientific
analysis, certainly had precursors outside of the West. Research agendas
ranging from doubts about hereditary historical accounts to the search
for objectivity had also emerged in world regions such as China, India,
and parts of the Islamic world.[99] The same is true for methodological
fields such as textual analysis, philology, epigraphy, and paleography.
The specific origins of such critical textual scholarship were locally
specific – for example, one of the major forces contributing to its
stronger role in eighteenth-century India were legal disputes over property claims for which archival expertise was required.[100] Later, epistemological schools of this kind could be presented as parts of
modernization efforts and blended into new nationalized forms of historical scholarship. In some instances, however, indigenous scientific
traditions were either ignored or even actively marginalized by a majority
of historians working in universities.[101] Here an emerging gap between

---

[95] Kuran (1962).   [96] Kafadar (1996).   [97] Tavakoli-Targhi (2001).
[98] For Persia see Mirsepassi (2000).
[99] For China see, for example, Elman (1984). For the Islamic world see Al-Azmeh
(2002); the same volume points out that earlier Islamic historiographies were also
characterized by proto-scientific methodologies.
[100] See Sen (2005). See also Guha (2004). For China see Chapter 4.
[101] See, for example, Chatterjee (2005).

more committed Westernizers and defenders of local traditions typically left rather little room for blending new and old approaches in the spirit of finding an alternative model of scholarship.

As already mentioned, the nation-state was not the only spatial category gaining global influence. Also, terms ranging from "continents" to notions of "cultures" and "civilizations" became globalized in the sense that they were accepted into the semantic patterns of many languages and served as guiding concepts for historians in different parts of the world. However, many of these concepts at least tacitly implied the existence of an unequal world order. This is exemplified by the dual meaning of the term "civilization," which in a wide variety of languages referred on the one hand to autochthonous cultures and on the other hand to universal development, a new stage of human progress typically embodied by the West.[102] Moreover, the concept of continents often operated on the basis that Europe represented the most advanced civilization. The idea that the European experience was exceptional enough to deserve the status of a continent became globally accepted, even though it was without clear geographical boundaries.[103]

In addition to conceptions of space, many other internationally influential historical categories such as the notions of "race" or "progress" were at least implicitly tied to the idea of European supremacy.[104] Significant was also the worldwide spread of Marxist categories ranging from the proletariat and other class-specific terms to ideas about historical stages such as feudalism. The international topographies of Marxist historiography were certainly far more complex than the Cold War concept of a divided world could possibly express. Its impact on world historical thinking was certainly not only confined to the Soviet zone of influence.[105] In Japan, India, and several Western countries, Marxist models became highly influential within the guild of historians, particularly after the Second World War.[106] Also derivative social scientific approaches à la Karl Mannheim, Antonio Gramsci, and

---

[102] See, for example, Duara (2002).

[103] See Wigen and Lewis (1997). Needless to say, such a geographical interpretation also subalternized many parts of Europe since the alleged core areas of the European experience were located in Western Europe.

[104] In many political and intellectual movements, which were openly rebelling against the idea of European supremacy, they were used in order to fight against a dominant status quo, thereby implicitly strengthening the tropes of global European dominance. See Geulen (2007).

[105] Taking the latter position: Erdmann (2005), chapters 14–17.

[106] About India see Sarkar (1997), pp. 1–49. About Japan see Conrad (1999b); and Hoston (1986).

Immanuel Wallerstein became rather important in different parts of the world.[107] Yet in many societies under communist rule, Marxist reformulations of national and world history took place under great governmental pressure. Here this often partified and petrified the innovative power of Marxist thought.[108] Methodologically rigid versions of Soviet historiography could be internationally spread through direct pressure, most notably to Eastern Europe, or through voluntary governmental adoption such as in China during the 1950s or in Cuba. In any case, entire cohorts of Chinese, Vietnamese, African, and Eastern European historians tried to fit the histories of their respective societies into Marxist categories and concepts.[109]

As the often antagonistic worlds of Marxism and more right-wing forms of developmentalism show, it would be wrong to assume that the "modernization" or "Westernization" of historical studies could possibly be understood as a homogenizing force. Already early in the twentieth century, one could observe contestations between rival ideologically rooted styles of historiography, which were often related to domestic political and cultural struggles over the future national system. In quite a number of countries in Latin America, East Asia, Europe, and elsewhere socialist and conservative, national and internationalist approaches to history competed for influence over the field. The span and intensity of rivaling approaches varied between different local contexts; their outcomes were often determined by political factors and acts of suppression.[110]

Global facets of historiography

The ways in which historiography as a supposedly scientific field spread all over the globe were not uniform. Rather, in many societies and world regions university-based historiography experienced hybridizations, selective adaptations, and contending schools of thought. Nevertheless, an array of complex global and local processes led to significant worldwide commonalities in the conceptual worlds and institutional features of academic historiography. They can be identified on the level of

---

[107] See Raphael (2003), Chapter 7. For the example of world systems theory in the West see Modelski, Denemark, Friedman and Gills (2000). See also the latter sections of this chapter.

[108] See, for example, Thomas (1994). In the Soviet Union the first wave of purges against "bourgeois historians" occurred during the 1920s, and Stalin intensified the pressure to produce streamlined histories during the early 1920s. See Shteppa (1962).

[109] See, for example, Service (2007). For the case of China see Chapter 4.

[110] Even in dictatorships certain earlier historiographical traditions could linger on – see, for example, Lehmann and von Horm (2003).

methodologies, patterns of professional behavior, institutions, and also conceptions of space.

For instance, many alternative visions of space were subordinated to the idea of the nation as the theater of history. National frameworks were dominant across the political and ideological dividing lines that characterized large parts of the twentieth century. Also in the Soviet Union and many other communist countries, a strong majority of historians remained loyal to the concept of the nation-state and clearly subordinated Marxist categories to it.[111] Likewise, many important efforts in former colonies to build modern versions of historiography were characterized by a primacy of national parameters. In a large number of South Asian, Latin American, and sub-Saharan societies, historians at the newly founded universities tended to accept the nation-state as the framework of their own local past. The history of colonial rule and dependency was often emphasized but usually not considered further in terms of global and transnational historical visions. In many cases the colonial heritage was presented in order to accentuate the goal of freeing a specifically national past from disadvantageous transnational entanglements.[112]

The "westward" orientation of many newly shaped historiographical systems implied a global surge of Eurocentric themes and topoi in world history. In this context one may, for example, consider the global prominence of the idea that Europe had become the most dynamic civilization on the planet and hence was destined to dominate the rest of the world. Equally influential was the notion that the "West" would eventually liberate humankind from its self-imposed shackles of tradition, oppression, and superstition.[113] While during the interwar and the early Cold War periods several Western powers promoted such right-wing Hegelian visions of history,[114] much world historiography in the Soviet zone of influence was characterized by tropes, which in many regards were not

---

[111] See, for example, Brunnbauer (2004). In some cases like in Latvia, themes of national awakening continued to remain important even under Soviet rule. See, for example, Dribins (1999). About Soviet historiography see Sanders (1998). Even many influential histories of the world communist movement were primarily divided into nationally specific chapters.

[112] For example, Nagano (2004).

[113] Several examples are discussed by Blaut (1993); Said (1989). Even though William McNeill's important work *The Rise of the West* was far from endorsing European triumphalism, the author stated with hindsight that it "shows scant concern for the sufferings of the victims of historical change." See W. McNeill (1990).

[114] For a politically embedded account of modernization theory see Latham (2003). Certainly, this is not to suggest that such outlooks remained uncontested within the United States and other Western societies. For a discussion of the US case see Chapter 2.

entirely dissimilar. Here too, influential narratives favored the European historical experience in general, and events like the Russian Revolution in particular, and treated them as the main sources of universal history. Needless to say, such visions were at least bent towards denigrating the non-Western world by consigning its premodern histories to the dark spots of the human past.

Generally speaking, the spread of academic historiography not only reshaped images of the past by projecting notions of linear time onto it. The belief in a scientific historiographical methodology also implied notions of geographical importance that tended to be nation- and Western-centric at the same time.[115] It was widely believed that, in order to construct a new national past, researchers would not only have to familiarize themselves with Western methodologies but also with the European past and, as the twentieth century progressed, increasingly with the United States as well. Within such an "Occidentalist" mindset many historians around the world assumed that studying Europe was a necessary precondition for national self-understanding whereas the study of other outside world regions was relegated to the background.[116] This means that in many cases ranging from Latin American countries to societies in East Asia, the new national histories could not be conceptualized as linear trajectories leading from an indigenous past into the future. Rather, the supposedly modernized visions of the past needed to follow far more complex paths that were also leading through the Western experience and the conceptual worlds ascribed to it.

In cases such as Japan the changes in historical reference spaces were particularly remarkable. Whereas the proto-national historiographies, which emerged from about the sixteenth century onwards, had been embedded in a Sinocentric worldview, the new national historiographies of the late nineteenth century were consciously modeled after a partly real, partly manufactured Western example.[117] At the same time, the

---

[115] This does not mean that the "West" was the sole reference system all over the world. For example, in China Japanese history and Japanese approaches to the study of the past were highly influential from the beginnings of modern historiography. For more details see Chapter 4.

[116] It should be pointed out that I am not using "Occidentalism" here in the manner of some important Latin American postcolonial theorists who refer to the term in order to emphasize that in Latin America discourses it was comparable to "Orientalism." See, for example, Mignolo (2000). About the category of "the West," which implied the idea of a transatlantic civilization, see Gowilt (1995).

[117] See, for example, Tanaka (2004). The turn towards European concepts had been proceeded by movements to center history on Japan, which started in the sixteenth century and also had parallels in Korea. See, for example, Haboush (2005).

nationalization of historical studies was accompanied by greater levels of attention to the Western world in education and research.[118] The central position of the "West" as a reference space in the new historiography of Japan would reach as far as Fukuzawa Yukichi's famed dictum "to leave Asia."[119] These new contextual geographies had great implications for the ambitions in which much of the new national historiography was being embedded. After all, nationalism seen from the East Asian experience seemed intrinsically connected with imperialism.[120] The identification with European tropes could hence also include patterns of justifying imperialism. For instance, a good number of influential Japanese scholars came to portray Korean history as a past of stagnation, backwardness, and dependency on China – from which a modern Japan would supposedly liberate it.[121] In other words, by defining Japan as the dynamic powerhouse in an allegedly backward East Asia, many Japanese historians during the decades after the Meiji Restoration staked political claims by quite consciously seeking to project Western versions of "Orientalism" onto the East Asian theater.[122] Against such colonizers' views of history, Korean historiography developed strands of national theories, many of which were written in a Social Darwinist spirit and assumed a cultural Korean essence from early times onwards. They drew their inspiration from modern European, Chinese, and even Japanese scholarship, but here too the "West" continued to figure as an important reference model.[123]

As can be seen from these examples, university-based historiography has certainly not turned into a globally homogenous system, but it developed some significant worldwide commonalities and entanglements. Apart from the level of concepts, methods, and ideas, such global similarities can also be detected at an institutional level. For example, degrees such as the doctorate carry meaning in many different societies ranging from the Global North to the Global South and from East to West. They are supposed to honor those who develop "new" perspectives and explore "new" facets of history through research and critical inquiry. In addition, methodological principles ranging from critical source analysis to the footnote have become global in the sense that academic scholars apply them regardless of their specific local academic community.[124] Furthermore, in numerous societies on all continents a strong national bias is reflected in the structure of history departments.

---

[118] See Schwentker (1997).   [119] Bonnet (2000).
[120] See, for example, Duara (2008).   [121] See, for example, H. Pai (2000).
[122] Tanaka (1993).   [123] See, for example, H. Lim (2001); and Y. Shin (2000).
[124] See, for example, Grafton (1997).

A large number of historians all over the world are experts in the history
of single nation-states or mono-cultural realms at best.[125] Today this is
even the case in societies in which academic circles have long actively
questioned facets of political nationalism.[126]

It is thus possible to detect many elements of a global disciplinary
culture in modern academic historiography. Yet the processes behind the
global spread of Eurocentric and national visions of history were not
solely driven by horizontal forces. Since in many countries the idea of
catching up with allegedly more advanced academic realms played an
important role in the establishment of university-based historical scholarship, the inequalities within the international academic and geopolitical system were a strong motor driving the global assimilation of
scholarly practices and standards. In many regards, the professionalization of historical scholarship was related to the overall professionalization of work in industrial and post-industrial societies.[127] Hence it is
small wonder that during the nineteenth and twentieth centuries, the
dominance of Western European and North American scholars in a geo-
academic context paralleled the power constellations among international technical and business elites.

These patterns of Western academic dominance unfolded even
though – and at the same time precisely because – important strands
of the new national historiography took the criticism of foreign domination as their points of departure. In many parts of the world,
academic historiography was to be anchored in nation-building projects, which is also why the field was supposed to be characterized by a
dominance of national over transnational or migrant groups. As part of
this endeavor, national citizens were often directly or indirectly priori-
tized in hiring processes for history faculty positions.[128] In some cases,
the nationalization of history faculty was even conducted as a purported reversal of earlier developments. For instance, during the nineteenth century, the large number of Syrian scholars at Egyptian
universities was perceived as problematic in government and

---

[125] Even in societies such as the United States, where history departments are characterized
by a strong regional diversification of expertise, national or macro-regional spaces still
frame much of historical scholarship. Up until recently, there has been a strong tendency
for fields such as US history, European history, Latin American history, or East Asian
history to be largely divided into separate research communities. Compare Wallerstein
(1996), pp. 33ff.

[126] See, for example, Iriye (1994).

[127] See, for example, Charle, Schriewer and Wagner (2004). On the European experience
prior to the nineteenth century: Reinhard (1996b).

[128] Some immigrant societies such as the US hired migrants (at first from Europe and then
increasingly from other parts of the world) more widely and systematically.

intellectual circles, giving rise to policies aimed at assimilating historians in terms of their national backgrounds.[129]

At the same time, the nationalization of history departments was not
only meant to lead to isolated scholarly communities. The nation-state
alone would have been insufficient as a source of legitimacy for historians as a professional type.[130] Even in nation-centered academic communities, international connections and transnational intellectual
networks were important to lend weight and prestige to academic historians.[131] The fact that linkages to the wider landscapes of scholarship
granted the profession authority to speak to the nation and for the nation
could also serve as a disincentive to criticize the international hierarchies
of knowledge in modern scholarship.

The modern scholar's uneasy position between national and international zones of professional belonging was often fostered by political
forces. For example, discourses of international competition often
helped – and still help – to raise funds for research on a national level.[132]
On the other hand, the main institutional realms in which historians
acted and interacted, ranging from associations to journals and foundations, long remained primarily national in scope, at least in most parts of
the world. Certainly, since the nineteenth century there have been
concrete efforts to bring scholars in different parts of the world to each
other through exchange programs, common projects, and international
conferences.[133] Yet in a large number of cases, events such as world
historical congresses, which date back to the late nineteenth century,
were conducted as gatherings of national representatives.[134]

Hence, like many other academic elites, modern historians found
themselves working within very peculiar spatial parameters. While
cosmopolitan in the sense that they belonged to a globally intertwined
professional culture, their main arenas of professional responsibility and
interests were usually confined to single nation-states, linguistic realms,
or regions. From the very beginning, a certain tension thus characterized
the social environments and epistemological claims of the modern

---

[129] Reid (1990). See also Iggers, Q. Wang and Mukherjee (2008).
[130] See Bourdieu (1988). About a – still rather adequate – description of the historian's
professional world see Bloch (1974).
[131] See, for example, Charle, Schriewer and Wagner (2004); and Bourdieu (2002).
[132] See, for example, Charle (1996); and Evans (1965).
[133] See, for example, Iriye (1997); Porter and Ross (2003); and Erdmann (2005).
[134] For example, the quinquennial conventions of the International Committee of
Historical Sciences, a worldwide association founded by Woodrow Wilson, have long
been structured primarily on the basis of national delegations. This situation continues
to be the case, even though transnational sub-organizations have started playing a more
important role. See Erdmann (2005), and for more recent information, www.cish.org.

historian. There was a tacit conflict in the notions that historians were supposed to serve as defenders of locality while at the same time they belonged to a transnational professional group. The allegiance to both the discursive worlds of scientific universalism and local belonging could create certain strains. On the one hand, historians drew a great deal of authority and legitimacy from being connected with international academic trends while, on the other hand, they were often involved in decidedly particularistic projects like, for example, efforts to imbue their emerging nation-states with narratives of primordialism or cultural authenticity.[135]

A global professional milieu and its hierarchies

The global condition of historiography has always formed a compound web of overlapping local, regional, national, and global formations. Yet even though the landscapes of historiography have always been subject to changes, they also continue older imbalances and patterns of dependency. Most notably, hierarchical relationships between different languages, countries, and institutions remain an essential part of historiography as a worldwide professional field. Today's scholarly communities are certainly not lined up into separate but equal westphalian units. For instance, the global environments of historiography still tend to privilege a few, typically Western, languages while tending to sink others into oblivion.[136] Despite the rising influence of postcolonialism and related fields, structural inequalities of this kind are still not sufficiently problematized, even in the theoretical debates surrounding the global historical trend.

More blatant still are the discrepancies between the material conditions of history departments in different parts of the world. For example, after much hope during the decolonization period, in entire world regions such as sub-Saharan Africa or parts of Central Asia, crises of the nation-state have led to a dramatic decrease in academic funding. This leaves many history departments and research infrastructures such as archives largely dysfunctional, and it does so across vast geographical territories, which are inhabited by significant parts of the global population.[137] In many instances, failures or problems of the nation-state deepened the patterns of intellectual dominance through scholarship

---

[135] See, for example, Appiah (1997).
[136] Generally on the topic of hierarchies of knowledge see Naylor (2005); and Pinch (1999).
[137] For Africa see, for example, Ajayi and Festus (1994). See also Eckert (1999).

emerging from rich countries.[138] For example, African history written in several Western societies continues to play a towering role in most university systems south of the Sahara. Similar observations could be made for other parts of the world, including rather large regions in Latin America, South Asia, and East Asia.[139] By contrast, approaches to North American history published in languages other than English usually play only marginal roles in US-based research.

Even more strikingly, global theories of Western origin that are written without any expertise in the intellectual debates in other parts of the globe continue to be widely influential in many world regions. For example, works such as Samuel Huntington's *Clash of Civilizations* or Francis Fukuyama's *End of History* evoked heated international debates even though both works hardly consider any scholarship from outside of the Anglophone world.[140] By contrast, theoretical perspectives and research agendas published in English strongly influence academic developments elsewhere; works in other languages are much less likely to transgress local academic boundaries without being translated.[141] Global theory produced in China or the Arabic world, for instance, carries only little weight in Europe and the United States even if it is available in English.[142] The patterns of an Anglophone-centered world can be further discerned by looking at the general book market. While the proportion of translated works in the United States has declined from 8.6 percent in 1960 to less than 3 percent today, it has risen to a margin of 15 to 20 percent in many continental European countries.[143]

Patterns such as the strong position of Anglophone literature reflects who can afford to ignore whom when theorizing about global constellations, including world history. For example, whereas a historian in Britain or the United States can become a leading theorist without even acknowledging the existence of works in other languages, a scholar working in Farsi, Chinese, or another language does not have the same privilege. Moreover, scholars in the United States can write general

---

[138] For a more detailed discussion of this problem see the Epilogue.

[139] See, for example, Hein and Selden (2000); and Cooper (2000).

[140] About the global influence of both works see, for example, Iggers, Q. Wang and Mukherjee (2008), Chapter 8.

[141] See also Mignolo (2000).

[142] See the next section for some examples of recent globally influential intellectual currents whose symbolic origin is located outside of the West.

[143] Cusset (2008), p. 38. Still, the numbers for Europe should not suggest a rising interest in global dialogues. The vast majority of translations appearing on the European book market are taken from other European languages.

research reports and review papers without specifying that they are focusing only on research in Anglophone countries. But a Japanese scholar, for instance, could not possibly deliver an alleged "global" overview of world history or any other field while only citing Japanese literature. Academics and public intellectuals in many parts of the world need to be familiar with the latest research in Europe and America in order to gain credibility – not only in an international academic environment, but first and foremost in their own local academic communities. These efforts are typically not reciprocated by scholars operating in the West.[144] Within this unequal world, it is primarily classics from the European past such as Marx or Weber that continue to serve as intellectual reference points. By contrast, local traditions in China, sub-Saharan Africa, and elsewhere are still often presumed dead in the sense that they are treated as objects of study, without carrying any epistemological significance for the present.[145]

Despite the strong position of English, it would be wrong to assume that all other languages and academic systems have an equally marginal status in the global landscapes of knowledge. For example, many countries and languages have a very strong regional influence, which replicates patterns of intellectual dominance within geographically more confined scopes. In some cases it is even still possible to identify lasting configurations of colonial dominance in today's global academic landscapes. For example, whereas scholarship produced in France continues to take a central position in the academic flows of Francophone-influenced countries ranging from Senegal to Vietnam,[146] it plays a much more marginal role in Anglophone or Luzophone societies.[147] Certainly, such colonial geographies may have become weaker due to factors such as the rising global connectedness of US academia after the Second World War. But they still have a lasting presence.

Also in other cases, which do not belong to the category of language realms created by colonialism, one can observe cascades of international influence. Germany is an illustrative case. Here many historians have voiced complaints that the scholarship produced in their countries is insufficiently recognized in the United States and other Anglophone countries. However, at the same time, the German academic system also has attributes of centrality vis-à-vis a number of countries. Scholarly

---

[144] For critical perspectives on this issue see, for example, Chakrabarty (1992).
[145] See, for example, Chakrabarty (2000), pp. 6ff.
[146] See Middell (2003).
[147] Of course, certain elements of French theory transcended many linguistic boundaries and became highly influential in different parts of the world.

literature published in German is still very influential in the historiography of its neighboring countries ranging from the Czech Republic to Poland, Denmark, or the Netherlands. However, in Germany, publications emerging from these countries are typically not recognized outside of specific area studies. In this manner they fail to influence the methodological turns, conceptual debates, and the formation of new research agendas even when they address European or global historical issues.[148] Except for French, proficiency in the languages of neighboring countries is not part of the standard repertoire of German intellectual life. Most importantly, there are no significant efforts to make scholarship from these countries available to the academic public through translations.

Also the academic relations between China and the West are still significantly shaped by hierarchies and inequalities.[149] For example, during the 1990s, thirteen times more academic books in the social sciences and humanities were translated from English into Chinese than vice versa. Another aspect of the same problem is revealed by a crude statistical analysis of important articles published on transnational and global historical themes in China during the 1990s and early 2000s: on average, more than 60 percent of the articles cited were Anglophone publications, which were partly available in translation.[150] Furthermore, the flows of Chinese students to the West are not reciprocated on an even remotely similar scale. For instance, whereas in 2008, 60,000 Chinese students studied in the United States and 26,000 in Germany, only 1,200 German and less than 5,000 American students were enrolled in PRC universities. The continued attraction of the West for Chinese students is also a cause for the continued intellectual migration or "brain drain" out of China. According to a 2009 statement of the Chinese Ministry of Education, China has sent 1,391,500 students abroad since 1979, of whom only 390,000 or about 28 percent returned to their

[148] In a selection of ten articles in the field of world history and transnational history, not a single citation was in the language of any neighboring country of Germany except French. See Chapter 3.
[149] This trend is also evidenced by polls conducted among Chinese world history students. For example, one recent survey conducted at thirty-seven universities revealed that Chinese students would like to receive more intensive training in foreign, predominantly Western "classics" of world history writing. The same study revealed that the five most frequently cited texts belonging to this group, which students read in their spare time, were all Western. See J. Xia and L. Wan (2006).
[150] This number is the result of my analysis of twenty articles in the field, which were published in leading journals such as *Shijie lishi* (*World History*) as well as in essay collections like Yu (2007b).

country.[151] Yet, ironically, it is not only the brain drain but also its exact opposite that is a strong indication of persistent academic imbalances. A high proportion of Western-trained history faculty in countries from Chile to the Philippines points to hiring patterns that are partly shaped by the continued reputation of North American or European institutions of higher learning in other parts of the world.[152] The same basic pattern is confirmed by the case of the United States. Whereas the country's academic system has become more open to immigrants from outside of Europe and North America, most of the faculty belonging to this group have usually graduated from Western universities and not from institutions of higher learning elsewhere.

The Western bias of the current academic system is upheld not only by material conditions, but also by implicit visions of world order and tacit assumptions about global intellectual gravity. Critical schools such as the subaltern studies movement have long problematized the fact that Western epistemological dominance has become an intrinsic part of the local intellectual, cultural, social and political fabric.[153] There is a strong awareness that even ways of conceptualizing national or regional history in India have been decisively shaped by colonialism and other global interactions.[154]

The same is even more blatant in the study of macro-regions such as "Africa" or "Latin America" which, even as geographical or cultural unities, are not historically rooted and have their origins in European projections, interventions, and inventions.[155] Here taking the West out of the historian's toolbox must necessarily be a purposeful act against a powerful academic mainstream. For the professional worlds of a Western historian of Europe, by contrast, it is still not a professional imperative to be familiar with the basic patterns of another world region's history, let alone let one's research be influenced by it.[156] This is particularly striking in the recent trend towards Europeanizing historiography in Europe, where the deconstruction of methodological nationalism has not led to similarly intensive challenges of Eurocentric tropes. Even many younger European

---

[151] *Xinhua news* release, March 25, 2009.
[152] See, for example, Nagano (2004). In some cases, at least the geographical scopes of Western-trained faculty have been changing. For example in India, the colonial monopoly is weakening in the sense that the proportion of historians trained in Britain is declining. An increasing number of foreign-trained faculty have received their training in the United States, Australia, and other countries. Compare Bayly (1997).
[153] Prakash (1994).   [154] Chakrabarty (2000).
[155] For example see Mudimbe (1988); and Mignolo (2005).
[156] See, for example, Dirlik (2002a); and Chakrabarty (2000), particularly Chapter 1.

historians opine that the inner history of the continent can be understood as largely independent from its global entanglements.[157]

Obviously there are gaps of importance, weight, and power in the current international academic system – gaps which at least in some regards cast shadows of the nineteenth- and twentieth-century world order onto the twenty-first century. In the face of this situation one may be tempted to liken the basic parameters of global academic historiography to the conceptual worlds of world systems theory and differentiate between global academic centers, regionally influential semi-peripheries, and peripheries that do not play strong roles in other languages. Such a model would even quite adequately reflect a situation in which countries in the academic periphery have long held only relatively minor connections with each other, hence strengthening the dominance of more central areas.[158] For instance, the degree of know-ledge transfers and academic exchanges between history departments in Latin America and East Asia is dwarfed by Western influence in both parts of the world. The lasting Western-centric legacy in the global sociologies of academic knowledge significantly limits the directions that its flows take. In this sense, Eurocentrism and the insufficient degree of global communication among historians are closely related problems.

Yet while using a language taken from world systems theory may help us to illustrate some key facets of the global academic environments, abstractions of this kind would certainly fall short of adequately depicting the global realities of historiography. The topography of aca-demic centers of worldwide influence is far more complex than any macroscopic model could possibly grasp, particularly if it uses nations and languages as its main units of analysis. For example, within single countries such as the United States or Great Britain, rich private univer-sities and community colleges can be worlds apart in terms of their professional opportunities and impact on academic discourse.

In addition, the persistence of worldwide academic hierarchies should not make us erroneously conclude that the global environments of historiography have remained largely frozen in time. Quite to the con-trary, they have been subject to profound transformations. For example, in some parts of the world, most notably East Asia, national govern-ments have started to invest significant amounts of funding in the university sector, which has already started to influence global patterns

---

[157] For a critical discussion see, for example, Sachsenmaier (2009b); and Osterhammel (2004).

[158] For example, in China the number of experts in fields like Indian history or Middle Eastern history is dwarfed by the faculty size in US, European, and Russian history.

of intellectual exchange.[159] For example, whereas two decades ago the globally most influential research centers of Chinese historiography were still located in the Anglophone world and Taiwan, departments in China are now gaining more weight. The future implications of these shifts in the global academic landscapes are likely to be profound, and together with other factors they may contribute to changing the balances of the global academic system.

Decentering movements and the Cold War

Ever since the spread of modern historiography there have been counter-movements to the modern academic canon and its inherent discourses of world order. Already at an early stage, challenges to Western intellectual supremacy were often closely related to various forms of political struggles in different parts of the world.[160] While these opposition movements often appeared as local forms of intellectual resistance, also transnational groups such as the Négritude School were influential during a time when European colonial order still seemed to be intact.[161] Despite such important antecedents, it was during the Cold War period, particularly from the 1970s, that movements seeking to break through the alliance of Eurocentric and nation-centric thinking gained more presence in various academic milieus as well as in their surrounding public spheres. As a result of very complex changes, a growing number of academic circles started to become more overtly critical of Eurocentrism and many other important paradigms of historiography as a scientific field. In contrast to the beginning of the twentieth century, today critiques of Western bias have become a more common repertoire in many academic communities throughout the world. However, as the earlier discussion of persisting global academic hierarchies has reminded us, this does not mean that Eurocentric structures and mentalities have disappeared from the global academic landscapes.

Critiques of Eurocentrism evolved in such kaleidoscopic patterns that it is impossible to present them in any other way than by sketching some important sample developments. In terms of a general outline, it is possible to crudely differentiate between two main stages in critiques of Eurocentrism without taking fully account of an immeasurably more

---

[159] For more details see Chapter 4.
[160] For a historical overview of such political and intellectual movements see Young (2001).
[161] See, for example, Wilder (2005).

complex reality. Whereas in the first two decades after the Second World War opposition to global power constellations was primarily voiced from alternative civilizational or national standpoints, epistemological concerns moved gradually closer to the foreground during the 1970s and 1980s. Concepts like nations or continents from which earlier forms of criticism had been enunciated now increasingly became the objects of intellectual scrutiny: they were being problematized as products of Western dominance. This is not to say, however, that the concept of the nation and national history came unequivocally under the attack during this period. For example, as the Chinese case will show, in some academic communities national history could even become more strongly accentuated during a mounting search for alternative, non-Eurocentric approaches to history.

In the history of intellectual oppositions to Eurocentric thinking, the world wars certainly were an important factor.[162] In particular, the Second World War and the experience of fascism deepened and widened intellectual doubts about the normative implications of European history. Thinkers such as Franz Fanon, Aimé Césaire, and Léopold Senghor, who all became strongly rooted in French society, academia, and politics, argued that the trajectories reaching from colonialism to fascism discredited Western civilization *in toto*.[163] For instance, in the eyes of Césaire fascism was a direct continuation of imperialism and thus a culmination of Europe's civilizational trajectories rather than a deviation from them.[164] Based on similar assumptions, Senghor called for new forms of humanism to pursue what the West had never achieved.[165] Many thinkers belonging to different schools argued that the logics of modernity such as progress, materialism, and rationalism were only a poor shadow of human existence. Reduced levels of human and humanitarian existence they also meant to discover in the lifestyles, habits, and values of the European bourgeoisie. At the same time, even important figures such as Césaire readily operated with spatial concepts such as "civilization" or "nation," which were markers of a global order shaped by the West.[166]

The widespread disenchantment with hitherto dominant ideologies of political order came to a first symbolic climax in 1968. when

---

[162] About transnationally circulating doubts about Western modernity in the aftermath of the First World War see Sachsenmaier (2006).

[163] Césaire (1955). On the general intellectual and political environment see Wilder (2004).

[164] See also Young (1990).   [165] Senghor (1997).

[166] Early currents of the négritude movements did not even seek to deconstruct discourses of race and ethnicity. See, for example, Wilder (2005).

anti-systemic protest movements became quite vociferous in several Western societies, Warsaw Pact countries, and China.[167] Certainly, these movements were not driven by homogenous motives, and their majority primarily operated within national frameworks. Nevertheless, the global flows of theories during that time period were remarkable in many regards, including their directionalities. For example, in societies from the United States to India and Southeast Asia, Maoism grew visibly present in public discourse even though in many cases it was far from being accepted by the mainstreams of public opinion. In many regards the popularity of Mao's *Quotations* and other works marked the first time at which an alternative vision of modernity formulated in China acquired a global appeal of such extents.[168] Certainly, the impact of 1968 can be exaggerated. Also after that year, theories emanating from the West continued to be highly influential on a global level. Yet as a general trend, the global patterns of scholarly flows had become convoluted enough as to defy the possibility of a clear separation between the origins and the receptors of many transnational intellectual movements.[169]

During the second half of the Cold War, the disintegration of European colonial empires and their concomitant state-formation processes meant that nationality was no longer an unrealized objective for large parts of the world. In many societies, this new global condition fostered attempts at gaining more local agency, which in academic circles stimulated debates on how to decolonize academia in conjunction with political liberation struggles. In the midst of a geopolitical setting dominated by two superpowers and ideological systems, such intellectual impulses were often channeled into Third World solidarity movements.[170] These were at least partly critical of both the development faith emanating from Washington and its opposing versions being propagated by Moscow.

The failure of development programs in many newly decolonized societies was just one of the reasons behind the doubts about the idea of the United States and the USSR as international models and tutors. The global academic climate was further impacted by more long-term transformations, ranging from the gradual decline of the West's proportion of global GDP to the growing significance of non-national actors in the political, cultural, and economic sectors.[171] In addition, in several

---

[167] Scholars hold different opinions on the global historical characteristics of the 1968 movements. Seeing them as a world revolution: Wallerstein (1993). A collection with different interpretations: Fink, Gassert and Junker (1988). See also Klimke (2009).

[168] See Sachsenmaier (2009a).

[169] A relevant sociological theory is Castells (1996).

[170] See, for example, S. Tan and Acharya (2008).

[171] On such long-term developments see, for example, Maier (2000); and Iriye (2002).

societies such as the United States, intellectual migration and the partial departure from ethnic notions of citizenship had a strong impact on academic theorizing.[172] Here particularly the humanities witnessed growing calls for the rise of subjugated forms of knowledge as well as increasing intellectual opposition to linear and universal master narratives.[173] All this raised the pressure on hitherto dominant tropes of world history and national history.

In the following, I will briefly discuss dependency theory and subaltern studies as two major transnational movements and examples of changes in the search for decentered visions during the second half of the twentieth century. Both schools were diverse enough to defy any precise definition, so it will only be possible to delineate some general patterns and tendencies. What the main currents of dependency theory and, slightly later, subaltern studies had in common is that they sought to strengthen the presence of alternative perspectives in historical inquiry. In both cases, this was related to specific political objectives and societal visions, with critiques of dominant world historical tropes playing an important role in the spectrum of intellectual topics covered. It will become clear that the main critiques of the dependency theory were often based on national perspectives. By contrast, critical re-evaluation of the nation and other concepts was a far more important part of the subaltern studies movement.

Precursors to – or early versions of – dependency theory emerged prior to the Second World War in Latin America. They were rooted in long intellectual traditions critiquing the reliance of Latin American countries on foreign political and economic powers.[174] During the 1950s and 1960s, public intellectuals in Latin America challenged development programs under the leadership of the United States. Like any major intellectual movement, dependency theory quickly branched out in different directions, some of which were more radical, while others were more moderate in terms of their overall political outlooks. However, most dependency theorists commonly held that the presence of a Western liberal market economy – and not its absence – was the root cause for economic misery and social crises in most countries south of the Rio Grande del Norte border.[175] In other words, scholars in this camp tended to argue that it was not local cultures and

---

[172] See Fahrmeir (2007). For more details about the US case see Chapter 2.
[173] An account of the wide range of positions covered by "postmodernism" and its history is offered by Taylor and Winquist (2001). See also Cusset (2008).
[174] For example by Lindström (1991).
[175] A good summary of the origins and evolution of dependency theories in Latin America is provided by Bernecker and Fischer (1995). See also Kay (1989).

structures that were to blame for the poverty of the Third World, but rather the structures and mechanisms of the global economic system. In this manner, concepts such as underdevelopment were no longer primarily seen as markers of a society's stagnation but as historically grown signs of disadvantageous relationships. The mere involvement of the West, it was argued, made it impossible for other societies to follow its historical trajectories.

The contrast between socialism and capitalism may have been an important aspect in the rhetoric of many dependency theorists,[176] but we should bear in mind the fact that the majority of thinkers in this camp did not primarily pursue any kind of internationalist solution. The main objective was often to gain local control over the ideas and mechanisms of development, which implied a radical critique of the directions and flows of international knowledge. Some took this position further and sought to break out of local habits of defining themselves in a subordinate position vis-à-vis Europe. In many countries, theoretical activities of this kind were linked to political efforts to forge a protectionist alliance between national business owners, the workforce, and an interventionist state. In the eyes of many dependency theorists this would reverse the terms of international trade, which had grown over long historical time periods and had progressively eroded the possibility of countries in the global periphery to act in their own interests.[177]

Since such disadvantageous global entanglements were not unique to Latin America, the dependency theory movement spread to other parts of the world, where it was adapted to new intellectual contexts. In Africa, for example, critical intellectuals referred to dependency theory when questioning the prospects of national liberation and its Western frameworks.[178] In fact, there was a certain overlap between the prominence of these positions and the appropriation of Soviet theories by leaders in several countries in the sub-Saharan part of the continent. During the 1960s, many African presidents including Sékou Touré (Guinea) and Kwame Nkrumah (Ghana) were at least partly influenced by the dependency movement.[179] Many prominent political figures maintained that their countries' underdevelopment was the direct result of colonial exploitation and imperialism. Yet whereas some leaders were closer to Soviet interpretations, others believed that primarily non-imperialist capitalist development provided a way out of their countries' condition.[180]

---

[176] Compare Packenham (1992).
[177] See, for example, Menzel (1994). See also Bernecker and Fischer (1995).
[178] See Cooper (1994).
[179] See Young (2001), pp. 46ff.   [180] Grundy (1966).

The paths and patterns in which dependency theory found its way to Africa and other parts of the world were certainly far more complicated than a direct transmission from Latin America. In fact, the reception in the United States, where dependency theory started enjoying a great prominence in the 1960s, was important for the further international spread of the movement.[181] Here, scholars such as Andre Gunder Frank moved dependency theory closer to the conceptual world of Marxism, albeit in modified forms.[182] Yet in spite of the important role played by American scholars, dependency theory came to represent an internationally prominent academic school that had emerged from partly non-Western contexts. This may have been more constructed than accurate, but it was important that a non-Western region and its intellectual circles were identified as the wellspring of global alternatives to the dominant theoretical positions of the Cold War. To put it in a different way, even though the approaches often subsumed under "dependency theory" were being produced in a translocal network of exchanges, Latin America continued to figure as the movement's symbolic and conceptual center of enunciation. An effort to make the experience base of areas outside of the West heard was basic to these approaches, and in that sense dependency theory implied a challenge not only to Eurocentrism but also to Western-centric critiques of Eurocentrism.[183]

While schools such as dependency theory were centered on economic and other material perspectives, it was particularly during the 1970s and 1980s when some left-wing theories brought allegedly "soft" factors into the foreground. This opened up new possibilities to combine critical approaches towards the cultures of academic scholarship with attempted interventions in global cultural, economic, and political realities. Some influential thinkers further developed the idea that the conceptual worlds employed by scholars were part of the mechanisms through which global hierarchies and imbalances functioned. Efforts to retrieve hitherto marginalized perspectives started heading in a direction that differed significantly from the positions of world systems theory and its precursors. For example, in the United States and some other academic communities, the so-called "cultural turn" was characterized by a growing interest in representations, identities, and symbolisms as objects of scholarly inquiry.

---

[181] An early but still accurate summary was provided by Cardoso (1977).

[182] An important work was A. Frank (1969). Compare Packenham (1992). An early US position of related ideas was Baran (1957).

[183] See, for example, Wolfe (1997), p. 405.

Many internationally influential theorists who sought to reinterpret global developments from the perspectives of the underprivileged actually shared a transnational background. A prominent figure was Edward Said, a Palestinian thinker teaching in the United States. His general hypothesis that the Western academy played a constitutive role in colonial projects by fitting previously rather autonomous societies into frameworks of dominance proved to have a strong impact among intellectuals from different parts of the world.[184] The debates that Said's main work, *Orientalism*,[185] provoked in many different societies were a strong indication of significant changes taking place in academic climates at that time. Compared to the decolonization years as well as the pre-war period, the international academic community was now more ready to problematize the social sciences in terms of their relations with patterns of global dominance and power. Also in the field of world history there was a greater readiness to "confront the philosophically certified 'higher morality' of world-history by asking some difficult questions about colonizers claiming to be the authorized historians of lands and peoples they have themselves put under a colonial yoke."[186]

In most academic arenas, the groups of scholars moving along these lines were intellectual minorities, but their voices were becoming stronger, particularly in the humanities. Another manifestation of this trend was the rise of movements that either labeled themselves as "subaltern studies" or were later associated with that term. "Subaltern studies" came to connote a very diverse research landscape, which by and large was far more closely entangled with history departments than other branches of postcolonialism.[187] The immediate roots of subaltern studies go back to the concrete context of the political, social, and cultural crises in India during the 1970s. At that time, the capitalist modernization programs under the government of Indira Gandhi had significantly widened the social, regional, and political gaps within the country. This trend was countered by growing waves of protest movements. Responding to this deteriorating situation, India's political leadership turned partly to repressive measures and partly to populist campaigns in order to gain support from the masses. The government's success in restoring its own authority was limited:

[184] See, for example, Freitag (1997); and Lütt (1998).
[185] Said (1979).   [186] Gran (1996), p. 5.
[187] For overviews of postcolonial theory see, for example, Young (2001); Gandhi (1998); as well as Loomba (1998).

the nation-state survived but in the eyes of many, the crisis eroded the legitimacy of national institutions such as the state administration and the legal system.[188]

The ensuing struggle over who could claim to represent India also became a dispute over who could speak for the Indian past. Pointing to the peasant uprisings shaking India during the early 1970s, thinkers like Ranajit Guha held that the underprivileged were being categorized and instrumentalized by the new national elites that had replaced the former colonial ones.[189] Despite their diversity of approaches, the subaltern studies group commonly argued that since elite discourses in India were either bourgeois-nationalist or Marxist, they were equally unmusical to the viewpoints and situation of the Indian peasantry. As a consequence, the argument went, potentially beneficial political mentalities and social structures within the Indian peasantry were relegated to a subaltern position.[190] National liberation, some thinkers further argued, may have fought against the stereotype of India being a passive society, but at the same time remained loyal to the former colonizers' categories of thinking.[191] Many intellectuals concluded that only if the subcontinent found its own ways of representing itself, particularly its masses, could it hope to find a dignified future.[192]

In this context, a significant amount of energy was spent criticizing the role of academic disciplines, most notably historiography.[193] A good number of scholars argued that both right-wing and left-wing approaches to history forced the Indian past into an iron cage of exogenous, Western concepts, and doing so at least tacitly implied asking how India "performed" vis-à-vis categories such as progress, modernization, and rationalization. While the argument went, "conservative" nationalist circles were attempting to write pride into the Indian past by equating its key concepts with Europe, Marxist circles were also unwilling to disentangle Indian history from Europe. This would have weakened the global power of concepts such as class and make it impossible to critique material dependencies.

According to many critics, applying European categories to India would mean perpetuating the intellectual patterns that had long supported European supremacy in the geopolitical arena. Based on this

---

[188] After Prakash (1994), particularly pp. 1474–76.
[189] See, for example, Guha (1982a); and Chatterjee (1993).
[190] See, for example, Guha (1982b); and O'Hanlon (1998).
[191] For example, Prakash (1990).   [192] Compare Inden (1986).
[193] For example, Gyan Prakash called for new post-foundational historiographies. See Prakash (1990). For more details see Young (2001), pp. 4ff.

assessment, a fair number of scholars initially set out to retrieve the voices of the "subaltern" and to explore them through the lenses of indigenous value systems, agendas and perspectives.[194] This notion was at least partly driven by the quest to regain authority over the logics with which India's past and the present were being conceptualized. Subsequently, the bulk of subaltern studies shifted its attention more towards studying the mechanisms of persuasion and coercion through which colonial and later national elites secured their own interests and power. For example, some research projects sought to show how, during the independence movement, the Indian elites marginalized certain forms of mass action while utilizing others.[195]

It is important to emphasize that subaltern studies were not – and never professed to be – a local counter-movement against global forces. Despite its initially local agendas, the subaltern studies group was mainly the product of translocal intellectual flows. Among other currents, French theory, the Cambridge School, postmodern philosophy, and Maoist elements were openly acknowledged as playing a constitutive role within this school.[196] Furthermore, the educational background of many early protagonists of subaltern studies oscillated between India and Western, typically Anglo-American societies. For example, Partha Chatterjee, who grew up in Calcutta and graduated from an American university, developed his main intellectual framework back in his hometown, where he stayed for several years during the 1970s. Subsequently, Chatterjee shifted his professional basis to the West, where he joined the faculty of prominent universities. Here he and other scholars with an Indian background such as Dipesh Chakrabarty, Gyan Prakash, and Gayatri Spivak quickly gained influence that reached far beyond academic circles in the United States and India. At the same time it was – analogous to the symbolic role of Latin America within dependence theory – important to construe India as the conceptual center, the locale of their critique's main concern and enunciation.

Epistemological doubts

The epistemological concerns articulated by subaltern studies and other intellectual movements have met criticism on different levels. For example, some scholars have argued that the purported

---

[194] An example discussed by Spivak (1998); and Bhabha (1994a).
[195] For example Chatterjee (1993). Heading in a similar direction: Sh. Amin (1984).
[196] See Lal (2002).

pluralization of perspectives boiled down to a marketization of difference within the academic ivory towers. According to them, the inclusion of gender as well as area-specific perspectives in primarily textually oriented research stabilized the fundaments of the academic system, moved synchronous to the logics of late capitalism, and hence abandoned the quest for radical emancipatory movements.[197] In this context, some critics interpreted the rise of postcolonial theory less as the search for subaltern voices and more as an expression of the power of intellectuals from the Third World who had acquired a rather high status in Western academia and were detached from the realities in poorer countries.[198] Coming from a different angle, other scholars argued that the success of subaltern studies and, later, postcolonial criticism was primarily in Western societies, whereas the main currents of academic theories in many parts of the Global South were heading in a different direction.[199]

Criticism of this kind has been mainly directed at subaltern studies and related academic agendas as they were being institutionalized in the West. It pointed to themes and problems which indeed may warrant further reflection, theorizing, and debate. After all, the privileged positions within the global hierarchies of knowledge from which many subaltern studies standpoints were being formulated were much less subject to the intellectual criticism of this movement. At the same time, subaltern studies or postcolonialism in the West have only been part of a geographically much wider nexus of strengthening doubts about the cultures, concepts, and structures of academic scholarship. Generally speaking, in many parts of the world there has been a rising problem-consciousness regarding the relationship between concepts, tropes, and languages on the one hand, and patterns of dominance or power structures on the other hand. This growing skepticism certainly did not form a coherent global intellectual movement,[200] so it remains a daunting task for future historians to map out its global paths and patterns during the last third of the twentieth century.

This estrangement between scholars and established academic concepts can be observed in many different areas of intellectual activity. The application of Western categories to local contexts outside of Europe has now been problematized in areas of research, which had long been quite immune to epistemological criticism. For instance, in

[197] For example Kaiwar (2004); Jameson (1991); and Appiah (1991).
[198] Dirlik (1994). About such criticism see Moore-Gilbert (1997), pp. 18ff.
[199] For example Mallon (1994).
[200] See also Chapter 4 as well as the Epilogue.

many countries even disciplines like economics have produced a small but at least increasing number of studies that shift away from the neo-classical models based on the idea of the universal *homo economicus* by gravitating towards embedded views and regionally sensitive perspectives.[201] In addition, at least partially globally oriented fields like development studies, environmental studies, and health studies now take local viewpoints and contextual approaches far more seriously than a generation ago.[202] Research projects which head in such directions have often been enriched by growing levels of international and interdisciplinary collaboration, even between the humanities and the natural sciences. As part of this development, a wide range of academic disciplines have demonstrated greater levels of sensitivity to the way in which local differences add complexity to the relationship between the subjects and objects of academic inquiry.

Together, developments of this kind could be regarded as disciplinary crises that many academic fields have experienced over the past few decades. For example, in the United States and some other societies, the main body of anthropology has become rather hostile to differentiating between civilized and less advanced societies, which originally had been foundational to the field. This change of disciplinary cultures has been quite significant, given the fact that during much of the Cold War the mainstreams of anthropology had still supported progressivist programs designed to help others to develop.[203] Moreover, during the same time period fields like sociology faced mounting levels of opposition to the notion of universal perspectives and the idea that future global models could be derived from the Western experience. The resulting disciplinary culture wars were often entangled with paradigm shifts within international organizations and even government circles. These had to face the failure of modernizing pedagogies in many decolonized societies in addition to the effects of macroscopic processes such as the decentering of the world economy. Although there had previously been critiques of universal worldviews, the distrust of Western-centric paradigms has become gradually stronger and more internationally connected over the past forty years.

Such epistemological discontent and critical awareness of the power structures could also be felt in many historians' workshops around the

---

[201] See, for example, Harvey and Garnett (2008); and Goodwin, Nelson, Ackerman and Weiskopf (2008).

[202] About activities in the field of environment and health studies see, for example, envhealthasia.aas.duke.edu. About development studies see, for example, Sachsenmaier (2009c); and Apffel-Marglin and Marglin (1996). See also W. Tu (2002).

[203] See, for example, Ferguson (1997).

world. For example, in large parts of sub-Saharan Africa there have been significant debates revolving around the question of alternative historical imaginaries to the nation-state paradigm, even though the latter continues to dominate institutions of higher learning.[204] While there had been earlier antecedents, already the 1980s witnessed a growing movement towards searching for more dignified ways of connecting African history with other world regions – ways that would see Africa not primarily through Western lenses and grant indigenous groups greater levels of agency than much of historiography had done before.[205] For example, on a methodological level, African and Western scholarship on African history witnessed more efforts to move away from the dominance of written source materials in Western languages, which in some cases could lead to a greater interest in oral traditions.[206] Furthermore, particularly in those states in which national universities have failed, secular, national, or scientific paradigms have been increasingly challenged as colonial or postcolonial impositions which do not correspond to the realities of social, cultural, and political communities on a local level.[207] In some cases, such processes have been paralleled by the increasing presence of Islamic and other alternative forms of knowledge. However, the scopes and impact of such currents should not be exaggerated. While they have become more influential, the dominance of Western intellectual life in Africa still constitutes a set of unresolved problems, especially within the confinements of academia. In many countries, the structures of university-based historiography continue to endorse an interplay of nation-centered and Eurocentric perspectives.

In other cases, national tropes of history have come under pressure from different directions. For example, in many societies historiography has been greatly influenced by pressure groups such as women's movements, who demanded that the field pay more attention to gender issues. This changed a discipline that in many societies had long been dominated by patriarchic outlooks. In addition, in some former colonies that had long been dominated by white segments of the population, there have been processes to decenter national history in the sense of putting more emphasis on the experience of hitherto marginalized ethnic groups. In addition to the United States, which will be dealt with in the next chapter, this has been the case in

---

[204] See, for example, Diouf (2000); and Cooper (2000).
[205] For example, Boahen (1987).
[206] See, for example, Feierman (1993).   [207] See, for example, Harneit-Sievers (2002).

Australia. Here, attempts to give the Aborigines and Asian immigrants a greater presence in academic research and state-sponsored history education provoked big public debates and even conservative back-lashes.[208] Also in Latin America, where some societies had long since failed to acknowledge a history of ethnic pluralism, there have been strong movements pushing towards greater levels of attention and appreciation of ethnic and cultural diversity. Particularly since the 1990s, indigenous and local groups launched more concerted activities towards a pluralization of society, which would allow greater levels of cultural self-representation and hence contribute to changing forms of historical consciousness.[209]

These examples suggest that, in many cases, unifying national histor-ical narratives came increasingly under pressure and now face opposition from identity groups that seek to gain a voice in politically endorsed forms of historical consciousness. New schools and movements stepped up their efforts to explore alternative social and cultural formations and, by implication, break with traditions of history that deal with nations as rather uniform entities. To a certain extent, this is certainly the result of social changes within academic environments. For example, in many countries the massive expansion of the education sector brought indi-viduals from new social and ethnic backgrounds to the academic ivory towers which, as a general development, put older elite-centered dis-courses under pressure.[210] Just as Eurocentrism and nation-centrism were usually part of the same conceptual package during the global spread of modern academic historiography, many of the more recent counter-movements have in fact turned against both, methodological nationalism and the idea of the West as the main global reference space.

It must be stressed, again, that growing academic critiques and research activities of this kind ought not be misunderstood as a majority discourse. In many parts of the world, national frameworks and Western-centrism continue to dominate academic environments, and in some cases critiques of national perspectives have met significant levels of scholarly opposition. Moreover, as discussed, the global land-scapes of knowledge remain in many regards hierarchical and still widely centered on privileged Western societies. Still, there have been changing patterns in global academic theorizing, many of which are highly relevant for the global historical trend. As already mentioned in the introduction, it is impossible to assess the complex dynamics

---

[208] See, for example, Haebich (2005); and Hearn (2007).
[209] See, for example, Millet (2006); and Jackson and Warren (2005).
[210] See Altbach (2007). From a different angle: Gibbons (1994).

behind these transformations while simultaneously taking account of global and local perspectives. Therefore, while this current chapter illuminated some general facets of global academic cultures, the following three chapters will focus more specifically on aspects of the global historical trend in the United States, Germany, and China. Combined with other factors, the concrete intellectual, public, and political forces feeding into this trend were not identical across these three cases. This in turn created specific paths, patterns, and centers of gravity in the field of global history.

2 A term and a trend: contours in the United States

Change in academic landscapes

As the previous chapter has shown, American universities were closely connected with several transnational movements criticizing facets of university-based historiography. While it would be erroneous to assume that the rising problem-consciousness regarding Eurocentric visions disseminated from the United States to other parts of the world, American academia played a significant role as a transaction hub in the global flows of theories. At the same time, many related academic transformations at US institutions of higher learning were not only caused by international movements of scholars: also a chain of domestic developments contributed to their growing presence. Since the specific rhythms of change were quite cacophonous, it is possible to sketch only some of the main forces which during the past half century were relevant for the significant changes in historical scholarship practiced on US campuses.

The history of area-specific research is an important example for some wider transformations within important segments of the humanities and social sciences in the United States. Ever since the 1940s, area studies at American universities were strongly promoted by the US government as well as by private foundations, with the chief aim of training a pool of skilled labor needed for the country's new international involvements and ambitions.[1] The institutionalization of area studies rose sharply in the 1960s, peaked in the 1970s, and went into a slow decline from the 1990s. In the eyes of many decision-makers, these fields were initially supposed to cater to political needs by providing training facilities and delivering information about strategically relevant parts of the world. In other words, the area studies were set up not with the intention of challenging the conceptual frameworks within which nomothetic fields such as sociology or political sciences operated, nor with the expectation

---

[1] See, for example, Palat (2000); and Manning (2003). Latin American history was already institutionally expanded in the aftermath of the First World War.

that they would have major implications for the study of history at large. Yet in the following decades, the growing academic expertise on world regions outside of the West was increasingly included in the portfolio of larger fields, including historiography. Particularly starting from the late 1970s, this changed the landscapes of several academic disciplines since many departments began systematically creating faculty positions with a regional focus on other world regions. As a consequence, the proportion of faculty at US history departments who primarily work on North America or Europe declined to about 66 percent nationwide and an even lower ratio at research universities.[2]

Together with other factors, structural changes of this kind put more pressure on dominant narratives in the study of world history and national history.[3] Needless to say, the pluralization of area-specific research did not evolve in a homogenous manner that would allow for blunt generalizations.[4] Yet as a general trend, this process facilitated cooperation and joint interventions of experts working on different parts of the world. Most notably, it made it at least easier to confront scholarship on Western history with research focusing on other parts of the world. In a very complex and certainly not linear set of developments, a growing number of scholars working on world regions outside of Europe and North America grew increasingly convinced that it was necessary to break out of the niches which originally had been ascribed to their research areas. For example, some influential academics problematized the Eurocentric categories with which different world regions such as China, India, or the Middle East were being assessed and analyzed. In a related step, more scholars based in the area studies or affiliated with them started to challenge the epistemological claims and research agendas that were widely supposed to frame their fields.[5]

The changes in area expertise at US universities were only one aspect of much larger, interconnected transformations that American academia experienced during and after the Cold War. An important development framing the overall historical context was the growing pluralization of universities – a process which, however, should not be confused with narrowing social gaps in the United States at large. As in many parts of the world,[6]

---

[2] See Townsend (2001); and Gräser (2009).

[3] An example is the growing criticism that "Western civilization courses" had to face, particularly during the 1970s and 1980s. See, for example, Allardyce (1982); and Naumann (2007).

[4] For example, single branches within the area studies tended to grow more critical offshoots than others; for example, the subaltern studies movement was much more forceful in South Asian studies than in East Asian studies.

[5] See, for example, Cumings (1998).   [6] See Scott (2006). See also Chapter 1.

institutions of higher learning in the United States were considerably enlarged during the postwar period, which meant that the number of professional academics and students grew rapidly.[7] The expansion of the university sector was granted political priority for a variety of reasons – for example, in many eyes strengthening the educated and highly trained parts of the population was seen an apt way of responding to the new geopolitical roles and ambitions of the country. Successive measures ranging from the GI Education Act of 1944 to the National Defense Education Act (1958) gave new social groups and classes access to higher education.[8] Against this background, it is remarkable that not only applied sciences and technical fields but also the humanities and social sciences experienced a rapid expansion of the faculty and student body. In the following decades, the idea of broadening access to higher education and widening its scopes continued to receive a high degree of political, societal, and private support. Even when the baby boom generation was reaching adulthood, the proportion of students among the overall population continued to rise.[9]

This process contributed to a diversification of scholars and students in terms of their social and cultural backgrounds, and it also had an impact on research and teaching agendas. Even though faculty numbers did not continue to grow significantly from the 1970s, US universities came to experience a social revolution that pluralized the ethnic, gendered, and social backgrounds of students to a historically unprecedented degree.[10] For example, at the University of California, Berkeley the proportion of students of Asian descent (both immigrants and citizens) went up from 7 percent of the graduate student population and 23 percent of the under-graduate body in 1983 to 17.6 and 41.7 percent respectively in 2007.[11] Similar things are true for the composition of history faculty, albeit to a lesser extent: not only women but also increasing numbers of scholars from non-European origins and quite divergent social backgrounds joined the ranks of the field.[12] US history departments certainly did not belong to the forerunners of the demographic transformations, and yet the pro-portion of Caucasian, that is, "white" faculty declined from 95.4 percent in 1988 to 85.3 percent in 2007.[13] Furthermore, while in 1980 women comprised 14 percent of academic historians, their proportion climbed to

---

[7] See, for example, Bender (1997).   [8] See Krige (2006).
[9] See Geiger (2005).   [10] See Higham (1989).
[11] Source: osr2.berkeley.edu/Public/STUDENT.DATA/set/set_registrants/html.
[12] Generally on the diversification of history faculty: Appleby, Hunt and Jacob (1995), pp. 206ff.
[13] Source: US Department of Education, National Center for Education Statistics, 2004 and 1988 National Study of Postsecondary Faculty.

30.4 percent in 2008.[14] As a consequence of these changes, the formerly widely dominant group of "white men" now only hold slightly more than half of the country's history faculty positions,[15] and the proportion of individuals from an Anglo-Saxon Protestant background has become even significantly lower than that figure.

These demographic transformations did not take place along identical lines across the entire nation. Some of the patterns of social change were regionally conditioned – for example, the sociopolitical situation in the American South was hardly comparable with the points of departure for universities in many other parts of the country. Furthermore, the pluralization of faculty and students could vary considerably between individual institutions, and it could be enhanced by different motivations ranging from sociopolitical pressure to economic interests. Some case studies have already started granting us insights into the intricate web of transformations that single US universities experienced during the Cold War and after.[16] Many instances, however, still require some more detailed historical investigation – among them Duke University, which evolved from a rather conservative segregationist Southern elite school in the early 1960s into an ethnically quite diverse university a generation later, where fields like cultural studies, postcolonialism, and neo-Marxism were well established.[17]

Building on a larger number of case studies, it would be worth historicizing the wider nexuses in which the developments at single universities were connected with each other and with society at large. Certainly, social changes in academia did not take place within an isolated ivory tower – much rather, they were entangled with wider social movements and political transformations. Most importantly, the waves generated by the civil rights movement and the Vietnam War heavily impacted US campuses and strengthened the demands to open the campus gates to hitherto underrepresented social groups. In a remarkably short period of time, the often rather open racist consensus at many American universities was forced onto the defensive. For growing segments of the US higher education system, pluralization rather than segregation became a calling of the time, which was so loud that it no longer could possibly be ignored by purveyors of economic interests, academic authorities, and political power.

---

[14] See Townsend (2008).   [15] See Townsend (2008).
[16] For example Lowen (1997); and Conkin (1995).
[17] Some interesting insights can be found in the autobiography of John Hope Franklin, the first African American president of the American Historical Association: Franklin (2005).

As a general development, the social changes and growing calls for inclusiveness at US universities had the most considerable impact on the conceptual worlds of the humanities and sections of the social sciences. In a number of disciplines such as literature and anthropology, rather hefty disciplinary culture wars erupted from the mounting pressure to move research and teaching agendas away from its Western-centric biases. Also history departments were the sites of significant contestations,[18] even though here academic counter-movements tended to be less extreme than in other fields.[19] During the second half of the Cold War, an increasing number of scholars and public intellectuals started to argue that the mainstreams of academic historiography were not doing justice to the diversity of the country.[20] There were growing doubts whether the ways in which history was commonly studied in the United States adequately represented the experiences of society or whether they were centered on privileged perspectives and elitist outlooks. In that sense, ideals conceived to democratize US universities in terms of their teaching and research agendas were at least entwined with the growing significance of academic currents such as the history from below movement.[21] Many groups advocating hitherto subaltern perspectives were becoming more strongly represented within US universities, and they often did so by rallying around identity causes or political objectives.[22] Among other developments, growing research fields, ranging from gender studies to African American studies, started challenging more vehemently the unity of the US past by posing questions such as "whose history?" In other words, they went against prevailing research agendas by shedding light on experiences and groups that did not easily fit into dominant tropes.[23]

Of course, ever since the late nineteenth century there had been several waves of movements striving to further broaden, pluralize and, by implication, democratize historiography and historical memory in

[18] Novick (1988).   [19] Compare Bonnelli and Hunt (1999).
[20] A very influential work was Zinn (1980).
[21] Research has increasingly come to address the connections between the changing geopolitical roles of the United States and its domestic struggles over race relations. In the context of Cold War competition over the Third World, even conservative forces in the country were at least under some pressure to demonstrate the United States was an inclusivist rather than an exclusivist society. See Borstelmann (2002); and Dudziak (2002).
[22] Bastedo (2005); and Searle (1994).
[23] In this context, critiques of widespread historical master narratives grew stronger and more concerted. For example, many scholars sharply turned against the idea that the American frontier marked the culmination of Western history, which in turn was depicted as an unfolding of freedom. See the reminiscences of W. McNeill (1995), pp. 10ff.

the United States.[24] Yet it was especially the transformations from the 1960s onward that diversified the fields of activity in US history departments to a degree that raised the objectivity question in history in new and politically palpable ways. Directly or indirectly, such movements as the "cultural turn" and, more generally, the rise of skepticism about reductionist generalizations could be felt across many academic disciplines.[25] In a related development, American universities became important arenas for critiques of Western-centric perspectives. Intellectual currents such as subaltern studies, post-colonialism, and postmodernism, which all espouse certain anti-hegemonic ideals, may have remained a minority discourse in the United States, yet their institutional bases have grown much stronger than in many other parts of the world, along with their impact on academic life in general.[26] It may be an overstatement that, during the rise of postcolonialism and other movements, Western institutions were deployed for the first time against the West.[27] Still, the academic changes during that time period were significant and caused the field in the United States to shift quite far apart from its hitherto dominant trajectories.

This brief outline of some social and epistemological changes in American universities since the 1960s needs to be seen as a general background from which many forms of global and transnational history emerged. The following sections of this chapter will primarily concentrate on more recent research developments in different branches of historiography. Addressing specific areas of research or even single publications, these sections will not search for direct causalities between social transformations and conceptual changes within the field of historiography. When investigating a wide array of academic literature, the rest of this chapter predominantly focuses on the United States but it will be impossible to operate with a narrow definition of "American" scholarship. This means that I will also consider many Anglophone publications produced in other countries which had an impact on historiography in the United States. As already discussed in the introduction, international entanglements are not unusual in any academic community. However, in cases such as Germany and China, the vast amount of Anglophone literature circulating on a global level is, *qua lingua*, more clearly recognizable

[24] See Novick (1988).   [25] Bonnelli and Hunt (1999).
[26] Critical accounts of the topic: Chomsky (1997); Robin (2001); and Cusset (2008).
[27] Young (2001), p. 64. One may think of the presence of Marxism during the nineteenth and twentieth centuries in some Western countries.

as emanating from different centers of enunciation, and it is often perceived as such. However, the availability of Anglophone literature from different parts of the world on the US market should not be taken as an indication of exceptionally tight connections between American academia and the pulse of research in many other parts of the world. Typically only a small segment of research produced elsewhere becomes available in English and, beyond that, is recognized within the community of US historians.

"Global history" – the rise of a new term

The diversifying nature of academic fields has profound implications for our understanding of the rhythms according to which they change. Some new intellectual developments rather quickly rally around an individual work, a thinker, or an identifiable school of thought. Movements such as world systems theory or the Orientalism school are examples of trends that already in their early stages developed a *locus classicus*, vis-à-vis which their supporting forces could articulate their cause. In most cases, however, the paths and patterns of emerging academic trends are much more diffuse and decentered. What later becomes a powerful transformation within an academic discipline often starts with shifting outlooks, interests, and individual predilections which are initially so diffuse and scattered that it takes a while before their first supporters or opponents articulate them as a new trend. In fact, an academic trend is usually already well on its way at the time when new terms are being coined to designate it as a distinct field of inquiry or methodological school. It is only at this stage that great academic controversies surrounding new concepts and approaches typically emerge.[28]

Within such a context, it is often almost impossible to precisely define the nature and core agendas of single academic schools. For example when newly coined terms such as "social history" or "cultural history" rose to prominence, they did not necessarily connote a coherent research spectrum. A brief look at some intellectual developments such as the rise of "social history" or "cultural history" in the past reveals that uncertain meanings and vague agendas are nothing out of the ordinary among newly emerging areas of research.[29] In fact,

---

[28] For some important academic debates in the field of historiography see Raphael (1990).
[29] Examples for theoretical literature seeking to characterize and further accentuate this movement are Hunt (1989); and Darnton (1984).

it is nigh impossible to define the intellectual contours of any academic movement by identifying a clear beginning and categorically distinguishing it from closely related fields. The problems incurred when mapping out a new field are manifold. For instance, only a tiny fraction of scholars who can be ascribed to a certain intellectual movement actually identify themselves with its new field designations and use them in their publication titles. Furthermore, most of the scholarship, which can be associated with a specific trend, usually remains closely entangled with a wide variety of other schools of thought.

Yet methodological pluralism and factitious dissent should not lead us to the erroneous conclusion that most academic trends are merely artificial labels. An example is the term "globalization," which during the 1970s was still referred to as a novelty[30] but in the meantime has become a key concept in social theory and a catchword in the public debates beyond.[31] Despite its wide range of attributes and meanings, research on "globalization" has been characterized by more shared agendas than critics pointing to its alleged lack of coherence might assume. Certainly, single academic schools and opinion camps tend to refer to "globalization in rather peculiar ways:[32] for example, whereas some scholars treat globalization as a culturally homogenizing force, others assume that processes subsumed under the same keyword generate new kinds of pluralism.[33] And while some neoliberal as well as neo-Marxist thinkers see globalization primarily as an economic process, other kinds of literature discuss it as a combination of closely tangled transformations, which can also include social and cultural forces as primary factors.[34]

Yet in spite of these contradictory interpretations, the keyword "globalization" has come to stand for an important development across a wide variety of academic disciplines. In its very core, it signifies the mounting importance of studies exploring transregional interconnections, transformative processes, and mutual influences across political as well as geographical boundaries. Just as in many other countries, also in the United States, research related to globalization has begun to be

---

[30] For example, Modelski (1972). See also Cox (1996), pp. 21ff.   [31] Mazlish (1998).

[32] A detailed study of the international semantics of globalization has yet to be undertaken. For some discussions see, for example, Scholte (2000).

[33] For a discussion of this problem see, for example, Robertson (1995). Even within a school such as world systems theory there can be quite different interpretations of globalization: for example while some see it as a process leading beyond established core-periphery structures, others argue that it further accentuates historically conditioned worldwide hierarchies. See, for example, Arrighi (2000).

[34] For example, various positions can be found in Applebaum and Robinson (2005); Ritzer (2004); and Chanda (2007).

institutionalized in fields ranging from anthropology to economics and from sociology to philosophy. The past few years even witnessed the founding of distinct study programs and institutes in "global studies."[35]

In many regards, the growing importance of global and transnational historical scholarship needs to be seen in the context of the rising interest in connections and webs of exchanges across a variety of academic disciplines. The journeys of the word "global" into the world of historiography were slower than in many other academic fields, especially the social sciences and economics. During the early 1970s, sociological titles in English referring to the term "globalization," for instance, were still about the same in number as historiographical publications. In 2001, by contrast, the former outweighed the latter by 800 to 900 percent.[36] Since then, the gap has been closing again. Some developments within the field of history were rather directly instigated by the debates on globalization in other academic fields as well as in the general public.[37] And yet, as I will show, there have also been significant transformations that were more specific historiography, which were feeding into this trend.

At the same time, it draws on a wide variety of developments that are rather specific to historiography. The various meanings and contents of "global history" are particularly hard to map out since this academic trend did not spring from a clear nucleus of theorists. Rather, the intellectual transformations and shifting research interests feeding into this trend were fairly diffuse in nature, and consequently the term "global history" came to be applied to a colorful landscape of research areas. Actually, long before the neologism "global history" was heard more often in the guildhalls of professional historians, compatible and supportive developments had already emerged in a wide variety of fields. A growing number of historians with highly divergent interests began looking for new ways to study the connections between certain types of local histories that had hitherto been studied rather separately from one another. As a consequence, the term "global history" is now as well known to historians of gender and culture as it is to experts in social or economic history.

---

[35] About the rise of global studies see Sachsenmaier (2004). For an extensive list of global studies institutes see the membership list of the Globalization Studies Association: www.gstudynet.com. Certainly, the institutional establishment of global studies and related fields should not be taken as a sign that there are no opponents to the idea of "globalization" as a concept relevant for research.

[36] For concrete figures see Guillén (2001), p. 241. Interesting statistics of the appearance of key terms such as "globalization" and "modernity" in scholarly publications can also be found in Cooper (2005).

[37] An overview of key debates among social scientists is provided by Guillén (2001).

Instead of attempting at a precise definition of global history as an evolving field, it is methodologically far more appropriate to investigate the phenomenon through separate lenses, which can capture some of its key characteristics in the American context. For example, it is important to illuminate the changing semantics leading to the growing prominence of the very term "global history" at the levels of research and institution building. In addition, it will be prolific to discuss the relationship between this rather young term and similar concepts ranging from world history to transnational history.

In the English-speaking world, the term "global history" seems to have first appeared in the year 1962, which coincidentally witnessed the publication of two separate books referring to "global history" in their titles. However, the works differed profoundly in the meaning, agendas, and contents which they attributed to "global history." In the first one, entitled *Age of Nationalism: The First Era of Global History*, authored by the renowned theorist of ideologies Hans Kohn, the term carried a decidedly modern connotation.[38] By contrast, the second book, *A Global History of Man* by Leften Stavrianos and several other authors, contained a textbook narrative depicting the entire past of human kind.[39] Hence, from the very beginning there was an uncertainty of what periods and kinds of historiography global history would actually cover. Still, both usages of the term "global history" shared certain elements in common since each of them was related to debates on how to gain new, less Eurocentric visions of world history. Yet at the time when both Kohn's and Stavrianos's works were published, there was no debate over possible definitions of "global history" and its potential distinctions from other fields. For a significant number of years expressions such as "world history" or "Western civilization were to remain the key terms in academic disputes over large historical master narratives.[40]

Over the following two to three decades, the expression "global history" remained quite dormant and was used only sporadically, most notably in some additional textbooks by Leften Stavrianos.[41] The situation changed around the time of the end of the Cold War when a number of scholars started promoting the expression "global history" as a particular approach to studying the past.[42] While at that time

---

[38] Kohn (1962). The work expounds on an alleged dichotomy between Western/secular and Eastern/mythical forms of nationalism.
[39] Stavrianos *et al.* (1962).   [40] See Middell and Naumann (2006).
[41] For example Stavrianos (1970; and 1966).
[42] Many positions are being articulated in Mazlish and Buultjens (1993).

"global history" largely implied postulates for future research, now an institutional landscape has emerged which draws on this term. University-based historiography has witnessed an increasing number of academic awards, conferences, and other professional activities devoted to "global history." For example, there is now a graduate minor program in Comparative and Global History at Rutgers University, a PhD program in Global History at the University of North Carolina, Chapel Hill, and a Global History and Theory program at Georgetown University.[43] Several book series and journals have been launched that focus either entirely on global history or certain aspects of it.[44] In addition, scholarly associations have been founded that refer prominently to the term "global history." This is, for instance, the case with *New Global History*, which was founded at Harvard and MIT during the late 1990s.[45] Furthermore, major scholarly associations have begun to operate with the expression "global history" or closely related terminological derivatives. For instance, in 2009 the American Historical Association's annual convention met under the guiding theme "Globalizing History."

The expression "global history" has also reached beyond academic work and has become more common within a wider public. The term can now be frequently found in high school textbook and college course titles,[46] in newspapers, on websites, and in other forums for public debates about issues related to history and historical memory. In September 2010, "global history" led to about 615,000 hits in a regular Google search. This compares to roughly 3.5 million entries found for a term such as "cultural history" which entered mainstream historiography at least two decades before and has long become disseminated outside of academic circles. In other words, the expression "global history" already generates almost 20 percent of the hits of a far more established branch of historiography. This needs to be seen as another indication of the broadening influences which global and transnational history experience in the United States. Due to its rapidly gaining currency and parallel institutional backing, the term will remain present for a significant time period, and its weight is even likely to grow, both in academic circles and societies at large.

---

[43] See http://history.rutgers.edu/index.php?option=com_content&task=view&id=135& Itemid=169; and http://history.unc.edu/fields/globalhistory/globalhistoryphd.

[44] For example, the *Journal of Global History* published by Cambridge University Press since 2006.

[45] See www.newglobalhistory.org for further information.

[46] An example for a high school textbook is Willner (2006). An example for the use of "global history" in pedagogical debates in the United States is Betterly (2000).

The necessary impossibility of defining global history

As a new pattern in the mosaic of historiography, global history invites curiosity about its shapes, contours, and qualities. As the popularity of the term grew during the early 1990s, there were first attempts to narrow down the meaning of "global history" to a clearly designated area of inquiry.[47] For example, in the eyes of scholars such as Bruce Mazlish, Raymund Grew, and Wolf Schäfer, the term was supposed to demarcate a new research field focusing on processes of globalization (as well as their historical antecedents) after the end of the Second World War. Opposed to Eurocentric narratives, they envisioned the study of modern globalization and its historical antecedents as the prime task of global history.[48] Yet, the use of the term "global history" quickly outgrew this and any other attempt to associate it with a specific research agenda.[49]

It might be tempting to try alternative definitions of "global history," but a look at the current literature reveals that the commonalities between publications referring to "global history" are rather sparse. For example, there is no consensus about the time periods the field is supposed to cover. While some scholars would be adamantly opposed to applying the term to the nineteenth century or even to the period before the Second World War, other works entitled "global history" refer exclusively to the ancient world.[50] There is equally little consensus about the amounts of time global history should be dealing with. Whereas some scholars opine that the macroscopic spatial category of the "globe" can only aptly be filled with the entire human past as an equally large frame of historical time,[51] others investigate much shorter time periods such as centuries, decades, or even single years[52] under the guise of "global history."

---

[47] See, for example, Mazlish and Buultjens (1993).

[48] A good overview of this position is presented in Mazlish and Iriye (2005).

[49] This forced some of its key protagonists during the early 1990s to change to the expression *New Global History* in order to specify their research agenda. For example, Mazlish (2006). According to Mazlish, the term pays homage to the fact that "something important has happened in the last fifty years or so, and ... this requires a new openness and a new mindset if we are to understand it enough to grapple with it effectively."

[50] For example, de Souza (2008).

[51] An example for this literature is: Kotkin (2006), which covers the entire period from 5000 BCE to the early twenty-first century.

[52] For example, Bentley (2009); Nussbaum (2003); Bayly (2004c); Weinberg (1995); Reynolds (2000); and Wills (2002). Arguing that the investigation of long transformations and processes needs to be understood as an intrinsic part of global history: P. O'Brien (2006).

Unlike intellectual movements such as subaltern studies or world systems theory, it is also impossible to define global history in terms of a core political agenda or societal commitment. In the literature operating with the concept of "global history," the range of worldviews, opinions, and positions is fairly wide. For example, while some scholars place emphasis on polycentric models and are openly opposed to teleological narratives,[53] others choose Western processes as the central storylines of their global historical perspectives.[54] In addition, whereas some historians apply the concept of global history to large-scale interpretations, developmental visions, or universal typologies in history,[55] many others have come to distance themselves from any kind of nomothetic ambition and attempts to generate global master narratives.[56] Furthermore, while some thinkers involved in debates on global history focus primarily on economics as the key factor of macroscopic historical developments,[57] others put more emphasis on topics such as cultural or religious flows and political processes.[58] Given such a plurality of visions, it would not even be possible to state that global history as an unfolding research landscape endorses a positive or negative interpretation of globalization.

The lack of a solid methodological core is reflected in the large variety of ways in which observers describe the field. For example, while some scholars group all large-scale historical thinking since ancient times under the rubric of "global history,"[59] others define it as a combination of rather recent methodological developments.[60] If no clear timeframe or methodology can help us to clearly outline the actual parameters of global history, it seems that at least it might be characterized by its "global" spatiality. Yet the matter is complicated by the fact that many publications appearing under the heading of "global history" are not global in the sense that they seek to take worldwide perspectives and planetary narratives. While some works carrying "global history" in their titles indeed aim to provide overviews of the human experience at

---

[53] For example, Hopkins (2002b); and Kossock (1993).

[54] For example, Black (2005); Riley (2001); Kotkin (2006); and Bodley (2002), which is based on the assumption of universal stages of development.

[55] For example Darwin (2007); and Fernandez-Armesto (2006).

[56] A discussion on global history and the problem of universalism is provided by Hopkins (2006).

[57] A good discussion of this literature (including references to global history) can be found in the introduction of Pomeranz (2001).

[58] For example Walters (1998); Chidester (2000); and Ferro (1997).

[59] Crossley (2008).

[60] This is, for example, the case with Pomeranz (2001), see particularly the introduction; and Grew (2000), which combines medical, cultural, sociological, and other perspectives.

large,[61] others focus on geographically far more limited sample cases.[62] In the latter group, the globe primarily functions as a reference space allowing historians to apply new spatial perspectives to local case studies. At first sight, it may seem counter-intuitive to observe that most literature on "global history" does not actually seek to cover our entire planet, but rather prefers to work with local samples. Yet one should keep in mind that also some of the most groundbreaking contributions to national historiography have not analyzed any given country in its entirety, but rather focused on single regions, cities, or provinces.

Precisely because global history has already started to mature into a commonly established concept, it is no longer possible to operate with an a priori definition, i.e. deriving its meaning from the combined connotation of the terms "global" and "history." The latter may be semantically more convincing and logically more coherent but it is also detached from the ways in which the term is being used in the real scholarly world. The term can only be defined a posteriori by sketching out the contours and possible future directions of the body of literature which may be ascribed to it. Only in that manner can we expect to grasp the kinds of historical conceptions and research that have come to be associated with this rather recent concept.

Instead of a clear demarcation, it is only possible to characterize some main facets of global history, both on a semantic and discursive level. In fact, the current landscapes of the field are complex enough for two seemingly contradictory statements to hold true at the same time. On the one hand, it is impossible to clearly outline the parameters of "global history" as a methodological school, an area of inquiry, or an interest in a certain period. On the other hand, it is perfectly justifiable to use the term as a marker for a wider academic trend which is actually much larger than the body of literature openly referring to the concept of "global history."

A critic of global history might hold that the field needs to be sufficiently different from older, established terms such as world history or international history. The same argument could continue that otherwise any claim for global history to mark a new trend would necessarily melt into the air. Yet any attempt to draw clear boundaries between terms such as global history and world history would bring us back to the futile task of pinning down precisely the core methodologies, theories, paradigms, and research perspectives of each field. The

---

[61] For example Bentley (2009); and Bulliet (2004).
[62] For example Stone (1994), which mainly focuses on the Atlantic dimensions of its main theme; and Pomeranz (2001), who operates with the term "global history" while primarily discussing single regions in Western Europe and China.

wide spectrum of meanings attributed to global history by its practitioners suggests that its parameters cannot be categorically distinguished from terms such as world history. Furthermore, since not all
research in global history or world history tries to cover the entire
scope of the planet and human kind in general, it is not even possible
to strictly differentiate it from "transcultural," "translocal," "transregional," or other forms of historical scholarship. Yet any such scholarly
keyword has implicit undertones, allusions, nuances, and accentu-
ations. Hence it is small wonder that, in the past, there have been
debates on the potential differences and commonalities of these terms.
While these were important to clarify different methodological choices
and possibilities, the spectrum of border-crossing research remains
interwoven in such complex ways that it is impossible to surgically
segment this research landscape into clearly distinguishable subfields.

Certainly, idioms such as "world history" or, for that matter
"universal history," have a history which profoundly differs from "global
history." While the former term is significantly older, both date back to
premodern times and, in the European context, long had Christian
connotations. These proved to have an impact on secular world historical outlooks which became increasingly popular from the eighteenth
century onwards.[63] Even though there have been alternative approaches
since the beginnings of modern academic historiography,[64] world history and universal history were long widely characterized by Eurocentric
narratives and teleological visions of progress. For the nineteenth and
large parts of the twentieth centuries, this was equally true for
scholarship in the West as well as in other parts of the world. For this
reason, some scholars have argued that the expression "world history" is
too burdened by its own past for it to be compatible with more recent
field designations like global history.[65]

In recent decades, the paths and patterns of world historical research
have taken directions that have caused the field to grow significantly
different from its previous shapes. It is interesting to note that as part of
this new orientation of world historical thought, the term "universal
history" has lost its significance in the United States. In its English
connotations, the term "universal" is often seen as rather closely wedded
to important Eurocentric and diffusionist worldviews, and many historians are rather reluctant to apply it to their own border-crossing

---

[63] A general overview of world historical writing prior to 1900 is provided by Manning
(2003), Chapters 1 and 2.
[64] For example, Hughes-Warrington (2009).   [65] For example, Mazlish (1998a).

scholarship.[66] The expression "world history" continued being used but under the weight of new scholarship and new critical debates, its connotations and institutional landscapes have significantly changed.[67] For example in his more recent works, the grand seigneur of American world history, William McNeill, greatly modified his original civilizational perspectives, which were based on the idea of "the rise of Europe," in favor of a storyline shedding more light on transregional entanglements.[68] Inspired by world systems theory, he came to conceive world economic changes as decisive factors that would trigger a chain of political, cultural, and social developments within geographically distant civilizations.[69] McNeill's most recent work and quite a number of other influential world historical studies are now more focused on metaphors of integration such as the "web,"[70] or similar concepts connoting entanglements and connectivity.[71]

Such developments are indicative of a wider trend that can be observed in many world historical publications. Even though earlier methodological traditions have not completely disappeared, the field of world history is no longer primarily characterized by civilizational tropes paired with Eurocentric assumptions or teleological timelines.[72] There have been considerable efforts to grant greater levels of agency to areas outside of the West.[73] For instance, responses to hegemonic powers and the searches for alternatives to Western order have received greater levels of attention.[74] In addition to abandoning the idea of teleological timelines, many "world histories" now operate with more complex patterns of space. The study of networks, interconnections and exchanges has clearly grown at the expense of narratives based on civilizations and nations as main historical units.[75] The latter two categories have not disappeared but they are often used more

---

[66] More recently, some research on large social systems, analyzing transregional patterns, laws, and regularities, has been conducted under the aegis of "macrohistory." See Galtung and Inayatullah (1997).

[67] See, for example, Manning (2003).

[68] See W. McNeill (1990). See also W. McNeill (2005).

[69] About McNeill's own account of this transition see W. McNeill (1995).

[70] W. McNeill and J. McNeill (2003).

[71] Needless to say, as Jonathan Spence has pointed out in his review of McNeill's "Human Web," world histories that structure their narratives around growing entanglements carry the danger of being rather detached and value-free analyses, which may not be able to adequately assess histories of colonialism, imperialism, and other trauma rooted in the past. See Spence (2003).

[72] See Feierman (1993); and Sachsenmaier (2007c).

[73] See Bentley (2003).   [74] For example, Duara (2004); Cooper (1997a); Aydin (2007).

[75] See, for example, Pomper, Elphik, and Vann (1998).

cautiously by treating them as historically conditioned rather than objectively given.[76]

While trade books and textbooks were long considered its main products, "world history" has increasingly acquired the character traits of a research field that is closely connected to recent work within other branches of historiography.[77] As part of this reform process, there have been significant attempts to change the academic structures underlying world history which, in the American context, had long figured primarily as a teaching field for colleges and smaller universities.[78] For instance, the annual meetings of the US-based World History Association have progressively attracted the participation of historians from a wide variety of research backgrounds. It is a notable gesture towards the goal of overcoming Eurocentric paradigms that the association holds half of its meetings in other parts of the world.[79]

Among other field designations in the vicinity of global history is the tradition of international history. A discipline with strong roots in the nineteenth century, international history has long been structured around the belief in the nation-state as the most important unit of historical inquiry. Consequently, international history used to be rather closely related to the disciplinary logic of international relations, with its emphasis on themes such as diplomatic exchanges and geopolitics. In many very influential studies, the world was largely treated as a stage for the clashes and alliances between national actors. But in recent decades, intellectual transformations such as the rise of social history or the cultural turn have also had a significant impact on the field. There has been a growing sense that a focus on international politics in a Westphalian manner was largely tantamount with taking rather Eurocentric perspectives, making the history of many other world regions look somewhat aberrant and deficient. After all, well into the twentieth century most parts of the globe were characterized by non-national forms of political order. These also included the European colonies which are hard to conceptualize as sources of historical agency when viewing the history of global interactions primarily from Westphalian perspectives.

In their attempt to make international history less Eurocentric, some practitioners of the field have tried to abandon the traditional focus on

---

[76] See Bentley (2006).   [77] A more detailed discussion is offered by Moore (1997).
[78] See Manning (2003).
[79] For more information about the World History Association see www.thewha.org.

Northern powers and include, for example, colonial, imperial, and economic formations in the picture. In addition, cultural and social historical approaches were injected into the study of international history, with far-reaching consequences for its conceptual foundations.[80] For example, the field was opened to such topics as the shared lifeworlds of diplomatic circles, the roles of media and other pressure groups in international decision-making processes, or racial discourses in international organizations. Some scholars now conceptualize international organizations no longer primarily as meeting places for the negotiation of national interests, but as social spaces with distinct cultures, networks and other features.[81] Generally speaking, a rising tide of literature is written in the spirit of "denationalizing history in order to internationalize it."[82] In a related development, international relations are no longer regarded only as the products of state action but, quite the contrary, also as important factors in the formation of nations. This has made many theorists of international history search for new ways of combining microscopic and macroscopic, global and local levels of analysis.[83]

The growing reluctance to define national powers as the main building blocks of international exchanges was one of the trends underlying the rise of another scholarly expression that has gained currency in English as well as several other languages: "transnational history."[84] Under different auspices, this term had experienced a first wave of prominence during the 1960s but it subsequently declined in importance. It became more commonplace again in the social sciences during the 1980s,[85] and finally started being frequently used among historians in the late 1990s. At its very basis, transnational history connotes research on topics such as the flows of ideas, economic exchanges, and organizations that cut across national boundaries without relying on nation-states as main agents. This includes the study of "situations in which national identities are joined, sometimes even transcended, by non-national, cross-national, and at times even anti-national forces."[86]

---

[80] See, for example, Iriye (1989); and Gienow-Hecht and Schumacher (2003).
[81] For example, Sluga (2006).   [82] Iriye (1989).
[83] Arguing that the new international history is no longer substantially different from branches of world history: Manning (2003). See also Lehmkuhl (2001), especially p. 423.
[84] For example, Milza (1998).
[85] For a historical overview of the concept of transnational history see Saunier (2008). See also Clavin (2005).
[86] Iriye (2008), p. 6.

Where do all these terms such as transnational history, world history, international history, and global history lead us in our search for field-specific clarity? Not very far. Certainly, on a pure terminological level, it is possible to draw some distinctions. As many scholars have argued, the expressions "transnational history" and "international history" still refer to the nation-state, even though this – especially in the case of the word "transnational" – can imply that these political units do not play central roles in historical inquiries. The same problem does not apply to the idioms "global history" and "world history," though a potential quandary of these terms is that, at least in a certain interpretation of them, they seem to refer to the entire planet in a rather holistic manner.[87] Yet again, a look at the ways in which today's historians handle these terms renders the quest for clear distinctions somewhat irrelevant. For instance, in current research projects the usage of the terms "global" and "transnational" often overlaps,[88] and the boundaries between "international history" and "global history" have also become blurred enough to make a precise separation between these fields neither possible nor desirable.[89] It is quite telling that the same historians became leading theorists of several of these terms. Akira Iriye, for instance, authored highly influential writings on the further development of international history, transnational history, and global history without ever seeking to distinguish clearly between them.[90]

While a high degree of congruence characterized such prominent terms as world history, global history, or transnational history, there have been many suggestions for alternative terms that express particularly well the complexity of spatial thinking in current border-crossing research. For example, some historians have started using new concepts from other social sciences, such as the term "intermestic" which depicts a merger of international and domestic concerns.[91] Others have promoted terms such as "interarea history"[92] which deliberately leave the

---

[87] For example, Nina Glick-Schiller differentiates between global and transnational levels of analysis, arguing that the former primarily address planetary phenomena while the latter term subsumes research analyzing processes across political boundaries: Glick-Schiller (2005). More than the term "world," the word "global" expresses an interest in the flows, exchanges, and mutual reactions between different world regions.

[88] A collection of the state of the art of transnational history: Iriye and Saunier (2009); and of transnational research in a variety of fields: Levitt and Khagram (2008).

[89] In some cases, the methodologies of new international history have been applied to the study of international relations by referring to the term "global history." For example: Young and Kent (2004).

[90] For example, Iriye (1989); Mazlish and Iriye (2005); and Iriye and Saunier (2009).

[91] French (2006b).   [92] Wigen (2005).

units in studies of interactive processes, exchanges, and common trans-formations open.[93] In addition, idioms such as "entangled histories"[94] and "connected histories"[95] were specifically coined to express the importance of transfers and outside contacts for the understanding of many kinds of local history, including the ones between colonized or colonizing societies. Concepts such as interarea history or entangled histories can be best understood as pointed theoretical interventions in the quest to experiment with new conceptions of historical space. The advocates of all these terms are explicitly drawing on a wide variety of schools of thought, and they usually do not seek to found new isolated fields of research.

In conclusion, many researchers operating on a translocal level do not worry about a precise classification of such terms, but rather use them interchangeably. In many cases, historians operate very flexibly with terms such as "world history," "global history," as well as a range of other concepts, and they tend to treat them as largely synonymous with each other.[96] Even publication forums such as the *Journal of Global History* or the *Journal of World History* do not act as adamant defenders of their flagship terms, but rather allow their authors to refer to a wide range of prominent and rare field descriptions. Despite their growing prominence during the past two decades, the various field designations have not crystallized into a set of rivaling schools but, on the contrary, have become increasingly enmeshed with each other. The reason for these overlaps is that – despite their different semantic connotations – many of these terms refer to the same intellec-tual trend. Because there is much common ground between the ways in which various field designations are being used and defined by scholars, it is not possible to categorically distinguish global history from fields such as transnational history or world history. Rather, global history – like many other terms – can be taken as shorthand for a larger academic trend which we may also choose to call the "global trend" in historiography.

---

[93] This openness can also express the idea that local identities and formations are often products of such translocal exchanges.
[94] For example, Cañizares-Esguerra (2007).   [95] For example, Subrahmanyam (1997).
[96] For example, series editor Michael Adas does so in his foreword to the American Historical Association's series Essays on Comparative and Global History. Another example is Pomper (1998), p. 3.

Global history as an intellectual trend: developments in established fields

As discussed in the section above, it would be methodologically incorrect to operate with a narrow and predetermined interpretation of "global history." Rather than artificially collapsing a complex academic reality into the fiction of a clearly defined field, it makes much more sense to take a wider perspective and shed light on a multitude of developments that have been tied to the global trend in historiography. Such an approach, which should also consider literature not referring to the term "global history," is not possible in a holistic manner since many relevant intellectual changes took place without being closely interconnected. It is a more promising methodological alternative to separately examine some relevant developments in various branches of historiography. A series of investigative looks through sample windows will therefore put us in a position to more clearly characterize the rhythms, directions, and patterns of global history as an academic trend. It will become clear that new, creative conceptions of historical space are a common characteristic of this intellectual movement.

It is important to note that the growing interest in global historical issues is not only the product of scholars who previously had been directly involved in international history, transnational history, or world history. Rather, historians from a wide variety of subfields ranging from economic history to social history increasingly developed a strong interest in reaching across national, regional, or even continental boundaries. Initially, these developments took place quite independently and were not part of a distinctly articulated intellectual project. Rather, they occurred as a trend *avant la lettre* or even *à côté de la lettre*, that is, before the times when global history was being articulated as a distinct project or during that same time, albeit without necessarily referring to concepts such as global history and its close terminological alternatives.

A rather typical development towards more complex conceptions of historical space can be seen in the field of comparative history. Even though comparative perspectives were far older, it was particularly after the end of the Second World War that many kinds of historical comparisons became important as declared research fields in historiography and historical sociology.[97] In their macroscopic approaches and preference

---

[97] See Berger (2007a); and D. Smith (1991). Many historical sociologists favored the analysis of societal and civilizational macro-structures over world historical analyses since, in their eyes, the latter did not allow for the same degree of abstraction. See Tilly (1984), particularly pp. 21ff.

for universal categories, which were supposed to fit all units of analysis, many comparativists continued Marxist or Weberian traditions of conceptualizing the past. For example, on topics such as political revolutions or the advent of fascism scholars abstracted social pressures, economic transformations, and other categories from specific historical contexts, so that they could be compared on a rather elevated level of analysis.[98] Given such a high level of theoretical abstraction and lack of interest in cross-regional exchanges, it is hardly surprising that a large number of studies actually conducted diachronic rather than synchronic comparisons.

Yet particularly starting from the 1980s, when cultural historical and postcolonial perspectives grew more influential in academic settings, abstract historical comparisons faced a mounting tide of criticisms,[99] not only among historians but also from sociologists. An increasing number of historians came to point to a methodological challenge which, during the late nineteenth century, was known as "Galton's Problem,"[100] namely the dilemma that comparative approaches must ignore the history of mutual interactions, transfers, and exchanges through which the objects of comparison continuously changed, evolved, and influenced each other. Furthermore, it was argued that structural comparisons often presupposed that transformative processes such as industrialization or political revolutions were characterized by common, if not universal patterns.[101] With this in mind, some scholars held that comparative approaches used concepts such as "nation," "civilization," and "culture" as predetermined categories and hence reaffirmed them, even though they were largely constructed through exchange processes and other translocal dynamics.[102] The idea that a scholarly observer can a priori isolate his or her objects of study from their historical contexts was particularly hard to justify in an age in which critiques of Eurocentric categories and methodologies had grown stronger.[103]

Given these developments, more recently the tide of comparative historical scholarship has shifted away from applying fixed sets of categories and has moved towards more complex case studies that are no longer centered on single, supposedly universal variables. New

---

[98] For example Skocpol (1979); and Moore (1966).

[99] Lamont and Thévenot (2000).

[100] The problem is named after an anthropologist who lectured on this topic at the Royal Anthropological Institute in London in 1889. See Kleinschmidt (1991).

[101] For debates in the field of sociology see Goldthorpe (1997); for history see, for example, Kocka (2003).

[102] On this and other forms of criticism, see Tyrell (1991); and Lorenz (1999).

[103] See, for example, Rueschemeyer (1991).

methodological possibilities emerged, particularly after comparative history started to gravitate towards cultural themes such as mentalities and intellectual movements – themes which had been the focal point of transfer studies. Here, there was a growing sense not only that comparative approaches needed to consider exchange processes but also that the historiography of flows, transfers, and shared transformations, if properly conducted, needed to open itself to comparative perspectives. The question of how certain ideas, movements, and institutions changed while moving between locations required comparison of the different contexts between which these entanglements occurred.

With structural comparisons declining in number and influence, comparative methods have increasingly become enmeshed with border-crossing historiography. As a consequence of these developments, comparative history has taken similar turns to international history and, in related steps, approached themes and topoi typically covered by transnational historical research.[104] As a partial result of such change, the term "comparative history" has been frequently used in conjunction with "global history." A telling example is that, in 1999, the *American Historical Review* added a "global and comparative" review section to its quarterly portfolio.[105] In addition, scholars like Patrick O'Brien have concluded that "comparisons and connections are the dominant styles of global history."[106]

The rising degree of scholarly self-reflexivity and attention to interchanges, similarities, and differences in comparative history went hand in hand with an increasing number of studies operating with more complex notions of historical space. In some influential cases, a combination of global and comparative historical approaches challenged the spatial attributes of continental and national histories. For example, Kenneth Pomeranz's groundbreaking study on China and Europe in the emerging world economy demonstrated that the bulk of literature on European economic history frequently refers to the continent *in toto* even though these studies are usually based upon relatively small, privileged regions.[107] The latter were usually single areas with high economic productivity, most notably – for the eighteenth and nineteenth centuries – England, the Netherlands, and some other limited parts of Northwestern Europe.

---

[104] For example Cohen and O'Connor (2004); and Seigel (2005).
[105] Another example for the joint usage of comparative and transfer-related approaches is Bayly (2004b). See also Washbrook (1997). See also Eaton (1997).
[106] P. O'Brien (2006).
[107] Pomeranz (2001). Deconstructing "Europe" and "Asia" as geographical entities in order to break with myths of Western exceptionalism, is Allen, Bengtsson and Dribe (2005).

While it may be accurate to understand these areas as the centers and nodes of larger economic flows, it is certainly not realistic to depict England and comparable regions as typical of the entire continent. It is also not appropriate to treat them as the center of a European nexus. In that manner, Pomeranz's and other scholars' arguments injected new perspectives into long intellectual traditions of explaining that the origins of the industrial revolution emerged, or at least unfolded, within much wider, transcontinental economic contexts.[108] As a result of such new and daring conceptions of historical space, which were partly gained from new comparative perspectives, European economic history is beginning to look more like an amalgam of spatial configurations than a solid geohistorical entity. Multiple, at times overlapping, economic macro-regions were connected with the world beyond in a variety of ways.

Particularly since more representatives of area studies have joined comparative history, the field has come to critique methodological Eurocentrism from different angles. Whereas in the past, much of comparative history had reified Eurocentric assumptions, important academic currents have now started flowing in the opposite direction. Many influential studies within this field have contributed to relativizing assumptions which take the Western experience as the standard with which all other history could be compared and analyzed.[109] A growing branch of comparative history has gone against the notion of European exceptionalism by pointing to a wealth of similarities in many world regions.[110] Yet many experts in the history of different world regions outside of Europe were not content to search for non-Western equivalents with European "modernity," but rather contributed to undermining holistic interpretations of this concept. For instance, one influential study argued that, in pre-eighteenth century East Asian societies, central features of an allegedly "modern" state bureaucracy could develop without being related to proto-capitalist transformations of the economy.[111] Another example is Philip Huang's work on civil justice in China between the seventeenth and the early twentieth centuries, which argued that – contrary to the assumptions held by the Weberian School – a rule of law could be practiced without formal rationalization.[112]

---

[108] An important recent position: A. Frank (1998).

[109] See, for example, R. Wong (1997); Allen, Bengtsson, and Dribe (2005); L. Liu (1999); and Lieberman (2003). For a discussion of recent scholarship on "surprising resemblances" see P. O'Brien (2003).

[110] For additional examples see Sugihara (1996); and P. O'Brien (2003). An example of new ways in the field of sociology to deal with similarities across cultural boundaries are the debates surrounding the concept of "early modernities." See *Dædalus*, 127–3 (1998), issue entitled "Early Modernities."

[111] See, for example, Woodside (2006).   [112] P. Huang (1996).

In addition, many important studies have come to emphasize the importance of outside influences on European history in order to break through long-established myths about the largely autochthonous historical development of the continent – a myth which was foundational to many comparative studies.[113] Moreover, some recent comparative and translocal studies have set out to newly explain the rapid decline of the Chinese, Indian, and other economies starting from the late eighteenth century as the outcome of complex global historical processes.[114] Their models and methodologies usually go far beyond the static frameworks of world systems theory and similar schools.

Comparative history is primarily a methodological approach that, in principle, is applicable to all branches of historiography. Seen in this light, comparative approaches were only a small aspect of a wider search for new spatial categories taking place in many other fields like, for instance, economic history. The latter has a particularly long tradition of tackling big problems such as the advent of worldwide economic systems, global interdependencies, and worldwide inequalities.[115] In their academic pursuits and methodological orientations, economic historians shared much common ground with economists and sociologists,[116] and it is safe to say that, for a long time, the proportion of macroscopic scholarship has been larger than in other areas of historiography. It was not only the character of their questions that made economic historians more prone to transgress national boundaries but also the nature of their source materials: a field relying for a large part on numerical data, after all, is less dependent on linguistic skills. Yet economic historians pursuing border-crossing work also faced the problem of the comparability of their source materials including, for example, the question of whether local historical data ranging from individual calorie consumption to gross economic products had been derived in similar ways.

In a process that was only loosely connected but still remarkably parallel to the developments in comparative history, many economic historians grew increasingly reluctant to regard nations, civilizations, or continents a priori as meaningful categories of space. For example, some

---

[113] For example Goody (1996; 2010).   [114] Washbrook (1997).

[115] An overview of recent discussions on global inequality is provided by Sutcliffe (2004). One should recall that the early economic classics written by scholars such as Adam Smith and David Ricardo were explicitly transnational and historical in scope: A. Smith (1776); and Ricardo (1817). The same is of course true for many works foundational to the Marxist tradition.

[116] For example, dependency theory and world systems theory proved to be influential across disciplinary boundaries. See Chapter 1.

studies sought to transcend nation-centered perspectives by putting
groups or processes operating across political boundaries in the spot-
light.[117] Furthermore, research on merchant networks as well as, more
generally, on the social and political formations underlying transregional
trade has become far more visible.[118] In addition, there have been efforts
to investigate multinational corporations and earlier translocal trade
organizations in terms of not only their economic impact but also their
social and cultural entanglements.[119] In this context, the word "global"
has become one of the main terms connoting efforts to see macroscopic
transformations no longer through nation- or Western-centered biases.
Compared with the status quo of economic history a generation ago,
single explanatory frameworks, which supposedly fit all local cases, have
become less influential.[120] The same is true for some prominent
neoliberal or neo-Marxist theories, which commonly interpreted
globalization as a rather cogent economic process emanating from a
small number of countries, particularly in Western Europe.[121] As part
of the same general development, the idea that the North Atlantic world
has served as the sole catalyst for modern economic development has
lost much of its cogency in academic circles.

A wealth of new translocal case studies contributed to challenging the
standing of holistic methodologies in global economic history. For
instance, detailed research shed new light on the highly divergent ways
in which economies outside the West were positioned within translocal
networks of exchanges.[122] Furthermore, many studies pointed to the
limited scopes of the European system by highlighting large economic
formations that did not involve the "West."[123] Most notably, there has
been a growing interest in further reflecting upon the ways in which
economic regions were globally connected and yet at the same time
significantly different from each other.[124] Some projects seeking to add
local sensitivity to our understanding of macroscopic economic activities
have gone as far as to propound the idea of local varieties of capitalism.[125] Usually, however, these specific economic systems are not seen

---

[117] Pomeranz (2008b); and Bairoch (2000).
[118] Examples are: Markovits (2000); Tracy (1990); and H. Liu (1998).
[119] For example, Mazlish and Chandler (2005); and Akita (2002).
[120] See, for example, Bordo, Taylor and Williamson (2003).
[121] A critical discussion of this literature is provided by M. Lang (2006).
[122] See, for example, Pomeranz (2002); and Acemoglu, Johnson and Robinson (2002).
[123] The most important study in this context has been Abu-Lughod (1989). Also:
Hamashita (1988). Generally on the topic: Dussel (1998).
[124] For example, Sugihara (2003); and Pomeranz (2008a).
[125] See, for example, Whitley (1999); Redding (1990); and Arrighi (2003).

as largely autonomous economic spaces but rather as varieties within worldwide economic nexuses and global capitalism.

Another research field which discusses how geographically distant communities came to be involved in transregional economic networks is the history of commodities. By analyzing the changing locations, modes of production, trade routes as well as markets for single goods, historians offer insights into the social and cultural consequences triggered by the globalization of trade. For example, in a study of the global dynamics and implications of the sugar trade, Sidney Mintz discusses the interconnections between several seemingly distant historical arenas, ranging from the forced migration of Africans to the New World and its sociocultural consequences to the effects of cheaply available sugar in parts of Europe since the eighteenth century.[126] Further studies have added a wealth of new insights into the effects of the globalizing sugar trade on regional markets and local communities.[127] Other global commodities have also been researched from a translocal perspective such as, for example, salt, cod, spices, and cotton, which all connected the social, economic, and cultural histories of different localities into nexuses of entanglements.[128] Together, these give us a better insight into some glocal processes which Eric Wolf characterized as follows: "through the expanding commitment to the production of commodities, changes on the level of the world market had consequences at the level of household, kin group, community, region and class."[129]

Fields like the history of commodities suggest that in addition to the rise of new transregional scholarship, there has at least been a rapprochement between economic history and other fields such as cultural or social history. At first sight, the greater levels of attentiveness to the spaces and contexts of economics seem to have developed rather independently from each other. However, both developments were rooted in a growing problem-consciousness about key arguments, concepts, categories, and institutional divides that had long belonged to the disciplinary fundaments of modern academic historiography in general and economic history in particular. The increasing search for new investigative spaces in economic history, which combine global awareness and local sensitivity, was often accompanied by a growing interest in the prism of social, political, cultural, and other environments

---

[126] Mintz (1985).   [127] Mazumdar (1998).

[128] For example Kurlansky (2002); Kurlansky (1997); Beckert (2004); Dalby (2001); and Topik, Marichal, and Frank (2006).

[129] Wolf (1982). For research on commodities since the 1970s, see Gereffi and Korzeniewicz (1994).

framing economic structures and interactions.[130] This is significant because for a long time, much of economic history had been prone to view economics in a rather isolated manner and exclude its wider contexts. Certainly, the role and impact of these contextual shifts should not be exaggerated. A belief in the primacy of data and material factors still characterizes much of the field and seems to support the assumption that social, cultural, and other factors can either be seen as a direct consequence of economic conditions, or are at least as so peripheral to economic processes that they can rightfully be ignored.[131]

Stronger cooperation between economic and other historians was further facilitated by the fact that many other branches of historiography had also experienced increasing levels of interest in spatial configurations which, a generation earlier, had still been unusual. A case in point is the wide spectrum of research that is often subsumed under "social history." For instance, in the study of migration there have been significant steps towards new perspectives that seek to combine transnational scopes of analysis with local sensitivity. This area of research long focused primarily on the fate of migrant communities with regards to single countries, and treated them either primarily as emigrant or chiefly as immigrant groups.[132] In that manner, the transnational sociocultural formations created by migration were rather neglected, even though these could even endure across such geographically wide distances as the Atlantic or the Pacific.

Some steps heading in a new direction were taken during the 1960s when Afro-American history, and subsequently other minorities such as the overseas Chinese, were studied under the aegis of the diaspora concept.[133] In the following decades, scholars moved the study of migrant communities closer to the spirit of transnational studies, and hence to a research agenda that no longer used nation-states as central units of analysis.[134] Many researchers from a variety of fields have come to regard transnational migrant communities as distinct social spaces characterized by particular identities, public spheres and, in some cases, transborder citizenship.[135] However, as Nina Glick-Schiller points out, some new perspectives on transnational

---

[130] For example, Held (1999); and O'Rourke and Williamson (1999).
[131] See, for example, Iggers (1996).   [132] Wimmer and Glick-Schiller (2002).
[133] See Schnapper (1999).
[134] For example Glick-Schiller (2004); A. Ong (1999); Morawska (2003); Bauböck (2003); and Faist (2000).
[135] This often changes national tropes significantly – for example, see Lewis (1995); and Kelley (1999).

communities risk replacing methodological nationalism with methodological transnationalism, that is, research perspectives focusing on single diasporic communities while neglecting their multifarious entanglements with other societies.[136] It is for such reasons that an increasing number of scholars now conceptualize diasporic formations less as seemingly autochthonous social spaces than as communities which are tightly intertwined with other groups, ranging from their home and host societies to other transnational communities.[137] The result of such research is a complex *jeu d'échelles*[138] between different conceptions of space, and more detailed studies have started exploring themes related to cultural history and other fields within that framework.[139]

Reaching beyond the study of diasporic structures in a narrower sense, some social historians have also come to study other migration patterns like forced relocation and temporal migration. A specific case is the study of labor movements which had its origins in the nineteenth century and, centered on the study of Western industrial labor, had long been characterized by Eurocentric bias.[140] Over the past few decades, the conceptual geographies in the study of labor have greatly changed from the nation- and Europe-centered visions which had dominated it in the past. There has been a strong tendency to relativize the Western experience in the history of labor and no longer regard it as the core of more universal paths and patterns. For instance, the field had only paid scant attention to agricultural labor, unfree labor, and other forms of work that did not seem to fit neatly into the supposed standard frame of the industrial workforce.[141] Influenced by a variety of intellectual currents including subaltern studies, movements such as the New Labor History[142] have become much more attentive to the multifaceted and often locally specific forms of free and forced labor, remuneration, contractual work, or mass recruitment.[143] For example, scholarship no longer operates solely with modern Western conceptions of exploited labor but has started paying more attention to comparable or related phenomena, such as chattel slavery or indentured labor.

---

[136] Glick-Schiller (2005), p. 442.
[137] A good overview of the field is provided by McKeown (2004); and G. Wang (1997). See also Ember (2005).
[138] After Revel (1996).   [139] For example, S. Zheng (2010).   [140] Lucassen (2006a).
[141] See, for example, Bayly (2004c).   [142] See Brody (1993).
[143] See the rich discussion of global labor history by Van der Linden (2008).

Furthermore, in conjunction with this new interest in local peculiarities, scholarship has increasingly come to view translocal entanglements from the perspective of alternative analytical frameworks. For example, new approaches have been adopted towards the transregional patterns in which various exploitative forms of labor have been structurally connected with each other – among entanglements, through multinational corporations, commodity nets, or consumption chains. In addition, historians have come to study workers' movements and momentums towards globally cooperative labor in ways that are no longer primarily centered on industrialized societies.[144] For instance, there have been promising attempts to broaden our understanding of the social forces underpinning major political movements and to consider frequently subalternized groups such as slaves as active agents.[145]

Similar or even closely related efforts can also be observed in other fields of study which can be grouped under the rubric of social history. Perhaps most significantly, this is the case with women's and gender history, which for a long time was an area of research in which only comparatively few transnational routes were taken. Yet, in recent years, this situation has changed, and several textbooks, trade books, as well as academic series discussing gender-related issues from global historical perspectives have appeared on the market.[146] Here, the growth of translocal perspectives initially took root in a combination of developments endogenous to the field and paradigm shifts within wider academic communities. As in economic history and labor history, also in the case of gender studies the search for new spatial parameters was tied to a growing distrust in the idea that historians could apply allegedly "universal" concepts to a wide variety of contexts. Most importantly, many scholars increasingly sought to abandon the idea of gender as a fixed category, and instead conceptualized it as a product of constructs and interferences from a large array of social, political, and cultural forces operating at both local and translocal levels. Likewise, fields such as the history of sexuality have experienced significant movements and debates related to the growing influence of transnational and global historical perspectives.[147]

---

[144] For example, French (2006a).
[145] For example, Linebaugh and Rediker (2000).
[146] For example, B. Smith (2004–2005); Stearns (2006); and Wiesner-Hanks (2001). In addition, the American Historical Association has started publishing a booklet series entitled *Womens' and Gender History in Global Historical Perspective*.
[147] See, for example, Canaday (2009); and Sigal (2009).

As part of this shift towards greater conceptual complexity, the number of historians interested in thinking about gender issues in spaces across and beyond national or regional boundaries grew significantly larger.[148] This trend opened up a plethora of fascinating and important questions that gender history needed to address as it granted more attention to the diversity of local experiences. Generally speaking, postcolonial and other criticism heightened sensitivities to questions such as, for example, whether the categories used by gender and feminist historians in the West are often characterized by hegemonic assumptions about the Third World. Many critics have charged that research in the United States and other countries does not pay due attention to the heterogeneity of sociocultural experiences of women.[149]

Among other developments, there has been growing pressure to abandon stereotyped visions which at least implicitly treat women in many non-Western societies as oppressed and passive victims awaiting liberation through supposedly more advanced societies.[150] Hence as a general tendency, scholarship in the field of gender history has become far more cautious about the contexts of power surrounding knowledge, academic pursuits and, more generally, claims to liberation.[151] Through such intellectual changes and other factors, gender historians have become increasingly reluctant to use abstractions and values from the Western experience as the yardsticks for analyzing the rest of the world. Similarly to labor history and other fields, however, it will be a major intellectual challenge to find ways to aptly combine global research agendas with sensitivity to local contingencies. This task is particularly important since through its connections with fields such as feminist studies, gender history can be seen as a research area that is publically engaged in a more immediate sense than many other branches of historical scholarship.

New approaches to political formations

During the rise of border-crossing approaches in many areas of research, also the study of nations and nationalism in a narrow sense has been taken into new directions. The most important trend is that today, an increasing number of historians no longer conceptualize national polities, societies, and cultures from endogenous perspectives. As the

[148] See, for example, Wiesner-Hanks (2007).
[149] See, for example, Mohanty (1988).   [150] Blom (2001).
[151] Examples of transnational research on women's movements are Gabaccia and Iacovetta (2002); and B. Smith (2000).

outcome of a wide variety of scholarly activities, the history of nation-building and national identities today looks distinctly less national now than a generation ago. Some prominent historians have further developed methodological frameworks to assess the advent of the nation-state as one of the most global and transnational phenomena of recent history.[152]

It is possible to crudely differentiate developments in the study of nations into four main fields of activity. Firstly, there have been significant efforts to move away from predominantly national and Western-centric frameworks of analysis in the study of legal concepts, social models, and discourses of political order.[153] An increasing number of historians have now come to investigate the transnational flows of ideas, networks of people, funding structures, as well as common socioeconomic pressures supporting the spread of various ideologies and global utopias in a wide variety of local contexts.[154] Even notions of internationalism and international order are now increasingly being understood as translocal discourses which were at least partly produced by the collaboration and competition between transnational and national players. These could encompass government circles, civil society agents, multinational corporations and intellectual networks.[155]

Secondly, there have been attempts to analyze the global spread of specific state institutions and policies, ranging from protectionism to the history of passports. In this context it has been convincingly argued that nation-building and internationalism, universalization and differentiation, went hand in hand with each other.[156] Heading into similar directions, many research projects have critically revisited discourses of national and cultural heritage in different parts of the world. New global perspectives and alternative geographies have put significant pressure on tropes of national cultures and societies. For instance, scholars have shown how supposed national traditions, ranging from specific cuisines to cultures of thrift, were being constructed under the influence of international discourses and their supporting networks.[157]

Thirdly, scholarship has again become more sensitive to the global frames – colonial, anti-colonial, and other – which were essential for the worldwide spread of systems of national order as well as the dominance of some states over others. For instance, detailed studies have added

---

[152] For example, Maier (2009).
[153] See, for example, Bright and Geyer (2005); and Hafner-Burton and Tsutsui (2005).
[154] For example Conrad and Sachsenmaier (2007); and Service (2007).
[155] See, for example, Geyer and Paulmann (2001); Akita and White (2010); and Conze, Lappenkuper and Müller (2004).
[156] See, for example, McKeown (2008).
[157] For example Appadurai (1988); and Garon (2000).

much substance to the argument that, rather than emanating from an uninfluenced European epicenter, modern national revolutions emerged in a complex Atlantic nexus.[158] Some scholars have argued that Atlantic entanglements contributed more to the emergence of discourses of freedom and rights than a strictly Europe-centered perspective would possibly be able to grasp.[159] In a somewhat related move, scholarship has come to further problematize nation-centered approaches to social history. For example, the notion of a "British society and culture" now looks increasingly complex due to an increasing number of studies illuminating the transcontinental dimensions of social classes, high and low, in the empire.[160] It would be equally hard to approach Russian history without paying due attention to the social historical consequences of its Eurasian expansions.[161] Coming from another direction, scholarship is still in the early stages of exploring the impact of colonial segregation on national identities in Europe and exclusionism in Western societies.[162] For example, some theorists argued that stereotypes of Englishness eroded and changed through the mimicry of the Indian upper classes who started to act in "white" ways.[163]

Fourthly, on a more general level, many historians have come to point to the fact that the growing spread of imperial and national order needs to be seen as having co-evolved since they were being produced by many co-dependent forces. Furthermore, several theorists suggested we view nation-states at least partly as enabling frames to deal with the challenges of growing global integration.[164] Furthermore, scholarship has again become more attentive to the colonial and other transregional spaces in which ideologies such as racism, Social Darwinism, ethnic bias, or genocidal thinking emerged and subsequently were disseminated to different parts of the world.[165] In addition, there have been suggestions to go beyond state-centered visions of world order by paying more attention

---

[158] See, for example, Kleinmann (2001).
[159] For new literature on this topic see Dubois (2000); Hafner-Burton and Tsutsui (2005); Gould (2007a); and Dubois (2004). "Classic" texts, which headed towards Atlantic perspectives: Palmer (1959); and James (1938).
[160] See, for example, Knight and Liss (1991); Driver and Gilbert (1999); C. Hall (2000); and Fischer-Tiné (2007).
[161] Dirks (1992).   [162] See, for example, Pollock (1993).   [163] Bhabha (1994b).
[164] Geyer and Bright (1995); and Maier (2000).
[165] See, for example, Ther (2004). Recent studies suggest that even the ideals of beauty during the Enlightenment age need to be understood against the background of colonial worldviews: Bindman (2002). In a certain way these more recent approaches relating colonialism to European racism and fascism lead back to theories that had been prominent in the years after the Second World War: for example, Arendt (1951).

to transnational power structures in the cultural, economic, and financial sector.[166] Such approaches often offer methodologically new ways of relating key processes such as imperialism and the spread of the nation-state more closely to each other as well as to other facets of globalization.[167]

In many ways, this renewed interest in the hierarchies of the international system and its intricate mechanisms of power might be considered as a return to neo-Marxist agendas which, in the United States and many other countries, had been particularly influential during the 1960s and 1970s.[168] However, much of the new literature exploring facets of global and local power is far less framed around structuralist perspectives or Marxist terminologies. In addition, it operates with a wider range of spatial concepts than many earlier theories of imperialism which tended to use nation-states and colonial formations as their primary units of analysis. Important new contributions have been made by studies of changing regimes of territoriality. For example, Charles Maier interprets the history of the nineteenth and early twentieth centuries as a period marked by the search for sovereignty, central government control, and the mobilization of internal resources through powers competing over a finite global space – a period which, according to him, was followed by an increase in pressure on territorially bound power, particularly from the 1960s onwards.[169] Others put more emphasis on the continuing tension between ever-changing territorializing and deterritorializing forces in an increasingly interactive world.[170]

Many of the academic movements described above could also be viewed as important intellectual transformations in the field of colonial history. According to one of its leading scholars, Frederick Cooper, colonial history was rather dormant between the 1950s and 1970s, since many historians of Africa had become wary of applying European perspectives to their field of inquiry and turned to explore either the pre-colonial or anti-colonial pasts. For many scholars, colonialism became an episode to be undone by modernization in political independence. Yet, in a rather complex process driven by intellectual

---

[166] Bright and Geyer (2005).   [167] See, for example, Weitz (2008).

[168] For example, Magdoff (1969); Mommsen (1977); and Lens (1971). Examples of more recent studies of nations and nationalism that are strongly based on Marxist perspectives are Hobsbawm (1990); and Anderson (1991).

[169] Maier (2000; 2006b). Maier is careful to point out that the more recent tendencies should not be understood as a finite development, and he sees the present situation as one characterized by a struggle between "globalist" and "territorialist" forces.

[170] For example, Sassen (1998). By contrast, Christopher Bayly sees the dominance of the nation-state as the central marker of globalization as it unfolded from the 1830s up until the present day: Bayly (2005).

transformations and new political experiences, scholarship in subsequent decades has seen a return of colonial and imperial history, albeit under new conceptual guises.[171] Speaking of a general trend, it is safe to say that the field has become very critical towards approaches which juxtapose an expansionist, dynamic West with a purely reactive rest. Many studies no longer treat colonies *grosso modo* as passive victims or recipients of Western dominance. Rather, they have come to accentuate a wealth of contact zones, mutual reactions, growing interdependencies, and other close entanglements between groups, ranging from elites to other social milieus, who were operating across the dividing lines between colonizing and colonized societies.

In other words, influential approaches have been careful to cross over the conceptual lines separating metropoles from colonies, and oppressors from subjects.[172] The rising interest in hybridization and creolization has led historians to pay more attention to many social groups in addition to privileged circles in urban colonial centers.[173] Furthermore, it turns out that the so-called colonial "hinterland" was usually not as detached from colonial exchanges as had often been assumed. Moreover, scholars are increasingly emphasizing the fact that colonial empires were characterized by a wealth of economic, religious, and other networks which certainly not all reached from the center to the peripheries. A progressive number of case studies have granted groups in the colonies more narrative space and historical agency in imperial formations.[174]

In addition to making our understanding of colonial histories more complex, the recent turns of the field have started to have an impact on visions of the European past. Most notably, one key trope in older world historical visions, namely the idea that European and, later, North American history can be widely understood as a historical development without significant influence from other world regions, has been challenged from a variety of directions. For example, scholars have started

---

[171] Cooper (2005), particularly Chapters 1 and 2. As Cooper argues, these transformations within the research landscape took place while the field became increasingly polarized between a gap between postcolonial positions and their critics. See also Howe (2001).

[172] Important in this context was the rise of subaltern studies. For example, see Chakrabarty (2000). An important debate between subaltern studies and other scholars revolved around the issues such as autonomy and authenticity in colonial settings. Examples of other positions of the 1990s are Nicholas B. Dirks (1992); and Cooper and Stoler (1997).

[173] See, for example, Stewart (2007).

[174] See, for example, Ho (2004); Aydin (2007); Lombard and Aubin (2000); and Sweet (2003).

taking greater interest in the reverse influences of the colonial system on the United Kingdom, Germany, and other societies.[175] Among other topics, some studies traced the origins of racism, factory organization, and class identities at least partly to colonial encounters and experiments which then made their way into the metropoles.[176] Moreover, historians came to emphasize that European regions changed or "modernized" according to various rhythms and stages, which often followed the logics of their connectedness to centers and resources in other parts of the world.[177] Other publications have shed more light on the multifaceted exchanges between Latin American independence movements and the quest for a new European order in the aftermath of Napoleon.[178]

As a general trend, historiography in the United States has witnessed a remarkable rise of interest in the history of empires. Many research projects in this field are not related to the American past but rather focus on European colonialism as well as imperial formations emanating from other parts of the world.[179] Yet there have also been a growing number of studies which seek to link the modern history of the United States to other imperial structures in the past.[180] Like the scholarship on empires and imperialism in general,[181] the relationships between America's global roles and European as well as other forms of imperial rule tends to be conceptualized in radically different ways.[182] Whereas some scholars treat the United States as an empire in disguise and even suggest potential benefits of colonial order, others opine that America's roles in today's world need to be critiqued from the context of new forms of empire that are no longer primarily territorially bound.[183]

Coming from a very different angle, recent years have witnessed mounting efforts to apply transnational and global perspectives to the history of the United States in a more sustained, coordinated, and integrative fashion. For example, some research projects have sought to combine very different branches of historiography which have commonly applied transnational perspectives to facets of US history. Indeed, for a rather long time, such fields as, for example, diaspora studies,

---

[175] See, for example, Codell and MacLeod (1998); and Thornton (1998). An earlier critique pointing to reverse flows of influence: S. Amin (1989).

[176] For example, Mintz (1985); Thorne (1997); and Stoler (1995), particularly Chapter 4.

[177] An influential article arguing this point is Geyer and Bright (1995).

[178] Gould (2007b).

[179] Examples for recent studies of empires, which did not directly involve European powers, are Duara (2003); Perdue (2005); and Powell (2003).

[180] Examples of works are Maier (2006a); and Burbank and Cooper (2010).

[181] Arguing that much of the scholarship about empires and imperialism is still largely divided along Marxist and liberal lines: Pomper (2005).

[182] Most prominently: Ferguson (2003).   [183] For example, Hardt and Negri (2006).

research on transnational elite cultures, global legal history, or new diplomatic history may have led to new, less-nation-centered visions of the United States and its history. According to the opinion of some observers, such endeavors may result in new attempts at synthesis in US history which – for a variety of reasons – has long been an exceptionally fragmented field.[184] Thomas Bender and some other scholars who in recent years endeavored to do so, were careful to emphasize the necessity of avoiding treating the United States as a microcosm of the world at large.[185] Going beyond that, they regard a greater emphasis on the global contexts of events and transformations such as the Civil War or the New Deal as a way to further abandon discourses of US exceptionalism.[186] At the same time, in the scholarship transnationalizing American history, important as they are, the US experience inevitably remains at the center of analysis.[187]

Gaining shape: growing fields and the condition of global history

The list of examples of new translocal approaches in American historiography could be widened almost indefinitely. For example, in fields that could be grouped under "cultural history," there is now a wide and colorful spectrum of research on global fashions, facets of pop culture, identity patterns, and related topics, many of which are being pursued not only by historians but also by scholars based in other academic fields like anthropology.[188] For instance, the study of artistic movements has produced some studies that investigate translocal dynamics without necessarily treating the nation-state as the main unit of analysis.[189] Likewise, the history of science and technology has undergone important developments to study global interaction patterns while at the same time moving further apart from its Western biases.[190] A related area of research is the history of technical innovations as well as the communication revolution,[191] from early postal systems to the internet, and its locally specific sociocultural consequences all over the

---

[184] For example, Gräser (2009).
[185] For example, Bender (2002; 2000); and Tyrell (2007).   [186] Bender (2006).
[187] Compare Beckert (2007).
[188] In this context, for example, the global connections of cities, their societies, economic structures, and cultures has been accentuated. For example, Cartier (1999).
[189] For example, Joyce (1993); and Jones (2001).
[190] See, for example, Schäfer (2003).
[191] An early work in this field is, for example, Kern (1983).

world. In addition, areas covered by medical history have seen continued interest in transnational and global scopes of analysis. While the history of epidemics and diseases has already figured prominently in earlier world historical accounts,[192] many more detailed studies have now appeared on topics such as the relationship between increasing global interaction on the one hand and the spread as well as control of diseases on the other.[193]

It is safe to say that much of what could be called the "global turn" in historiography took place within established fields such as social or economic history. But the rise of translocal perspectives also generated fresh opportunities for interdisciplinary cooperation and scholarly networks. For instance, new scientific communities have started forming around hitherto marginal themes such as the history of international non-governmental organizations or global environmental history. The members of these research constituencies come from a wide variety of disciplinary backgrounds. In addition, the growing presence of global historical themes also evoked debates which were wide enough to attract the attention of scholars from very different branches of historiography. Many theoretical questions emanating from global historical considerations are now being discussed in key journals like the *American Historical Review* as well as a large number of more specialized periodicals catering to specific parts of historiography.

Some debates surrounding global historical problems generated rather unusual public spheres within the field since they became influential among very different types of historians. One example of a theoretical question of this kind has been the problem of periodization in global historical contexts. An aspect of this issue was the somewhat artificial question about the beginnings of globalization. Many participants in this debate agreed that it is impossible to define clear global historical watersheds since a multitude of local and translocal histories were entangled with each other in profoundly divergent ways.[194] In the debates on how to conceptualize global epochs and stages, most scholars argued that it should be possible to reflect upon important transregional transitions without claiming that these affected the entire world evenly and synchronically. Since the patterns in which knives cut and divide tell us quite a lot about the hands holding them, the debates on topics such as the "beginnings of globalization" actually provided opportunities to

---

[192] For a discussion see W. McNeill (1992).
[193] Examples are W. McNeill (1976); Mann (2005); Oldstone (1998); Watts (1999); and Engel (2006).
[194] For a discussion of this problem see Bentley (1996a); and Manning (1996).

exchange opinions on a much wider range of issues which global and transnational historians had to face. For example, one of the fundamental questions looming in the background of periodization problems was how to weigh economic, political, military, cultural, and other perspectives against each other when reflecting upon the question of time within a global space.

Suggested timelines for the beginnings of "global history" are manifold,[195] and some scholars suggest that they reach as far back as the early stages of long-distance human migration during the Neolithic Period.[196] Others hold that globalization began with the inclusion of the Americas into the global trading system during the sixteenth century. They argue that cross-Atlantic exchanges quickly led to a Columbian exchange of plants, animals, and people,[197] which was followed by a global assimilation of silver prices, leading to great socioeconomic repercussions in many parts of the world.[198] This proposed periodization reaches back at least to Adam Smith who deemed the European "discovery" of the Americas and the passage to India to be the "two greatest and most important events in the history of mankind."[199] Much closer to the present is the idea that such developments as the growing importance of global organizations and institutions, the end of colonial empires, technological revolutions such as the internet, and the step into space make the postwar period a new epoch in human history.[200]

Many representatives of different fields, however, agree that the nineteenth century was a major transition period in the history of the globe, even though they differ in their reasons and the exact timelines they suggest. For example, some economic historians hold that, during the 1800s, local markets all over the world became so tightly connected with international currents, fluctuations, and developments that they can no longer be properly understood when isolated from the larger picture of a global economy. In this context, some scholars have suggested that, during the 1820s, global price convergence came to characterize such a wide spectrum of commodities that it is no longer possible to view trade

---

[195] Some scholars have tried to bridge the gaps between different possibilities for global periodization and rather sought to identify different stages of globalization. See Hopkins (2002b), p. 1.
[196] For example, Clark (1997).
[197] See, for example, Crosby (1972); Gunn (2003); A. Frank (1998); and Green (1998).
[198] Flynn and Giráldez (2004).   [199] A. Smith (1776), vol. I, p. 121.
[200] See, for example, Mazlish (1993). See also Schäfer (2003). This periodization is in line with many sociological and economist interpretations of globalization. An overview of the latter is provided by Guillén (2001).

from regional perspectives alone.[201] Coming from a different direction, a group of historians identified the spectrum of nineteenth-century revolutions in transportation and communication technology – and their social consequences such as mass migration – as an important transition period for the history of the world as an integrated space.[202] From yet a different angle, other scholars have pointed to the global entanglements of the European power struggles between the 1760s and the 1830s as well as to their mutual transcontinental influences. According to Chris Bayly, for example, this age was characterized by a multi-centric order that continued many facets of earlier periods, but at the same time was increasingly impacted by transregional social forces and ideologies. In an increasingly complex global arena, Bayly argues, many localized conflicts in different parts of the world started directly or indirectly affecting each other, leading to political destabilization in many regions.[203] Some historians such as Michael Geyer and Charles Bright noted that the second half of the nineteenth century, specifically the period between the 1840s and 1880s, was a time in which many national and imperial structures were being reshaped in violent and drastic ways. Many empires, for instance, started to develop more central power structures as colonial policies began shifting away from mere surplus extraction towards socio-political engineering.[204]

Most attempts to sketch epochs within global frameworks have not been written from absolutizing perspectives. The course of the debates on global periodizations reflects the aforementioned tendencies to operate with rather flexible notions of time when thinking about history in macroscopic dimensions. This can be observed also in some recently published global historical overviews. For example, some excellent global and transnational accounts of such crucial periods as the nineteenth century have been written from multi-angled visions in order to accommodate the different timelines of economic, political, social, environmental, and other processes. They also remain sensitive to the diachronic character of local experiences, even if they are tightly entangled with global formations. Most importantly, however, approaches to

[201] O'Rourke and Williamson (2002). The advocates of the idea that globalization in the modern sense had its origins in the nineteenth century often assume that economic integration receded around the time of the two world wars and then proceeded again during the Cold War era. For example, O'Rourke and Williamson (1999); and Bordo, Taylor and Williamson (2003).
[202] For example, Therborn (2000); and McKeown (2004).   [203] Bayly (2004b; 2005).
[204] Compare Geyer and Bright (1996), particularly pp. 623–53.

the question of global timelines have been largely centered on networks beyond national boundaries, or on global processes that affected a large number of national and imperial polities. In that manner, the debates surrounding global historical conceptions of time have been inseparably connected with scholarship operating with translocal parameters of space.

Parallel to the emergence of new approaches to rethinking the history of long-term developments through new conceptions of globality and translocality, some fields operating with rather unconventional conceptions of space have experienced new levels of significance. This applies, for instance, to historical research that explores human interaction along geographical settings that do not match national, continental, or other culturally and politically defined boundaries. One example of such an area of interest is maritime or oceanic history. Certainly, the study of oceans, seas, and rims as arenas of historical interaction is not new, and generations ago produced such epigone figures as Fernand Braudel, whose work has been influential in the United States.[205] But for a long time, maritime historiography followed in the footsteps of world history in the sense that it primarily gave rise to historical overviews such as textbooks or trade books which, moreover, often used nation-states as the prime units of analysis. In addition, oceanic interpretations often played an important role in Eurocentric visions of world history – such as, for instance, the idea that the Atlantic world constituted the primary, if not the sole agent in a globalizing world.[206]

Analogous to the development within some other fields, a large number of new research projects and detailed studies has significantly changed the character of maritime and oceanic history.[207] The wealth of topics pursued from the perspective of maritime history includes translocal studies of trading communities, exchange processes in nautical technology, the transformations of gender and ethnicity discourses, as well as mechanisms of imperial expansion and dominance.[208] There is

---

[205] See, for example, Osterhammel (1994b).

[206] For a critique see Geyer and Bright (1995).

[207] Detailed studies also influenced the character of larger synthesizing studies emerging out of these fields. See Wigen and Lewis (1999); and Bentley (1999).

[208] An impression of the width of fields being pursued can be gained at Hattendorf (2007). Important theoretical issues were discussed in the *American Historical Review*'s June 2006 forum on "Oceans of History" as well as the forum "Entangled Empires in the Atlantic World," *American Historical Review*, 112–13 (2007), pp. 710–99. Important synthesizing studies or collaborative research projects on different oceans have appeared. For example: Bentley, Bridenthal, and Wigen (2007); Bose (2006); Bailyn (2005); and Cunliffe (2001).

now a tendency to deal with maritime rims as regional systems and to explore the ways in which different coastal communities were involved in dense networks of exchanges and mutual interaction. This shift of perspectives does not deny the importance of land-based state actors such as nations, but it adds a new dimension to their genesis and evolution. With challenging perspectives and alternative conceptions of this kind, many maritime historians have come to operate in larger, often global scopes of analysis.[209]

To a certain extent, the growth of maritime history has reintroduced geographical tools and considerations into the workshop of historians. This does not mean, however, that recent scholarship reconnects with earlier traditions of historical geography. For instance, most of today's historians are far more cautious when applying the logics geographical determinism to the study of the past.[210] However, scholars are becoming more interested in the physical, topographical, and climatic worlds in which human beings live and interact with each other. A major example of this trend is the increasing weight of research directions that have come to be grouped under "environmental history."[211] It was during the 1970s that a multitude of works on issues related to the human habitat began to be established through the foundation of scholarly associations, programs, and journals. Much of the growing energy within this new branch of historical scholarship grew in conjunction with international movements that addressed environmental concerns.[212] From the outset, environmental history was a likely candidate to develop perspectives cutting across national boundaries. The geography of environmental problems hardly matched the world's political topographies at any given point in time. In addition, a large number of researchers who became active in the field were in fact not historians but scientists whose training had exposed them to a lesser degree to the methodological nationalism and other spatial paradigms which had been foundational to historiography.

Nevertheless, nation-centered perspectives continued to weigh heavily on environmental history, particularly since much of the supplied data was generated at a national level and framed in a corresponding way. Yet while many studies in environmental history remain confined to single

---

[209] See, for example, Eltis (1999); Seeman and Cañizares-Esguerra (2007); Jones, Frost, and White (1993); Gilroy (1993); and Matory (2005).

[210] A prominent exception to the tendency to avoid geographical determinism is Diamond (1997).

[211] Important institutionalized subfields include, for example, forest history, the history of climate change, and the history of national parks.

[212] J. McNeill (2003).

national arenas, new global historical perspectives have grown in number, and some recent overview works have sought to transgress the nation-state as a unit of analysis when possible and plausible.[213] Some detailed studies have even moved towards focusing on alternative spatial boundaries, for example by investigating the paths of environmental destruction along river systems or wind currents.[214] The move towards new conceptions of space in environmental historical research has been greatly facilitated by the fact that the field has branched out to new areas of inquiry such as social or cultural history. Topics like demographic growth, energy consumption, the global impact of economic expansion, or the transmigration of plants and animals through human beings have become far more common, and have often lent themselves to new translocal approaches.[215] Furthermore, some global and comparative studies have addressed sociocultural ways of conceptualizing the environment and human ways of interacting with it.[216]

Environmental and maritime history remained characterized by geographical considerations in the widest sense, but this was not necessarily the case with other research fields that rose in conjunction with increasing transregional interests. One example of such an area of inquiry is the scholarship on global governance and global civil society.[217] As a result of a growing body of literature, a much clearer and more nuanced image of the growth of transnational activist movements is emerging, ranging from environmentalist groups and women's rights groups to anti-globalization forces.[218] Other kinds of global non-governmental organizations such as the International Olympic Committee or the Parliament of the World's Religions have also received historiographical attention.[219] In addition, the study of intergovernmental organizations ranging from the League of Nations to the International Commission for Air Navigation has explored new topics in ways that go far beyond the

---

[213] Examples of works providing global historical perspectives on environmental issues and problems are Radkau (2008); J. McNeill (2000); and Chester (2006). See also Hughes (2001).

[214] For example, Grove (1998); and Glasso (2008).

[215] For example, Crosby (2004); M. Hall (2005); and Weller (2006).

[216] See, for example, the series Religions of the World and Ecology, edited by Evelyn Tucker and published during the 1990s. Some macroscopic works have approached a spectrum of themes ranging from attitudes towards nature in different world regions to failed sociopolitical responses and to environmental problems as well as their disastrous consequences. An example of the history of environmental failures which gained a lot of attention in the wider public is Diamond (2005).

[217] For an overview of positions see, for example, Lipschutz (2006). An example for studies related to global governance and its history is Connelly (2008).

[218] See, for example, Keck (1998); Paxton (2006); and Eschle and Maihguashca (2005).

[219] See, for example, Seager (1993).

parameters of diplomatic history.[220] For example, a fair number of studies illuminated the complex entanglements of such organizations with the world beyond. For instance, some publications investigate the relationship between interests of empire and newly founded organizations such as the United Nations.[221] Other historians have begun exploring the intricate networks between non-governmental activities and governmental organizations.[222] New concepts and methodological developments of this kind have also had an impact on the history of peace as well as its underlying processes, structures, and efforts.[223]

Many of the most influential contributions to the study of global organizations and civil society have actually not emerged from history departments but rather from other disciplines, ranging from anthropology to sociology. Many publications in the latter field, for example, rely on interpretation of past developments, but are actually often tied to future-oriented visions ranging from neoliberalism to postmodernism.[224] For example, some works interpret the growth of non-governmental movements as the beginnings of cosmopolitan governance in a stage of history at which the difference between domestic and foreign policy is becoming less relevant.[225] Other influential books assess patterns of transnational activism in terms of their potentials for a future global democracy which, in the opinion of some theorists, would be characterized by traits such as a growing influence of "cosmocratic" forces and a global pluralization of power.[226] Heading into a similar direction, some groups of observers consider international NGOs to be the beginnings of world citizenship or even of a singular global polity characterized by decentralized facets of authority.[227] Other studies regard the numerical growth of global organizations as a separate, more promising, storyline which unfolded independently from the world wars and other great traumas of the modern age.[228] No matter what position is taken, scholarship related to global civil society and global

---

[220] A historian's account of the growth of intergovernmental and non-governmental organizations is Iriye (2002). See also Boli and Thomas (1999); and Murphy (1994).
[221] Mazower (2009).   [222] For example, Iriye (2002).
[223] This is a field which was important during the 1960s and 1970s and, after a period of relative decline, has recently experienced a surge of interest. For more details see, for example, Clinton (2005); and Jones (2002).
[224] For a classification and discussion of various positions see Kaldor (2003).
[225] For example, Held et al. (1999), and, heading into similar directions, Giddens (2000).
[226] See Keane (2003); and Hardt and Negri (2004).
[227] For example, Boli and Thomas (1999).
[228] According to Akira Iriye, international organizations need to be seen as "civilized societies" that have the potential to turn the world into a civilized community: Iriye (2002), p. 193; and Iriye (1997).

governance has been characterized by efforts to overcome both nation- and power-centered visions of world politics in visions of globalization.

Concluding observations – in lieu of a definition

As can be seen from the wide variety of research discussed above, in many established fields of study, ranging from economic history to the history of gender, historical space is now being conceptualized in far more complex ways than a generation ago. As a result of many influen- tial case studies challenging methodological nationalism and Eurocentrism, the mental maps of historical scholarship look increas- ingly kaleidoscopic and are convoluted in the sense that they are less structured in clearly separable units. Since in the US research landscape the global trend builds on a multitude of detailed research projects in all branches of historiography, it would be tempting to conclude that now "most historians are global historians. The problem is that they don't know it yet."[229] Yet when identifying an intellectual trend, it would hardly be convincing to equate global history with the state of the art of historiography at large. The days in which representatives of an *histoire totale* could proclaim their field as the integrative queen of the social sciences[230] are gone. Global history as a larger academic trend is certainly far from reaching out to a great synthesis, even though indi- vidual scholars may indeed see it as the final edifice built by large numbers of historians. As an academic transformation, global history is far less and, therefore, at the same time far more than the sum of historiography in its current state. For instance, global history excludes the wide range of studies which operate within more established con- ceptions of space such as nations, even though many of these may indirectly contribute to expanding the frontiers of border-crossing research.

One main characteristic of global history in the United States is a critical reconsideration of those conceptions of space that had been foundational to modern academic historiography. This has major implications since ideas of space convey notions of contingency and autonomy, distance and closeness, as well as centrality and marginality. An increasing number of scholars have become either directly or

---

[229] Bayly (2004a).

[230] About *histoire totale* see the "classic" study by Stoianovich (1976). It should be mentioned that the *histoire totale* also operated with flexible conceptions of space and dimensions of reality that were commonly applied to the same object of study. See Chartier (1989).

indirectly involved in emancipating their field from the political and intellectual regimes of territoriality that have long dominated its professional structures, academic communities, and scholarly pursuits. However, this has not been a uniform process since not all historiography was dominated by the same conceptions of space; the segmentation of territoriality tended to be field-specific. For an expert of the European Middle Ages, for example, explorations of intra-European interactions were hardly ever revolutionary, yet until recently investigations of historical dynamics between Islam and Christendom were hardly present in the field. By contrast, the action radius of most historians working on the modern era tended to be framed around the concept of the nation-state.[231] For a long time, even colonial or world historical approaches to modern history were primarily channeled through the idea of states and their boundaries as the main units of the past.

The search for alternatives to methodological nationalism, culturalism, and similar paradigms has taken a multitude of directions, so it is certainly not the case that one new set of spatial categories has replaced another one. Rather, experimenting with alternative conceptions of space, breaking through disciplinary boundaries, and transgressing political or mental borders has become in vogue within the community of historians. Many case studies now focus on linkages which scholarship had long relegated to the background because it primarily studied single nations, world regions, or other spatial configurations which were long primarily regarded as rather independent historical arenas. Concepts like flows, webs, connections, entanglements, and mutual influences have now become part of the standard repertoire of historical scholarship.

Spatial thinking in the field of global history has reached a sufficient degree of complexity for certain types of methodological or conceptual problems to no longer play a central role on the field's public stages. This applies, for example, to the question whether locality needs to be seen as an alternative to globality, which had long figured as a prominent theme in several academic fields.[232] The global historical trend has not let the "local" disappear, but it certainly has made it far more complex. Much of what before had been primarily treated as local now appears to be dependent on – or even result from – wider processes and interconnections. In an increasing number of studies, territorial formations and deterritorializing processes are hardly juxtaposed with each other but

---

[231] See Wigen and Lewis (1997). The civilizational perspective of world history has experienced a certain public revival following the publication of Huntington (1998).
[232] For more details and a historical assessment of these debates M. Lang (2006), pp. 902ff.

remain rather interwoven in such complex nexuses that they cannot be properly conceptualized in a separate manner.[233] Among the consequences of such change is the fact that the history of the United States now increasingly gives the impression of being "simultaneously that of a sovereign and a global nation."[234] In addition, concepts such as "globalization" and "culture" are often treated in ways that do not consider either side as absolutes or fixed points.[235]

Despite some concerns of its critics,[236] most of global history as an academic trend has been far from blending all local perspectives into a chimera of amorphous connectivity. If we regard the mental cartographies emerging from a multitude of recent approaches we see not a holistic globe emerging but much rather a dynamic realm of overlapping, entangled, and interacting spaces, as well as long-term and short-term hierarchical relations. In the main, the "globe" of emerging from global and transnational historical scholarship in the United States is not a fixed entity waiting to be filled with new master narratives but primarily an open question addressed by a myriad of individual research activities. The vast majority of relevant projects do not operate on a planetary scale but nevertheless the multifaceted and open character of this scholarship influences our images of globalization and history.

Under the impact of the global trend, many spatial categories that tended to be seen as given have now increasingly become a focus of critical inquiry.[237] Generally speaking, historiography as an academic field has become more immediately interested in its own disciplinary conceptions of space, on both macroscopic and microscopic levels. One aspect of this growing self-reflectivity is the surging number of publications investigating topics such as the constructions of national historiographies, myths of continents, and tropes of civilizations. Another facet is the appearance of studies which examine the global spread of modern academic historiography and its conceptual worlds from a wide variety of angles.[238] Together, such research raises awareness that the very spatial concepts with which historians operate are products of historical developments rather than given frames of the

---

[233] For a more thorough discussion of this subject see A. Amin (2002).
[234] Bright and Geyer (2002), p. 73.   [235] Cooper (2001).
[236] An early example is McGerr (1991).
[237] For example, this has been the case with the transdisciplinary literature pointing to the invented character of world regions. For example, Wigen and Lewis (1997); Wolff (1994); Mignolo (2005); and Bassin (1999).
[238] In recent years, many important works have discussed the emergence of modern historiographical cultures in many parts of the world as the results of global and local encounters, conflicts, as well as hybridization processes. For example, Iggers, Q. Wang, and Mukherjee (2008); and Woolf (2011).

past. This certainly contributes to making the relationship between history and historiography more complex.

In other words, in American academic circles, the global historical trend has been connected to a growing reluctance to operate within alleged monolithic visions of the nation. Already before the rise of global and transnational history, historical research about the United States had already undergone a pluralizing or even fragmenting process.[239] During the 1980s in particular, a progressive number of scholars sought to add another layer of complexity to their studies, dealing with the ways in which reality was being perceived and constructed by distinct historical groups as well as individuals.[240] For example, this implied that scholars grew more hesitant to accept the notion of historical objectivity, which had a significant impact on the ways in which concepts such as "society" or "culture" were used among historians. Even before global history and related terms were articulated as an academic project, historians of gender, social milieus, religious groups, and many other fields of study had increasingly criticized the idea of the nation as a container of historical contingency. While many movements turning against elite-centered visions of the past initially operated on a subnational level, their new emphasis on diverse historical spaces made it more acceptable to think about the nation in terms of more flexible geographies.

Due to its major methodological implications, one might assume that the global trend in American historiography was largely driven by new theoretical reflections and conceptual debates. Until now, however, theoretical works have only been a small part of the developments towards greater spatial complexity in the field. Decisive for the growing prominence of global and translocal perspectives was a multitude of small and large publications cutting across established conceptions of historical space. In a slow and largely inadvertent process, this has started altering historiographical research landscapes as well as many images of the past arising from them. The diffused character of the global historical trend may also account for the fact that it spread in rather uncontroversial ways, without evoking the staunch opposition that many other academic trends faced in the past. True, there have been critics of certain types of global history but the rise of translocal perspectives has in itself neither stirred significant levels of disciplinary

---

[239] On the growing diversification of historiographical journals into specific research communities see Middell (1999).

[240] For more details see Hunt (1989). Many of these intellectual movements were related to what came to be referred to as the "cultural turn" in the humanities and social sciences.

anxieties nor encountered high levels of resistance. In addition, global history has experienced only few tendencies to polarize into feuding camps, each operating under high pressure of conformism.

While the changing cultures of historiography have been tied to changes within US universities and American society at large, they do not necessarily reflect clear changes in majority opinion. Among large segments of the American population there is strong resistance to deconstructing national history and world historical narratives by shifting away from topoi such as the idea of US exceptionalism or the primacy of Western civilization on the global stage. In fact, there has been a growing market for right-wing textbooks that portray history in ways that run diametrically counter to many ideas and values shared by central currents in academic historiography.[241] In a rather polarized political landscape, an overwhelming majority of faculty in the social sciences and humanities vote for the Democratic Party.[242] In that sense, the changing opinion climate at American institutions of higher learning reflects transformations of public opinion only within part of the US population. It may be worth reflecting further upon the question whether the increasing internationalization of American universities has been structurally related to their growing estrangement from large parts of US society.[243]

Needless to say, even within academic circles, not all recent border-crossing historiography has sought to reverse the spatial categories and normative lenses that characterized much academic history writing for a long time. Some recent scholarship offering global interpretations of the past has even endeavored to reaffirm ideas of Western exceptionalism and derivative claims to ethicopolitical superiority.[244] Nonetheless, the main currents in the recent discussions surrounding terms such as global history, translocal history, and even world history have led into very different directions. Among other developments, an increasing willingness to deconstruct concepts like "Europe" as part of a search for alternatives to Western-centric worldviews and hegemonic storylines has become an important trait within today's research communities.[245] Attacking theories of convergence, narratives of Western-led progress,

---

[241] See Bentley (2005).

[242] According to one survey, the Democratic–Republican ratio among US faculty is 9.5 to 1 in the field of history and 28 to 1 in sociology. See Klein and Stern (2004).

[243] Generally about the anti-intellectualism and anti-internationalism within large parts of the political right see T. Frank (2004).

[244] For example, Ferguson (2003); Landes (1998); and Headley (2008).

[245] As Michael Geyer and Charles Bright point out, even many critical world histories tended to depict constructs such as, most notably, "the West" as the sole active centers in global contexts: Bright and Geyer (2005).

and challenge-response models has become common to a degree that the major contestations in global historical scholarship are no longer situated on the linear trajectories of these theories. As an academic trend, global history is thus far from fostering the deterministic and homogenizing interpretations of globalization which continue to enjoy rather strong support in other academic fields like economics.

The close connection between global history and a research landscape which has been pluralizing while at the same time reconnecting begs the question about the future trajectories of this trend. For example, is global history in the process of becoming a solipsistic community of aficionados or like-minded scholars, another research community in an increasingly fragmented field? If this is the case, the global turn in historiography would evolve into a specialized subdiscipline such as economic history or the history of gender, both of which after periods of maturation developed their own field-specific infrastructures, career paths, and methodological debates, even though they remain closely related to other historiographical fields. Another, profoundly different possibility is that global history will play an integrative rather than an aspectual role in the future. After all, disciplinary insularity does not seem suitable to a field which emerged out of a much wider academic trend.

Yet more important than the potential future standing of global history within its larger academic environments is the question regarding its potential contribution to historical thinking. Precisely because terms like "global history" or "translocal history" have gained considerable academic authority, this is not the time for mutual back-slapping and blind endorsements of a process that is still unfolding. Certainly, the huge diversity of studies, positions, and projects that can be subsumed under "global history" make it almost nonsensical to ask whether this movement should be regarded in positive or negative terms. For instance, the critique of Eurocentrism or intellectual imperialism that has been voiced in response to global and world historical literature[246] has been important but it actually only touches upon a small fraction of this intellectual trend.

Nevertheless, in any kind of globally oriented thinking, it would be far too careless to disregard such criticism by arguing that the bulk of publications in the field are written in a spirit counter to privileged Western perspectives. Particularly in such an internationally connected and diversified system as the United States, it is tempting to interpret the pluralism of positions discussed on a domestic level as a reflection of global academic opinion climates. Yet,

---

[246] Dirlik (2002a).

as outlined in the previous chapter, most global historical scholarship published in other languages and countries is hardly even recognized by its peer group in the United States. Although the declared aim to "let others speak" may have been applied to the study of the past, there are strong indications that our international academic communities remain as hierarchical, Western-centric, and imbalanced as they were a hundred years ago. Seen from this angle, global history as an academic trend may run the risk of deconstructing boundaries in history while inadvertently contributing towards the preservation of many of the old structures of privilege and disadvantage, which above all favor the United States in the global landscapes knowledge.[247] In that sense, the open rejection of Eurocentrism by the vast majority of researchers in the United States does not necessarily mean that it has ceased to exist.

[247] On this point see also Feierman (1999).

3   On the margins of a troubled
     nation – approaches in Germany

The primacy of the national past

Although global memory may not exist, there are certain aspects of the past that have transcended their original spatial confinements and entered historical consciousness in different parts of the world. Among the most well known and symbolically charged aspects of the human past are certainly the crimes and traumas of the Nazi era. In many countries, the atrocities committed during the Third Reich, particularly the *shoa*, occupy an important place in textbooks as well as in popular historical consciousness as they are transmitted and reinvoked on television, in newspapers, and other media. German fascism has also become an important subject of academic research and intellectual debate, even in regions such as East Asia or South Asia that were not directly affected by it. In many parts of the world there have been debates about the implications of the Nazi experience for notions of such fundamental concepts as modernity or Europe and its place in the world as well as – in some cases – human nature and God.[1] The historical discourses surrounding the National Socialist past are certainly far from identical in different public spheres. However, this does not change the fact that important facets of the history of Nazism and its victims have been globalized in terms of their historical implications, connotations, and symbolism.

These worldwide dimensions of German history's fateful years stand in sharp contrast to the thin presence of non-European and global history in German academia. The poor representation of these fields may be seen as somewhat surprising in light of the complex ways in which German society, economy, and politics are connected to the wider

---

[1] In this context one may, for example, think of the works of Hannah Arendt, Aimé Césaire, and Frantz Fanon.

110

world.[2] As the Chicago historian Michael Geyer remarked, "the truly strange thing about Germany is that German lands and their peoples have been so deeply entangled with the world and, yet, Germans, and German historians at that, have such tremendous difficulties in coming to terms with that fact and its consequences."[3] Indeed, at first glance it may seem somewhat counter-intuitive that, in the face of such an international presence, the main orientations of German historiography have remained tied quite closely to the nation-state. One might be tempted to point to the brevity of Germany's imperial experience in a search for an answer to the question why transcultural historical research has remained rather small. Yet if the comparatively short history of German overseas expansions were the main cause for its Eurocentric historiographical cultures, other former colonial powers would, by implication, necessarily be characterized by more diversified patterns of area expertise in history departments. Yet world, non-European, and transcultural history are only slightly more present in countries like France, Great Britain, and Belgium.[4]

This suggests that the marginality of world and translocal scholarship in Germany could be understood as part of a wider, commonly European phenomenon. Certainly, in the past Eurocentric visions which arose in an age of the continent's global dominance also contributed to the fact that much European historiography remained quite unmusical to the world beyond. For a long time, notions of cultural superiority have made politicians and academicians throughout Europe less likely to study the rest of the world. We can see manifestations of this mindset, which rendered the world almost irrelevant to the understanding of Europe and its polities, in the structures of many history departments between the eastern shores of the Atlantic and the Ural Mountains.[5] As some scholars have argued, many European societies did not choose to diversify their regional expertise, even after the end of the colonial age. This has been the case, they allege, because – in contrast to post-war global players such as the United States – the great social, cultural and political questions faced by many European societies were primarily regional or national in nature.[6]

While keeping such European commonalities in mind, it is also important to consider national factors that have been contributing to

[2] For example, Wirz (2001); and Patel (2004).   [3] Geyer (2006), p. 4.
[4] A comparative overview is provided by Loth and Osterhammel (2000).
[5] See also Chapter 1.   [6] For example, Middell (2002a). See also Kaelble (2004).

the rather introverted scopes of historical research in Germany. This is even more the case since, while the European Union is becoming an increasingly influential actor on the academic stage, German academic institutions, public spheres, and funding structures continue to widely shape the basic parameters of its historical research. It is particularly the dark shadows cast by the Nazi past that for a long time made transnational approaches appear less relevant or even problematical in the eyes of many German historians. Coming to terms with the Nazi heritage and creating an apt historical consciousness for a liberal democratic culture has certainly been the main concern of historical research on the modern period. This implied addressing the enormous question of how to place the Third Reich within longer historical timelines and patterns of the past. For a long time it seemed as if answers to this question were necessarily limited to the confinements of national history, since many transnational approaches could be interpreted as efforts to relativize the responsibilities stemming from the German past.

For these and other reasons, much of German historiography remained quite closely wedded to the concept of the nation-state ever since the *Kaiserreich*. Moreover, history departments never made significant efforts to add capacity to the study of world regions outside of Europe and North America. Yet this situation may not be ascribed to the fact that German history departments experienced unbroken traditions in political climates and attitudes towards nationalism. Rather, the national bias towards historiography in Germany continued despite – or exactly because of – great ruptures in attitudes towards the nation and its past. By implication, the status of transnational and particularly transcontinental scholarship has also experienced some remarkable continuities ever since the late nineteenth century.

The long dominance of nation-centered perspectives in historical scholarship should not make us assume, however, that the spatial concepts preferred by German historians remained frozen in time. Particularly since the late 1980s, there have been growing efforts in Germany to explore the hitherto quite unchartered territories of transnational history. This process can be divided into five main branches, of which the strongest is formed by attempts to look at the German past from new global, transregional, and comparative angles. Secondly, there have been attempts to Europeanize history, which involve critical considerations of German as well as many other national histories. Thirdly, mounting efforts were made to grant more prominent research space to non-European history within the institutional worlds of German historiography. Stemming from this movement, there have been, fourthly, proposals to intensify the cooperation between Europeanists and scholars focusing on other world regions in order to open up new kinds of research possibilities. Fifthly, the field has witnessed new activity in world historical scholarship, which in some cases has significantly departed from earlier traditions.

An important context of global and transnational history between the Rhine and the Oder rivers is the changing relation between German historians and their colleagues in other parts of the world. While nineteenth-century German history departments were often seen as international forerunners, as conceptual and methodological epicenters of the entire profession, the same has hardly been the case during the second half of the twentieth century and after. Today, scholars from Germany no longer serve as the conceptual and methodological vanguard for the study of history. With a few exceptions, the main international audience for German historiography lies in the circles of experts in German history. In many fields, among them transcontinental history as well as many regional studies, Anglophone literature has long come to have a strong influence on the paths and patterns of German research. Even though the networks of academic transmission have been far more complex, it is to a certain degree accurate to say that, while in the nineteenth century Germany was among the main exporters of national conceptions of history,[7] it now imports many transnational ideas.

Marginalizing the world: modern German historiography

Over the course of the nineteenth century, German historical scholarship shifted away from Enlightenment cosmopolitanism.[8] Particularly in the newly formed research universities of the Second Reich, national history was promoted by the state, and transnational perspectives were marginalized. The same was true for historiographical work on the world outside of Europe. Nevertheless, at certain times, the German academic system witnessed important, wider debates over world historical topics. This was, for example, the case with the so-called "Lamprecht controversy" named after the famed Leipzig scholar who, around the turn of the twentieth century, advocated more holistic, civilizational approaches to the human past.[9] Among other ideas and projects, Lamprecht

---

[7] Today's scholarship has come to revise the stereotype of the global influence of historicism and German historiography in general. Citing the most important literature: Fuchs (2002), particularly p. 5.
[8] For more details see Chapter 1.   [9] See, for example, Schleier (1993).

suggested that one should differentiate between the terms world history and universal history by making the former a marker of the history of European hegemony and the latter a designation of the human past at large.[10]

Within this disciplinary culture of historiography, it was possible for established scholars to become involved in world historical projects, though these endeavors were usually regarded as excursions from the strict standards of academic work. In general, the central importance attached to primary source work and detailed local analyses made it impossible to consider such towering figures as Karl Marx, Max Weber, or Oswald Spengler as being close to the centers of innovation within the field of historiography.[11] They were either regarded as representatives or founders of other disciplines, or as public figures operating largely outside academic cultures. Many historians believed that their own social role was less to explain a rapidly changing world than to solidify the notion of Germany.

The experience of the First World War pushed German academic history writing even deeper into the camp of national history. The loss of colonies ended the global ambitions of the former Second Reich, and the prolonged domestic crises of the Weimar Republic absorbed much scholarly energy.[12] Moreover, many scholars became involved in efforts to disprove the Versailles notion that the Reich was solely responsible for the war. Most historians were ideologically rather close to various right-wing currents, which were highly fragmented but united in their opposition to the internationalist tendencies of the political left. The main areas in which international historical research was institutionally expanded were Eastern European and, to a lesser extent, Latin American history – reflecting the somewhat shrunken foreign ambitions within which German politics maneuvered. Also under the Nazi regime, historiography did not put much emphasis on imperial or world historical scholarship in the strict sense of the terms.[13] At the same time, Social Darwinist or even racist categories of thinking became lead paradigms for many national, international, and world historical texts. In addition, anti-modern discourses were

---

[10] Kossock (1993), pp. 94ff.
[11] After the Second World War, particularly since the 1960s, Weber became far more influential in German historiography and yet his transculturally comparative approaches remained rather marginalized. Generally on the topic see Kocka (1986).
[12] See Lambert (2003).
[13] See, for example, Haar (2000); and Schulze and Oexle (2000). About plans to cluster the research on world regions see Hausmann (1998).

even further instrumentalized as a way of legitimizing the movement's racial ideologies and expansionist ambitions.[14]

1945, the big watershed year in German history, did not wash away many ways of conceptualizing the German nation-state and its history. After the war some older doubts about the suitability of the Prussian-led state project, which had been enunciated from many Catholic regions including the Rhineland, reemerged but failed to establish significant schools of alternative, cross-border visions of the past.[15] In any case, the majority of prominent scholars reinvented themselves as liberal, pro-democratic historians in a society that, they now claimed, had been pushed off its historical trajectories between 1933 and 1945.[16] It is interesting to note that in order to be able to delink the Nazi era from the main patterns of German history, many histor-ians resorted to transnational perspectives and abandoned strictly endogenous visions of the past.[17] For example, Gerhard Ritter focused his analysis of National Socialism on the Jacobin elements of mass-based democracy and militarism.[18] Several other historians, including some representatives of the political left, saw the root causes of National Socialism in a depersonalized, technocratic age.[19] Rather influential scholars opined that the Third Reich was primarily a symptom of a major civilizational crisis shaking much of the European continent.[20] Floating on this tendency to treat the Nazi experience as a discontinuity of German history with transnational root causes, some of the main historiographical schools in Germany, including Rankeanism and folkish histories, could continue without major disruptions.[21]

A big break with older traditions of history writing occurred during the 1960s, when a new generation of historians, which had been too young to be actively involved in the Nazi regime, started to become influential within German academic circles and the wider public. This generational break was further enhanced by the rapid expansion of the

---

[14] Oberkrome (1993). See also Middell and Sommer (2004). Anti-modernist ideologies partly underpinned the *völkish* or folk histories with their emphasis on customs and daily life which emerged in the late nineteenth century and gained currency during the 1920s.

[15] See Conrad (1999a).

[16] See also Schulze (1989).

[17] For more details see Assmann and Frevert (1999); and Wehler (2001), pp. 45ff.

[18] For example, Ritter (1954).

[19] For an overview of the positions see Iggers (1997a), Chapter 8.

[20] An overview of East and West German research on fascism is provided by Caplan (1997).

[21] This is also true for the tradition of *Volksgeschichte*, which had essentialized the nation by focusing on the history of – usually highly constructed – motions of the German people.

academic sector, which fed into the shakeup of the country's old cultural and academic elites.[22] Partly encouraged by US modernization theory,[23] scholars such as Hans-Ulrich Wehler and Jürgen Kocka professed to expose the errors and crimes of the past, and rebelled against the silences of those who had lived as adults under the Nazi regime.[24] The main vehicle for this journey became social history or "societal history" (*Gesellschaftsgeschichte*). Social history in Germany was somewhat different from the social turn in Anglo-American universities, which put greater emphasis on the study of social milieus that were of new interest to academic research, particularly minorities. In the German case, the social historical movement did not seek to contribute to a further fragmentation of the field but rather aimed at a holistic perspective of the national past. Patterns, transformations, and constellations of social forces were investigated in order to gain all-encompassing visions of sectors such as politics and culture in German history.[25] The young social historians wanted to break with both elitism and apologetic nationalism by uncovering the crimes and atrocities of the Nazi past.[26]

Hence, unlike with their peer group in the United States, the growing presence of social historical studies did not lead to efforts to decenter hitherto dominant national frameworks in favor of transnational perspectives. Through the rise of social history, historical evaluations of the Nazi period changed decisively in the sense that now many historians started to interpret Hitler's regime not as an aberration from the trajectories of the German past but as their very consequence. This meant that research on the historical contexts and root causes of fascism started to take decidedly nation-centered turns. Comparative perspectives with other liberal Western democracies played a certain role, but were often meant to further accentuate the hypothesis of a German *Sonderweg*, an allegedly unique path to modernization.[27] The renewed commitment to conceptualizing German history primarily from inside out also had significant implications for the ways in which Germany's cultural and political interactions with the world beyond Europe were being depicted.[28] For example, some prominent studies sought to explain

---

[22] See P. Nolte (1999); and Schulze (1989), pp. 302ff.
[23] On American influence see, for example, Schulin (2002).
[24] See Dahrendorf (1965), pp. 431ff.
[25] See, for example, Schulze (1990); and Kocka (1997).
[26] See, for example, Marcuse (1998).   [27] Welskopp (2002).
[28] The marginalization of Germany's international entanglements can also be observed in overviews of German history such as Wehler (1987–2008), which largely follows a nation-centered Weberian framework. See also Rürup (1984), which treats German history largely as a sequence of societal formations.

the history of German colonialism primarily as the outcome of domestic tensions.[29] In many cases, factors contributing to colonialism, such as the logic of power politics and the international spread of colonial ideologies, were moved to the margins of historiographical considerations.[30]

In a somewhat ironic way, Germany's new social historians thus continued older tropes that juxtaposed an "other" Germany with a modern West, albeit under a profoundly different value system. Even after the relative decline of social history during the 1970s and 1980s, it seemed necessary to primarily stick to national historical outlooks in a struggle against apologetic tendencies vis-à-vis the Nazi past. It remained politically sensitive to relate the National Socialist experience to an international context, particularly in an intellectual and public climate that was wary of attempts to dilute a postwar consensus founded on the acknowledgment of the uniqueness of Nazi crimes.[31] Generally speaking, large academic circles felt that the young Federal Republic had only recently dropped anchor but not fully found a harbor in the Western world. Indeed, during the 1980s, some prominent studies written from a transnational perspective smacked of historical and political revisionism. Michael Stürmer, for example, explained German authoritarianism largely with the idea that the country had been situated in a very precarious geographical situation.[32] Going further that that, it was the Berlin historian Ernst Nolte who ignited the famed historians' controversy (*Historikerstreit*).[33] In a newspaper article, the prominent scholar of fascism called for a "normalization" of German national identity and argued that the Holocaust and other Nazi crimes not only were comparable to the Soviet Gulag, but also needed to be understood as a historical transfer from the East. This right-wing conservative position sparked outrage among prominent German thinkers and historians ranging from Jürgen Habermas to Hans-Ulrich Wehler, Wolfgang Mommsen, and Christian Meier.[34] The ensuing debates revealed bitter divisions over questions such as whether the Nazi past and its crimes should be treated as structurally related and morally equal

---

[29] Wehler (1969).   [30] Compare S. Conrad (2002), particularly pp. 158ff.
[31] See Giesen (1993); M. Greiffenhagen and S. Greiffenhagen (1993); Fulbrook (1999).
[32] Stürmer (1983).   [33] E. Nolte (1986).
[34] A collection of key texts related to the *Historikerstreit* is Augstein, Bracher, and Broszat (1987). A detailed analysis of the key positions taken in the controversy is Kailitz (2001); also Diner (1987). See also Maier (1988).

to other atrocities under dictatorships ranging from Stalin to Pol Pot.[35]

During the late 1980s, there were some indications that historical research would increasingly abandon the nation-state framework.[36] Yet after the high tides of the *Historikerstreit* receded, some time in the decade after 1989, as an immediate consequence of German unification, significant scholarly energies were channeled back into national history.[37] Among other factors, the acute challenges and tensions in national institution building may have prevented many key actors from internationalizing historiography in Germany. Furthermore, German unification also rekindled fears that Germany would now loosen its close cultural and political ties with the West. During the early and mid-1990s, there were concerns that growing segments of intellectual life would abandon the historical identity of Germany as a social and cultural space in which the Nazi experience had been once possible.[38] This, in turn, had implications for the standing of research seeking to transnationalize aspects of the modern German past.

Still, while many worries about impending historical revisionism could still be heard, the times had changed. The *Historikerstreit* during the 1980s was actually the last case of a public discussion on the directions of the entire field. After that, the public sphere in general and historiography in particular became far more fragmented than during the Cold War, and the role of university-based historians as the gatekeepers to appropriate forms of national political consciousness declined. This process was partly characterized by the growing presence of new forms of political concerns such as gender advocacy within German history departments.

As some later sections of this chapter will show, such developments and the diversification of historiography eventually created new possibilities for global and transnational historical scholarship. Not unlike in the United States, growing interest in global and transnational history did not primarily emerge from earlier world historical traditions. In spite of this fact, a closer look at the hardly crowded paths of world history in Germany will help us situate more clearly the changing landscapes of various kinds of transregional scholarship there.

---

[35] See Kailitz (2001). See also Maier (1988).
[36] See the following sections of this chapter.
[37] An overview of some contentious issues is provided by Jarausch and Middell (1994).
[38] See Maier (1988), p. 57. Examples from the debates during the 1990s: Gessenharter (1994); and Lohmann (1994).

Trajectories of the sidelines: the paths and positions of world history in Germany

Even though world historical reflections played an increasingly marginal role in nineteenth-century German history departments,[39] around the turn of the twentieth century they experienced a boom among the wider public. The popularity of world historical texts within German political circles, the business world, and their surrounding classes was certainly conditioned by the specific contexts of the time.[40] The nation-building project, which had been greatly enhanced after unification in 1871, was now largely consolidated, and the Second Reich under Wilhelm II started to actively pursue a global colonial role.[41] The sense of worldwide competition, which intensified when discussions of European expansionism gave way to the idea of a finite world, generated a great demand for historical orientation. Hence, around 1900, more than twenty different world histories, most of which had been produced outside of or on the margins of academic departments, were available to the general public.[42] While some world histories remained characterized by Christian or cosmopolitan perspectives, the strongest trend was to see world history through Social Darwinist lenses. Works written under such conceptual premises also outgrew the genre of Marxist-materialist scholarship in that field.

Social Darwinist, ethnically biased, and Eurocentric paradigms were brought out even more strongly during the Nazi era. Also after the Second World War, such presumptions about history did not immediately become the subjects of strong intellectual criticism and epistemological reflection. Actually, the most important world historical overview published shortly after 1945 was the *World History of Europe*,[43] written by Hans Freyer, who – on account of his ties to the Nazi regime – struggled to find an academic position after the war.[44] When the book was published in 1949, it was widely acclaimed and praised by fellow historians[45] as a major contribution to the field. In his introduction, the author emphasized that the work was largely created during the Second World War in Europe but that, after 1945, he made only minimal

---

[39] Compare Bergenthum (2002). See also Chapter 1 of this book.
[40] See Mollin (2000).   [41] Vom Bruch (1982).
[42] See Bergenthum (2004). A bestseller until the beginning of the twentieth century was the *Weltgeschichte für das deutsche Volk* (19 vols.) by the Heidelberg historian Christoph Schlosser.
[43] Freyer (1949). Also containing world historical theories: Freyer (1955).
[44] On Hans Freyer, a Leipzig historian, see Middell (2005b), vol. II, pp. 650–807.
[45] See Schulze (1989).

changes to its overall composition.[46] As the title "World History of Europe" suggests, Freyer owed certain elements of his world historical interpretation to Hegel, including the idea that world history needed a subject, and that Europe had served as the dynamic entity which, through its own self-realization, had turned the globe into a coherent "world."[47] The work was also filled with tropes such as the depiction of Indo-Germanic peoples as epicenters of strength and the will to power.[48] Freyer even depicted national leaders like Napoleon and Bismarck as the best means to translate the self-destructive potentials of modernity into energy, future, and progress.

Yet the 1950s and particularly 1960s also experienced some conscious attempts to change foundational theories, models, and visions of world history. This search for new paradigms and concepts was at least entangled with a growing interest in the development of world historical thought in other countries.[49] A similar development also took place in the genre of edited multi-volume world histories written by academic historians for a general audience, which dates back to the nineteenth century.[50] For example, a new edition of the *Propyläen Weltgeschichte* (Propyläen world history), published in ten volumes during the early 1960s, sought to further develop the liberal and cosmopolitan branches of German historiography.[51] The editors distanced themselves from strong currents that had characterized much world historical scholarship in Europe in general, and in Germany in particular. For example, Golo Mann argued that the tragic events under Nazi rule had dealt a final blow to the credibility of many ideas, including the notion that the rest of the world only mattered once it came into contact with European civilization.

---

[46] Freyer (1949), pp. 10–12.

[47] For a more detailed discussion of the *World History of Europe* see Middell (2005b), vol. II, pp. 772–807.

[48] Particularly after the First World War this intellectual current, which in Germany was represented by such renowned thinkers as Rudolf Eucken, became rather influential on an international level. See, for example, Sachsenmaier (2006).

[49] For examples for German histories of world history during the first decades after the Second World War, see Löwith (1953); Vogt (1961); Wagner (1965); and Schulin (1974). All of these works focused either predominantly or exclusively on Western conceptions.

[50] Important early examples of this remarkable genre is the nine-volume world history co-authored by thirty-six mostly professional historians and edited by the publicist Hans Helmolt between 1899 and 1907: Helmolt (1899–1907), and von Pflugk-Harttung (1907–1910). For more details see Bergenthum (2004); and Middell (2005b), vol. II, pp. 604–27.

[51] Heuss, Mann, and Nitschke (1960–1965). The earlier version had been edited by the Leipzig historian Walter Goetz between 1929 and 1933. Among other points, it was meant to endorse liberal-democratic master narratives. For more details see Middell (2005b), vol. II, pp. 637–49.

Along with the other editors, he emphasized that world historical overviews could no longer be structured along either all-encompassing Eurocentric narratives, nor could they merely be an assembly of local histories.[52] This conceptual trend has been further accentuated in some recent world historical publications.[53]

These recent examples should not obscure the fact that many influential world historical overviews published in German continue to take strong Eurocentric perspectives. One example is *A Little World History*, authored by the renowned historian of antiquity Alexander Demandt.[54] The work follows a familiar framework: after two chapters on early civilizations since the Stone Age, the historical account professes to focus on single world regions but implicitly accentuates the idea of the primacy of Europe.[55] For instance, whereas about 100 pages depict European history from the ancient Greeks to the Reformation, the entire South Asian and East Asian experience up until the seventeenth or eighteenth centuries is crammed into a twenty-page chapter. Africa and Latin America are not even treated in separate chapters or subchapters. The nineteenth and twentieth centuries are primarily framed as a history of European expansionism, which is presented as a dark but necessary past allowing for the possibility of the worldwide spread of liberal democracies.

Heading in a similar direction, another book, *Five Crossroads of World History* by the Freiburg historian Gottfried Schramm, focuses on turning points of supposedly universal significance. However, the work actually discusses the rise of monotheism, the emergence of Christianity, the advent of Lutheranism, the American constitution, and the beginnings of communist ideologies in nineteenth-century Russia.[56] This means that none of the supposed great watersheds of world history is located outside the scope of many teleological, Hegelian and other, interpretations of Western history. By implication, entire world regions ranging from East Asia to Latin America are deemed to lack agency of true world historical significance. Many similarly Eurocentric narratives can

---

[52] See, for example, Mann (1960); and Heuss (1960). Since at least two-thirds of their own edition focused on European history, the editors acknowledged that their theoretical postulates were not quite matched by the realities of their own work.

[53] For example, a new edition of the *Fischer Weltgeschichte* (*Fischer World History*), following the one published in thirty-six volumes between 1965 and 1981, is supposed to place more emphasis on transregional approaches.

[54] Demandt (2003).

[55] See, for example, the critical reviews by Eckert (2004b); as well as Nippel (2003).

[56] Schramm (2004).

be found in a whole range of world histories that have appeared in increasing numbers in a rather receptive German market.[57]

The institutional parameters of German historiography

Eurocentrism has long not only been a conceptual but also a structural problem of historiography in Germany. As mentioned, the areas of expertise represented at German history departments are still predominantly related to the study of the national and – to a lesser extent European – past.[58] While the regional distribution of area expertise has not experienced any revolutionary change during the past 100 years, there have been significant continuities in the national origins of historians. Certainly, German faculty have become far more diversified in terms of gender and class backgrounds, yet historians of foreign descent have remained a minuscule minority in the country's universities. In addition, institutional maneuverability has been significantly limited by budget cuts since the 1990s, which heavily affected the social sciences and the humanities. After all, in a shrinking academic system there are usually rather few opportunities for profound structural changes.

Data surveys on the institutional structures of history departments reveal the extreme Eurocentric biases of German historiography. A statistical analysis conducted in 2002 that was financed by the German Association of Historians is very telling. This study, which partly relied on polling and partly on bibliographic, especially online, research, found that only 28 out of 541 German historians were classified as experts of "non-European history" – that is just over 5 percent of the overall sampled body.[59] My own sample of tenured and long-term positions at fourteen history departments representing a wide spectrum of regions[60] came to a similar conclusion. The survey, which reflects the

---

[57] For example Mai (2006); Lexikonredaktion Brockhaus (2006); and Schulz (2004).

[58] Certainly, the ratio between German and other European expertise varies according to the time period studied. Whereas the history of the nineteenth and twentieth centuries is dominated by faculty focusing on German history, the fields of ancient, medieval, and early modern history are characterized by different geographical emphases. But also here, research expertise in other parts of the world (including the southern shores of the Mediterranean and the Middle East) is extremely rare.

[59] Lincke and Paletschek (2003), particularly pp. 45–47. A similar proportion was also found for non-tenured historians where only 33 out of 683 (about 4.8 percent) were working on non-European history.

[60] The surveyed departments were Bielefeld, Munich, Münster, Freiburg, Leipzig, Potsdam, Tübingen, Kiel, Erlangen, Frankfurt (Main), Hamburg, Marburg, and Heidelberg as well as Humboldt University in Berlin.

status quo of 2006, found that, out of a total number of 460 historians,[61] 390, i.e., 84.8 percent, were historians of Western Europe, the vast majority of whom were primarily working on German history. Another 47 historians (10.2 percent) were mainly doing research on Eastern European history, which means that 95 percent of the historians surveyed were chiefly – and in most cases exclusively – dealing with an aspect of European history. A mere 5 percent of historians working at these sample institutions were experts on areas outside Europe. Among these, a little less than half (2.4 percent of the entire body) were historians of North America, while another twelve scholars, i.e. 2.6 percent, covered the entire rest of the world ranging from Latin America to Africa, the Middle East, South Asia, and East Asia.

According to statistics provided by the German Science Council, a publicly funded advisory body that advises the federal and state governments, only two history departments have professorships in East Asian history.[62] Despite the importance of the United States as a reference space for the *Sonderweg* literature, in all German history departments there are only eight full-time professorships in Anglo-American history.[63] In fact, only few history departments do not conform to this general pattern. For example, the University of Hamburg, which actually has its origins in a research institute in colonial studies,[64] has traditionally devoted some teaching and research capacity to non-European history. Today, there are three full professors as well as a number of untenured faculty working primarily in a distinct area of study entitled "Extra-European History" (*"Aussereuropäische Geschichte"*).[65] But even in Hamburg the proportion of scholars exploring history outside Europe has usually been below 20 percent of the entire department's faculty. Some newly founded universities experimented with a greater regional diversification of historical research, but so far they have failed to become forerunners of a wider trend. This is, for example, the case at the Fern-Universität Hagen, Germany's only

---

[61] The fact that transcultural historians in Germany constituted only a tiny minority necessitated a methodological choice in order to avoid double counting: those scholars working with non-Western sources were categorized as experts on the "rest of the world" whereas, for example, historians of colonialism focusing on Western source materials were counted as experts in Western European history. I categorized historians of Greco-Roman Antiquity as historians of Western Europe; scholars working on Byzantium as experts on Eastern European history.

[62] These are at the University of Freiburg and the University of Erfurt.

[63] Wissenschaftsrat (2006), particularly pp. 53–69.

[64] See Ruppenthal (2007). See also Eckert (2005), especially p. 44.

[65] See Brahm and Meissner (2004). On the Hamburg Institute for Asian Affairs see Schütte (2006).

state-sponsored distance university, where a small history department places a very strong emphasis on non-European and transcultural history.[66] In a very remarkable case, the University of Erfurt established a department of history with a declared mission to move beyond Eurocentrism and towards transcultural as well as global historical research. However, budget cuts and the concomitant merger of the university with a pedagogical school of higher learning marginalized the Erfurt experiment within the national academic landscape.[67]

The task of studying Africa, Asia, the Americas, and the Middle East is largely relegated to small specialized fields such as Islamic Studies or Sinology. However, up until the present day, these small disciplines have tended to nurture their own forms of academic training. Furthermore, they entertain their own disciplinary public spheres through separate journals, conferences, and associations. As a consequence, the bulk of area expertise in Germany remains rather fragmented, which prevents researchers focusing on other parts of the world from building an intellectual counterweight to predominantly Eurocentrically structured fields such as historiography. In other words, many institutional settings have perpetuated an academic culture in which research on non-European world regions continues to play only a marginal role. As a Swiss-French scholar recently observed, regional studies have a larger number of professorships in Germany than other European countries, yet at the same time their status in the social sciences and humanities is much more marginal than, for example, in the French academic community.[68]

The epistemological impact of the regional studies is constrained by two additional factors. Firstly, high-level academic positions are almost exclusively filled with scholars of German descent.[69] Secondly, large area studies programs, which would be able to serve as forums for compatible expertise in other departments, have remained rather exceptional.[70] For example, the subject of Sinology still has an average of merely 2.2 professorships at those universities in which it is represented. This means that, with few exceptions, Sinological expertise and related library resources are scattered across the country.[71] As a consequence,

---

[66] See Wendt (2004).

[67] A point also made by Marc Frey in his review of Klein and Schumacher (2006): Frey (2007).

[68] Zufferey (1999), p. 583.

[69] Pertaining to Chinese studies, see, for example, Martin (1999), p. 8.

[70] Two of the main exceptions are the universities of Bochum and Heidelberg. See Schütte (2004), p. 300. A general overview of the situation in Europe is provided by Cartier (1998).

[71] Osiander and Döring (1999), pp. 126 and 143. More generally on area studies see Puhle (2006).

professors in "area studies" are required to serve as generalists with the task of representing and teaching an entire field – a field defined by nothing less than the study of a macroscopic region with its history, literature, present-day politics, economics and cultural formations.

Given such structural demands, it is perhaps small wonder that fields such as Sinology or Japanology are still characterized by strong philological traditions. Certainly, the regional studies have also witnessed a rising number of scholars interested in social scientific methodologies, which in the recent past has led to rather sharp disciplinary divides.[72] There has been a growing insecurity about the methodologies and nature of these fields, which generated intense discussions about their present nature and future agendas. For example, while acknowledging the need for greater institutional entanglements, many scholars warned that a greater rapprochement with other academic disciplines could make the status of regional studies potentially decline until they become merely auxiliary disciplines.[73] While many representatives of area studies ruled out institutional marriages with larger fields to avoid a misalliance between unequal partners, they flirted with new ideas of partnership and partial cohabitation.[74] Pointing to Anglophone debates, some scholars maintained that research on European and non-European history needed to be critically reconsidered as part of one and the same academic community. For example, a group of Africanists argued that the sub-Saharan part of the continent needed to be seen from new spatial perspectives that had escaped the narrow lenses of research on colonialism and decolonization, which had often been either Euro- or Africa-centric.[75]

Reflecting the rising interest in spatial concepts beyond disciplinary boundaries, the number of collaborative projects between representatives from area studies and history departments has been growing slowly but steadily. In many cases, expanding fields such as maritime history, the history of diasporas, or the study of global transformations served actually as disciplinary meeting grounds.[76] This process met with the support of influential academic and political circles, which came to promote interregional and interdisciplinary research. For example, in 2005 the German Science Council recommended that some universities establish interdisciplinary area studies centers, which could inject area

---

[72] On cultural studies and area studies in Germany see Lackner and Werner (1999).
[73] See, for example, Nettelbeck (2005).   [74] Compare Osiander and Döring (1999).
[75] For example, Harneit-Sievers (2000).
[76] Puhle (2006). See also Deutsche Gesellschaft für Asienkunde (1997).

studies expertise into the debates about themes such as globalization.[77] In a very daring vision, the council also addressed the possibility of establishing binational, co-sponsored professorships as a way of cultivating transnational research landscapes.[78] At the time, a few research institutes already covered several world regions, such as the Hamburg Institut für Asienkunde (Institute for Asian Affairs), the German Institute of Global and Area Studies,[79] and the Zentrum Moderner Orient (ZMO) in Berlin. The institutional roots of the ZMO, which has evolved into an internationally connected research center,[80] reach back to a branch of the GDR Academy of Arts and Sciences. While it focuses on North Africa, the Middle East, South Asia, and Southeast Asia, it hosts many research projects that purposely transcend local, regional, and disciplinary boundaries.[81] Translocal historical research, at least on a bicultural level, was also promoted by the federally sponsored German Historical Institutes in cities such as London, Tokyo, and Washington.[82] During the past few years, a richer institutional landscape has started to emerge, with the possibility and purpose of strengthening interdisciplinary cooperation by fostering global and transnational historical research.[83]

In the spirit of transnationalism: protests against the status quo

During the past two decades, global and transcultural history in Germany has become more influential and taken new turns. There were many developments ranging from new academic trends to changing political mentalities, which fostered historiography beyond national or continental boundaries, and several of them have been interconnected. As one needs to separate in order to be able to narrate, the following segments will discuss single arenas of intellectual and other change, which all contributed to the rising prominence and the locally specific contours of global history in

---

[77] Wissenschaftsrat (2006). See also *Freiburger Memorandum zur Zukunft der Regionalstudien in Deutschland am Beispiel ausgewählter Weltregionen*, which postulates the formation of research and teaching clusters in regional studies.

[78] Wissenschaftsrat (2006), p. 45.

[79] This institute, which evolved from the Hamburg Overseas Institute in 2006, is largely divided into separate area studies but it also encourages cross-regional and comparative research, which, however, is more focused on the social sciences than on historiography. See, for example, the discussion paper by Basedau and Koellner (2006).

[80] These and other examples are in Schütte (2004), pp. 179ff.

[81] See www.zmo.de. See also Eckert and Reinwald (1999).

[82] See Wissenschaftsrat (1999).

[83] See the section "Towards new world and global historical spaces."

Germany. At the same time, this will help us to map out in further detail the locally specific contours of global history and similar research trends in Germany.

Particularly since the 1980s, the edifice of German historiography has witnessed several efforts to open new windows onto the outside world. There is now a certain tradition of protest against the Eurocentric foundations of the field, which led to a series of short victories and subsequent setbacks but all in all has contributed towards a growing and widening problem-consciousness within the guild of German historians. A good observation ground for the complex inroads of global agendas into German historiography are the biannual *Historikertage*, conventions that now draw more than 3,000 participants and are therefore comparable to other national historical associations' general meetings. These events traditionally focus on German and European history, yet their concrete scope and thematic focus usually depends very much on the organizational committee, including the acting president of the German Historical Association (Verband der Historiker Deutschlands).

It was in 1988, under the leadership of Christian Meier, a specialist of ancient history, that the *Historikertag* saw the first systematic attempt to remove the Eurocentric blinkers from the community of historians. After controversial discussions within the organizing committee during the run-up period,[84] it was decided to focus the general theme of the meeting on "non-European" history. The use of the term *Aussereuropäische Geschichte*, which is usually translated as "non-European history" but literally means "extra-European history," is actually telling in the sense that it reflects some of the core structural and intellectual problems of German historiography. As some critics have argued, the idea of lumping together all of the rest of the world into one category actually continues older Eurocentric visions, which denied historicity and a plurality of experiences to the outside world.[85] Only in an extremely Eurocentric academic system can "non-European history" become its own, separate category.

Terminological questions notwithstanding, the 1988 gathering in Bamberg was certainly revolutionary in several regards. For example, about half of all panels were at least partly dedicated to the world outside of Europe, and there was a particular emphasis on transcultural and interdisciplinary scholarship. This also meant that a high number of scholars from area studies participated in the event. Topics ranging from ethnic minorities on the American continent to comparative assessments of historiography in Europe and East Asia were covered. Also highly

[84] As mentioned by Mommsen (1989).   [85] Osterhammel (2001a), p. 8.

unusual was the fact that the opening lecture, held by the Swiss world historian Rudolf von Albertini, did not deal with German or European history, but with decolonization in the British Empire.[86] Furthermore, in his opening and closing statements, Christian Meier spoke very clearly against the narrow, nation- or culture-centered expertise in German history departments which, according to him, were so tied up with older intellectual preferences that they were incapable of addressing the burning questions of an ever-more tightly interconnected world. In this context, he expressed the hope that the Bamberg meeting would initiate an expansion of historical research on other world regions as well as closer levels of cooperation with area studies. Meier also advocated the idea of abandoning Eurocentric world histories in favor of approaches inspired by the notion of a "world of histories."[87] During the convention, Meier's suggestion to open up historiography to the study of other parts of the world was specifically endorsed by German president Richard von Weizsäcker.

Plans and visions were flying high in Bamberg, but they did not have a lasting effect on the program agendas of the *Historikertage*. The following convention, 1990 in Bochum, had a special section for non-European history, but not more than 10 percent of the overall events focused on transcultural topics or the history of other world regions.[88] A more systematic effort to break through the Eurocentric boundaries was again undertaken during the 1992 meeting in Hanover, which carried the motto "unity and plurality." The main objective of the meeting was to historically approach the radical changes facing the European continent after the fall of the Iron Curtain as well as the accelerating pace of the then West European integration processes.[89] Some scholars sought to include the "non-European" world as well as the history of European colonialism and imperialism in the picture.[90] Consequently, in 1992 the majority of the panels was transnational in scope, and about 20 percent of the topics dealt at least in some capacity with other parts of the globe.[91]

---

[86] For more information about the program and the single sections see Schumann (1989).

[87] In Schumann (1989), pp. 18–24 and pp. 38–45. An extended version of the final statement was published in Meier (1989).

[88] For more details see Schmale (1991).

[89] Nevertheless, few of the great global questions resulting from the disintegration of the Warsaw Pact and the crisis in China were being reflected in the convention's overall agenda.

[90] For example, Mommsen (1994b), p. 415.

[91] For an overview of the sections see Averkorn (1994).

As a reflection of this new emphasis, a number of prominent representatives of various area studies played an important role during the convention.[92]

The momentum from Bamberg and Hanover proved to be hard to sustain: during most of the subsequent biannual meetings, the focus was again narrowed down to the core themes of German historiography. In face of a rapidly changing global, European, and German context, the organizing committees obviously saw it as their primary responsibility to address issues related to Germany and its European neighbors. Consequently, the special section on non-European history, which had been designed partly as a kind of affirmative action plan for underdeveloped fields, was again abolished during the mid-1990s. More specifically, at the conventions in Leipzig, Munich, and Frankfurt, which took place between 1994 and 1998, the stream of history beyond European boundaries was again reduced to a narrow trickle of about two panels per meeting. This situation did not change during the first *Historikertag* of the new millennium in Aachen, which took place under the promising motto "One World – One History?" In spite of this overarching theme, the "world" had hardly been present at this convention – except for a panel on Chinese historiography and one panel offering internationally comparative perspectives of contemporary historical writing.[93] Also the subsequent three meetings in Halle, Kiel, Constance, and Dresden (2002–2008) did not genuinely reverse this trend. Panels focusing on themes beyond European boundaries remained quite rare, even though their proportion is higher than during the mid- or late 1990s.[94] Topics such as images of European modernity seen in an intercultural context (Halle), transcultural communicative spaces in modern African history (Kiel), or the relationship between colonialism and the social sciences (Constance) were rather exceptional. The dominance of panels dealing exclusively with German and European historiography can be easily expressed in numbers. For example, in Halle in 2002, 84 percent of the panels focused on Europe, 5 percent on North America, and none on any single world region such as East Asia or the Middle East. Of the 11 percent of panels that primarily addressed issues from a transcultural perspective, all but one discussed primarily European issues.

---

[92] For example, the prominent Sinologist Helwig Schmidt-Glintzer organized a panel on "Europe and China: Two Models."

[93] For more information see Kerner (2001).

[94] For the 2002 meeting in Halle see Ranft and Meumann (2003). For the Kiel gathering (2004) see Reitermeier and Fouquet (2005). For the Constance convention see www.uni-konstanz.de/historikertag.

The 2010 convention in Berlin witnessed greater levels of attention to global and transnational themes, but it remains to be seen if this development will continue. During the decade before, the regional focus of the German *Historikertage* has almost habitually been subject to criticism. For example, at the 1998 meeting in Frankfurt, Helmut Bley pointed to the dangers of intellectual isolationism in a disciplinary culture that regarded transcultural and global approaches as an area of expertise without any implications for the main field.[95] Two years later, in her Aachen keynote speech, Nathalie Zemon Davis (then at the University of Toronto) held that a global consciousness and the familiarity with non-Western perspectives needed to be a part of any historian's intellectual horizon and advocated research projects spanning across macro-regional spaces.[96] Following the 2002 meeting in Halle, Andreas Eckert, an Africanist and global historian, voiced his opinion in an article entitled "Imprisoned in the Old World," which appeared in the weekly *Die Zeit*.[97] Characterizing German historiography as "provincial beyond hope" and caught in an ivory tower, he lamented the inability and unwillingness of his field to face the great questions of the time ranging from migration to September 11.[98] Before the *Historikertag* in Constance in 2006, Middle East historian Birgit Schäbler pointed to the scarce attention which this event as well as in German historiography in general paid to the outside world.[99] Others argued that, given the lack of non-European history in academic departments, the general public in Germany could hardly be adequately informed about global processes and their historical dimensions.[100]

Such recurrent disapproval voiced around the time of the historians' conventions must be seen as symptomatic of a mounting sense of discontent among some German historians. The chorus calling for a greater presence of global and transnational history in Germany has grown more concerted and louder, but its message remains characterized by the structural conditions of the field. For instance, in many cases global history and related approaches are still advocated as partisan voices from the margins addressing an unreceptive center. In addition, many scholars postulate the expansion of "non-European" historiography and global history as part of the same package.[101] Indeed, the limited maneuverability within a shrinking

---

[95] Bley (1999). The paper was part of a panel on modernity in a global historical context.
[96] Davis (2001).   [97] Eckert (2002), p. 40.
[98] Heading in a similar direction: Ogle (2004).
[99] "Geschichte darf keine Selbstbespiegelung sein" (interview with Birgit Schäbler), *Süddeutsche Zeitung*, 2006.
[100] H. Nolte (2005a), especially p. 138.
[101] See, for example, Eckert (2004a); and Schleier (1997).

field means that it is more likely that, if at all, professorships in global and transcultural history will be created rather than positions with a strict focus on single areas outside of the European world. For this reason, few young German historians seek to qualify themselves exclusively in the history of single world regions such as East Asia or Latin America but seek topics such as colonialism or globalization, in which it is possible to build a profile in both European and non-Western history. As part of this trend, several scholars have come to complain about the fact that, in the German case, job descriptions such as "modern history" or "contemporary history" are usually equated with Western European history or even German history.[102]

Beyond the *Sonderweg*: comparisons, transfers, and cultural history

Not only supposedly "exotic" research fields focusing on other continents but also changes within the very centers of German historiography opened spaces for new perspectives beyond the nation-state. An important venue of changes was the field of social history, which long had remained explicitly nation-centric by its insistence on the endogenous origins of the Nazi past and the uniqueness of the developments leading up to it. Within conceptual frameworks such as the *Sonderweg* ("special path") hypothesis, the German experience had often been contrasted with selected Western cases, which allegedly represented "normal" ways to modernity.[103] During the late 1970s, the challenges to the idea of a German *Sonderweg* grew more significant. Very influential was a book by the two British neo-Marxist historians, David Blackbourn and Geoff Eley, that in several regards went against the notion of exceptionalities in the patterns of the German past.[104] Many scholars agreed with these two authors that it was conceptually flawed to assume a "normal" way of modernization, since each nation was differentiated by unique paths and processes.[105] Subsequently, a wealth of detailed studies focusing on themes such as the tensions between liberal and feudal social milieus came to deconstruct the idea of fundamental differences between German history and its western neighbors during the nineteenth and early twentieth centuries.[106]

---

[102] For example, Brenner (2004).

[103] See Kocka (1999; 2000); and Bauerkämper (2003).

[104] Blackbourn and Eley (1980). Both authors still argued that there were continuities in German history that led to the Third Reich, albeit not in a deterministic sense.

[105] Some British, French, and other historians even applied the concept of the *Sonderweg* to their own societies. For example Furet (1991); and Weisbrod (1990).

[106] See, for example, Puhle (1991); and Tenfelde and Wehler (1994). In the 1980s the idea that a uniquely challenging geopolitical position between the West and an

This criticism from the left suggested that historians needed to embed the German past in more complex and multifaceted understandings of "modernity" and the "west" than the *Sonderweg* historians had done. Scholars like the Frankfurt historian Detlev Peukert argued that modern civilization was more Janus-faced and could not be solely associated with universal normative standards since it carried its own destructive potentials. In his interpretation, which was influenced by postmodern theories[107] but in many important regards reached back to intellectual debates immediately after the war, modern elements – rather than "failed modernization" – were the main roots from which fascism grew.[108] This research trajectory culminated in a rather intensive debate about whether Nazi Germany could be understood as a modern society.[109]

During the 1990s, many historians abandoned the terms "modernization" and "modernity" altogether as tools of analysis. Furthermore, since it was no longer possible to crudely juxtapose a crooked German path with "Western development," the outside world became more relevant for the study of German history. At the same time it needed to become more complex. The changing international political situation of Germany also made it increasingly unconvincing to confine one's perspectives of German history to the nation alone. As Jürgen Kocka pointed out, the events around the time of the fall of the Berlin Wall in 1989, which no German historian had anticipated, were a clear reminder of the fact "that the inner history of single countries is decisively codetermined by changes within the international arena."[110] The social historical focus on domestic structures and conditions obviously needed to be widened by a wide range of international and transnational variables. This loss of a tight national frame of analysis, however, made almost unfeasible the holistic claims of those who practiced history as a social science. While maintaining that the nation-state could not and should not be completely deconstructed, many prominent social historians held that historiography needed to increasingly study the entanglements between single societies within a globalizing world. This would quite consciously lead to an internationalization of social historical research paradigms in ways that differed profoundly from some pre-war assumptions about the primacy of foreign politics for understanding the national past.

underdeveloped East (*Mittellage*) determined many trajectories of German history enjoyed a certain prominence, but a larger trend headed in different directions.
[107] See, for example, Jarausch and Geyer (2003), pp. 97ff.   [108] Peukert (1987).
[109] Summaries of the debate are found in Alber (1989); and Frei (1993).
[110] Kocka (1997), p. 68. Kocka argues that historical comparisons are the most timely ways to move historiography to a transnational or even global level.

An important interim step towards more contextualized approaches to the German past was the rising interest in comparative history. In fact, this field of research became more popular in Germany during the 1990s than in most other Western countries.[111] While many scholars initially drew heavily upon American comparative sociology, soon close exchanges with other areas of research were established, ranging from demographics to political history.[112] The bulk of social historical comparisons focused on Western European sample cases as well as the United States, which played an important role as a contrast for the German experience.[113] When comparative studies covered areas outside the West, they tended to be largely structured around macro-theoretical concepts and explored themes such as revolutionary movements or trajectories of development.[114] After 1989 an increasing, albeit still rather small number of studies comparing Germany to societies in Eastern Europe further eroded the idea of a dichotomy between the West and the rest. There were hopes that systematic comparisons between facets of the Nazi past, Stalinism, and other regimes could enrich the field in ways that were far removed from the apologetic tendencies that could be observed during the *Historikerstreit*.[115]

Around that time, some major theoretical works discussing comparative history in terms of its schools, types, possibilities, problems, and challenges appeared on the market.[116] As in the United States and some other countries, however, comparative history found itself exposed to mounting tides of concerns from various directions. At the same time, increasingly complex methodological approaches made it harder to clearly separate international from domestic units of analysis. In the German case it was particularly a new school studying the "history of transfers" that positioned itself as both a challenge and an alternative to systematic comparative approaches. In a narrow sense, the transfer study movement had its origins among representatives of German studies in France during the 1980s, and became very influential in Germany a decade later.[117] Even though the conceptual parallels in other academic systems were plentiful, the study of "transfers" remained a field designation that was initially largely confined to the study of Franco-German interactions.[118] As the term "transfer" indicates, the field sought to bring the flows of ideas, people, and goods,

---

[111] Examples for large-scale research projects are Kocka (1988–1989); Tenfelde (1986).
[112] Haupt (2006).
[113] Examples for influential works are Kocka (1977); and Welskopp (1994).
[114] For example, Schölch (1982); and Dahlmann (1986).   [115] Kocka (1990).
[116] For example, Kaelble (1999a); and Haupt and Kocka (1996).
[117] See, for example, Espagne (2003).   [118] See Middell (2000).

as well as other exchanges, to the foreground of scholarly analyses. In contrast to scholarship focusing on diffusionist processes, it particularly centered on intentional translations, inculturations, and adaptations as well as their agents who incorporated ideas from one context in another.[119] The professed research agenda of transfer studies also included ways in which certain societies tried to differentiate themselves from others through transferred concepts such as "culture" or "nationhood." Yet, by and large, the history of transfers remained largely wedded to the concept of the nation-state as the main unit of analysis, and usually researchers tackled only exchange processes between two European societies.[120] While there were important exceptions, the field did not culminate in a study of transnational milieus and other social, cultural, or political spaces beyond the nation-state.[121] In addition, the vast majority of publications in these fields remained focused on the European experience.

Still, while many global historical projects chose a different terminology, a fair number of publications applied terms such as "transfer history" to global and transnational themes. This has been, for example, the case with studies focusing on cultural transmissions and perceptions of difference.[122] Moreover, there have been some efforts made to create dialogue and cooperation forums for researchers of transfer processes focusing on Western and non-Western history.[123]

In a rather parallel process, comparative history has experienced a geographical widening of its research agendas. In recent years a number of strictly comparative studies have appeared that contrast parts of Europe with other world regions.[124] Since comparative history and non-European history have been both regarded with a certain degree of skepticism within parts of the German academic community, theoretical contributions often defended the importance and practicability of what is often connoted as "transculturally comparative history."[125] A common charge was that macroscopic comparisons would inevitably sacrifice methodological accuracy. Many scholars responded that comparative historical research would not necessarily have to follow the footsteps of historical sociology and deal with huge units of analysis. Rather, partial comparisons could

---

[119] See, for example, Werner (1995).
[120] An example of a compilation of bilateral studies is Muhs, Paulmann, and Steinmetz (1998).
[121] Compare Kaelble (2005); and Middell (2000), particularly p. 20.
[122] For example, see Lüsebrink (2005).
[123] See, for example, the special issue of *Comparativ*: Schulte (2006). See also Kaelble (2006b).
[124] For example, see Dillinger (2008); Krämer-Lien (2004); and Radkau, Fuchs, and Lutz (2004).
[125] Osterhammel (1996b; 1996a); Kaelble (1999b). See also Matthes (1998).

focus on clearly demarcated topics and draw on a small number of case studies – which would still necessitate primary source work and sensitivity for local contingencies.

While trans-local scholarship grew in both fields, the debates between comparativists and scholars interested in transfers became less polarized,[126] and the gap between the two areas of research began to narrow. The emerging conflictual partnership of these fields helped to generate some important energy not only for transnational but also for transcontinental research.[127] It helped to open the straitjacket of national perspectives and to think in new categories of space when addressing questions that were relevant to German history. Some scholars even argued that new forms of global and world history would be the best possible framework to create links between transfer studies and comparative scholarship – a combination that Johannes Paulmann considered to be a "seductive drug" for researchers.[128]

Such a combination has become reality in the sense that in many globally oriented research projects, comparative and transfer-related studies tend to show significant overlaps. Ever since the mid-1990s, within a climate more conducive to global historical pursuits, combined activities in transfer-related and comparative approaches have been small but remarkable. Some scholars pointed out that certain processes, such as the spread of global fashions could only be viewed from transregional angles, which implied comparative perspectives.[129] Moreover, there have been discussions of how certain trajectories and aspects of German history can be related to experiences in other parts of the world through a combination of comparative and transfer approaches.[130] For example, Chicago historian Michael Geyer, who also publishes a good number of articles in German, argued that some parallels between facets of the German and the Japanese past were contingent upon their shifting positions in a global system, and thus needed to be studied from global historical perspectives.[131] Scholarship on such patterns, according to Geyer, needed to include methodological elements from comparative history and transnational history but could not be reduced to them. Rather than adhering to notions of singularity and linearity, he held, research ought to explore commonalities and

---

[126] See, for example, Paulmann (1998).
[127] For example, the comparative history of empires has now also been very active in the study of comparative semantics – see, for example, Bosbach and Hiery (1999).
[128] Paulmann (1998) (quote: p. 686); and Middell (2000), particularly pp. 39–41.
[129] Osterhammel (1996b), p. 296.   [130] See, for example, Sachsenmaier (2003).
[131] Geyer (2004). Focusing on approaches in Japan: Conrad (1999b).

connections between the two nations in the context of shared transformations and an emerging international system.

One of the most active research fields that has recently offered
comparative perspectives while at the same time paying attention to
cross-continental transfers[132] has been the history of historiography.
Here, there has been a rising interest in contextual comparison that also
considers political influences on scholarship, the structure of institutions, the social role of historians, and other factors.[133] For example,
single-authored comparative studies have touched upon issues ranging
from the trajectories of German and Japanese historiography after the
Second World War to the rise of "New History" in the US and other
countries during the early twentieth century.[134] Also a growing number of
edited volumes have offered comparative accounts on topics such as the
politics of history or historiographical traditions in various nations.[135]
However, most chapters in these collections focus on single national
traditions, and comparative tasks such as the creation of typologies or
the definition of commonalities and differences are largely left to the
reader.[136] The same is true for a single-authored global introduction to
historiography by Markus Völkel, which treats India, China, Europe, and
other traditions in separate chapters.[137] Yet this textbook and several
transculturally comparative volumes are a remarkable indication of the
fact that non-Western scholarship is no longer being ignored in overviews
of historical scholarship. Until recently, this was hardly the case.

One book which shifts from comparative to more genuine global
historical perspectives is *Geschichtswissenschaft im Zeitalter der Extreme*
(*Historiography in the Age of Extremes*) by the Trier historian Lutz
Raphael.[138] This work not only pays attention to the global institutional
and intellectual transformations underlying the emergence of national
historiographies but also describes local traditions and contingencies.
To put it in a different way, Raphael aims more at depicting the international and transnational facets of the field rather than assessing various
national realms. As he writes, "this approach appears legitimate to me
since the national developments have been documented best thus far, and
also since an international history of the field is more than a mere addition
of histories of national disciplines."[139] Within this methodological

---

[132] Osterhammel (1996b), p. 271; and Conrad (1999b).
[133] Rüsen (1998); and C. Conrad and S. Conrad (2002a).
[134] Conrad (1999a); Raphael (1997).
[135] An example of the latter is the special issue of *Comparativ*: Zimmerer (2004b).
[136] For example Küttler, Rüsen, and Schulin (1993–1999): Fuchs and Stuchtey (2002);
and C. Conrad and S. Conrad (2002a). See also Kaelble and Rothermund (2001).
[137] Völkel (2006).   [138] Raphael (2003).   [139] Raphael (2003), p. 22.

framework, Raphael includes geopolitical developments such as the wave of decolonization in the picture, particularly when discussing topics such as the global rise of certain historiographical schools. His work still compares different scholarly traditions, but it treats them as nodes in an interactive system, which cannot be convincingly analyzed by comparing selected cases or studying bilateral exchanges. In studies of this kind, the instruments of comparative history and the study of transfers have become part of the same global historian's toolbox.

Yet the developments in comparative and transfer-related historiography have only been part of a wider trend towards more complex spatial parameters in the study of history. A major movement, which emerged largely independent of comparative approaches and opened up possibilities for new transnational perspectives, was the rise of cultural history from the 1980s onwards. Cultural history or *Historische Kulturwissenschaft* ("historical cultural studies"), which is how some of its main currents came to be referred to, was partly rooted in distinctively German academic traditions dating back to the early twentieth century.[140] At the same time, however, cultural history in Germany needs to be situated within the context of an international academic trend, which was partly characterized by an interest in the history from below and a growing importance of deconstructivist approaches. In several regards, the cultural turn in German historiography followed methodological rhythms that could also be observed in the United States, France, and other countries. A particularly influential current was the rise of micro-history, which was mainly imported from Italy during the 1970s and was closely related to fields such as historical anthropology, the history of everyday life, and the growing attentiveness to facets of the past hidden beneath the previously dominant master narratives.[141] Historical research started to put more emphasis on the history of women, children, and many other segments of society, which typically had not been the subject of major research projects before. From the late 1980s onwards, research on segments of German society became even more complex through the use of categories such as ideas, worldviews, perceptions, interpretations, or symbolic acts.[142] As a general trend, different branches of cultural history as well as their surrounding theoretical frameworks[143] contributed to visions of national history becoming far more pluralistic than they had previously been.

---

[140] See, for example, Oexle (2004).
[141] For an overview see Medick (1994); and Schlumbohm (1998).
[142] Compare Mergel and Welskopp (1997).
[143] For example, about the influence of postmodern thought see Niethammer (1993).

Going even beyond that, the cultural turn in German historiography fostered ways of thinking about the German past in spaces that no longer matched the boundaries of the nation-state. Some influential voices even now went as far as to suggest that it was impossible to write one unified history of Germany.[144] This, in turn, greatly antagonized many other leading historians, who opined that the growing fragmentation of historiography might jeopardize the Federal Republic's political consensus, which they saw as strongly based on the acceptance of national responsibility for the Nazi past. For this and other reasons, the rise of cultural history in Germany resulted in debates which in many regards were more vehement and had an even deeper impact on the field than in the United States and many other countries.[145] At stake were not only conceptual problems but also the role of historians within a society that still defined itself by the distance it had gained to the pre-1945 period. Leading representatives of social history, for example, argued that an erosion of social and political concerns among scholars was the true force behind postmodern doubts of holistic narratives.[146] On the other side, some scholars countered that the predominance of structuralist interpretations of the Nazi past in social historical research before the 1980s systematically excluded the agency of perpetrators from the historiographical picture.[147]

In Germany, the bulk of cultural historical studies operated on a subnational rather than a transnational level,[148] and the field did not produce a similar interest in diasporic groups and transnational networks as in the United States.[149] In fact, the reception of research agendas and methodologies from scholarship abroad was highly selective. For example, a very influential study published by Hans Medick

---

[144] For gender see, for example, the overview by Sachse (1997). See also Frevert (1991).

[145] Overviews of the debate are, for example, provided by C. Conrad and Kessel (1994); Mergel and Welskopp (1997); and Daniel (1993).

[146] Compare Wehler (2001).

[147] Berg (2003). Berg ascribes the largely structuralist interpretation of the Nazi past to German historians and intentionalist perspectives to Jewish historians – a bifurcation that was received rather critically in the debates following the publication of his book. In the reactions to this hypothesis many scholars pointed to the difficulty of measuring the status quo of historiography before the cultural turn by using the yardsticks of later scholarship. More recently, there has been a growing interest in the perspectives of the victims, which includes their modes of contact with perpetrators. About new currents in Holocaust research see Gerlach (2004); and Herbert (2000).

[148] See, for example, the overview of studies related to a cultural history of politics provided by Mergel (2002).

[149] Compare Daston (2000). As an example for research see Zips (2003). More generally about the transatlantic divide and the selective reception of international trends in German cultural history, see Eley (1998).

during the early stages of the cultural turn referred to the rebellion against Eurocentric tropes and ethnic bias among anthropologists and historians in the United States. But the author mainly aimed at applying alternative, "subaltern" perspectives to social groups and milieus in German history – a scope of research that did not transgress political boundaries.[150] At the same time, the combined weight of studies and theoretical interventions of this kind made it more acceptable to think in social and cultural geographies other than the nation-state. This, in turn, prepared the grounds for new transnational approaches to the German past.

In the meantime, a growing number of research fields, which can be ascribed to cultural history, have sought to strike a balance between national and transnational perspectives. This has been, for example, the case with the growing research community exploring facets of "Americanization" in Germany and other parts of Europe during the twentieth century.[151] Generally speaking, this field seeks to help scholarship further depart from strictly nation-centered understandings of social changes and cultural practices in twentieth-century Germany. At the same time, it does not move to genuinely transregional frameworks of analysis since the German experience remains at the investigational center. Similar things could be said about historical research on processes underpinning the Western orientation of the Federal Republic of Germany.[152]

Transnational history in a pluralizing society

The increasing pressures for transnational perspectives were not only generated by academic changes but, to a significant degree, by transformations of society at large. One of the most obvious developments making the multifaceted and transnationally entangled nature of German society and its history ever harder to deny has been immigration. In particular, postwar flows of migrants from Turkey, Yugoslavia, Vietnam, and several Southern European countries have greatly changed the composition of German society. Today, about 20 percent of all residents in the country have a migrant background,[153] and the proportion of permanent foreign residents between the North Sea shores and the Alps stands now at about

---

[150] For instance, Medick (1984).
[151] For example, see Doering-Manteuffel (1995); Linke (2006); Füssel (2004); and Jarausch and Siegrist (1997).
[152] For a general overview see Görtemaker (2002).
[153] A large proportion of this number, however, is composed of evacuees and resettled persons after the Second World War and, some time after, ethnic Germans "returning" to the Federal Republic.

7 million people, i.e. more than 9 percent of the entire population. This number is expected to climb to about 13 percent in 2030 – a figure which excludes the rising number of German citizens of foreign origin. This has led to significant changes in local cultures. For example, Cologne, a historical stronghold of Catholicism, is now home to 120,000 Muslims, i.e. about 12 percent of its entire population. Furthermore, immigration has produced some new hybrid communities that have created close sociocultural ties between regions in Germany and some other countries such as Turkey or Greece. Today, three-quarters of all Turks and 80 percent of all Greeks living abroad, for example, reside in Germany, and this situation has created tight networks of interactions across all societies involved.[154]

Just like in other European societies, the impacts of migration have become subject to public debates[155] on how to finally come to terms with the lasting implications of immigration and pluralization. Starting from the 1970s, it was undeniable that a large proportion of the so-called *Gastarbeiter* ("guest worker") families would not return to their home countries but stay in Germany. In addition, low birth rates suggested that Germany would need to rely on a continued influx of foreign labor in order to stabilize its employment sector and retirement systems. Yet the reality of continued marginalization of certain groups, particularly the 2 million Turkish and other Muslim residents, challenged the idea of a German melting pot, which was underlying some models of social integration. These and other developments warranted new definitions of Germany in a Europeanizing and globalizing world.

Influenced by international discourses surrounding the aftermath of September 11 and the question of whether Turkey should join the European Union, the debates on the implications of immigration grew increasingly politicized and laden with polarizing forms of rhetoric. On one side of the spectrum, which was usually – but not exclusively – close to the political right, many politicians and other public voices advocated the idea that integration could only be achieved through assimilation. Anti-foreign slogans and exclusionary mechanisms that had previously been directed at other minorities in Germany and then widely critiqued as incompatible with the idea of an open Federal Republic[156] became again more intellectually acceptable when they were projected onto new immigrant groups. Among some opinion leaders there was a tendency to

---

[154] See, for example, Münz, Seifert, and Ulrich (1999).
[155] Despite some Europe-wide commonalities, the debates in Germany differed somewhat from the ones in former colonial powers such as Great Britain, France, or the Netherlands because Germany had long been more characterized by an ethnically rather homogenous society. More general on the topic: Malik (2004).
[156] Schneider (2004).

conflate religious extremism with Islam. In some extreme but remarkably prominent cases, public voices expressed concerns about a Turkish "conquest" of Germany through birth rates and even about the effects of migration on the gene pool of German society.[157]

Academic circles certainly did not come to endorse radical positions of this kind but already during the late 1990s and early 2000s, several prominent scholars resorted to civilizational rhetoric when discussing problems surrounding immigration. This was, for example, the case with the social historian Hans-Ulrich Wehler, who on most issues strongly identified himself with the political left. In a series of articles he declared Islamic societies to be incompatible with the West, which – according to him – had been primarily characterized by the Enlightenment tradition and a long heritage of tolerance.[158] Furthermore, in his opinion the future of immigrants in Germany and the prospects of Turkey in the European Union became the same question.[159] In his and quite a number of other contributions to this topic, the prospect of pluralization tended to be at least implicitly treated as a cultural and political threat.

On the other side of the spectrum, public figures started to actively advocate more multifaceted visions of society[160] that put the burden of change not only on immigrants but also on the majority. For example, some organizations of Germans with a foreign background began to demand a stronger role for themselves in actively shaping a new society – a role that would significantly go beyond the common expectation to fit into an alleged cohesive and homogenous sociocultural pattern. In this context, the cardinal question "whose history?" which in the US and some other societies went against narrow forms of national historical memory, could also be heard in Germany.

The fact that Turkish organizations and other groups have become more established in the German public sphere[161] will quite likely accelerate the pluralization of historical consciousness in Germany. As in many other countries it is typically not immigrants but their indigenized descendents who are powerful and influential enough to voice their perspectives in public discourses.[162] In that manner, history and historiography in

---

[157] This was most prominently the case with a book by a board member of the German Central Bank, Thilo Sarrazin (Sarrazin (2010)). Following the publication of his book, Sarrazin had to leave his post but in various opinion polls about 18 percent of the German population expressed sympathies for his views; also several media channels and major newspapers were rather supportive of his ideas.

[158] Wehler (2002).   [159] More generally on this topic: Leggewie (2004).

[160] See, for example, Bade and Bommes (2004).   [161] Çetinkaya (2000).

[162] Jarausch and Geyer (2003).

Germany may become the subjects of further societal and political debates, which are profoundly different from the earlier struggles over how to live with the memory of the Nazi past.

Thus far, the social forces pushing for more dynamic boundaries of German history have mainly gathered outside of the academic world. In the historical scholarship focusing on Germany, themes related to immigrant groups and their transnational connections continue to play rather marginal roles.[163] At first sight, one might suppose that the history of Turkish, Vietnamese, and other migrant flows is too recent to be considered by historical research. Yet a comparative look at the burgeoning historiographical literature on East Germany shows that this is not the case. A more significant factor lies in the fact that in Germany there are hardly any history professors with a migrant background.[164] In addition, the growing ethnic and cultural pluralization of society did not lend itself to the academic and political efforts of nationally coming to terms with the Nazi past.[165] Up until the present day, pedagogical guidelines for history education hardly discuss how students of foreign descent can be included in the education about the Nazi past, as well as their central meaning for the political culture of the Federal Republic of Germany.

Certainly, more academic attention has been paid to some questions surrounding migration in Germany. German political theory has prominently addressed these questions,[166] and ethnological, sociological, and other literature on topics such as migrant communities and the social consequences of immigration has been growing slowly but at least quite steadily.[167] In addition, a number of research institutes have opened that analyze migration from demographic, cultural, and other perspectives.[168] Also historians have not completely shunned the field, having produced scholarship on topics ranging from minority politics to discourses of immigration and studies of integration.[169] Some recent

---

[163] Among the exceptions is Thränhardt (1995).

[164] For example, in regular faculty positions there are no German historians of Turkish descent. About the continued low education levels of a high proportion of Turkish and other foreign-born immigrants in Germany see Thränhardt (2000).

[165] See, for example, Georgi (2000). See also Ehmann (2002).

[166] For example, on the topic of including alternative perspectives and minority groups: Habermas (2000).

[167] Generally on this field: Ackermann (1997). See also, for example, Bergmann and Römhild (2003).

[168] For example the Institut für Migrationsforschung und Interkulturelle Studien (Institute for Migration Research and Intercultural Studies, IMIS) in Osnabrück; or the Berlin Institut für Bevölkerung und Entwicklung (Berlin Institute for Population and Development). Examples for literature: Thränhardt and Hunger (2004); or Münz (2007).

[169] Important works are, for example, Herbert (2001); Schönwälder (2001); Lucassen (2004); Oltmer (2004); and Motte, Ohliger, and von Oswald (1999).

developments suggest that parts of the history of migration and minorities in Germany are increasingly shifting towards transnational perspectives, some of which are influenced by postcolonial and related paradigms.

For a long time, the scholarship on migration to modern Germany largely focused on domestic settings. Typical research topics included the role of migrant workers in communities, factories, and trade unions in Germany.[170] However, a number of young historians with Turkish language skills have added new facets to the history of Germany's largest minority groups by developing an interest in the transnational connections of certain sociocultural milieus.[171] Going beyond strictly Germany-centered visions, some studies have brought facets of Turkish civil society as well as its transnational social networks, public spheres, and identity formations as agents into the picture.[172] A few scholars have begun to combine the history of domestic minority politics with research on foreign policy and diplomatic history, and in that manner also various aspects of the Turkish state have been included into the picture.[173] Similar conceptual turns have also been taken in the study of minorities such as Gypsies or Afro-Germans,[174] and the history of Judaism and Jewish communities in Germany has visibly gravitated towards plural and transnational perspectives.[175]

While opening up new areas of research, some studies focusing on minorities have also come to challenge mainstream historiography in the sense that they were written under the aegis of internationalizing German history.[176] An important part of such attempts has been the aim to depict minorities as active, transnationally entangled agents within German society and its political cultures. Hence, as a general trend, the history of migration has started to become a rather important forum of activities that critically reconsider hitherto established conceptions of space in German historiography. The history of migration in and of itself is largely based on European perspectives, which also include Turkey in the picture. Yet other research fields have also begun to make other parts of the world more relevant – both as

---

[170] A research overview is provided by Hunn (2004).
[171] For example Rittersberger-Tiliç (1998); and Wilpert (1992). About US influences on these fields see Ackermann (1997).
[172] For example, Hunn (2004).   [173] For example, Steinert (1995).
[174] For example, Giere (1996); and Campt (2004).
[175] For example Diner (2006); and Heil (1999).
[176] See, for example, Bade and Oltmer (2004). An overview and a transnational interpretation of migration during the *kaiserreich* is provided by S. Conrad (2006).

independent research fields and as a source of perspectives with great implications for historical conceptions of Germany and Europe in general.

Colonial history and new perspectives on the German past

In many European societies such as Britain, France, and the Netherlands, the history of ethnic minorities is strongly connected with the colonial past. Here historical questions arising from a plural society have been increasingly related to the heritage of imperial rule. Colonial history long played a very different, lesser role in German historiography and public memory, which can be partly explained by the patterns of the country's past. In its narrowest sense, the German colonial endeavor was rather short, merely covering the decades between the 1880s, when Bismarck modified his opposition to overseas expansionism, and the end of the First World War, when the country lost all of its overseas territories. Furthermore, German colonialism did not generate waves of migration comparable to the settler colonies of the British Empire or the flows of people into Europe during the decolonization period. Based on such comparisons with other European powers, German scholars usually treated colonial history as a brief interlude, as an addendum to the main storylines of German history.[177]

Yet the rather brief time span of German imperialism is only one reason why academic historians and the general public in Germany took relatively little interest in colonial history. For a long time, it did not seem to befit the academic and political cultures of German historiography to consider the colonial past as a research field of equal importance to modern European history. Particularly during the 1960s and 1970s, when many German historians were committed to nation-centered visions of the modern past, colonial history was often seen through domestic rather than transregional lenses. For instance, in many studies German expansionism was treated as an outlet for domestic tensions. In particular, non-Marxist theories of social imperialism were framed around the assumption that colonial thrust in Germany was mainly destined to cover up or even pacify emancipatory movements within German society.[178] Other groups of studies treated expansionist visions of world order largely as the projection screens of homegrown

[177] Compare van Laak (2005).   [178] For example, Wehler (1969).

social and cultural developments[179] such as an alleged proto-fascist political culture during the *Kaiserreich*.[180]

However, especially since the late 1990s there have been different efforts to relate German colonial history to the history of Germany as a nation. To a certain extent, this new movement followed a research trend that was clearly visible in several other countries such as Great Britain or the United States.[181] The rising interest in European, particularly German, colonialism emerged in a reciprocal relationship with the wider public, which grew more attentive to the subject. Television media began to produce a fairly large number of programs and series covering German colonial endeavors and related historical themes. Before that, daily and weekly newspapers had become much more willing to publish book reviews and general articles related to the history of German colonialism.[182] These developments were accelerated by events such as the ones surrounding the centennial of the Herero genocide in Namibia in 1904, most notably a restitution claim issued by the Herero People's Reparation Corporation in 2001.[183] Three years later, after a controversial debate within the German government and society at large, the minister of development, Heidemarie Wiezcorek-Zeul, publicly apologized for the atrocities committed by the German troops and commemorated their victims in Namibia. While the public discussions about Germany's colonial past remained focused on the genocidal acts in Namibia, they started to have wider effects on modes of historical memory and political cultures in Germany.[184]

Generally speaking, the general readership of historical works became more willing to consider works dealing with colonialism. Before, there had been a small but very solid scholarly tradition of colonial history built by scholars such as Wolfgang Reinhard and the Swiss historian Rudolf von Albertini.[185] Even though their scholarly activities were often

---

[179] Mommsen (1969) and Gollwitzer (1972–1982). Heading in a similar direction: W. Smith (1986).

[180] This was also a trend in the aforementioned discussions surrounding the above-mentioned Fischer controversy: see Moses (1975).

[181] For the Anglophone world see, for example, Hull (1993); and Fitzpatrick (2008a; 2008b).

[182] Such articles were (and still are) often authored by professional historians.

[183] In 1904 the local Herero population was systematically expelled into the desert and dwindled to 16,000 from an original level between 60,000 and 90,000. The restitution claim resulted in a class action claim in the United States in 2001. For more information see Krüger (2005).

[184] See Krüger (2005), p. 47. Up until the present day the German government refuses to pay any restitution and reparation to the Herero people.

[185] Important works during that period were, for example, Reinhard (1983–1990); von Albertini (1976); and Osterhammel and Mommsen (1986).

regarded as rather separate from mainstream historiography, they culti-vated an important circle of students which would eventually enhance the cause of transnational history in German-speaking countries.[186] After the mid-1990s, more comprehensive or general accounts of coloni-alism targeting academic and public audiences appeared on the German book market. These works ranged from theoretical interpretations and typologies of various Western, Russian, and Japanese forms of colonial-ism[187] to general histories of mainly European forms of colonialism.[188] However, given the overall context, it is hardly surprising that the German overseas expansion made up the lion's share of the newly appearing literature.[189] Within that framework, single facets of colonialism such as imperial wars, ideologies, or developmental projects were now being increasingly explored.[190] In addition, a rising number of edited volumes in the field pointed to growing research activity in the study of colonialism.

Colonial history has now experienced the growth of a scholarly com-munity in Germany which is sizable enough to build networks and initiatives in the field.[191] Certainly, not all recent scholarship has taken new, daring perspectives; as a matter of fact, many publications actually have not abandoned but rather confirmed the nation-state paradigm, since they primarily focus on the experiences of Germans overseas. Nevertheless, the study of colonialism has become one of the few meet-ing grounds where historians and representatives of area studies interact with each other and pursue compatible research agendas. As some observers have argued, this trend may help to discover new, more flex-ible, and pluralistic approaches, which together can help this area of research to further depart from some macroscopic theories in the study of colonialism.[192] In any case, the history of colonialism has turned into one of the main arenas challenging prominent Eurocentric and nation-centered assumptions in German historiography. The study of German colonies provided an especially good angle from which the

---

[186] See Middell and Naumann (2006).

[187] For example, Osterhammel (1995b). The work also offers ways of periodizing various stages of colonialism.

[188] For example Reinhard (1996a), which was published in several translations; and Eckert (2006a).

[189] Indeed, most German colonies, even small territories in the South Sea or in China, have been subject to new studies. See, for example, Hiery (1995). For example regarding German colonialism in China see Leutner and Mühlhahn (2007); Kim (2004); and Mühlhahn (1997).

[190] See, for example, Barth and Osterhammel (2005); Klein and Schumacher (2006); and van Laak (1999).

[191] For an overview of initiatives, projects, and institutions see www.deutscher-kolonialismus.de.

[192] Compare Barth (2000); and Osterhammel (1995a). See also Mommsen (1994a).

non-European past could be related to the central areas of interest within the historians' guild. The push to move non-European history away from the margins of academic and public discourse had to be closely connected with efforts to widen the conceptual boundaries of German national history and its transregional contexts. Seen in this context, it is hardly surprising that some scholars have suggested extending the time-lines and geographies of the colonial experience in German history. For example, some studies widen the notion of German colonialism by including Hitler's conquests in Eastern Europe in the picture.[193] Others extend the periodizations and definitions of German imperialism by pointing to the various German, usually private, colonial endeavors prior to the *Kaiserreich* or during the early modern period.[194]

Important parts of the new historiography on colonialism were thus at least implicitly motivated by objectives to deconstruct both Eurocentric visions and national historiographical traditions. Through this development, postcolonial elements began to gain influence in German historiography even though it constituted an intellectual environment which was profoundly different from the societies where the movement had flourished before. Some scholars worked on introducing postcolonial perspectives[195] and related schools of thought such as the Orientalism debate to a German academic audience. Particularly in the eyes of some younger scholars, postcolonial thought seemed to be an apt weapon to counteract the widespread assumptions that Europe had allegedly never been significantly impacted by its own global endeavors and that hence national historians could continue to neglect the colonial past. As an alternative program, some scholars started to define new field demarcations such as "entangled histories" or "shared histories."[196] These were driven by the idea that the paths and patterns of modern European societies were directly impacted by colonial and other global experiences.[197] The search for alternative historical spaces facilitated the new receptivity to fields such as "Atlantic history" in the German aca-demic community.[198] In addition, some researchers sought to critically rethink very localized spaces in the light of colonial and postcolonial

---

[193] For example, van Laak (2005); and Graichen and Gründer (2007).

[194] Fenske (1991); and Zantop (1999).

[195] Most notably the essay collection edited by S. Conrad and Randeria (2002b), in which the editors advocate applying colonial and postcolonial perspectives to German history. About the Orientalism debate see, for example Osterhammel (1997a).

[196] For example Randeria (1999); and S. Conrad and Randeria (2002a). See also Lepenies (2000).

[197] See, for example, S. Conrad (2002).

[198] See Pietschmann (1999); and Reinhard (2005).

perspectives. For example, one project tried to map out the wide array of colonial factors influencing the local history of small inland cities such as Freiburg near the Black Forest Mountains, which had previously hardly been associated with the history of overseas expansionism.[199]

The movement to widen the parameters of European, especially German, history by seeing it through the lenses of the colonial experience was based on efforts to break up the firm conceptual boundaries between the colonizers and the colonized. In conjunction with that, there have been attempts to view colonial encounters in ways that no longer reduce the colonies to little more than passive settings for German and other European activities.[200] Important for undoing some of the earlier narratives surrounding the study of colonial formations have also been projects that investigate the impact of colonialism on German university systems and their academic canon.[201] These contribute to the necessary self-criticism of a field, which for a variety of reasons has recently come to critically reconsider its own conceptual fundaments.

The growing interest in new outlooks on colonial history was entangled with attempts to rewrite aspects of modern German history from transnational perspectives. For example, there have been a growing number of projects seeking to critically reconsider some interpretations of the *Kaiserreich* on which many *Sonderweg* theories had focused in the past. For instance, an international conference on transnationalizing the history of Germany between 1871 and 1914 brought together various approaches ranging from economic history to gender history.[202] Furthermore, Sebastian Conrad's habilitation thesis opened up several transnational and global perspectives on the Second Reich. For example, he argued that the notion of work as an important facet of German national identity developed far more global ambitions and parameters than previously assumed – parameters which included the mobilization of labor at home and in the colonies.[203] This is significant since the transnational dimension of German and other nationalisms has been largely neglected by the field of historiography.[204]

---

[199] See www.freiburg-postkolonial.de.

[200] For example, Speitkamp (2005). Also applying multiperspectivity in his narrative: Eckert (2009). See also Lüsebrink (2006); and Reinhard (1997).

[201] See, for example, Pollock (2002); and Stuchtey (2005). Showing that even failed colonial ambitions, for instance in the Near East, could foster the establishment of new research fields: Fuhrmann (2006).

[202] S. Conrad and Osterhammel (2004).

[203] S. Conrad (2006).

[204] An overview of research about German nationalism is provided by Langewiesche (1995).

Some scholars even suggested that aspects of modern German history including the Third Reich should be understood less as national history and more as imperial history – not only when viewed from the colonies but also from parts of Eastern Europe.[205] Such ideas have been tied to attempts to widen the study of historical trajectories leading into the Nazi era. For instance, a growing number of historians now argue that many mechanisms to enforce social order, ranging from racial segregation to mass destruction, developed in a dynamic interchange between Germany and its colonies.[206] Indeed, a wide range of techniques commonly associated with modern state rule had first been set up in some colonies before being transferred to the European continent.[207] Examples of the colonies serving as the laboratories of European modernity range from the use of fingerprints by the police and mass internment to certain forms of urban planning and mass immunization.[208]

Tackling another aspect of colonial entanglements, some case studies have investigated how colonial triumphalism contributed to an opinion climate, which in Germany as well as in many other European societies proved fertile for the rise of racism and politicized biological ideologies.[209] Several representatives of the field have also become interested in the colonial sources of currents flowing into Nazi ideology ranging from imperial ambitions to the goal of acquiring foreign land at the expense of allegedly inferior peoples.[210] Recent studies have found more evidence for the idea that programs such as cleansing society through eugenics, or the forced resettlement of supposedly superfluous parts of the population, had already been drafted during the German colonial period.[211] Some scholars even opined that there were direct continuities and significant similarities between genocidal practices under German colonial rule

[205] For example, Ther (2004); and Zimmerer (2004a).
[206] See, for example, Eckert and Pesek (2004).
[207] Mühlhahn (1999). More critical of the concept: van Laak (2004b).
[208] For example, Mühlhahn (2009); Wright (1991); and Eckart (1997).
[209] See, for example, Geulen (2004); Berman (1996); and Honold and Scherpe (2004). See also Kundrus (2003b). About colonialism and German historical consciousness see Zeller (2000). Ascribable to the same category of literature are also studies on the types of identities and forms of racism emerging in particular historical contexts. Among those are, for example, the massive protests in German cities against being occupied by troops that included soldiers from French African colonies. See, for example, Wigger (2007).
[210] Already at the time of the colonial age, colonial visions were being projected onto Eastern Europe. See, for example, Geulen (2004); and Friedrichsmeyer, Lennox, and Zantop (1998). About the dreams of a "German India," a trope that Hitler applied to the Ukraine, see van Laak (2005).
[211] For example, Kundrus (2003a); and Patel (2004).

and the Holocaust.[212] In addition, a number of studies have traced the transmission channels that linked colonial rule to the Nazi occupation in the East.[213] For example, it has been argued that there were direct connections between colonial forms of mass internment and Nazi concentration camps.[214] In this context, it is important to note that the new interest in alternative spaces and timelines of imperialism is not only limited to the Nazi era and its pre-history. For example, a study by Dirk van Laak addressed the continuities between earlier German colonial ambitions and Cold War plans to build new infrastructure under moderate colonial regimes.[215]

Such theses concerning direct connections between the colonial and the Nazi experience have met with criticism. Contextualizing the "final solution" by relating it to other historical cases remains an academically problematic and socially sensitive subject matter.[216] Some scholars have pointed to the significant differences between the industrial extermination of European Jewry and acts of genocide in the colonies, particularly because the latter were launched in a very different way and at the time heavily criticized in the German public sphere.[217] Moreover, the suggestion that there existed unilinear connections between German colonialism and Nazism has provoked considerable doubt, particularly since historical interpretations of this kind may result in yet another German *Sonderweg* hypothesis if the exceptionality of German colonial acts is not proven systematically.[218] When tracing the impact of the colonial experience on German political culture during the first half of the twentieth century, research will not be able to neglect more complex transmission channels that go beyond direct sets of exchanges between single colonizing powers and the colonized.[219] After all, discourses on global hierarchies, civilizing missions, and supremacy were generated and exchanged in complex transnational networks reaching across different colonial powers and world regions.

In many regards, the search for connections between colonialism and fascism revitalizes some approaches that were propounded not only by

---

[212] About the argument of direct continuities see Zimmerer (2003); and Bühler (2003). A critical response to such positions: Malinowski (2007).
[213] For example Zimmerer (2004a). Others have suggested that some experiences of the Second World War are more comparable to the early forms of colonialism on the European continent: Lindquist (1999).
[214] Eckart (1997).   [215] Van Laak (2004a).
[216] Friedländer (1993). See also Jarausch and Geyer (2003).   [217] See Kundrus (2004).
[218] For example, Fitzpatrick (2005).
[219] Similar: van Laak (2005), pp. 18 and 176. An example of a study on some international dimensions of racism is Kühl (1997). For exchange processes between colonial powers see Geyer (2004).

theories of imperialism but, particularly during the postwar period, also by such towering intellectual figures as Hannah Arendt, Frantz Fanon, and Aimé Césaire.[220] Despite significant differences between their philosophical backgrounds and proximity to Marxism, these thinkers all regarded the Nazi era at least partly as the result of a brutalization of European culture brought about by colonial expansionism. Yet while there are some basic similarities, the current drives to globalize facets of German history are heading towards slightly different epistemological shores. Whereas more than half a century ago, materialist perspectives were deemed to be the main keys to understanding the links between colonialism and fascism, today's researchers devote more attention to cultural historical topics. In addition, they usually do not operate at a level of macroscopic theorizing but rather pursue much more detailed research agendas.

Across a wide spectrum of research interests, the recent scholarship on colonial encounters predominantly investigates Germany-related themes. This bilateral approach to Germany and its former overseas territories is partly conditioned by the structures of an academic system in which scholars with an overseas research agenda can only hope to establish themselves if their own research is at least partly related to German history. The strong focus on Germany makes large chunks of what is often categorized as "global history" or "transnational history" in Germany actually more comparable to the project of globalizing American history[221] in the United States than to more recent branches emerging from world history proper.[222] Many new transnational perspectives aim less to deconstruct the nation-state as a modern invention than to establish a more accurate historical understanding of the forces, processes, and contexts that shaped or characterized the German past.

Within this framework, the impact of transnational and transcontinental perspectives can increasingly be felt in important subfields such as, for example, social history. Here too, more scholars have joined the ranks of those who argue that historiography needs to operate with far more dynamic and delocalized understandings of social formation which favor the study flows over the analysis of structures.[223] They point out

---

[220] Arendt (1951); and Césaire (1972).   [221] See, for example, Bender (2002).

[222] In the US, world history and the debates on globalizing American history are quite separate, even though they share important elements. Compare Fuchs (2005).

[223] For example, Wirz (2001); and Spiliotis (2001). Earlier, the sociologist Friedrich Tenbruck had argued that it was erroneous to analyze single societies as isolated entities and held that more attention should be paid to transfers, flows, and other translocal social structures. In an influential article Tenbruck emphasized that many social transformations did not occur in single societies but in the spaces between them,

that essential aspects of society, ranging from intellectual networks and political groupings to public spheres, were often characterized by transnational connotations.[224] More moderate voices suggest that, rather than exploring transnational spaces in a separate field of inquiry, the current parameters of social history should be widened at first to a European and then potentially to a global level.[225]

The transnationalization of German history does not abandon the nation-state as an operative concept, though it does decisively change the nature and definition of its boundaries. Paying more attention to topics such as migrant communities and colonial history certainly moves historiography further away from the main contours of the German past as it was conceptualized in public memory and academic research a generation ago.[226] It is important to note that in contrast to some movements during the Cold War today's transnational research perspectives do not come from the political right and are not connected with a national agenda to alleviate German society's responsibilities for the Nazi past.[227] Rather, they are part of international research trends offering new viewpoints to the study of modern history including twentieth-century dictatorships and genocides. These perspectives may cut across national experiences, but they do not directly seek to relativize and deconstruct them.

Further trends feeding into global and transnational history

Most of the research which came to be associated with global history in Germany has been tied to new ways of conceptualizing the German past. At the same time, developments in other, previously rather marginal research fields has also contributed to the growing global and transnational trend. For example, there have been significant reform movements within international history which have moved this field closer to problematizing the nation as the sole container of

---

and he advocated a spatial paradigm change for sociological and historical inquiry. Tenbruck's article, however, primarily focused on early empires and their assessments by macrosociologists and world historians. See Tenbruck (1989). An earlier sociological theory heading into a conceptually similar direction was Dahrendorf (1958).

[224] Examples for research projects heading into this direction: Kaelble, Kirsch, and Schmidt-Gernig (2002); as well as Gosewinkel et al. (2003); and Charle, Schriewer, and Wagner (2004).

[225] Osterhammel (2001d).   [226] Eckert and Wirz (2002).

[227] See, for example, Kundrus (2003a).

history.[228] In particular, some younger international historians, who had not experienced the great methodological controversies during the Cold War, became more attentive to ways of combining cultural and new social historical perspectives into overarching methodological frameworks.[229] For these and other reasons, international history in Germany followed similar patterns and rhythms as in the Anglophone world.[230] This, in turn, often led to a search for alternative conceptions of historical space which no longer drew on the nation-state as the dominant unit of analysis. Given such trends, it is hardly surprising that some scholars used terms such as international history and global history in conjunction.[231]

In addition to international history, the search for potential parameters of a new European history has generated significant transnationalization efforts. Even though there is a wide spectrum of positions that can be considered to be a part of this rather recent project, they commonly assume that European history can no longer, and ought no longer, be written as a compendium of national experiences. On the contrary, a growing number of academics are now inquiring into alternative perspectives that allow them to conceptualize European commonalities or regional entanglements across and beyond national levels. Moreover, some scholars expected that, when lifting comparative frameworks onto a global level, Europe as a whole and no longer the nation-state needed to be the unit of analysis.[232] There were some hopes that – following the visions of Marc Bloch, Otto Hintze, and other towering figures of earlier generations – comparative history would prepare the grounds for a transnational European history *in spe*.[233]

The search for a Europeanized history is conceptually related to other transnational currents, and yet it is unusual in many regards. This is most blatantly true for the institutional landscapes within which it is being generated and promoted. For instance, in the case of European history, a transnational political force has come to actively support new ways of conceptualizing the past. Driven by the concern that the

---

[228] Important theoretical debates can be found in Loth and Osterhammel (2000); and Conze, Lappenküper, and Müller (2004). See also Lehmkuhl (2001); and Ziebura (1990).

[229] For example G. Müller (2005); Herren (2000); and Gienow-Hecht (1999). Several examples for studies can be found in Gienow-Hecht and Schumacher (2003).

[230] See Chapter 1.

[231] For example, Leipzig University Press started publishing a book series on international and global history which is edited by Ulf Engel, Frank Hadler, and Matthias Middell.

[232] For a critical discussion of the literature on Europeanizing history see Chapter 1.

[233] Haupt (2004); and Kaelble (1999b).

new Europe needs to gather more active support from the general public,[234] the European Union launched several campaigns aimed at fostering commonly accepted symbols, along with documentaries and other measures deemed helpful to promote a European identity. As far as the study of history is concerned, the EU has been heavily involved in establishing transnational institutions and funding structures facilitating cooperation between historians of different countries. Among those institutions are, for example, a European university with a graduate program in history[235] as well as the European Standing Conference of History Teachers (EUROCLIO). Of growing importance is also the European Science Foundation, which – in addition to other projects – funds research projects and academic exchanges[236] ranging from transnational European research networks to graduate programs.[237] Of particular note in this context is the European doctoral program "Building the Past" in the social history of Europe and the Mediterranean, which is operated by a consortium of ten universities.[238] European history textbooks have also been either directly or indirectly sponsored by the European Union. Such intervention in the production of history has been subject of much criticism. For example, a common argument is that many textbooks deconstruct national narratives while at the same time seeking to manufacture Europe as a new historical unity.[239]

Despite such efforts, support for a European past is not evenly distributed across the European Union. While, generally speaking, historians in Eastern European societies and in the United Kingdom are more reserved about this project, its intellectual motors have been

---

[234] For an overview of EU activities aimed at creating a common historical consciousness see, for example, Shore (2000).

[235] Among the many activities dedicated to exploring the parameters of European history are – in addition to conferences and graduate education – summer schools for students on new forms of European history.

[236] For the European Science Foundation see www.esf.org. More examples are provided by Schmale (1998); for European textbooks see Stobart (1999).

[237] For example, see the ESF research networking program, "Representations of the Past: The Writing of National Histories in Europe," which was funded from 2003 to 2008 and involved historians from many European countries. The main objective was to understand and in that manner problematize the formation of national histories in a transnational, European dimension. See www.esf.org/esf_article.php?language=0&article=363&domain=4&activity=1.

[238] For more information see hsozkult.geschichte.hu-berlin.de/chancen/type=stipendienandid=1621.

[239] Examples for textbooks: Jones (1981); Mendras (1997); and Heater (1992). Additional examples are provided by Shore (1999). See also Pingel (2000); Schmale (1998); and Haupt (2002). More book series and other projects are listed on the European History database: www.lrz-muenchen.de/bib?9332aa/webserver/webdata/webbib.

mainly based in Germany, France, and the Benelux states.[240] In any case, activities in Germany need to be seen as part of an evolving European academic structure that has come to interact with national systems in very complex ways. It is important to note that the debates surrounding the historical questions posed by the European unification project still predominantly occur on a national level.[241]

Particularly since the mid-1990s, a steadily growing number of European history surveys have appeared on the German book market. Much of this literature does not apply alternative perspectives to the European past in the same manner as they are being developed by oceanic, colonial, and other historians. In many, if not most, overviews of European history produced in Germany, for example, Europe's connections with the outside world including imperialism and the world wars are being reduced to a brief addendum that fits comfortably onto a few pages.[242] This conveys the idea that Europe's global expansion was not a genuine part of its own past and had very few repercussions for it.[243] In that sense, the literature on Europe inadvertently continues older world historical tropes that tended to portray the history of the European continent as an experience that could and ought to be understood as an independent past.[244] Even though the triumphalist overtones of the European past are largely gone, the idea persists that Europe greatly influenced the rest of the world while the opposite was not the case.[245]

In the same spirit, several studies published in German apply comparative methods not in order to explore how the European past was truly unique, but rather to further accentuate a previously existing assumption of European exceptionalism in a global context.[246] For example, in a widely acclaimed study the recipient of the prestigious triennial German historians' award, Michael Mitterauer, professes to explain the medieval foundations of the allegedly special path of European history which he labels as a *Sonderweg*. In his introduction, he places his work explicitly in

[240] Altrichter (2006).
[241] In this context, German historians have taken positions on questions such as the cultural boundaries of Europe and the prospect of Turkey joining the European Union. An insightful discussion of the topic is Kocka (2005).
[242] Examples are provided by Osterhammel (2004). See also Pingel (2000).
[243] A critique of the Eurocentrism in most of the new historiographical research on Europe is A. Eckert (2004a).
[244] For the tradition of world history see Fuchs and Stuchtey (2003). For a general critique see, for example, Blaut (1993).
[245] For more details about the genesis of Eurocentrism see Chapter 1.
[246] According to some critics, this reduced comparative agenda has a long tradition in European scholarship, of which Max Weber was an important part. See Kalberg (1994).

the tradition of the Weberian quest to explain why only the Occident generated universalizable civilizational facets. He does so by unfolding a European master narrative in which he compares single elements of the European past such as family patterns or aspects of the medieval legal system with their alleged equivalents in other cultures.[247] Such selective or partial comparative approaches are methodologically problematic since they cut out chunks from the European nexus and contrast them with alleged functional equivalents in other cultures.[248]

Equally questionable are attempts to outline a unique European development culminating in the tragedies of the twentieth century.[249] This often translates into suggesting that a continuous and holistic historical logic permeated the European experience – an approach which, in turn, tends to marginalize the role of entanglements with the outside world. In that sense, the growing literature on the history of European political culture[250] could greatly benefit from research which is attentive to colonial and other transcontinental spaces in which ideologies such as Social Darwinism, ethnic bias, and genocidal thinking emerged.[251] Similarly, some important studies analyzing facets of social histories of Europe focus almost exclusively on the myriad of intra-European structures and processes.[252] This approach warrants a greater dialogue with research on transatlantic family connections, networks, and public spheres that had a significant influence on European social and cultural history.[253] For example, at least during the period prior to the First World War, the social history of Britain, Ireland, and some other countries was in many regards more closely connected with North America than with much of Eastern Europe.[254]

Paying more attention to the plural interactions and co-dependencies between parts of Europe and other world regions would be a significant step on a journey away from tropes of European exceptionalism which, as the first chapter has shown, have not only characterized modern historiographical traditions in Europe, but also been tightly woven into

---

[247] Mitterauer (2003), particularly pp. 8–16. Mitterauer acknowledges that other cultures also had special experiences. He also distances his book from the project of constructing European history and holds that his work stands in the tradition of scholarship seeking to understand the parameters of European history.

[248] A similar argument is made by Haupt (2002).   [249] For example Meier (2002).

[250] For example Reinhard (2001).

[251] See the section "Transnational history in a pluralizing society" in this chapter.

[252] For example Crossick and Haupt (1998). Another example is Kaelble (2004).

[253] See, for example, Davies et al. (2000); and Hoerder and Moch (1996).

[254] See, for example, C. Hall (2000); or Burton (1994). Important theoretical debates can be found in Loth and Osterhammel (2000).

the textures of the global academic system. In addition, through spatially more complex research perspectives it would become more difficult to portray single regions of Western Europe as sample cases of an alleged continent-wide experience.[255] After all, many historical narratives surrounding the concept of "Europe" were focused on several Western European societies. This implicitly degrades the Eastern European experience to a deviation from a standard pattern – a line of interpretation that has already been criticized as another form of Orientalism.[256] A rapprochement with schools such as colonial history or entangled histories would require historians of Europe to be more attentive to the divergent developments of the Eastern and Western halves of the continent, particularly during the modern period. It would also be more compatible with ideas of an evolving European model based on more integrative and cooperative forms of political culture.[257] For instance, it would be promising to further head into the direction of studies that have shown how European regions changed or "modernized" in various rhythms and stages which followed the logics of their connectedness to the world beyond.[258]

Towards new world and global historical spaces

After the Second World War, many world historical publications were more geared towards the general book market. Certainly, critical interpretations such as theories of imperialism[259] or world systems theory attracted some attention, albeit without having a major impact on the big conceptual and methodological debates of the time.[260] On the other side of the Iron Curtain, the field was represented at several institutions of higher learning, such as the University of Leipzig.[261] It is hardly

---

[255] A critique and a more nuanced set of comparative and other research agendas is proposed by Duchhardt (1997).

[256] For example Todorova (1997). See also M. Müller (2004).

[257] See Sachsenmaier (2009b).

[258] An influential article arguing this point: Geyer and Bright (1995).

[259] An overview of the spectrum of approaches subsumed under "theories of imperialism" is provided by Mommsen (1977).

[260] An overview of world system theory in Germany is provided by H. Nolte (1994). See also Elsenhans (2001i); Feldbauer and Komolsy (2003); and Bornschier and Suter (1996). A recent history of the world from the fifteenth through the nineteenth centuries, which draws on world systems theory, is H. Nolte (2005b).

[261] See Middell (2005b), vol. III.

surprising that, in East German academia, world historical research was predominantly framed by Marxist approaches, with degrees of government interference varying over time. After the fall of the Berlin Wall, some scholars with an East German background predicted that new Marxist approaches would become more prominent in German research. In their eyes, the epoch-making events concluding the Cold War necessitated a stronger role of world historical studies and all-encompassing utopias, which postcolonial and other, related perspectives would not be able to deliver.[262] Others were more critical of holistic master narratives but argued that East German some world historical traditions would become an important landmark within a pluralistic historical research landscape *in spe*.[263]

Despite such hopes, Marxist and other East German approaches were not continued to the extent that had been expected. On the contrary, most transnational and world historical traditions in the so-called five "new states" of the Federal Republic were discontinued in rather abrupt ways. Such a rupture in the early years after reunification was caused by the vast majority of East German incumbents being removed from their chairs and replaced with scholars from the West.[264] This process, which seen in a particular East German context could somewhat ironically be called a "Westernization" of the social sciences and humanities, not only rapidly transformed the research orientations of history departments but also those of the area studies. In the latter case, the influx of scholars from the western parts of the country even led to a resurgence of philological traditions, which offered only limited possibilities for cooperation with history departments, let alone work on world historical themes. Nevertheless, some locations in the eastern part of the country evolved into significant centers of activity for new forms of border-crossing scholarship.

Particularly since the mid-1990s, much of this new research was more and more often referred to as *Globalgeschichte*, which is a direct equivalent of the English term "global history." Not unlike its Anglophone counterpart, *Globalgeschichte* was often used in Germany in order to distinguish it from *Universalgeschichte* and *Weltgeschichte*, both of which carry problematic connotations in the German context. The term *Globalgeschichte* owes much of its new prominence in Germany to the debates on globalization, which in turn were spurred on by the great

---

[262] Küttler (1992); see also Kossock (1993).
[263] Middell (1992). Generally on the topic: Iggers (1994).
[264] About the marginalization of East German perspectives and the decline of Marxist narratives see Jarausch and Geyer (2003). See also Berger (2002).

transformations after the Cold War.[265] It catered to the feeling among many scholars that it has become vital to critically reconsider the outlooks of academic historiography that often treated the world as no more than a residual category.[266]

There were other suggested neologisms, one example of which is *translokale Geschichte* ("translocal history"), which was coined by Ulrike Freitag and other researchers at the Zentrum Moderner Orient.[267] According to its creators, the new term expresses the desire to treat neither "cultures" nor "regions" nor "nations" as fixed entities, but to view all definitions of locality as constructs and – at least partly – as the results of global entanglements. Other scholars prefer the term *transnationale Geschichte* ("transnational history"), which in their eyes should be differentiated from fields such as international history or global history.[268] Against such terminological skirmishes, scholars like Andreas Eckert warned that, in Germany, the movement exploring cross-border histories is too recent and the circle of scholars too small to become engaged in fights for "theoretical air supremacy" between different subfields.[269] Indeed, there is a risk in defining and differentiating transcultural, global history and other programs at a time when a solid institutional grounding for actual research projects has not been fully established. Partly because of such terminological debates, some critical observers in Germany have argued that the global history movements were characterized by postulates rather than by actual research projects. This has not necessarily been the case since there is a growing landscape of actual research projects in the field. The contours of this landscape will eventually determine the contact zones and overlaps between different fields and their designating terms.

Most proponents of transnational and global history in Germany emphasize that they do not aim to construct a separate field along the lines of older universal histories.[270] In their eyes, terms such as *Globalgeschichte* should mainly connote various reform movements, academic developments, and paradigm changes that apply new spatial perspectives to the study of the past. This is perhaps one of the reasons why the concept of mental maps has also received increasing levels of attention in Germany.[271] Along similar lines, the small number of publications in German which specifically address issues related to the history of

---

[265] An influential German sociological overview of globalization theories is Beck (1998). See also Hübinger, Osterhammel and Pelzer (1994).
[266] Osterhammel (2000a).   [267] Freitag (2005).   [268] Patel (2004).
[269] Eckert (2006b).
[270] For example Patel (2003); Rothermund (2005); and Eckert (2000).
[271] Bruns (2009); and Schenk (2002). See also Osterhammel (2001c).

globalization[272] does not usually treat the term as a marker of an objective process. In that sense, only a minority of historians in Germany see "global history" as a program to rewrite the history of the modern period as the story of globalization. Rather, the history of globalization is portrayed as a fresh and timely set of perspectives, as a set of angles from which processes that otherwise are easily ignored by historians can be tackled. According to such perspectives, which do not claim to be totalizing, the historiography of globalization should focus in particular on transregional processes and interconnections. These can include transformations such as industrialization, the surge of migration, the mechanization of agriculture and its varying local impacts, the emergence of global cultural facets, and transnational social structures. In this sense, many proponents of global history in Germany emphasize that the history of globalization does not replace national narratives but poses new questions in relation to them, which, however, may lead to many new spatial conceptions beyond the nation-state.

A major landmark for the field of global history in Germany was the publication of Jürgen Osterhammel's *Transformation of the World*, a volume of more than 1,500 pages which lists more than 2,500 titles in its bibliography.[273] The work pursues global historical perspectives of the nineteenth century but avoids both universal modes of periodization and monolithic notions of space. As the author writes in his introduction, "treating space and time equally counters the impression that world history would necessarily be connected with a de-specification of time and a spatial turn ... The book shifts its emphasis from synthesis to analysis – two narratives styles, which are anyhow not characterized by significant contrasts."[274]

Within this conceptual framework, the author accentuates the unique timelines and geographies that characterized different historical processes ranging from the growth of cities to imperial formations or evolving patterns of global exclusionary mechanisms. At the same time, the author considers more protracted developments that characterized much of the long nineteenth century such as, for example, the intensifying aspects of Western-centrism and the world's growing interconnectedness through revolutions in transportation technology. Osterhammel's work had a significant impact within the field of historiography as well as

---

[272] For example, Osterhammel and Petersson (2003); Wendt (2007); and Fischer (1998). On methodological approaches to globalization see especially pp. 7–15. See also Grandner, Rothermund, and Schwentker (2005).

[273] Osterhammel (2009). An English version will be published by Princeton University Press.

[274] Osterhammel (2009), pp. 21–22.

among the general public. Soon after its publication it was widely reviewed in all major German newspapers and academic journals. Important representatives of the field referred to the book as a "milestone of German historiography, one of the most important books during the past few decades"[275] or as "the most significant achievement by a German historian of the modern period during [the first decade of] the twenty-first century."[276] In that sense, its publication can serve as an indication or a symbolic event for the rising status of global historical literature within the German academic system.

As a general trend, there is now a growing amount of literature available that provides the interested reader with insights into the global historical dimensions of certain time periods.[277] Below the level of macroscopic accounts, there are reasons to assume that the surging interest in transnational or transcultural themes will provide new connecting points between the field of history, area studies, and hybrid subfields such as oceanic history or continental history.[278] In this way, the historiography of China, India, the Americas, and other parts of the world may ultimately start to lose their character as a garden of marginal "orchid fields" and gain significance within the professional community of German historians. It is quite clear that a more intense dialogue between historiography and the area studies, hitherto rather separate fields, could explore many new territories for research. As Margrit Pernau pointed out, the rise of global and trans-cultural history carries the danger of a resurgence of Eurocentric perspectives if representatives of area studies are not included in this endeavor.[279] This necessitates, however, a greater willingness of historians in fields such as Sinology or Indology to actively engage themselves in this endeavor and collaborate with experts in European history.

No movement can gain momentum solely from good intentions and intellectual declarations. During the past years, a growing institutional fundament has been built that can support a further expansion of historical research at a global and transnational level. This process has

---

[275] Kocka (2009).   [276] Lenger (2009).

[277] An example is the series Global History – The World, 1000–2000, which in eight edited volumes provides global historical accounts of the past millennium. Examples are Thomas and Limberger (2009); and Feldbauer (2009).

[278] See, for example, Pietschmann (1999); Lehmann (2006); Rothermund and Weigelin-Schwiedrzik (2004); and H. Nolte (2000).

[279] Pernau (2004). Arguing that overcoming Eurocentrism needs to imply taking on current debates on global and transcultural history in other parts of the world: Sachsenmaier (2005b).

been aided by the fact that a small but growing number of newly opened positions in some area studies and in modern history have been filled with scholars who, in their own work, no longer operate exclusively within the traditional boundaries of their fields. In German academic life, public foundations, especially the Deutsche Forschungsgemeinschaft (Federal German National Research Foundation), play an exceptionally important role in supplying scholars with funding for research projects. One of the traditional roles of foundations has been to supply entire academic divisions at single universities with considerable research funds that pay for an array of additional untenured positions, staff, and conference expenses for a number of years. In order to acquire funding for these competitive programs supporting collaborative projects (most notably the *Sonderforschungsbereiche*), several departments have to jointly file an application and pledge to collaborate with each other for a number of years. This has led to a number of projects in which area studies departments have worked together with history departments. This has, for example, been the case with the Berlin-based project Changing Representations of Social Order – Intercultural and Intertemporal Comparisons, in which different fields joined forces.[280] In addition, a number of other foundation-sponsored programs ranging from interdisciplinary networks among young scholars[281] to research training groups (*Graduiertenkollege*), that is, groups of graduate students from different academic fields, have proven to be relevant for the field of transnational or global history.[282] The same has been true for government-sponsored institutions such as the international research center Work and Human Life Cycle in Global History, which is based at

---

[280] The project has been sponsored since 2004 and is directed by Kaelble and Schriewer (both Humboldt University Berlin). For more information see www.repraesentationen. de/site/lang__en/3846/default.aspx. A list of *Sonderforschungsbereiche* with a transregional focus during the early 2000s can be found in Wissenschaftsrat (2006), p. 49.

[281] For example, the transatlantic research network on "Conceptions of World Order, 1880s–1930s. Global Historical Perspectives," which brought together nine young scholars with different area expertise between 2004 and 2007. See Conrad and Sachsenmaier (2007).

[282] Generally on the topic of interdisciplinary graduate groups related to the field of history: Zimmermann and Mönkemöller (1997); and Middell (1997). An example for transnational graduate student groups is the transatlantic research project on "History and Culture in the Metropolises of the Twentieth Century," which is centered on a collaboration between four universities in New York and Berlin: www. metropolitanstudies.de. Another important graduate group works on transnational media events from the early modern period to the present (see Gerbig-Fabel (2006)). Those groups were mainly sponsored by the Deutsche Forschungsgemeinschaft (German National Research Foundation, DFG) and the Volkswagen-Stiftung (Volkswagen Foundation).

Humboldt University in Berlin and provides fellowships for international researchers from various academic disciplines.[283]

Moreover, the federally sponsored "Excellence Initiative," which started in 2005 and selected a small number of elite universities to receive special government funds, facilitated the growth of research landscapes that are more supportive of transnational and global historical themes.[284] Among the sponsored projects are the University of Constance's Institute of Advanced Study, which explicitly includes global historical perspectives in its agenda,[285] as well as the Heidelberg interdisciplinary research cluster Asia and Europe in a Global Context.[286] Such efforts started to create public spheres in which history departments and area studies come to interact with each other. They also put scholars in Germany into more sustained dialogues with researchers in other countries. Important in the latter context are also the bilateral cooperation projects between foundations in Germany and other European countries, which actively promote transnational European research and education projects.[287]

In addition to endeavors of this kind, there have been various initiatives to strengthen the institutional ties between researchers focusing on different parts of the world. For instance, as early as the 1980s, historians who identified themselves as experts on "non-European history" started to become more organized, first with separate meetings at the *Historikertage*, which was then followed by the founding of a special workshop in the field.[288] In the context of these efforts, *Periplus*, a journal for non-European history, was founded in 1990, and as such was related to a sense of "inner mission" with regards to the community of German historians.[289]

During the past two decades, the University of Leipzig has become an important center of activity in transnational and global historical research in Germany. Here an institute for cultural and universal history was

[283] See www2.hu-berlin.de/arbeit/das-kolleg.html.
[284] See, for example, Winnacker (2005).
[285] See www.exc16.de/cms/kolleg.html?&L=1.
[286] See www.asia-europe.uni-heidelberg.de/en/home.html.
[287] For example, this is the case for a cooperation between the largest German and French foundations, the DFG and the Agence Nationale de la Recherche (National Research Agency, ANR).
[288] This workshop is called Arbeitskreis für Aussereuropäische Geschichte (Non-European History Working Group). See also Dietmar Rothermund's interview with Andreas Eckert: Rothermund (2003).
[289] *Periplus. Jahrbuch fur Aussereuropäische Geschichte (Periplus. Yearbook for non-European History)*. About the sense of "inner mission" see Dietmar Rothermund's interview with Andreas Eckert: Rothermund (2003).

reestablished in 1994, having initially been founded at the beginning of the twentieth century.[290] As a precursor, the Karl-Lamprecht-Association was founded in 1991 which sought to continue local traditions in world history dating back to the late nineteenth century and further develop East German research in transcultural history.[291] One of the declared aims of the association was to promote new kinds of transregional historical research which would remain deeply embedded in area expertise. The Karl-Lamprecht-Association publishes the bimonthly *Comparativ* – a journal that has become an important organ for global historical research in Germany and covers important topics in the field.[292] The same association and its president, Matthias Middell, were also one of the main and its president driving forces behind the founding of the European Network in Universal and Global History, which held its founding congress in 2006 and quickly grew into an important biannual forum for the field.[293] Leipzig has also become the site for graduate programs and international summer schools in global history.

Outside of the Federal Republic, the University of Vienna was actually the first German-speaking university to set up an emphasis in global history within an MA program.[294] Global history in Vienna is also part of Erasmus Mundus Global Studies, an EU-sponsored transnational graduate program in global studies, in which several universities participate.[295] Furthermore, parts of the Vienna faculty played a major role in producing some of the first textbooks carrying the term *Globalgeschichte* in their titles.[296] Generally speaking, during the past fifteen years there have been rather lively debates on how to introduce global or world historical perspectives into German university education.[297] There are similar projects targeting high school history education, from which non-Western history or world history traditionally has been virtually absent.[298]

---

[290] Institut für Kultur- und Universalgeschichte (Institute of Cultural and Universal History). Middell (2004).
[291] See www.lamprecht-gesellschaft.de. Since 1994 the association has been connected with the Leipzig Institute for Cultural and Universal History. Since 2002 it has been affiliated with the World History Association. See also Middell (2004).
[292] For example, international civil society (1997–2), world exhibitions in the nineteenth century (1999–5), transatlantic slavery (2003–2); and ways of teaching world history (2006–1).
[293] For more information see www.uni-leipzig.de/~eniugh.
[294] See www.univie.ac.at/Geschichte/Globalgeschichte.
[295] See wwwm.uni-leipzig.de/zhs/index.php?option=com_content&task=view&id=466&Itemid=358.
[296] Edelmayer, Feldbauer and Wakounig (2002); Grandner and Komlosy (2004).
[297] For example Popp and Forster (2003); Bley (2000); Osterhammel (2005); and Riekenberg (2005).
[298] See, for example, Riekenberg (2005).

Furthermore, in Hanover, a Verein für die Geschichte des Weltsystems ("Association of the History of the World System") was founded in 1992 to promote historical research on a larger scale.[299] Since 2000, the association, whose agendas and activities go far beyond world systems theory, publishes the *Zeitschrift für Weltgeschichte* (*Journal of World History*), which has brought many important international debates to the attention of its audience.[300] Other journals have also begun to publish special issues related to global historical topics – among them, perhaps surprisingly, *Geschichte und Gesellschaft*. Even though this key journal of the social history movement in Germany has long focused almost exclusively on German national history and European history, since the early 2000s it has dedicated more space to non-Western and transregional history.[301] By contrast, such disciplinary icons as the *Historische Zeitschrift* have remained rather hesitant to publish large numbers of articles reaching beyond the boundaries of Europe.

Besides journals, the general book market has also witnessed a growing interest in transnational and global history. In Leipzig, a book series on universal history and comparative history of societies was launched in 1992.[302] New approaches within the field of international history have been the subject of a book series published by Oldenbourg in Munich.[303] In 2007, Campus publishers in Frankfurt started a book series on global history that is designed to provide a forum for outside perspectives on Europe.[304] An important medium for exchanges is the online forum geschichte.transnational/history.transnational, which was founded in 2004 and which after two years already had more than 1,800 subscribers. The forum provides book reviews, conference reports, and announcements, and it has also become an important site for theoretical exchanges in the field.[305]

---

[299] See H. Nolte, "Der Verein für die Geschichte des Weltsystems," in www.vgws.org/Texte/nolte-verein.html.

[300] An overview of the issues can be found at www.vgws.org/ZWG.html.

[301] An expression of this trend is that Jürgen Osterhammel, a historian of China and global history at the University of Constance, is now one of the three managing editors of the journal. A statistical overview is provided by Raphael (2000).

[302] See Middell (2004). In 2006, Leipzig University Press also launched a book series in English entitled "Global History and International Studies."

[303] The editors are Anselm Doering-Manteuffel, Jost Düffler, Wilfried Loth, and Jürgen Osterhammel.

[304] The first volume, a reader on global history, has been put together by the three series editors: S. Conrad, Eckert, and Freitag (2007).

[305] A debate on conceptualizing transnational and global history invited many leading German and international scholars in the field, and important parts of the discussion were subsequently published as a book: Middell (2006).

Positions of global and transnational history in Germany

While it is easy to conclude that the research environments of global historical research in Germany have been deepening and broadening, it is far more difficult to describe their position within the international academic landscapes. Compared to the nineteenth and early twentieth centuries, the global influence of German historiography has been greatly reduced. Certainly, in the field of German and Central European history German historiography carries enough weight to build internationally influential centers. Yet in the long run, a condition in which – to paraphrase the Cambridge scholar Richard Evans – there have been many experts on German history in other countries, while there were very few experts on other countries in Germany,[306] was bound to marginalize the field within the international communities of historical research.[307] This situation may eventually change if German universities continue to foster internationally connected and interdisciplinary research centers in fields such as global and transnational history. In these areas of research more border-crossing methodological exchanges can be expected in the future.

Until the mid-1990s, transnational and, more generally, non-European history had even less of a home base in Germany than today. In most cases, leading representatives of non-European or transnational history relied on a scholarly community abroad rather than at home. For example, Dietmar Rothermund, a specialist of modern Indian and transregional history, reminisced about this situation in an interview conducted around the time of his retirement. His work, which includes a widely acclaimed world history of the consequences of Black October in 1929,[308] was very prominent in India, England, and the United States. By contrast, in Germany Rothermund was rather isolated between a very Eurocentric historiography on the one hand and an Indological tradition centered on philological Sanskrit studies on the other hand.[309] Yet precisely because of its enduring marginal status, his and other, comparable experts' research activities in Germany were not confined to the periphery of the German mainstream. The small number of scholars working on global historical themes often found their academic environments in international circles. For

---

[306] Evans (1998), pp. 172–73.
[307] About the question whether American and German approaches to German history will become increasingly divergent see Jarausch and Geyer (2003).
[308] Rothermund (1996).
[309] See Dietmar Rothermund's interview with Andreas Eckert: Rothermund (2003).

these reasons, the rhythms of non-European and world history were not necessarily connected with the conceptual evolutions of German historiography at large; rather, they were often characterized by their own patterns of development that were attuned to the rhythms of research communities abroad.

Up until the present day Anglo-American literature has played a highly influential, if not even dominant role in German global and translocal historical scholarship. Individual German historians have made remarkable attempts to establish dialogue forums between Western and non-Western historians[310] but, in general, recent works produced in China, Africa, and other parts of the world are hardly even noticed by German global historians, even if they are available in translation.[311] Much of the literature quoted in important theoretical and practical German publications related to global history is predominantly in English. A recently published important German essay collection in the field of global and transnational history consists almost exclusively of articles previously published in the United States.[312] This shows that research trends on the other side of the Atlantic are an important benchmark for many global historians in Germany.

The reasons for this strong attachment to research in Anglo-American societies are not only conditioned by academic factors. They are also deeply related to intellectual mentalities and political cultures as they developed in the Federal Republic of Germany, which have come to be characterized by the *Westbindung*,[313] that is, bonds with a partly real, partly imagined West. In contrast to the nineteenth and early twentieth centuries, the desire to develop alternative global visions does not play a strong role in today's German academic milieus. Rather, the German movement of transnationalizing history situates itself primarily within

---

[310] For example, the historian Jörn Rüsen organized several conferences, which brought together scholars from Germany and the non-Western world. See Rüsen (2004; 2002; 1996); Gottlob, Mittag and Rüsen (1998). During his time as the president of the International Committee of Historical Sciences (ICHS/CISH), Jürgen Kocka initiated several transcultural historical dialogues. For example see: Sachsenmaier (2005a).

[311] See also Chapter 1. One may see the growing trend of reporting about world historical conceptions in other countries as a precursor to more international interactions. Still, the number of publications on world history in the United States by far outweighs reports about other countries. See, for example, Fuchs and Middell (2006); Fuchs and Stuchtey (2003); Gräser (2006); Fuchs (2005); and Middell and Naumann (2006).

[312] Budde, Conrad, and Janz (2006); and S. Conrad, Eckert, and Freitag (2007). The introduction to the volume refers to debates on world history in East Asian societies.

[313] For the debates on *Westbindung* and political identities in Germany during the 1990s, see Berger (1997), particularly pp. 185–205. About the future of transatlantic relations pertaining the study of history see Geyer (1990). See also Kocka (1992).

a transnational scholarly discourse in which research centers in the English-speaking world hold a very influential position.

The fact that – in Heinrich August Winkler's words – Germany finally arrived after a long journey to the West[314] may be one of the chief reasons why scholars have been reluctant to launch a wider debate on potential German or European perspectives of global history and related fields. This may be a missed opportunity, particularly in a situation in which global historical approaches from the English-speaking world are often used in order to transnationalize research on the German past. For example, thus far there has hardly been any debate about the potential limitations in the ways in which postcolonial concepts can be taken from Anglo-American contexts and applied to the research interests of historians in Germany many of whom, after all, tend to study colonial experiences of the Second Reich and their postcolonial effects. There have been a few movements heading in this direction, and some scholars have tried to encourage their colleagues to start reflecting on specific European, national, or local continuities in world historical thought.[315] Yet these attempts have not developed into a wider debate on the potential contours of German or European approaches to world history in today's world. For instance, there has not been an intellectual exchange on questions such as whether the German tradition of responsibly coming to terms with a traumatic past could inject some important new viewpoints into the debates on the heritage of colonialism, imperialism, and Western supremacy.

There have been a few creative attempts to apply methodologies developed within a German historiographical context to the study of transnational history. For example, in one article Jürgen Osterhammel related Hans-Ulrich Wehler's social historical categories, which were developed in order to gain a comprehensive vision of the German past, to the modern Chinese case.[316] Another example is Adrian Gerber's suggestion that the approaches to conceptual history developed by Reinhart Koselleck and other scholars should be used in order to develop transcultural dictionaries bridging the semantic gaps between different historical contexts and area-studies-related traditions of

---

[314] Winkler (2000).
[315] See Middell (2005a), particularly pp. 64–66. Also mentioning such a potential: Kaelble (2004), www.zeithistorische-forschungen.de/16126041-Kaelble-3-2004; or H. Nolte (2005a), p. 126.
[316] Osterhammel (2002). An important outcome of the study was, however, the limited applicability of Wehler's conceptual world to the Chinese context since its lenses failed to capture the strong role of international forces and other factors.

studying them.[317] In addition, the rather German tradition of multi-authored world history volumes has continued up until the present day, and even started to become more influential in international academic environments. For example, a *New World History*[318] book series jointly published by Beck (Munich) and Harvard University Press is partly rooted in the tradition of reputed German series such as the Fischer and Propyläen world histories. However, the new Harvard/Beck series also departs from the parameters of many previous German series since its authors primarily explore topics from global historical and translocal perspectives rather than delivering area-specific contributions.

Nonetheless, the bulk of transnational and global historical literature in Germany applies formats and concepts that have not emerged from local academic traditions, but are rather common in wider, usually Western, scholarly contexts. Yet global historical research in Germany is by no means a copy of research activities in the United States or even a province of them. As this chapter has shown, there are several reasons why the topics chosen by transnational historians in Germany differ profoundly from global historical scholarship in neighboring countries as well as in other parts of the world. The same is true for the modes in which the field has come to be institutionalized, particularly during the past decade.

In addition, the wide spectrum of transnational and global historical scholarship in Germany plays a very peculiar role in wider public debates over the future of migration and society, political cultures, and forms of historical memory. For example, the question of how global and transnational history relates to the postwar consensus is certainly an important one. This is particularly the case at a time when the ranks of the war generation are becoming thinner and public memory of the Nazi past is changing from personal forms of memory to historical ones, without losing its highly moral meaning in large parts of German society.[319] Furthermore, even though one may not share the overly celebratory tones in some accounts of postwar German democracy,[320] today totalitarianism or even extreme forms of ethnic nationalism are no longer immediate dangers. The younger generation of German historians enjoy the luxury of no longer needing to see their social and political roles in the same way as their predecessors did, namely as the guardians and defenders of a democratically committed historical consciousness. During the past ten years, the great public contestations among academic historians have become less intense, even though they have

---

[317] Gerber (2005).   [318] Edited by Akira Iriye and Jürgen Osterhammel.
[319] For a discussion of the topic see Jarausch and Geyer (2003).
[320] Critical of this trend: Winkler (2004).

not completely disappeared. The proclivity towards defining ideological opposites in attitudes vis-à-vis the Nazi past, which had been dominant during the Cold War period, has diminished. The group of scholars advocating transnational positions[321] has certainly met with criticism. For example, some prominent representatives of the older generation of historians have bitterly complained about the boom of postcolonial concepts among a younger group who – in their opinion – have not sufficiently considered the strong forces of national history.[322] But such arguments have not spilt over into the political sector, nor have they triggered new versions of the famed historians' controversy of the 1980s. Rather, they have generated some academic debates, with little in the way of wider impact.

As a general trend, the rise of global and transnational history in Germany has opened up new ways for a pluralization of perspectives in historical research, and it has increased the number of roles that historiography can play in a changing environment.[323] For example, scholarship can help to reconceptualize history in a society that is still struggling to find patterns of identity befitting an age of migration and Europeanization. An open society and non-ethnic forms of national belonging can only prosper if new viewpoints, alternative perspectives, and different spaces are allowed into the German past. Thus far, there has been no close cooperation between academic attempts to transnationalize national history and politicized struggles of minority groups to gain visibility or a "voice" in German society.[324] One of the reasons why the transnational turn has not established strong connections with forces in civil society is that hardly any leading academic position in German departments is filled with scholars of a foreign background. Still, at least the project of transnationalizing German history has already started affecting wider segments of society, for example through changes in textbooks or shifting interests in historical themes covered by the media.

As discussed in the first chapter, the challenge of making the study of the non-Western world seem relevant to the majority of the historians' guild is not untypical in a disciplinary culture which, in terms of its basic structures, was at least in part founded on

---

[321] In the eyes of many scholars, the great themes for future scholarship remain almost always tied to the nation. See, for example, Wehler (1991); Sabrow (2004) (recorded panel discussion among several historians).
[322] For example Wehler (2006).
[323] Making a similar observation: C. Conrad and Kessel (1998). For a general interpretation see Marcuse (2001).
[324] Fuchs (2005).

Eurocentric premises. By contrast, intellectual and academic elites in many world regions outside of the so-called "West" have long been unable to maintain similar solipsistic outlooks. This fact will be further illustrated with the case of scholarship in mainland China, which is the subject of the following chapter.

4   Another world? Thinking globally about history in China

Patterns of Chinese historiography prior to the mid-nineteenth century

In many Western societies, central currents of academic scholarship have long treated the main patterns of the European past as a largely autochthonous process. In particular, present cultures of historiography in Europe are often portrayed as outcomes of homegrown traditions and conceptual innovations. For Chinese scholars and public intellectuals, however, such professional negligence of global entanglements and influences from the outside world has no longer been possible for generations. In contrast to many popular notions of continued cultural solipsism in the East, forms of global consciousness have played much more central roles within the community of modern Chinese historians than among their peers in most Western academic systems. Since the late nineteenth century, it has been almost impossible to conceptualize Chinese history without paying attention to the wide spectrum of discontinuities and influences, which in some cases have been referred to as the "internationalization of China."[1] Even the most patriotic accounts of modern Chinese history cannot deny the massive impact of international powers and global transformations on the former Middle Kingdom, particularly from the mid-nineteenth century onwards. Because the ensuing waves of changes also reconfigured China's institutions of higher learning and sociologies of knowledge, it is almost impossible to argue that Chinese historical scholarship in its present state is primarily the product of endogenous developments.[2]

This is striking since China could look back at a long historiographical tradition and in its history exerted several waves of influence on neighboring societies such as Korea, Japan, and Vietnam. As a consequence of the Middle Kingdom's dominant position within the political and

---

[1] See, for example, Kirby and D. Niu (2007); Kirby, Leutner, and Mühlhahn (2006).
[2] See, for example, D. Liu (1998); and H. Wang (1994).

172

cultural flows of East Asia, the idea of China as a wellspring of commonly human knowledge, norms, and values was a recurrent theme throughout many historical epochs. Of course one should beware of holding an overly monolithic view of Chinese history and assuming that in premodern China culturally centrist views remained completely static and unchallenged.[3] For example, during the crisis-ridden late Ming dynasty (late sixteenth/early seventeenth centuries) Chinese Buddhist texts were openly critical of Sinocentric worldviews and interpretations of history.[4] Centuries before that, some Buddhist authors in China had suggested that India and not China deserved to be called the true "Middle Kingdom" since it had given birth to the teaching of Siddhartha Gautama.[5] In general, research has become increasingly sensitive to the spirit of *curiositas* that was shared by significant segments of the Chinese upper classes at various stages of history.[6]

Nevertheless, as in many other parts of the world, the main schools of imperial Chinese historiography tended to view the Middle Kingdom's past as largely independent from other cultural realms.[7] For example, the very diverse landscapes of Confucian historiography tended to maintain a vision of the past that was centered on a tension between ancient ages and the present but not on a net of exchanges between China and the world.[8] The guiding idea was that the proper cultivation of the "Way" (Dao) had been lost and needed to be restored, particularly through a return to high morality, a spirit of social responsibility, and proper codes of conduct.[9] Confucian historiography then focused largely on the moral lessons that could be derived from the past.[10] In later periods, particularly from the seventh century onwards, much of Confucian historiography was steered towards official purposes, with a main direction of scholarly activity aiming at classifying and recording the previous dynasties and deriving moral lessons from them.[11] Following

---

[3] Also, definitions of China varied significantly over time – for instance, under the Manchu-ruled Qing dynasty ethnic tropes did not play any role in official articulations of Sinocentrism whereas in other times they were more important. The purely ethical and culturalist definitions of "China" under the Qing only heightened the degree of pretensions vis-à-vis the East Asian "periphery". See Q. Wang (1999a).

[4] See, for example, Weidner (2001).

[5] For more details see the "classic" work by Zürcher (1959).

[6] See, for example, Waley-Cohen (1999); and Mungello (1999).

[7] See Chapter 1 for more details.

[8] Generally on historiography in imperial China: Ng and Q. Wang (2005).

[9] See, for example, Schwarz (1985); and Ng and Q. Wang (2005).

[10] A brief introduction is provided by A. Cheng (1993).

[11] In the neo-Confucian era, starting from the Song dynasty, the moral implications were increasingly embedded in anthropocosmic visions, which were seasoned by Buddhist ways of thinking about the world.

a similar impulse, a few centuries later many historical narratives produced in official circles largely focused on the emperor and other distinguished individuals. To a certain extent, this was also true for the genre of independent histories, which flourished particularly during the boom of a private book market in the seventeenth century and usually covered regional topics and events.[12]

As in most other civilizations, attempts to write histories of the then known world played a rather marginal role in the Chinese context, even though the Middle Kingdom produced some very remarkable examples of this genre. The most famous one is certainly the work "Historical Records" (*Shiji*) by the Han-dynasty historian Sima Qian (d. 86 BCE), who during his lifetime undertook extensive travels throughout the Middle Kingdom in order to collect materials.[13] Sima's magnum opus not only included topical chapters on fields like music, ceremonies, and religion but also shed light on China's neighboring peoples by even including their pasts on synchronized tables.[14] However, at the same time he left no doubts about the primacy of the Middle Kingdom's civilization to the "barbarian" satellites encircling it. Similar cultural identities can also be observed in the case of many great historians from the Tang, Song, and other periods,[15] including the neo-Confucian Song scholar Cheng Hao (d. 1085).[16] One of the most influential works of the Song period, Sima Guang's (d. 1086) "Contemporary Mirror to Aid in Government" (*Zizhi Tongjian*), a massive tome of about 3 million characters, was written as a universal history but actually remained almost exclusively focused on China. Its purported objective was to serve as a source of moral guidance for good governance for imperial and literati circles.[17] In this capacity, it was for a long time a standard reference work and guiding example for the official historiography to come.

Many aspects of Chinese historiography were based on cyclical notions of time, which in turn tended to be closely wedded with Sinocentric perspectives. This was the case because the rise and fall of dynasties were seen as the main stages in the rotations of time, which narrowed the possibilities of ascribing important roles to foreign connections.

---

[12] About the genre of local gazetteers, which goes back to the Song period but greatly grew during the late Ming, see, for example, Moll-Murata (2001).
[13] See, for example, Durrant (1995).
[14] Interesting reflections on Sima Qian's methodology: Hardy (1994).
[15] See Q. Wang (1999a).
[16] Cheng also emphasized that different countries have different timelines. For more details see Sato (1991a).
[17] See X. Ji (2005).

At the same time, however, cyclical visions of the past did not monopolize Chinese historical scholarship. For example, Sima Guang's main history as well as many influential works that followed in its wake were at least partly written from different chronological principles. Also the general Confucian perception of time was not solely oriented after the rhythms and patterns of single dynasties. Rather, the cultural and political *telos* of restoring the "Way" in China was at least as a general tendency tied to an eschatological understanding of time. Some scholars have thus observed a certain tension in Confucian attitudes towards the temporal logics of history.[18]

Conceptions of timelines in traditional Chinese historiography grew highly relevant during the late nineteenth and early twentieth centuries, when Western and Japanese scholarship got widely disseminated within the Chinese intellectual elite through translated texts and personal studies abroad. During that time, Western progressivist visions were not necessarily understood as an abrupt change in perceptions but rather as new forms of epistemological and political optimism in themselves familiar to the Confucian tradition.[19] Likewise, many Chinese historians regarded important elements of modern critical source work as "new" in various regards but not necessarily as completely exogenous in the sense of impossible to connect with earlier Chinese traditions. Indeed, many comparable and compatible methodological elements had been well known in the Middle Kingdom before the nineteenth century, even though they had emerged from contexts that differed profoundly from the European experience. For example, some grand historians of old such as Sima Guang and even Sima Qian had made great efforts to distill historical facts from a great number of written sources and archeological evidence.

Furthermore, while there were some precursors in the Song period, critical source work had been given a new boost of significance from the first half of the seventeenth century onwards when the "School of Evidential Learning" (*kaozhengxue*) was rising to prominence.[20] The Kaozheng School grew from the spirit of great political and cultural disillusionment during the crisis of the late Ming dynasty.[21] At that time

---

[18] See, for example, Schwarz (1996). Generally on the notion of time in ancient Chinese thought: Q. Wang (1995).
[19] Arguing that the Chinese academic environment is, for historical and contemporary reasons, characterized by higher levels of epistemological optimism than its Western counterparts: Metzger (2005).
[20] See, for example, Quirin (1996).
[21] For the general context see Y. Zhao (2006). See also Wakeman (1985).

more members of Chinese elite circles came to blame Buddhist emphases on spirituality for the evils of their time. Among other developments, the desire to return to the alleged original Confucian agenda gave a boost to efforts to reach out to the true meaning of classical texts through careful source work. As part of this quest to sort fact from fiction, fields like philology, phonology, etymology, and phraseology were widely expanded during the seventeenth and eighteenth centuries.[22] Since this critical source work challenged state-endorsed neo-Confucian outlooks, the School of Evidential Learning was not as strongly rooted in official circles as previous Confucian schools had been.[23] Nevertheless, its rise was aided by significant socioeconomic transformations such as the growth of an independent merchant class, the mounting importance of independent academies, and the formation of what was quite likely the largest book market in the world.[24]

While it would be futile to ask for direct functional equivalents between the European and the Chinese experiences, it was certainly the case that historiography in China witnessed some developments which – at least in terms of their methodological principles – did not look completely different from the growing importance of critical source work and systematic historical studies in Europe between the times of humanism and the Enlightenment period.[25] Kaozheng traditions went into decline around the turn of the late eighteenth century but at that time they already had had a lasting impact on many official and non-official forms of history writing in China. About a hundred years later, they again received increasing levels of attention within China's intellectual community when the presence of "Western" scholarship and institutions of higher learning could increasingly be felt. They became an important connecting point within a scholarly community, which increasingly defined itself by referring to both the idea of national tradition and the nimbus of progressive, intellectually connected research.

---

[22] See, for example, Elman (2001); and Ng (1993).

[23] At the same time, one should be careful not to overemphasize the polarization between kaozheng circles and the Chinese governments. Leading representatives of the School of Evidential Learning were being recruited for government services. Dai Zhen, for instance, was an editor for the Qianlong emperor's massive encyclopedia project, the *Siku Quanshu*. See, for example, Guy (1987). Nevertheless, several Kaozheng scholars were severely punished by the imperial court for their intellectual positions.

[24] A concise summary of the Kaozheng School can be found in, for example, Iggers, Q. Wang, and Mukherjee (2008). See also Chow (2005).

[25] Q. Wang (2003b).

Enmeshment with the world: historical thinking before and during the Chinese Republic

Particularly from the turn of the twentieth century onwards, the series of economic, political, social, and cultural crises that China had experienced for decades became more acute. With the growing presence of Western powers and the expansion of Japan, the regional order was transformed as quickly as China's domestic system. Moreover, a combination of official policies and market developments changed China's knowledge sector profoundly during the last years of the Qing dynasty and the subsequent attempts to establish a functional republic. This also had a great impact on historical scholarship, particularly within the revolutionized systems of higher learning.[26] Factors such as the abolition of the imperial examination system in 1905, the mass movements of Chinese students abroad and the growth of Western-style schools in China ended the role of Confucianism as a state orthodoxy.[27] Furthermore, the cultural center of the country shifted to exponentially growing urban centers, many of which were the theaters of widening public spheres, growing book markets, and emerging modern universities.[28] It was also here that new social prototypes such as the independent intellectual were emerging, and they did so partly as a result of international influences.[29] In addition, the landscapes of knowledge were altered by the growing number of translated foreign works dealing with topics ranging from Western philosophy to Social Darwinism and a wide spectrum of political ideologies.[30]

Due to these and other facets of the country's "internationalization," it became increasingly difficult to assert that the conceptual world of China was largely free from outside influences.[31] A symptom of the growing sense of historical rupture was the increasingly politicized question of whether "tradition" constituted a hindrance to modernization or

---

[26] Certainly, the decline of the literati class, which had been the sociocultural backbone of imperial China, was not a clear-cut process. In many parts of the countryside traditional forms and institutions of scholarship continued throughout that time period. See, for example, Esherick and Rankin (1990).

[27] See, for example, H. Huang (2002); and W. Ye (2001).

[28] See, for example, Vittinghoff (2004); and Z. Luo (1999).

[29] See, for example, Weston (2004).

[30] See, for example, Wright (2001). See also Huters (2005); and Y. Xiong (1994).

[31] As research during the past few years has shown, the semantic changes that the Chinese language experienced in the late nineteenth and early twentieth centuries were massive, leading to great levels of entanglement with other languages. See L. Liu (1995); and Lackner (2001).

a treasure to be preserved.[32] In this general climate, almost all leading intellectual and political circles came to share a strong sense of nationalism with the general public – a sense of nationalism which was often based on strong feelings of humiliation by outside powers.[33] During the early twentieth century, many important proponents of national identity in China were quite open about the exogenous character of this ideology and related discourses ranging from mass mobilizaton to citizenship. Transforming the former Qing territory into a national body was often understood as a way of emulating successful players in a brutish geopolitical environment.[34] This is not to say that Chinese elites were in favor of radical Westernization, or that their outward gazes remained fixated upon the West. Already early in the twentieth century, some Chinese observers followed closely the developments in colonized societies in Africa, Asia, and other parts of the world,[35] which strengthened the close relationship between anti-imperialist discourses and visions of nationhood.[36]

Given the strong dedication of many leading circles to a mass-based nation-building project, it is small wonder that the study of history also started serving purposes that lay outside the spectrum of earlier Confucian approaches. Visions of the past deemed suitable to nation-building efforts were also propounded through media such as newspapers, novels, films, and general histories (tongshi) published by a burgeoning world of commercial presses. A large factor in the public dissemination of a new historical consciousness was the spread of citizen-building projects, most notably the establishment of a public education system.[37] Some key facets of the nationalization of history were modeled after the allegedly successful experiences of other modernizers in the world. For example, during the institutionalization of academic history departments, Japanese universities served as important models since in the eyes of many Chinese observers they had successfully integrated Western (Rankean and other) elements into an East Asian context.[38] Japanese and several Western systems also

---

[32] See, for example, G. Sun (1994); Mitter (2004); and X. Tang (1996).

[33] See Cohen (2002).

[34] For China, see, for example, Duara (1994); Esherick (2006); and Dabringhaus (2006); and Dittmer and Kim (1993).

[35] See Karl (2002).   [36] For the latter see Zanasi (2006); and Duara (2009), pp. 23ff.

[37] See, for example, Hon and Culp (2007). See also G. Li and B. Wang (2000), and L. Liu (2001).

[38] Generally on Chinese perceptions of Japan see Masuda (2000).

served as benchmarks for the history curriculum within the newly created public education sector.[39]

Generally speaking, the basic outlooks of modern Chinese historiography became characterized by a high degree of global consciousness,[40] and, embedded in it, territorial understandings of China were being developed. Both global and national-territorial forms of thinking had still been highly unusual in Chinese historiography one or two generations before. At the same time, many important schools of Chinese historiography acquired a highly future-oriented, linear character.[41] Certainly, some important aspects of Qing historiography were being continued,[42] and many important historians like Liang Qichao or Hu Shi did not go as far as to believe that Chinese historiography needed to completely break with earlier traditions in the quest to "reorder the national heritage."[43] Yet in their as well as many other scholars' eyes the public role of historiography needed to change dramatically. Its new versions were supposed to contribute to future-oriented politics, to help to mobilize the masses and build a modern Chinese state. A new type of historian staked a claim for social prestige and political influence through his or her alleged ability to provide orientation within a rapidly changing domestic and international environment.[44]

For example, Liang Qichao (d. 1929), a leading historian and public intellectual, argued that for the first time in its history China needed to continue transforming itself with a close eye on the examples of outside models, including Japan.[45] In his mind, there had been revolutionary changes in dynastic governments before but no profound alterations in China's political, cultural, and social structures. The sudden transformations of the present, Liang argued in his *Xin Shixue* (*New Historiography*),[46] needed to be supported by a new historical

[39] See, for example, Z. Ou (2003).
[40] For a general discussion of the emergence of levels of global consciousness (many of which remained Western-centric) see Geyer and Bright (1995).
[41] Duara (1995), pp. 36ff. and 138ff.; and L. Kwong (2001).
[42] See Mazur (2007). Moreover, in many scholarly circles there was a reappreciation of Kaozheng traditions, which were seen as compatible with the new Western forms of scholarship. Prominent examples of scholars holding this position were Hu Shi and, to a lesser extent, Gu Jiegang.
[43] See, for example, X. Tang (1996); and Sachsenmaier (2007a).
[44] See, for example, Hon (2007). See also C. Hsü (1993).
[45] On the influence of Japanese national historiography such as the works of Fukuzawa Yukichi on Liang's thought see Q. Wang (2003c). See also Fogel (2004).
[46] Q. Liang (1902a); see also idem (1902b).

consciousness, which was no longer centered on the elites and, by implication, on granting political stability to the dynastic order. According to him, future forms of Chinese historiography should also no longer focus on dynastic cycles but reveal the forces of development and dynamism inherent in the Chinese past. Liang further argued that historiography could play a central role in awakening the people and arousing national sentiments among them. In fact, he opined, history writing needed to be credited with being at least half the force behind the powers of nation formation in the West.[47] Heading in a similar direction, many other historians around the same time, such as Huang Jie (d. 1935) and Zhang Taiyan (d. 1936), advocated a historiographical revolution in which the Chinese people would replace the imperial court as the center of scholarly inquiry.[48] That this new programmatic vision was inspired by outside experiences even became apparent on a terminological level. For example, the term "renaissance" came to play an important role in the intellectual debates in China during the first decades of the twentieth century, with its meaning shifting increasingly towards exploring the Chinese past through critical modern scholarship.[49]

The high degree of international awareness within which the nationalization of Chinese history was embedded caused the genre of world history to play a relatively important role from the inception of modern academic scholarship. Already in the middle of the nineteenth century scholars such as Liang Tingnan (d. 1861) or Wei Yuan (d. 1857) produced works that sought to give an account of the world and also included some historical perspectives. For example, the latter's *Haiguo Tuzhi* (*Illustrated Treatise of the Maritime Countries*)[50] needs to be seen in the context of efforts undertaken within some circles to ward off the threat of imperialism by suggesting that people learn from "the West."[51] Consequently, many reformist accounts of the "world" were based mainly on Western sources, and in their narratives they focused on the global powers of that time. Such works that were supposed to help

---

[47] See, for example, X. Tang (1996). See also Duara (1995); and X. Meng (1985).

[48] See Q. Wang (2001).

[49] For Liang's new historiography and his modes of periodizing the Chinese past see Q. Wang (2007a), particularly p. 139.

[50] Y. Wei (1844–52). See Leonard (1984); and Y. Xiong (1996).

[51] Wei Yuan's and some other works were also at least partly related to the growing concern to tie the vast territories in China's West more closely into the Chinese state, through administrative measures as well as cultural and historical sensitivity.

initiating a more internationally aware Chinese intellectual tradition typically aimed at both understanding a changing world and adapting China to it.[52] They were mainly produced by an increasing number of scholar-officials who sought a more practicable applicability of historical and other forms of empirical knowledge, particularly for the purpose of refining and expanding mechanisms of statecraft.[53] Nevertheless, authors like Wei Yuan were certainly far from being committed to the dramatic "modernizing efforts" which scholars two or three generations later voiced when they were involved in the Chinese nation-building project. Even though Wei departed from the styles of annal-biographies, his thinking certainly was not meant to abandon the idea of a Sinocentric world order resting on Confucian norms and ideas.[54]

Little more than half a century later, when linear notions of the past were gaining more presence in China, national and international historiography were jointly thriving in the Chinese context. Already during the late Qing dynasty, the first foreign history textbooks were being produced for the public education system and the private market.[55] After the Chinese Revolution of 1911, studying Western history for two out of four years of history education became part of the middle school curriculum.[56] There were similar requirements for university-level history education, and it was not uncommon for students to study the history of the West with materials published in foreign languages.[57] The textbooks available in Chinese either were direct translations from Japanese works or heavily relied on Western sources.

Hence, already during the first half of the twentieth century, the strong emphasis on globally aware historical education and research in China did not mean that the entire world was covered equally and unequivocally.[58] As in the case of national history, large regions were being marginalized

---

[52] See F. Hu and W. Zhang (1991).
[53] See Dabringhaus (2006), particularly pp. 31ff. This quest was also related to the growing importance of historical geography and frontier studies.
[54] Individuals such as the scholar and translator Wang Tao (d. 1897), who collaborated with European scholars and spent several years in England, went further and actually advocated greater ranges of cultural learning from the West. However, during Wang's lifetime such positions remained rather marginal in Chinese political and intellectual circles. See Q. Wang (2001), pp. 36ff.; and D. Yin (1985).
[55] S. Ji (1991).   [56] See Y. Zhu (1992), p. 359.
[57] See L. Xu (2010). See also P. Yu (2006).
[58] For example, prior to 1949 only eight books in the field of African history were published in China, and all of them dealt with Egypt. See F. He (2000).

and many possible ways of thinking about world history suppressed when the field became established within academic environments and the general education system. Many authors of world historical texts belonged to the growing group of intellectuals who had been trained in modern institutions of higher learning or at Western universities.[59] This may have contributed to the fact that several widely disseminated texts were largely based on the idea of Europeanization (*ouhua*) as a universal project. For example, during an initial period, most nationwide curricula and textbook accounts of world history were mainly centered on the North Atlantic world and often referred to Japan as a successful importer of key Western elements.

These particular spatial preferences were embedded in linear or even Hegelian conceptions of the past: history as a dynamic global process was often presented as the product of Western powers.[60] Some texts even portrayed colonialism as a natural consequence of development gaps – an idea which was then related to the notion of learning from the West as a measure to avoid subjugation under imperial rule. According to many widely read historical works, the revolutions in the Atlantic world had triggered a process by which pre-existing nations were transformed into a new political and economic order. According to the same train of thought, the resulting self-empowerment of European societies had major implications for the outside world. Typically, the global spread of what was taken as Western modernity was not only described as a danger for China but also as a significant opportunity to imbue its society with greater levels of energy and agency. In the eyes of a growing number of Chinese historians, the transformation of China into a nation-state was far more than a necessary measure to avoid the fate of colonization. Many saw in a supposedly universalizable modern civilization the potential for liberation and the betterment of the human condition within the Chinese context.

The emphasis on the West as the main source of a global storyline continued throughout the Republican period, even though there were historians like Lei Haizhong who were critical of Eurocentric visions of world history and postulated that scholarship pay more attention to China's roles in world history.[61] Critical voices of this kind may have contributed to the fact that a few years after May Fourth, officially endorsed world historical narratives were somewhat mitigated in terms of their main interpretative lines. For instance, works published during

---

[59] See Culp (2007); and S. Qi (1994).
[60] For a theoretically sophisticated account of the problems and dilemmas surrounding the rise of linear historical conceptions in China see Duara (1995).
[61] See P. Yu (2007a).

the Nanjing Years (1927–1937) tended to pay more attention to colonized and semi-colonized societies in other parts of Asia, Africa, and Latin America. Here the fate of China was more related to other "weak and small peoples" struggling against foreign domination – an idea which had already been prominently espoused by Sun Yat-sen.[62] Yet while this vision had been partly inspired by Lenin, both communism and Pan-Asianism received little favorable treatment during the Chiang Kai-shek era.[63] During that time, world historical master narratives were predominantly based on the idea of the liberation of societies through national independence. In this context, compatible notions of modernization received much more favorable treatment than others.

In any case, the great emphasis the Chinese nation-state placed on the history of other world regions marks a great contrast with the United States and Germany, where experiences in the non-Western world were not much more than a residual category within history departments and the general public.[64] As discussed in Chapter 1, these different geographies of historical interest need to be partly understood as mirror reflections of divergent types of modernization rhetoric in more and less industrialized societies. Whereas for the intellectual and political mainstreams of Western societies, visions for the future were usually not tied to programs of learning from other cultures, the opposite was the case in many other parts of the world, including China. Here intellectual opinion makers and political decision-takers commonly agreed on the necessity of becoming familiar with other, allegedly more advanced societies in Western Europe and North America. Furthermore, large groups within the upper strata of Chinese society were convinced that it was necessary to gain knowledge from Japan, which was often seen as the product of a successful process of Europeanization.

The sense of urgency surrounding the study of history caused world historical interpretations to become closely tied to political struggles over the question of domestic order. In a society without a widely shared political consensus, some fundamental questions needed to be clarified, and many prominent historians or historically inclined public intellectuals were involved in them. For example, a choice existed between different political and economic systems such as liberalism, communism, and even fascism, which were all represented by various international powers. A derivative question was how to decoct a universally applicable essence

---

[62] See Culp (2007).
[63] See, for example, W. Yeh (1990). About history textbooks in the Japanese-controlled areas of China during the Second World War see W. Chan (2007).
[64] See for France and Germany: Schleier (2003), p. 207.

from such exogenous models in order to make them applicable to China. This was in turn related to the more general question of how compatible "newness" was with "Chineseness" and what elements of the Chinese past ought to be transposed into a modernized future.[65] Another burning issue of the time was the problem of whether China would need revolutionary acts or gradual change.[66]

Even though the camp of individuals seeking to fully copy any outside model was rather small and the majority of Chinese thinkers were in favor of finding a specific, suitable way for China into modernity, international reference systems played a crucial role in these debates. At the same time, however, prominent political visions for China also started to have an impact on the study of Western history and world history. Due to these close entanglements between inside and outside perspectives, between the study of the past and visions of the future, national history and world history became regarded as being engaged in a closely related duet in the Chinese context. Ironically, this implied for the future that both fields became rather strictly divided in terms of their institutional settings.

Communism and Chinese historiography

Marxism further strengthened the role of international outlooks and world historical perspectives within China's intellectual and political landscapes, and it took them into new directions. The centrality of Western history and world history for developing new visions of the Chinese past was a strong component of most Marxist interpretations of history as they became more visible in China from the 1920s onwards. In the decades to come, much scholarly energy in China was dedicated to fitting the Middle Kingdom's past into Marxist categories and modes of periodization, which were commonly derived from the European experience. However, here the strong emphasis on European history and historiography was not meant to emulate any Western example but rather to help China find ways of overcoming imperialist dominance and move to a new stage of modernity. Furthermore, in many Marxist world historical outlooks written in China the concept of a world revolution played only a rather subordinate role. Actually the anti-nationalistic interpretations of "classic" Marxist historiography never became a

---

[65] About contending visions of Gu Jiegang and Chen Yinke see Schneider (1996).

[66] A famous example was the debate between Hu Shi and Li Dazhao over the question of "isms" and the choice between gradual transformations and revolutionary approaches. See Dirlik (1978).

dominant trope in China, where the idea of a communist revolution was closely wedded to the objective of national liberation.

Nevertheless, the mental maps of Marxist historiography in China remained largely fixated upon the West. Since the keys to revolution were supposedly to be found in the Western experience, much of Chinese communist world historiography tended to marginalize the historical experiences of other parts of the world.[67] Certainly, for rather long periods Russian and then Soviet history received a high degree of attention in China but, generally speaking, the same was not true for colonized or semi-colonized regions in Africa, Latin America, South Asia, and elsewhere. Similar patterns could be observed for the flows of modern historical scholarship into China: here a strong influence of publications from the Soviet Union was usually not paralleled by greater levels of receptivity for publications produced outside of the West. At the same time, the commitment to allegedly global modes of inquiry was even further accentuated in Marxist historiography in China. After all, its strictly materialist perspectives had been highly unusual in the Chinese intellectual context and proved more difficult to embed in the idea of continuing epistemological traditions in China.

As a general tendency, early Marxist circles in China tended to emphasize the political implications of history and historiography even more strongly than other progressivist or reform-oriented camps. One of the reasons was that the future visions espoused by this ideology were based on a radical reinterpretation of history. The first widely disseminated account of Marxism in the Chinese public, an article written by Li Dazhao for the journal *Xin Qingnian* (*New Youth*) in 1919, already contained some basic world historical interpretations that would remain influential in the future.[68] In this piece, Li, who had been exposed to Marxist-Leninist ideas during his studies in Japan, argued that the disadvantageous conditions of China were not the result of internal historical developments but rather were largely caused by the exploitative powers of imperialism. As a result, Li held further, the entire country of China had become part of the world proletariat, which in turn qualified it to participate fully in the impending world revolution.

While, generally speaking, the 1920s were a period of unsteady but growing influence of Marxism in Chinese academia, by the 1930s, Marxism had found a stronghold there. In Chinese historiography, the Marxist "historical explanation school" gained more ground and set itself apart from other forms of scholarship that put an emphasis on

---

[67] See, for example, Crozier (1990).   [68] See Meisner (1967).

careful source analysis. Particularly through the "social history controversy," which lasted from about 1929 to 1933, Marxist historical categories such as class struggle and relations of production received more attention in Chinese intellectual circles.[69] During the war years, Marxist historiography was gaining further influence due the prestige which the communists' guerilla war against Japanese troops funneled among growing segments of the Chinese population. Also its revolutionary optimism combined with anti-imperialist outlooks resonated well with the fears and hopes of the time. Still, Marxism and Leninism by no means dominated the intellectual climate and the writing of history.

After winning the Chinese Civil War in 1949, the Chinese Communist Party (CCP) rather quickly took what it deemed to be necessary steps to modernize the country. While the late 1940s had witnessed the liberation of China from imperialist aggressors, the official government rhetoric went, now the country also needed to be rid of domestic suppression. This included a governmental push towards new forms of historical consciousness. For example, as part of campaigns against "feudal" elements and "superstitions," the party also sought to eradicate traditional understandings of time and beliefs in auspicious dates that had survived the introduction of Western time units in 1912.[70] On a more general level, it also attempted to mold the public sphere and the academic system according to its ideological outlook, and in that manner it greatly reshaped the field of historiography.[71]

All in all, throughout the entire period between 1949 and the late 1970s, the study of history as well as public debates about the past were far more tightly controlled by the central government than was the case either beforehand or afterwards. Many leading figures of the field like Hu Shi or Fu Sinian left mainland China, and others such as Guo Moruo or Gu Jiegang were placed under stricter political control. During most years of the Mao period, maneuverability was very limited for efforts to find alternative historical periodizations and master narratives. That there was a desire to do so within the Chinese historians' community, however, can be seen from the repeated movements to emphasize the peculiar nature of Chinese history during times of political relaxation. Among many representatives of the field there was obviously a degree of reluctance to holistically project exogenous concepts, periodizations, and assumptions of historical development onto the Chinese past.

---

[69] See Dirlik (1978), p. 197; and Leutner (1982).   [70] See L. Kwong (2001), p. 188.
[71] Weigelin-Schwiedrzik (1993).

Yet even though the CCP greatly narrowed down the range of national and world historical interpretations circulating in China, some important trends of the Republican period continued.[72] For example, national history defined largely by the territorial confinements of the Qing dynasty remained the basic framework for studying the Chinese past. Furthermore, the "world" studied at history departments stayed a place of unevenly distributed attention. As had already been the case with foreign history during the 1920s, the expertise represented at Chinese world history institutes was far from being global but rather focused on selected parts of the world. While before the revolution of 1949 such divisions had mainly hosted experts in Western European and North American history, now a strong research capacity on Russia and the Soviet Union was being added. This reflected the geopolitical orientation of the new People's Republic of China, which could be felt in many professional realms and academic fields.[73]

While there were some basic continuities, the institutional frameworks of foreign and international history changed significantly after 1949. In fact, the field was profoundly restructured in terms of its institutional bases and chief contents. Most notably it was now that world history officially replaced Western history as a field designation in Chinese curricula.[74] As a field, world history came to enjoy institutional importance in the sense of being established as one of the main branches of academic historiography. Whereas many universities divided history departments into national history and world history sections, the influential Chinese Academy of Social Sciences in Beijing set up a division of ancient, modern, and world history.[75] All in all about a third of China's university-based historians actually belonged to world history institutes or comparable centers dedicated to this specific field.[76]

Initially, after the CCP victory in China the reins imposed on universities could be rather lax, which enabled earlier forms of world historical scholarship to play a certain role after 1949. For example, Lin Judai's textbook *Outline of Modern Foreign History* was reprinted in 1950 and 1951, albeit with a preface cautioning the reader that the work relied heavily on Western perspectives, and its narrative structure was not oriented after Marxism.[77] Also Zhou Gucheng's three-volume world history, which relied heavily on Anglophone scholarship and had been first published before the revolution, was reprinted in 1950 as well as in 1958.[78] The work was partly driven by the idea that it was necessary to include

---

[72] See Q. Wang (2000a).   [73] Q. Wang (2003a).   [74] See L. Xu (2010).
[75] See Q. Wang (2000b).   [76] See Martin (1990), p. 22.   [77] J. Lin (1952).
[78] G. Zhou (1949).

other, non-industrialized parts of the world in the picture, yet at the same time it largely neglected the dark sides of colonialism.[79] For these and other reasons, during the 1960s the work was heavily criticized as an example of scholarship that endorsed Western perspectives on the global past.

Despite such reprints, the 1950s and 1960s were a time in which Soviet party historiography started to dominate Chinese world historical research, with many foreign advisors being involved in the reshaping of academic institutions and the directions or research practiced at them. However, in spite of the period's relatively narrow spectrum of methodological options, many Western world historical texts were translated into Chinese during the 1950s and particularly in the early 1960s – officially in order to demonstrate the superiority of Marxism to the Chinese audience but in reality to foster quite lively and at times rather open debates as well.[80] Still, the school and university history education curricula increasingly reflected the credo in a communist force against imperialist countries.[81] Many important theoretical and historiographical works were being translated from Russian into Chinese in order to bolster the methodological shift China was supposed to take. This also encompassed party propaganda works such as the piece *Dialectical and Historical Materialism*, which was attributed to Stalin himself. Of equal influence was also the *History of the Communist Party of the Soviet Union (Bolsheviks): Short Course*, which had been developed under Stalin and quite randomly defined the stages of historical development Marx had outlined in his *Preface to a Critique of Political Economics*. Moreover, many works produced at the Soviet Academy of Sciences History Institute became highly influential in the Chinese setting, including the four-volume *Course in Modern History* (1950–1953) or the two-volume *Course in the Modern World* (1953–1954).[82]

Rather than following Marx in deriving new theories from the study of history, many Chinese historians vigorously tried to apply his basic ideological framework to Chinese and global contexts.[83] Identifying the same stages of development within an allegedly universal historical scheme was now the main way of connecting the Chinese past to European, Russian, and other historical experiences. In any case, it became almost impossible to study Chinese history without bringing other histories, or certain interpretations of them, into the picture. For instance, in many Chinese works

---

[79] Martin (1990). Generally about world history in China see Q. Chen (1991).
[80] See Q. Wang (2003a), particularly pp. 335–41.
[81] See G. Wang (1975).
[82] See Martin (1990), p. 23. See also H. Zhang (1992).
[83] See Weigelin-Schwiedrzik (1996). See also Pilz (1991).

the Paris Commune of 1871 was portrayed as the first proletarian revolution – as a process which then led to the triumph of the October Revolution less than half a century later.[84] The global condition of imperialism, the same narrative thread continued, made it possible for a socialist revolution to emerge and succeed in an agrarian country such as China. In this context, the Chinese Revolution of 1911 was usually seen as an old-style democratic revolution, which a few decades later was followed by a genuine communist revolution against both imperialism and reactionary rule. As these examples suggest, there were significant intellectual challenges involved in questions such as how to demarcate the transition from slavery to feudalism in the Chinese context or when to define the origins and beginnings of capitalism there.

At certain periods, especially after Mao's failed Great Leap Forward, academics were freer to bend communist theories in order to gain narrative space for the particularities of the Chinese experience. At the time scholars like Jian Bozan, Wu Han and Liu Jie went as far as to argue that, in the Chinese context, class concession rather than class struggle had advanced history.[85] Such a search for new, locally specific conceptual categories was greatly aided by the gradual Sino-Soviet split, which had began during the second half of the 1950s and which slightly later grew into an open political polarization. Now the Chinese government accused the USSR of being a part of imperialist power structures. During that time, there was a greater need for historiographical and intellectual paradigms that would support China's Three Worlds policy and its declared aim to build a block-free alliance guided by the example of the Chinese Revolution.[86]

In this context, the problem of Eurocentrism in world history reemerged as a controversial issue in the academic as well as the general public sphere.[87] Many leading scholars such as Zhou Gucheng were openly pleading to change the focal points set by PRC world historical scholarship standards.[88] One major work appearing during this period was the *Shijie Tongshi* (*General History of the World*), a volume edited by Wu Yujin and Zhou Yiliang, both Harvard-trained scholars who were then teaching in Beijing.[89] The work was influenced by a Soviet text and remained conceptually very loyal to Marxist stages of development; yet it granted the "Third World" in Asia, Africa, and Latin America about a

---

[84] See Martin (1990).
[85] Generally about Chinese historiography during the early 1960s see G. Wang (1975).
[86] See Martin (1990).   [87] See, for example, L. Wang (2002); and L. Xu (2004).
[88] For example G. Zhou (1961). See also Q. Wang (2003a), p. 333.
[89] For more details see L. Xu (2007). About Wu's academic life see Z. Li (1994).

third of its narrative space and hence much more than most world histories that had been published in China before that. Zhou and Wu not only relied on Soviet methodologies but also drew heavily on Geoffrey Barraclough's *History in a Changing World* – a work that they regarded as an alternative to Eurocentric approaches. At the same time, both authors criticized Barraclough for failing to recognize that Western capitalism was doomed whereas the socialist societies had found a key to the future.[90] Since the *Shijie Tongshi* tried to trace universal developments in single societies, the text was quite typical for contemporaneous world historical writing in that it almost completely neglected trans-regional interactions or related topics. In line with these nation- or civilization-centered perspectives, the 1962 edition omitted Chinese history from the picture.

Even though Chinese scholarship had gained more maneuverability during the 1960s, scholars were still required to operate primarily within the confinements of rather strictly applied Marxist periodizations and categories.[91] Many prominent scholars like Gu Jiegang had to go through lengthy processes of supposed "thought reform," leaving few possibilities to further advance independent scholarship.[92] Academic historiography came to a virtual standstill during the Cultural Revolution in the late 1960s, when Chinese universities were closed and scholars such as the renowned world historian Zhou Yiliang were being sent to work in the countryside.[93] Even after the high tides of the Cultural Revolution had receded from the country during the early 1970s and students were being readmitted to universities, scholars remained extremely cautious, which – in addition to material factors in a crisis-ridden society – greatly reduced publication levels in the field. This was so despite the fact that the diplomatic opening of China to the United States and Yugoslavia increased official demand for world historical interpretations.[94]

During that time, political pressure could sometimes lead to rather strange outcomes. For example, in many textbooks Napoleon was largely excluded from the condemnation of feudal sovereigns in order to make it at least implicitly possible to liken Mao's historical impact to his.[95] It was only several years after the end of the Cultural

---

[90] For a discussion in a Western language see Littrup (1989).

[91] A prominent example is the harsh criticism that Fan Wenlan, the director of the Institute of Modern History at the Chinese Academy, received when arguing that Chinese nationhood might be older than its counterparts in Europe. See Q. Wang (2000a).

[92] See, for example, Y. Sun and X. Wang (2000).

[93] Generally on the Cultural Revolution: MacFarquahar and Schoenhals (2006).

[94] See Martin (1990). In 1972, Zhou Yiliang's and Wu Yujin's edited world history was reprinted in China.

[95] For the depiction of French history in China during the past fifty years see Y. Gao (1997).

Revolution that the field started to reconstitute itself as a vibrant research environment.

History and the world in the intellectual climate after Mao

With the Gang of Four arrested and Deng Xiaoping in power, China experienced a strong change in policy making, which over the years amounted to profound transformations in the economy and the society. The focus on mass-based struggles was abandoned in favor of a state vision that saw China only in the initial stages of a truly socialist society gradually evolving towards this objective.[96] Within this framework, socialism and the market economy were no longer deemed incompatible with one another, and in a new way technological modernization became portrayed as a central aspect of Marxism. A blending between a state-led and a liberal economy was seen as the basic program that would propel China towards, as key slogans expressed it, *Socialism with Chinese Characteristics* or the *Four Modernizations* of agriculture, industry, science, and technology. The government's goal was to connect China with economically more "advanced" societies such as Japan and the United States while at the same time not attempting to copy any of them.[97]

The political changes led not only to growing levels of international entanglements but also to a diversification of China, with special economic zones booming in the new market while other regions experienced much lower levels of change. It was particularly in the economically privileged areas where the university system was profoundly affected by Deng's reform policies. In addition to growing levels of funding and international exchange efforts, many key institutes were restructured and important new academic centers founded. For example, in 1979 the World History Institute at the Chinese Academy of Social Sciences was established on the basis of institutional predecessors. Its bimonthly journal *shijie lishi* (*World History*) rather quickly turned into a major forum for introducing and debating a wide range of new world historical and other theories from foreign, mainly Western countries.[98] The influx of new academic theories needs to be seen in the context of the gradual,

---

[96] A. Hu (2008).   [97] See, for example, Shirk (1993); and Z. Wei (2002).
[98] Another important journal was *Shijie yanjiu tongxun* (*World Historical Research Newsletter*).

government-led opening process, which found the support of many university-based historians.[99] The official line under Deng Xiaoping made it a declared aim to develop a new Chinese model by closely cooperating with the rich capitalist countries of East Asia and the West: a new China was to be created as it became connected with the world in new ways. By contrast, political discourses in China during the later Mao years had been centered on the notion of self-reliance and the idea of anti-imperialism in close identification with the Third World.

Given changes of such magnitude, the question of how to conceptualize the relationship between theory and history was gaining new vibrancy among historians. Many representatives of the field opined that in the past few decades Chinese historiography had not sufficiently reconsidered its own methodological foundations, which in their eyes had led to intellectual stagnation.[100] A growing number of scholars now openly went against the rigid theoretical frameworks, analytic categories, and modes of periodization that had characterized much of Chinese historiography during the decades before.[101] Such efforts also found institutional support, with many centers of higher learning now openly supporting theoretical and methodological work.

The quest for new cultures of historiography was greatly aided by the changing ways in which Chinese academic life was connected to other parts of the world. During the 1980s, rapidly expanding academic exchange and cooperation programs brought large numbers of Chinese students to universities abroad, most notably to neighboring countries in East Asia as well as to the West.[102] In addition, an increasing number of Chinese scholars got the possibility to conduct research overseas while at the same time prominent academics from other countries started visiting China. Also several internationally renowned historians came to China and received significant degrees of intellectual attention.[103] While some patterns in this academic internationalization were not too dissimilar from developments during the first decades of the twentieth century, the global academic environment that China reentered in the 1980s differed significantly from the one during the early 1900s. For example, now a substantial number of scholars of Chinese descent had joined the faculty

---

[99] For example Z. Chen (1979).   [100] See, for example, P. Yu (2000). p. 159.
[101] See Weigelin-Schwiedrzik (2005).
[102] For example, the number of US student visas issued to citizens of the PRC swelled from 1,330 in 1980 to 13,414 in 1987. See Orleans (1988), p. 88.
[103] An interesting account can be found in the essays of the prominent Chinese world historian Zhang Zhilian, who is fluent in English and French and introduced the Annales School to China. See Z. Zhang (1995).

of Western universities, particularly in the United States.[104] During the 1980s and early 1990s some leading scholars belonging to this group gained a rather strong presence in the People's Republic's intellectual life. Developments of this kind seemed to make it possible to speak of the "periphery as the center" in the contemporary cultural landscapes of China.[105]

Moreover, unlike during the Republican period, this time there existed highly established academic systems in Hong Kong, Taiwan, and Singapore, which at least partly operated in the Chinese language and were each characterized by specific emphases and research emphases.[106] For example, in Hong Kong the study of transnational encounters and hybridizations has long held a rather prominent place in historical scholarship, which at least can be partly ascribed to its peculiar local history and the widespread bilingualism of its academic sector.[107] In Taiwan, a society that particularly since the early 2000s has experienced heavy political struggles over the question of national independence versus commitment to the idea of Chinese unity, historiography came to experiment with a wealth of alternative spatial approaches. While textbooks were often influenced by the shifting weights of a polarized political landscape, several scholars developed some rather sophisticated theories that sought to transcend the problem of nationhood by situating different aspects of Taiwan in various regional, trans-regional, and global contexts.[108]

The intensification of academic connections between Hong Kong, Taiwan, and the mainland during the 1980s still needs to be historicized in terms of its intellectual flows and impacts on all participating sides. As a consequence of growing contacts more and more academics from the PRC became exposed to alternative forms of Sinophone scholarship. This process was rather slow but steady since the availability of Chinese materials published outside of mainland China was still quite restricted.

---

[104] See Chapters 1 and 2.
[105] W. Tu (1991). Tu's statement also expressed the idea that during much of the twentieth century many facets of Chinese cultural had been better preserved outside the mainland.
[106] Compare Q. Wang (2010a).
[107] See Y. Jin (1997); and S. Guo (2003). About Macao studies as a bridge between European and new Chinese studies: Z. Wu (2002).
[108] See Q. Wang (2002); P. Hsiung (2005); Z. Du (2002); and S. Zhang (2001). Advocating new theoretical rigor and a focus on themes such as the entanglements of Taiwan and Japanese colonialism: M. Lin (1996). Discussing the complexities of writing Taiwanese histories by pointing to the history of US historiography and German local-national histories: H. Zhou (2000). In Taiwan, the journal *Xin shixue* (*New Historiography*) sought to create a forum for cultural, social, and other historical approaches.

At the same time, an increasing number of foreign works now became available in China through translations and had a strong effect on historiography there. New literature available in fields such as social history, cultural history, gender history, and the history from below movement fed into a heightened problem-consciousness about the concepts and categories that had dominated historiography for decades under Mao.[109] In the field of world history, Chinese versions of a wide range of texts by Western world historians such as William McNeill's *Rise of the West*[110] generated intense discussions. Moreover, as universities were creating courses in foreign historiography, several readers appeared, introducing the Chinese audience to Western historiographical traditions and recent developments in various fields, including world history.[111]

The greater presence of foreign historiography at Chinese universities did not, however, usher in another quest to apply a seemingly monolithic and universal Western model to the Chinese context. A large proportion of scholars maintained that the Chinese academic community needed to be highly selective in order to avoid lapsing into another search for exogenous orthodoxy.[112] The idea that China needed to find its own world historical approaches was greatly aided by the obvious diversification of scholarly work and the strong critiques of Eurocentrism in much of the literature that now found its way into China.[113] At the same time, Marxist narratives in general and historical materialism in particular remained highly influential among significant groups of historians in the People's Republic.[114] During the Deng period, many senior figures in the field resorted to reform Marxist world historical narratives that were closer to the critical Chinese positions of the early 1960s than to the latest ideas translated from Western languages.[115] Moreover, many experts in Western history, who decades before had received their training abroad, were not fully willing or able to accept the scope of new theoretical positions that now arrived in Chinese libraries and seminar rooms. In addition, a large number of scholars were not philologically equipped to fully engage with the new literature in its proper contexts and scopes.

In this situation, a certain generation gap emerged, with many younger historians supporting a more profound departure from the historical paradigms that had been prominent in China throughout

---

[109] A more recent perspective is, for example, J. Sun (2004).
[110] See W. McNeill (1963).   [111] For example, S. Guo (1983); and B. Sun (1984).
[112] For example, Z. Chen (2003), p. 131.   [113] See Q. Wang (1991).
[114] X. Liu (1995).   [115] Compare Q. Yue (2003).

much of the twentieth century. It is important to note that their critique was not only directed at post-1949 approaches in China but, more generally, went against alleged patterns of *longue durée* in Chinese culture and historiography. In fact, the tendency to conflate critiques of Maoism and Chinese tradition was an important character trait of the so-called "culture fever" (*wenhua re*), a vague term comprising a wide variety of intellectual currents in universities as well as in the wider public, particularly during the 1980s.[116] At the core of this rather heterogeneous movement stood the idea that, as part of a new beginning, China needed to enter the world and transform its culture accordingly. This was related to a new acclaimed commitment to scientism as well as interest in the Enlightenment and Western humanism – which in some cases was quite consciously portrayed as a return to the agendas of the May Fourth Movement.[117]

In this opinion climate there was a renewed trend to understand the main facets of Western history as a civilizational success and, by contrast, the Chinese past as a history shattered by domestic failures, distortions, and foreign intrusion.[118] An oft-cited example for this intellectual current is the success of a Chinese TV series which had been produced with the support of party reformers and advised by prominent historians like Jin Guantao. As this piece expressed it, a blue, ocean-oriented culture would need to replace the yellow, isolationist traditions of China.[119] In many regards, the series was remarkably loyal to Western stereotypes about the alleged stagnation of Chinese culture, which had been accepted by many Chinese intellectuals during various stages of the twentieth century. Its historical outlook was further based on ideas such as nationhood and civilization, with added components like the assumption that the quest for wealth and hegemony constituted principles that were intrinsic to the human experience.[120] According to the series narrative, the geographical location of China fostered a centralized society, which never sought to free itself from the constraints of nature. By contrast, Europe was portrayed as a civilization harboring nations with open, dynamic, and hence more progress-oriented cultures. Like many historical book publications during that time, this series either downplayed or largely ignored the multi-layered interactions between China and the outside world in the past. In that sense it also clung to a monolithic vision of Chinese history and paid hardly any attention to

---

[116] For more details see J. Wang (1996). See also E. Gu (1999); X. Chen (1995); and X. Zhang (1997).

[117] See, for example, Z. Li and Z. Liu (1987). About contemporary debates on the relationship between the 1920s and the 1980s see J. Wang (1996).

[118] See Q. Wang (2003a), pp. 343ff.; M. Lin and Galikowski (1999); and L. Xu (2002).

[119] See X. Su and L. Wang (1991).   [120] See J. Wang (1996), chapter 3.

the great differences between single Chinese regions such as the inner Asian provinces or the southeastern coastal areas – differences which were partly conditioned by their specific topographies of interaction with areas outside of the Middle Kingdom.

Jin Guantao's decidedly Eurocentric outlooks of history need to be seen in the context of an atmosphere in which more influential voices postulated to open up the political system along with the economy and industry. Around this time an idea which had already been prominent during the Cultural Revolution regained vibrancy and was taken in very different directions. A growing number of academics and public intellectuals became rather vocal in their opinion that the Communist Party had not managed a full revolutionary break with the past but rather continued some problematic traditions. Some suggested that in particular the Cultural Revolution and other traumatic aspects of the Mao period had been shaped by older patterns of suppression and autocracy. In particular, a younger generation at universities tended to regard a rather vaguely defined Westernization as the best way out of what they saw as historically conditioned structures and habits. Tropes of this kind became part of the growing political tensions that started building up within the party and society at large during the second half of the 1980s. These eventually culminated in the student and social protests on Tiananmen Square as well as in many other parts of the country during the spring of 1989.

In many regards the Tiananmen Movement of 1989 and the ensuing crackdown on June 4 needs to be seen as a significant event for China's intellectual and academic flows during the post-Mao period.[121] The events at Tiananmen were followed by much tighter control of intellectual and university life, which included the arrests of many prominent thinkers as well as the termination of academic journals.[122] Still, the period of massive state restraints on intellectual life proved to be rather brief, and many academic publishers and institutes could resume their work a few years later. Nevertheless, in many regards the late 1980s and early 1990s proved to be an important transition period for academic and intellectual circles in China. For instance, since then university faculty and students have widely abandoned their engagement in

---

[121] Today there is are a number of widely divergent interpretations about the origins and the key thrust of the Tiananmen Movement. For example, interpreting Tiananmen mainly as a protest movement: H. Wang and Huters (2003). Seeing it primarily as a democratic movement: Goldman and Nathan (2000).

[122] Among the journals closed was *Lishi yu lilun* (*History and Theory*), edited by Chen Qineng (Beijing). However, two years later Chen was able to open the journal under the new name *Shixue lilun yanjiu* (*Historiography Quarterly*). About the impact of Tiananmen on Chinese historiography see also Iggers, Wang, and Mukherjee (2008).

political activism – a social role that had been at least latently significant ever since the May Fourth period, albeit in very diverse ways.[123] The retreat of universities into academic expertise was greatly aided by other developments, most notably the increasing competition for jobs and social status within the upper and middle echelons of Chinese society, which profoundly changed the outlook of Chinese students to academic life. At the level of faculty, the stratification of universities in China and the stiffening academic competition has led to a greater emphasis on strictly academic skills. In this regard, Chinese universities have grown more similar to centers of higher learning in North America, Western Europe, Japan, and other countries where the idea of political movements emanating from academic life has been reduced, particularly during the past generation. With academic joint ventures mushrooming and Chinese students having become the largest national contingent at US institutions of higher learning, the increasing professionalization of academic life in China may even be partly explained as a result of its internationalization.[124]

At the same time, university life has not been entirely disconnected from society and politics in China but continues to be linked to them in several important regards. These linkages include political constraints: today, academic institutions, teaching, and publications are certainly far from facing the same ideological control as during most periods of the Mao era but governmental watch remains a significant factor to be reckoned with. There are varying degrees of state censorship on intellectual publications, which largely impact the spaces for the enunciation of alternative viewpoints.[125] Somewhat entangled with new forms of government interference – but certainly not fully explicable by them – are the new forms of nationalism and jingoistic visions of history, which have gained more presence across large portions of Chinese society, including many students abroad.[126] Also in some academic circles tropes of humiliation as well as the overall idea that nationalism ought to enhance the power of the Chinese state have become again far more influential.[127] There has also been a growing market for historical book publications and film productions dealing with events such as the Nanjing massacre of 1937 and the Korean War, which appeal to both, forms of victimhood nationalism and triumphant

---

[123] A good depiction of the transition of intellectual life from the 1980s to the 1990s is C. Wang (2003). See also J. Xu (1999), p. 10.
[124] An interesting discussion on related topics: Lee (1998).
[125] See, for example, Brady (2008).
[126] See, for example, Des Forges and L. Xu (2001); Gries (2004); B. Ren (2004); and J. Xu (2005). See also Gries (2004); and M. Zhao (2006).
[127] See X. Chen (1995).

nationalism.[128] While those sentiments reach at least back to the early twentieth century, the growing emphasis on newly gained national strength and global influence[129] needs to be seen as a rather new element.

Certainly, many scholars continue to distance themselves from jingoistic tones one frequently encounters within the wider public.[130] It would also be erroneous to assume that even within smaller sectors of society such as academic circles the nationalism of the 1990s and 2000s is rather monolithic in character: its manifestations range from scholars with a new interest in Chinese "tradition" to theorists operating with postcolonial paradigms.[131] In the face of such diversity, the growing presence of nationalism in Chinese academia and society at large needs to be explained from various angles. While some observers emphasize the government's role in fostering nationalism, others interpret the tides of nationalist sentiments at least partly as an outgrowth of late capitalist development, while a third group sees them primarily as reactions to injustices in international order.[132] In any case, the progressive internationalization of Chinese academia in terms of study abroad opportunities, translations, and the general availability of information about the changing world has not generated a strong academic trend shifting away from national towards transnational outlooks. Rather, a shrinking world contributed to greater levels of support as well as concerns for China's place, image, and reputation within that world.

Compared to the 1980s, levels of identification with Western academic circles have significantly declined within the Chinese intellectual elite.[133] In a parallel development, the impact of intellectual circles which push for a rather sudden political liberalization have declined decisively in favor of a zeitgeist prioritizing incremental change over a return to sudden ruptures and dramatic new experiments.[134] One of the

---

[128] See Fogel (2000); Gries (2007); and Z. Sun (2005).

[129] See Duara (2009), pp. 23ff. Patriotism and consumerism were already entangled during the Chinese Republic; however, the means of commercial activities in this sector were more limited. An example of research on this aspect of Chinese society during the 1920s and 1930s is W. Tsai (2006).

[130] For example, S. Le (2004).

[131] For the 1990s see, for example, Fewsmith (2001); and Schubert (2001).

[132] For the first position see Hughes (2006); for the second one see, for example, K. Liu (2004); for the last position see, for example, Y. Zheng (1999).

[133] See, for example, H. Wang (2003).

[134] M. Zhang and S. Li (1999). Certainly, some groups such as the scholars behind the founding of the influential journal *Xueren* in 1991 (Chen Pingyuan, Wang Hui, and Wang Shouchang) called upon intellectuals to embark on projects of greater self-historicization and -contextualization in order to better understand their roles, influences, and responsibilities in China and elsewhere. This implied a certain degree of distancing from both the role of serving the nation-state and advocacy of a heavily stereotyped "West."

main political fault lines is now running between "liberals," i.e. those intellectuals who support a free market development without major government interference, and so-called "conservatives," who believe in the importance of state intervention in the forces of capitalism. Both groups, however, back central aspects of the current Chinese model, at least in principle. Even within internationally connected academic circles, there is now broader support for the idea that political stability should be maintained rather than China's central government opposed.[135] In a related move, concerns over American cultural imperialism and the injustices of a Western-dominated international system have moved closer to the center of many nationalist discourses in China.[136] There has been a growing problem-consciousness regarding the power gains of the United States and the growth of unilateral politics in the aftermath of the Cold War.[137] In this context, many key protagonists of the Chinese public intellectual scene became highly critical of the Chinese academic climate during the 1980s, which they interpreted as an age of insecurity and unjustified adoration of the West, playing into the hands of cultural imperialism.[138]

Developments of this kind also had a strong effect on academic work, particularly in the social sciences and humanities, including historiography. For example, in many theoretical accounts the acclamation of the West as a source of global models has declined significantly during the past two decades. This had effects on the ways in which the discussions of Western philosophy and political models were being framed. For example, whereas during the 1980s the Enlightenment was primarily discussed as a philosophical achievement with great implications for China, the following decades witnessed rising doubts about its alleged universality.[139] In academic circles, these changing dynamics contributed to an increasing interest in historicizing the Western Enlightenment, which included efforts to shed more light on its diverse or even rather fragmented character.[140] In addition with growing misgivings about the idea of a coherent, universalizable "West," there have been mounting intellectual efforts to develop new theoretical

---

[135] In fact, this trend has raised concern among some Taiwanese scholars – see, for example, Q. Lin (2004).

[136] A critical perspective: J. Xu (1997).

[137] Examples are provided in, for example, Fewsmith (2001).

[138] For example, X. Wang (1996). See also Q. Liu (2001).

[139] See, for example, J. Xu (2000).

[140] An important contribution to this was the book series Xifang xiandai sixiang congshu (Series of Modern Western Ideologies) and Gonggong luncong (Public Debate Series), which both have been published by the Academy of Social Sciences' publishing house (Beijing).

frameworks that would be specifically suited to grasp the Chinese experience.[141] In fact, the growing problem-consciousness of bluntly referring to "the West" as a reference space for Chinese theory and politics[142] is one of the remaining common grounds for an intellectual scenery that has arguably become far more fragmented than it has ever been since the 1920s.

Framing the study of world history: the question of modernity and tradition

In the debates about the future order of China and its international roles, the history of Sino–foreign interactions often figures as a prominent theme. While the idea that China needs to leave the trauma of the past 150 years behind remains highly influential, there has been a renewed interest in the pre-nineteenth-century past. Within academic circles, the so-called "national studies fever" (*guoxue re*) of the 1990s and later was characterized by a growing interest in pre-revolutionary Chinese history and its intellectual traditions.[143] A related trend has also been visible in the general public, where there has been a growing demand for anchors of historical identity, with many TV series focusing on past dynasties and a flourishing market for popular historical works stressing Chinese values and the 5,000-year-long duration of Chinese civilization.[144] Many works and television productions also revolve around the topos of the Qing dynasty's humiliation, and here usually it is no longer China's masses but, more generally, Chinese culture and the state as a whole that are being portrayed as the victims of history.[145]

Needless to say, particularly in academic circles such a reappreciation of the earlier Chinese past, or certain facets of it, opens up a plethora of challenging historical issues. One of them is the rather precarious

---

[141] See, for example, D. Jiang (1996).
[142] For a discussion of the intellectual and political climate during the 1990s see Fewsmith (2001).
[143] See, for example, B. Xu (1999). In this context, also the current project to write a new dynastic history of the Qing dynasty, which at least in some regards would follow the tradition of histories of earlier dynasties, should be mentioned. See, for example, Q. Wang (2009/2010).
[144] About popular historical works and trade books see Spakowski (1999).
[145] See, for example, Hevia (2007). In addition, the critique of culture industries, which had been more prominent in China during the 1980s and 1990s, has lost vibrancy and influence. See, for example, Y. Zhao (2005). For some wider reflections on the memory nexus in China see B. Wang (2004).

question of how to deal with China's revolutionary heritage as well as the political and historical discourses revolving around it.[146] This in turn is related to the problem what aspects of "culture" and "tradition" ought to be salvaged or even revitalized in a country that has experienced dramatic changes, particularly from the times of the Opium Wars onwards. After all, there is the problem that, after more than a century of historical ruptures, the breakdown of central political and religious institutions, of changing state ideologies, global entanglements, and outside influences, it is not easy to define the meaning of being Chinese today. A now rather long history of internationalization makes it almost impossible to reconnect with certain patterns of the Chinese past without considering the problem of China's changing place in the world.

An increasing number of scholars and public voices have been quite eager to relate reflections on a Chinese modernity and future world orders to a renewed esteem for Chinese "tradition," most notably Confucianism. Such efforts to reappreciate Confucianism are usually not accompanied by strong reservations about the idea of modernity as a societal transformation and an intellectual discourse. In this intellectual camp, many scholars espouse the idea that certain patterns and value systems of the Chinese past carry increasing levels of significance precisely because China is experiencing rapid transformations which are often subsumed under the rubric of "modernization."[147] Some thinkers have even voiced the idea that a return of China to its roots of practical rationality would – together with a more elevated status in the world – enable the country to mediate between civilizations such as Islam and Christendom.[148]

The willingness to again value Confucian traditions initially largely emerged from outside of China, for example from scholars in Taiwan, Hong Kong, Singapore, and the United States.[149] However, particularly since the 1990s ideas of this kind have found growing levels of resonance in mainland China – not only among scholars but also in official circles as well as within the wider public.[150] Even though there have been steps to include Confucianism in the general education curriculum and in some symbolic state acts, it remains to be seen

---

[146] A summary of recent contested issues is F. He and P. Yu (2005).
[147] See for example Z. Li (1995); and Chen (2009).
[148] For example Z. Li (2002).
[149] See, for example, Y. Jin and X. Zhou (2003); and W. Tu (1994).
[150] See Y. Tang (2001). See also W. Tu (1996); and Bell (2008). For a critical discussion and contextualization see Mazumdar (2009).

how influential Confucian thought will be in China in the future. While there has been no widespread attempt to reestablish Confucian institutions, far more conferences are now dedicated to this teaching than to Marxism or Maoism.[151] At the same time, the growing interest in Chinese history and thought has thus far hardly been accompanied by a quest to return to allegedly "traditional" narrative styles and modes of historical inquiry.

The question of how to connect China's historical pathways and future trajectories has received significant levels of attention across several segments of society, reaching from the political leadership and the economic realm to the wider public. Within academic circles such overarching themes are too large and the implications for the future of China too great to be monopolized by single disciplines. Furthermore, the debates over *problematiks* of this kind are not clearly divided into opinion camps that could be neatly identified and categorized; rather they constitute highly dynamic environments. These are further complexified by factors ranging from state control to the impact of internationalization and commercialization on public and intellectual life. Due to the intricate nature of these debates, it is only possible to delineate a selection of some core themes, key concepts, and issues of contention. Before focusing on developments within the study of history, I will also take developments in other academic fields such as historical sociology into the picture.

Among the key terms in the debates touching upon China's entanglements with the world were the binary concepts of "modernity" and "modernization." Both terms regained significance through changes in government policies and rhetoric after the death of Mao.[152] Starting from the 1980s, Deng Xiaoping endorsed the concept of "modernization" in order to express the idea that gradual reforms rather than revolutions were the keys to development and progress.[153] At that time, a large number of scholars supported this position in principle and argued that modernization did not fully depend on revolutions, even though the latter were often an aspect of the former.[154] This overall context proved very suitable for the aforementioned opinion that many facets of communism in China had not truly broken with the Chinese past. The proponents of the "feudal communism hypothesis," which

---

[151] On the declining interest in Marxism and the growing presence of Confucianism see, for example, Dirlik (2002b).

[152] A critical discussion of modernization as a new paradigm in Chinese historiography is Dirlik (2000).

[153] Compare D. Tao (1999).   [154] See, for example, X. Wang and J. Li (2003).

gained currency during the 1980s, argued that post-revolutionary China continued many problematic elements of Chinese "tradition," ranging from the high prestige of party leaders to corruption in the bureaucratic apparatus.[155] Going further than that, prominent scholars like Li Zehou even cast shadows of doubt on the revolution of 1911 by suggesting that modern China's emphasis on political struggles had impeded true change in its sociocultural and political fabrics.[156]

In conjunction with the rising interest in historical continuities, a growing number of studies came to question the year 1949 as the clear historical watershed, as which it had usually been described in previous Chinese scholarship. For example, some publications focused on modernizing processes initiated by the Guomindang government prior to the end of the Second World War, while others dealt with the beginnings of a modern Chinese civil society during the late Qing and Republican periods. Furthermore, there was a growing interest in exploring the history of Chinese metropoles, most notably Shanghai, from the perspective of modernization.[157] In academic literature of this kind many central tenets of the Mao period appeared implicitly as relapses of rural or traditional elements destroying many of the modern seeds that had started germinating before 1949.[158]

Even though the expression "modernization" has figured prominently in critical accounts of the Mao years, it is difficult to ascribe the term to any particular political camp or intellectual direction. What often remained a contested issue was the question of what kind of modernization, a primarily economic or also political-democratic one, ought to be pursued. Nevertheless, since the 1980s the idea that China needed to develop along clearly definable trajectories of "modernization" came to be shared by rather large circles across a wide social spectrum, spanning from many government circles to visionaries of radical change. The popularity of linear or even teleological theories of development within Chinese intellectual circles needs to be understood from the specific contexts of Chinese academia and society at large. Not too far removed from the predictions US modernization theorists made during the 1960s, many parts of China quickly developed from pre-industrial economies into consumer societies. Furthermore, positions related to the critical branches of modernization theory could

---

[155] See Sullivan (1993). See also H. Wang (2000a).
[156] Z. Li (1995); and Z. Li and Z. Liu (1987). Others argued that the reform movement of 1898 largely failed because of the impatience on the reformers' side: see, for example, G. Xiao (1995). An insight into the debates of the 1980s is provided by R. Luo (1990).
[157] For a critical perspective see Dirlik (2002b).
[158] See, for example, W. Yuan (1996). See also Cohen (2003).

help to grasp other developments in China such as the widening gap between the rich and poor segments of the population.

In academic circles, the concept of modernization was usually rather closely tied to linear or at least decidedly future-oriented perspectives of history.[159] Some prominent Chinese scholars even referred again to the classics of American modernization theory such as the works of W. W. Rostow or Cyril E. Black.[160] This is not to say that Chinese historians and other social scientists sought to blindly apply US approaches from the 1960s to the contexts of a rapidly transforming China several decades later. For example, scholars like Xu Jilin and Chen Dakai took many elements from US modernization theory but distanced themselves from the idea of modernization as a global spread of a tightly packed Western socioeconomic and cultural model. In addition to specifically Chinese social, economic, and political factors they also stressed the anti-hegemonic patterns which in their eyes characterized the developmental patterns of China as a late modernizer.[161] Others opined that China needed to deviate from earlier patterns and Western models by undergoing two historically separate waves of modernization in one step: industrialization and the turn towards a knowledge society.[162]

While a strong part of the Chinese intellectual community continues to operate with linear perspectives of history, there have been significant changes pertaining to the conceptions of space within which these visions are being embedded. Particularly from the 1990s onwards, Chinese specificities were seen less as a hindrance than as an enabling framework of modernization.[163] For instance, the idea of an "Asiatic Mode of Production" was now often treated more favorably and no longer primarily portrayed as a disadvantageous deviation from Western norms.[164] In addition, theoretical frameworks that were centered on concepts such as multiple modernities or alternative modernities now received some attention in China.[165] In general, there have been growing levels of support for the idea that China's recent experiences constitute a

---

[159] Compare H. Wang (1999).

[160] See the special issue of *Chinese Studies in History*, 43–1 (2009) on *Modernization Theory in/of China*, edited by Q. Wang.

[161] J. Xu and D. Chen (1995). Both authors remain also critical of positions that view Chinese modernization primarily as a response to Western impact.

[162] For example, Y. Zhang and C. He (2004).

[163] See, for example, X. Xie (1994). There was also a rising interest in the so-called Qinghua School around thinkers like Feng Youlan and Zhang Dainian. See W. Hu (1994).

[164] See Karl (2005); and X. Xiang, F. Song, J. Wang, and H. Li (1999).

[165] For example, Q. Li (1990); and R. Huang (1997). See also Sachsenmaier, Riedel, and Eisenstadt (2009).

special, successful path to modernization and development – a path supposedly unique enough to defy any attempt to understand it through theories derived from the West. Also the challenges and constraints of China's modernization are often portrayed as so locally unique that Western models can only be of limited use.

Many theories of modernity have become rather state-centric in nature, often in conjunction with a rather openly expressed desire for international recognition of China's recent developments. In a large number of academic speeches and articles one finds references to the idea that after 150 years of failed attempts, China now found a suitable path to "modernity."[166] This special way, many Chinese historians have come to opine, was eventually guided by a spirit of creative blending between Chinese and other elements. The determination to find a suitable pattern of modernity, the argument often goes, allowed China to blend various ideological elements ranging from socialism to a liberal market economy into a rather unique model. Certainly, the idea of a locally specific form of modernity is not entirely new since it had already been advocated early in the twentieth century by intellectual figures ranging from Liang Shuming and the late Liang Qichao to Wu Mi, Mei Guangdi, and Chen Yinke.[167] Also central tenets of Mao's thought were based on the concept of blending both universal and particular elements into a new mass-based revolutionary ideology, which would propel China into a hitherto unknown future.[168] Yet in one key regard these early and mid-twentieth-century ways of conceptualizing a Chinese form of modernization differ significantly from basically similar themes, debates, and topoi during the past two or three decades.[169] Today, ideas about China's future are often no longer primarily voiced as utopian visions; rather they are based on the assumption that a specifically Chinese model has already proven to be possible.[170]

In many cases, the new prominence of China-centered perspectives was tied to interdisciplinary debates about the changing international environments of the country as it was searching for a new place in the world.[171] Particularly since the 1990s, many scholars have come to point to the parochialism of the Western experience and the untenability of any

---

[166] For example W. Yuan (1996).
[167] See, for example, Sachsenmaier (2007b); and Schneider (1997).
[168] See, for example, Z. Mao (1969). See also Knight (1990).
[169] See B. Lin and Z. Dong (1998).
[170] This is a general character trait of more recent forms of Chinese nationalism, which is different from the main currents of national sentiments during the early twentieth century. See S. Zhao (2004), Chapter 6.
[171] See, for example, X. Chen (2004).

claim to universalism.[172] Moreover, there has been a growing interest in theoretical positions criticizing Eurocentric facets in global academic culture. For example, a certain number of intellectuals, many of whom were later associated with the school of "post-ism" (*houxue*), referred to postmodern and postcolonial criticism when problematizing the influence gaps between globally dominant discourses from the West and intellectual visions produced in China.[173] At the same time, the influx of such theories did not necessarily usher in critiques of nationalist constructs of the Chinese past.[174] In fact, many representatives of the *houxue* movement have themselves operated rather closely to ideas of cultural nationalism. Some branches of Chinese "post-ism" were partly connected with public discourses of national self-strengthening against Western hegemony.[175] For example, some historiographical works that referred to postcolonial thinking sought to accentuate national viewpoints in research fields such as the history of Christianity in China.[176] On a more general level, many currents of the *houxue* movement took rather essentializing positions when trying to recover supposedly timeless Chinese elements from the ruins of the twentieth century.[177] Positions of this kind, however, also found their critics, who argued that discourses of "tradition" need to be seen as part of modernity and not as alternatives to them.[178]

Thinking the global and the local together

Many scholars in China's social sciences and humanities departments have not supported the journeys back to traditional roots. Yet even a broad spectrum of thinkers who remained rather reluctant to grant Confucianism and other Chinese traditions more sociopolitical significance were eager to add more historicity to their visions for China's future. For example, some theorists who described present-day China primarily as the result of hybridization processes between globally

[172] For example Y. Tang (2002). See also B. Li (2001).
[173] See K. Zhang (1999); and L. Zhang (1998), particularly Chapters 5 and 6. An interesting comparison between the reception of postcolonialism in the "Three Chinas" (in Taiwan, for example, postcolonial theories were used to critique the One China Policy) is X. Zhao (2004).
[174] See, for example, C. Wang (2003), particularly pp. 19–21; and X. Zhang (1999).
[175] See S. Zhao (1997).
[176] See, for example, L. Wang (2003).
[177] For example, F. Zhang, Y. Wang and Y. Zhang (1994). About the general background see B. Xu (1998). For more details see Schneider (2001). See also S. Li (1999). At the same time, many scholars in this camp kept a distance from postmodern theories because of their foreign origins.
[178] For example, D. Tao (1999; 1996). In the latter piece Tao also provides a critical discussion of theories that Chinese tradition should enrich Western modernity.

circulating ideologies emphasized that many important elements in the present did not grow only during the nineteenth and twentieth centuries. One very influential historiographical intervention argued that some ultrastable structures of Chinese society such as the commitment of the country's bureaucracy to an ideological system had survived the turmoils of the twentieth century.[179] Several theorists argued that certain social mores stemming from premodern periods were highly compatible with the demands of a modern system. Among such practices, which in their eyes needed to be taken into the picture when reflecting upon the reasons underlying China's rapid development since the 1980s, were alleged cultural peculiarities ranging from a high appreciation of education to a commitment to social harmony within the overall population. Other scholars put more weight on the idea that many foreign ideologies including socialism could only be successful on Chinese soil because it was possible to relate them to compatible elements within China's historical fabric.[180]

Certainly, quite a number of scholars were opposed not only to revivals of tradition but also to the objective of finding living traces of the past in today's China. For example, some critics argued that new intellectual trends of this kind amounted to a reverse Orientalism that sought to overturn imagined hierarchies of world historical thinking without undoing equally problematic modern categories such as the nation or "civilizations" – categories that also needed to be understood as products of the modern age.[181] Yet also within such opinion camps it has now become far more common to emphasize the idea that China's present and future cannot possibly be measured by supposedly universal standards. However, here the specificity of the Chinese model is more likely to be conceptualized as a unique combination of modern and counter-modern elements, with little impact from earlier "traditions." Some prominent social historians, for instance, argued that the official program of reform socialism rests on such a unique combination of seemingly incompatible elements like socialism and a market economy that it in and of itself needs to be regarded as a unique way into the future.[182]

A few thinkers such as, for instance, Wang Hui try to combine internalist and modernist explanations of a specifically Chinese form of

---

[179] G. Jin and Q. Liu (1993). The book further developed some ideas both authors had already published during the 1980s.

[180] For example G. Jin (1994).

[181] For example, H. Yu (2001); and B. Zhang (2001). See also Zurndorfer (1997).

[182] For example Z. Wei (2002).

modernity into one congruent framework.[183] Wang's thinking is at least partly characterized by a reluctance to think in terms of exclusive dichotomies, which in turn allows him to apply different, seemingly incompatible perspectives on the question of Chinese modernity. Hence on the one hand, he regards the late Qing dynasties and the two Chinese republics through the guiding concept of a worldwide crisis of modernity characterized by a complex interplay of repressive mechanisms and counter-movements.[184] On the other hand, Wang points particularly to the Song dynasty as the origin of a proto-modern Chinese state formation, which shared certain character traits such as the centralization of government, economic rule, and early facets of nationalism with what later was to become the Western experience. At the same time, Wang opines that there have been continuities from the Song dynasty far into the twentieth century which were more specific to the Chinese experience. For example, according to him older concerns for political order and common wellbeing resonated with core agendas of Chinese socialism.

On the basis of such dual perspectives Wang approached the idea of possibilities for China that would go beyond the options of blindly endorsing or opposing seemingly worldwide programs like "modernity" or "tradition." While warning of nativism as a modern ideology, Wang nevertheless invites the academic community to uncover facets of Chinese history that in his eyes had been repressed by the forces of modernity. In this context he emphasizes that such an enterprise could not only lead to a greater awareness of peculiar sociocultural habits and economic patterns but also to possibilities of critical reflection on modernizing processes – intellectual possibilities that had been rendered subaltern during the late Qing dynasty and after. Wang argues that particularly some core ethicopolitical visions of neo-Confucianism developed during the Song dynasty would open possibilities for new forms of critical intervention. In contrast to most twentieth- and early twenty-first-century criticism of modernity and the West, the latter would not be framed around categories such as the nation, development, or progress. Such a search for alternative intellectual standpoints, Wang maintains, would not be anti-modern in nature. In this context, his understanding of neo-Confucianism as part of a Song proto-modernization process carries particular significance. Rather than advocating a blunt program of returning to "tradition," his intellectual visions aim more at

---

[183] For a contextualizing discussion see Murthy (2006).
[184] See especially H. Wang (2004–2007). See also H. Wang (1998).

reconnecting with at least the critical potentials of a largely abandoned Chinese historical path that could be labeled as proto-modern.

Given this critical spirit and emphasis on the problem that most Chinese critiques of modernity remain framed by Western categories and concepts, Wang Hui's thinking has deviated from the theories of Luo Rongqu, a prominent Beijing University historian who died in 1996 and whose work on Chinese modernity and modernization remain widely influential today. In several of his writings Luo sought to uncover some continuities across the ruptures and revolutions of Chinese modern history.[185] Furthermore, he shifted away from the idea that the constitutive forces of Chinese modernity had primarily emanated from Western or Soviet models. Quite to the contrary, Luo opined, the recent developments in East Asia had revealed the limitations of these models, which had long dominated Chinese ideas of progress and development.[186] While critical of the political and economic role that Japan had played in the region during the first half of the twentieth century, Luo sought to revive the idea that this first modernizer in East Asia had already provided a very successful example of blending traditional and modern elements into a new combination. In a subsequent but related step, he encouraged Chinese historians to pay more attention to the specific conditions and forces of the Chinese past, which – together with outside influences – have contributed to its distinctive historical pattern over the past two centuries.

In his own quest to outline the basic pattern of a distinctively Chinese path into modernity, which would follow the lines neither of twentieth-century socialism nor of capitalism, Luo accepted the idea that in principle certain Chinese customs and traditions could contribute to a new form of capitalism.[187] Like other thinkers, in this context he explicitly referred to such Confucian values as duty-consciousness, group responsibility, and the importance of education. Nevertheless Luo thought Confucianism as a holistic moral, societal, and institutional system to be incompatible with any modernization process. Rather than conceptualizing Chinese modernity *in spe* as an encounter between a supposedly static China and a mono-dynamic "West," he thus suggested that China's modern history had already been the result of complex local and translocal influences. According to Luo, China's future would also

---

[185] See R. Luo (2004); and R. Luo (1992). See also G. Jin and Q. Liu (2001).

[186] In this context it is worth noting that there has been a lively debate on Hong Kong's and Taiwan's contribution to the trajectories of China since the late 1970s. See, for example, G. Liao (1993).

[187] For some philosophical interpretations of Confucian capitalism see, for example, H. Yeh (2003). Critical of the idea of Confucian capitalism: H. Wang (2000b).

need to be envisioned as a hybridization process between highly diverse elements, ranging from the opposing ideologies of socialism and capitalism to local Chinese mores. In other words, while he maintained that Chinese modernity was the result of global interactions, Luo nevertheless accentuated its peculiar character.[188] His pluralistic visions of modernity, however, did not lead Luo to question the idea of modernization as a transformative process that would follow the same basic patterns across space and time. More specifically, Luo assumed that world history had thus far witnessed three main phases of modernization, each of which was centered in different geographical regions:

From the late eighteenth-century beginnings of the Industrial Revolution in England to the middle of the nineteenth century emerged the first wave of the world's industrialization and modernization. The center was in Western Europe. From the second half of the nineteenth century to the beginnings of the twentieth century emerged the second wave of the world's industrialization and modernization. The center extended from Western Europe to Eastern Europe and North America; also territories in Latin America were greatly influenced. At the same time it spread across the European continent and spread to East Asia, where it was uniquely successful. After the Second World War, from the 1950s to the 1980s, emerged the third wave of the world's industrialization and modernization. This time the great wave extended to big regions in Asia, Africa, and Latin America, but the center was in East Asia.[189]

While this model of spreading waves may appear to be based on a uniform understanding of global change, Luo repeatedly stressed that in his view modernization was not solely an outcome of European agency, which is why modernity acquired regionally specific characteristics. In line with this assumption, Luo argued that future world historical scholarship should portray less the European expansions of the sixteenth century but rather the shrinking global spaces of the industrial and communications revolutions as the origin of modernization as a global force.[190] He primarily understood the transformations of "modernization" as culturally neutral forces that are related to specific economic systems and technological developments.

Other scholars shared this basic interpretation of modernization,[191] and many understood also the term "globalization" (*quanqiuhua*), which has become more popular in historical and social scientific publications,[192] along similar lines. In many cases, globalization has been

---

[188] R. Luo (2004), Chapter 6.   [189] R. Luo (2004), pp. 211–12.
[190] R. Luo (2004), Chapter 3.
[191] For example C. Qian, Y. Yang, and X. Chen (1997).
[192] See Q. Wang, "Globalization, Global History, and Local Identity in Greater China", in www.japanfocus.org.

portrayed as the outcome of modernization, and as a process that the West will ultimately not be able to control, hence granting greater levels of agency to China and other parts of the globe.[193] Similar ideas have become important paradigms in the study of transformative processes and structures, which are often interpreted as important components of modernization. For example, the historiography of capitalism has further accentuated regional differences in areas such as business–government relations or the distribution between private and public property.[194]

Not unlike Luo Rongqu's thought, many additional theories surrounding the concepts of modernization and globalization in China have been based on the assumption that a continued internationalization would ultimately benefit the Chinese society, economy, and polity. For example, whereas some observers primarily deal with globalization as a development opportunity providing poorer nations with the ability to narrow international power gaps, others regard it as a process that may eventually result in the democratization of China, or at least might remove alleged social habits such as despotism and nepotism from its social fabrics.[195] While there are many additional visions, it is safe to conclude that, in the Chinese case, usages of the term "globalization" are tilted towards positive connotations.[196] For example, some scholars have come to argue that, in a globalizing world, China will gain more transformative influence while it itself will also be the subject of significant forces of change.[197] Luo Rongqu has mused on the question of whether the new Chinese model could not only be seen as a successful local adaptation to global transformations but rather as a system that had many advantages over other forms of modernity – advantages which eventually would alter the structures of global politics and the economy.[198]

Generally speaking, the idea that global integration puts much pressure on the nation-state did not gain a high currency in China. The Zhejiang historian Wang Jiafeng's words "the more national, the more global" express a worldview that is shared by many of his colleagues in

---

[193] See, for example, D. Yao (2002); P. Yu (2001); W. Yu (2002); and G. Feng (2000).
[194] A summary can be found in X. Xiang, F. Song, J. Wang, and H. Li (1999).
[195] An example for the latter position are C. Pu (2002); H. Li (2003); T. Cao (2003); and X. Li (2003). For a more general discussion see Y. Yan (2002).
[196] See, for example, K. Liu (2004). More generally on the topic of the impact of globalization on China: Y. Zheng (2004). An example for a critical interpretation of globalization as a force eroding cultural differences is S. Li and J. He (2000).
[197] For example, P. Pang (2000).
[198] For example R. Luo (2004), Chapter 4.

mainland China.[199] This is significantly different from many societies in the West, where both advocates of neoliberalism and their critics basic- ally shared the idea that the growing worldwide entanglements of the economy and financial sectors shake many frames once held by the nation-state.[200] Yet the centers of gravity in Chinese debates on global- ization and modernization also deviate from the intellectual majority opinions in many poorer and often formerly colonized societies. Here a large number of thinkers and politicians have come to argue that the forces of globalization actually strengthen patterns of dependency and exploitation rather than mitigate them.[201]

As during the wave of revolutions and reform movements at the beginning of the twentieth century, many Chinese intellectuals see growing levels of global connectedness and nation-building not as two mutually exclusive processes but rather as complementary trans- formations. In fact, Deng Xiaoping's and his successors' "open door policy" is credited by many intellectuals and large sectors of the general public with successfully reaching the century-old goal of national "wealth and strength" (fuqiang). This, however, should not be taken as uncritical endorsements of governmental policies – in fact, groups of intellectuals such as the New Left (xin zuopai) have become more vociferous in their criticism of China's current sociopolitical and eco- nomic trajectories.[202]

Nevertheless, in a climate of opinion which is, generally speaking, in favor of nationalism and globalization at the same time, alternative political imaginaries to the nation as a historically grown and territorially defined body do not play a very prominent role.[203] At the same time, the academic landscapes of China continue to change and diversify at a fast pace, and many research movements have emerged that ultimately will prove to be hardly compatible with nation-centered visions of the past. Before taking an exploratory journey through the historiographical environments of China, it is first important to take some institutional changes into consideration, particularly the ones which have an impact on historiographical research and teaching.

---

[199] J. Wang (2009), p. 92.

[200] For Anglophone debates about globalization during the 1990s see Guillén (2001).

[201] For an insight into some of these positions see, for example, Jameson and Miyoshi (1998); and Bello (2002).

[202] Generally on public political cultures: T. Shi (2000).

[203] Also the greater visibility of minority politics has not weakened the dominance of an ethnic nationalism based on a strong territorial consciousness. See, for example, Karmel (2000); and Leibold (2006).

World history during the 1990s and after

World history has a strong presence at Chinese universities and even high schools.[204] Almost all history departments contain world history as one of their subdivisions, and according to one estimate during the 1990s about 40 percent of all Chinese historians qualify as world historians.[205] This number might be too high[206] and, moreover, one should be aware of the fact that "world history" is institutionally defined as the history of the outside world. This means that all historians of Japan, Europe, Africa, and other parts of the world qualify as "world historians," even though their own research is often confined to single-nation states. Thus the regional expertise of the vast majority of "world historians" is the West, with Russia and the Soviet Union very strongly represented among an older generation of Chinese scholars.

While there have been some changes, the institutional parameters of world history in China continued endorsing nationally framed views of history throughout the 1990s and even after. Given these official parameters of the field, the Chinese past has long remained marginalized or even excluded from much of the world historical activities. This is still, for example, typically the case in the compulsory "general world history" courses where, as a recent assessment found, the history of China usually continues to play a very subordinate role.[207] In general, the current structural conditions of historiography provide few incentives to move across the divisions between world history and Chinese history by accentuating connections and interchanges. Consequently, as Xu Luo astutely observes, a good number of "China's 'world' historians believe that the responsibility of writing world history rests on their shoulders and theirs alone, and they have not reached out to cooperate with Chinese history specialists."[208]

Nevertheless there have been an increasing efforts to build bridges between the study of China and the world at large.[209] On the one hand, many scholars have come to pay more attention to the various levels of interconnections and interdependencies between China and the

---

[204] On the rise of required world history and related courses in Chinese high schools since the late 1980s (roughly 40 percent of the curriculum) see Jones (2005).

[205] S. Qi (1994).

[206] According to Q. Wang, the number of Chinese university-based historians working on the outside world is closer to 25 percent. See idem (2010a).

[207] See J. Xia and L. Wan (2006). See also C. Qian (2009).

[208] L. Xu (2007), p. 342.

[209] Particularly during and after the 1990s, the problem became a subject of debate in the Chinese community of world historians. See, for example, C. Hu (1995), p. 128.

world.[210] On the other hand, analogous to developments in the literature on modernity and modernization, there have been new attempts to gain distinctively Chinese visions of world history. During the mid-1990s, both routes were taken by an elder statesman in the field of world history, Wu Yujin, who in 1962 had served as the co-editor of an influential world history series and who had published widely on world historical themes, ranging from the relationship between nomadic and farming cultures to industrializing processes. In a series of articles Wu went against the tradition of understanding world history largely as an integrative discipline which would merely assemble different national experiences.[211] Rather, for him the field would now need to specifically focus on those processes and transformations that intensified mutual exchanges. By conceptualizing world history as an objective process of growing entanglements and not primarily as a perspective, Wu certainly followed Hegelian and Marxist patterns of thinking about the past. Yet at the same time he was adamant about overcoming the heritage of universal historical perspectives, which in his eyes had characterized much of the social sciences and humanities in twentieth-century China. He encouraged his colleagues to try to develop Chinese narratives of the power constellations, dependencies, and transfers that had characterized essential aspects of world historical processes. For him, Sinified visions of Marxism were one of the key elements that could frame such potential Chinese outlooks.

Together with Qi Shirong, Wu Yujin edited a new three-volume series that was published posthumously in 1994 under the plain title of *World History*.[212] In terms of the textual space granted to the non-Western world, the 1994 edition was even more Eurocentric than the edition of 1962.[213] Yet there were various important changes, reflecting some key political developments that China had experienced after the 1970s. Most notably, Wu's and Qi's work followed some main currents of Chinese scholarship by abandoning the idea of revolutions as keys to understanding historical watersheds. While they did not break with the idea of the fifteenth and sixteenth centuries as the dawn of a new world historical epoch instigated by Europe, in their text Western revolutionary moments such as the English Bourgeois Revolution no longer figured as important world historical landmarks. As an alternative, much more narrative space was granted to more drawn-out changes such as the

---

[210] For example, during the early 1990s: Z. Li, M. Gao, and X. Tang (1991).
[211] See, for example, Y. Wu (1995); and Z. Li (1994). See also L. Xu (2007).
[212] Y. Wu and S. Qi (1994). For a critical discussion see L. Xu (2007).
[213] See L. Xu (2007).

"agricultural revolution" or the "industrial revolution" in order to support a linear yet at the same time more gradual understanding of the forces of history. In line with this approach, the work did not treat the October Revolution but, more vaguely, the time around the turn of the twentieth century as an approximate transition between the periods of contemporary and modern history.[214] According to Qi's and Wu's text, contemporary history was characterized by a shrinking importance of space due to technological and scientific developments as well as, later, the breakdown of colonial order.

Moreover, both authors emphasized that the forces leading to translocal integration in the contemporary period should not be understood as vectors pointing to an increasingly assimilated world but rather as global transformations manifesting themselves in locally, respectively nationally specific ways.[215] For the purpose of analyzing this interplay between localism and globalism, Wu and Qi suggested that one should operate with a combination of vertical and horizontal perspectives. The former were supposed to trace long historical constellations and changes within single nations, and here the categories of analysis remained closely oriented after Marxist concepts such as modes of production. The latter focused on the growing intensity of transregional exchanges, influences, and common transformations which, according to the authors, caused hitherto separate histories to be increasingly entangled with each other. Through these combined horizontal and vertical perspectives China grew highly present in Wu's and Qi's work, and some of its interconnections with East Asia and the world at large were being accentuated.

As can be easily seen from its guiding ideas and key tropes, the *World History* of 1994 was rather congruent with the historical outlooks espoused by theorists of modernity like Luo Rongqu. Heading in similar directions, other recent world historical approaches which share an emphasis on the idea of global transformations have brought concepts such as modernity and modernization into the foreground. For example, scholars like Qian Chengdan, a prominent world historian based in Beijing, argued that during the past few hundred years modernization processes constituted the core of world historical developments.[216] Yet the prominence of the modernization paradigm has not necessarily

---

[214] In fact, the work dedicates an entire volume to "contemporary history": Y. Wu and S. Qi (1994).

[215] See also F. Dong (1996). For the following see L. Xu (2007).

[216] C. Qian (2003). Arguing that intercultural connections have always been a part of world history: Y. Zhang (2001).

sparked a movement to decenter world historical outlooks pertaining to all periods of time. In fact, in the historiography of premodern periods it frequently confirmed some core Eurocentric assumptions. For example, while accentuating the idea of modernization as a powerful global transformation, many standard world history texts in China tended to portray early modern European history as advanced and progressive while depicting the same period in East Asia, Africa, and other parts of the world as ages of stagnation.[217] A related and common topos is the portrait of China as the world's most continuous civilization, which started falling behind during the sixteenth century.[218] Moreover, in many works Europe is presented as the cradle of modernity and capitalism, and other parts of the world are primarily treated in terms of their contacts and experiences with an expanding Europe.[219] In world historical writing approaches such as the concept of early modernities, which offer a very different interpretation of capitalism, public spheres, and standards of living in pre-nineteenth century China, have thus far had only a limited impact.

Still, while Europe is often described as the epicenter of global modernization processes, in China there is now more support for historians who no longer accept the view of Europe as the sole creator of the modern world.[220] In addition, most works at least tacitly endorse the view that modernization, as it becomes global, does not equal Westernization. Like in the case of the modernization literature, many world historical accounts are now primarily written from the perspective of a country that has supposedly now found an adequate way of combining modernity and tradition, the self and the West, as well as the global and the local. In world historical texts one increasingly encounters the idea that, decades after the decolonization period, the world reached a stage of emerging multipolar patterns of global power and the world economy. Due to intellectual developments and changing political expectations of this kind, there is now a rising interest in the history of China's entanglements with other world regions. Since modernity is no longer primarily conceptualized as a universal transformation but rather as a complex pattern of global and local interactions, for many historians it no longer makes sense to categorically separate the history of the "advanced world" from the study of China.

---

[217] For example Y. Wu and S. Qi (1994).   [218] X. Li (1997).

[219] For example R. Pan and C. Lin (2000). The work starts with the seventeenth-century English revolutions and ends with the Russian Revolution. Most narrative space is devoted to intra-European history, and the rest of the world is mainly covered in terms of colonialism or anti-colonial struggles. See also Z. Li (1996).

[220] See, for example, W. Ruan (2001). See also L. Xu (2007), particularly pp. 342–45.

As part of this process, educational policy making has made efforts to put more emphasis on the study of interconnections between nations and world regions. For example, in 2000, history curriculum standards added more emphasis on educational goals such as respect for other civilizations and holistic perspectives (*zhengtishi*) as an alternative to dualistic models based on the idea of Western agency and Chinese responses.[221] In the 2003 curriculum standards additional efforts were undertaken to remove the barriers between Chinese and world history.[222] Among other points, it was recommended that chronological units rather than world regions form the subjects of single chapters, allowing for more narrative possibilities of including translocal interactions into the picture.[223]

Likewise, the Chinese academic community has witnessed significant institutional changes, which are aimed at fostering new forms of transnational and world historical scholarship. For example, at Capital Normal University (Beijing) a Research Center for Global History was founded in 2004,[224] and several courses have been created in this field. According to some of its key protagonists in China, "global history" (*quanqiu lishi*) is supposed to overcome the divide between world history (*shijie lishi*) and Chinese history and, in addition, move scholarship towards more decentered modes of analysis.[225] The fact that the driving forces behind these developments at Capital Normal University are no solitary figures in the Chinese academic landscape is evidenced by a recent survey conducted among thirty-seven faculty members, each representing individual institutions in China. Here thirty-five respondents indicated that they had familiarized themselves with the field of "global history," which they see – among other points – as a step towards overcoming Eurocentric narratives.[226] In such a changing atmosphere, there was a favorable reception of translations of recent Western global historical textbooks, which tried to abandon the idea of epicenters of world historical developments and were rather centered on topics such as cross-regional interactions.[227]

---

[221] See Y. Jiang and K. Wu (2005); and A. Huang (2000). See also Jones (2005).
[222] This was even more decidedly the case in the Shanghai curriculum standards, which differed from the national ones.
[223] See H. Che (2004).   [224] See Q. Wang (2010b); and X. Liu (2007).
[225] See W. Zhang (2008). See also M. Cheng (2009).
[226] See J. Xia and L. Wan (2006).
[227] For example, this was the case with Bentley and Ziegler (2002). In Chinese, the text was published under the title *Xin quanqiu shi* (*New Global History*), (2007). The modern history part of S. Qi (2006–2007) is in many regards oriented after the narratives in Bentley and Ziegler (2002). On Bentley's reception in China see also Q. Wang (2010b).

While the term "global history" has gained enormously in popularity, there are significant differences in the ways in which the expression is being used in the current academic literature. For instance, whereas some authors operating with the term show their affinity to postcolonial theories, others use the same concept when applying rather linear or developmental visions to the study of history.[228] In the face of such a variety of interpretations, it is small wonder that many authors do not carefully distinguish between "global history" and "world history" and use both expressions as rather interchangeable with one another. Despite some efforts to the contrary, the present research landscapes in China are certainly not characterized by a clear programmatic divide between world history and global history.[229] A large number of scholars agree with the objective to pay more attention to transnational entanglements but they prefer to use the term "world history" or even other field designations. Hence, as in Germany and the United States, in Chinese scholarship the field of global history needs to be seen as part of a vibrant research landscape whose terms and trends are tightly interwoven with each other.

It would be erroneous to assume that in the Chinese context, field designations such as "global history" are treated as largely congruent with critical perspectives of nationhood or nationalism. In fact, some prominent and politically influential scholars like Yu Pei, the former director of the World History Institute at the Chinese Academy of Social Sciences, have come to operate with the term "global history"[230] and yet at the same time sought to actively defend nation-centered perspectives. In Yu's eyes, Chinese world historical writing should beware of trends that could challenge the idea of a contingent, largely autochthonous Chinese past.[231] Based on the idea that the nation is the most apt container for most historiographical investigations, Yu Pei and some other scholars argue that the conceptual turns of world historical thinking in China should finally overcome the student–teacher relationship, which had long characterized much of Chinese intellectual outlooks towards the West.[232] They hold that, while China in the future would

---

[228] In some cases, Chinese global outlooks on history are portrayed as a commitment to historical materialism and the interest of the global proletariat. For example, L. Wang (2002).

[229] See, for example, the following anthology of forty theoretical articles that were originally published between 1990 and 2006: P. Yu (2007b). The articles are grouped into three main sections, dealing mainly with "Marxism and world history," "globalization and history," and "global outlooks on history." The volume's editor has been a prominent proponent of patriotic approaches to world history.

[230] P. Yu (2007b).   [231] P. Yu (2004). Also: P. Yu (2009).

[232] P. Yu (2003); and P. Yu (2001).

need to further open itself to flows and ideas from abroad, its world
historians also ought to strengthen their efforts to overcome Eurocentric
traditions in academic scholarship.

In many cases, demands for new world historical perspectives of this
kind have been tied to the idea of a changing world order and China's
rising status in the international system.[233] The notion that historical
studies needed to return from the cosmopolitan interests of the culture
fever period to the service of the nation-state has also been promoted
heavily by the National Education Commission and the patriotic
education (*aiguozhuyi jiaoyu*) campaigns starting from the early
1990s.[234] Yet it would be wrong to assume that government pressure is
the only force behind the strong role of national outlooks in Chinese
historiography. As already discussed, it is for a wide variety of reasons
that concepts such as globalization or modernization are widely used
among Chinese scholars, however without being understood as processes that challenge ideas of nationhood or civilizational belonging.
Equally marginal in the current Chinese academic literature are theories
pointing to the modern, transnational, and constructed character of
national as well as civilizational identities. In many publications, the
concept of the nation and civilization in China are treated as rather
timeless.[235] Nevertheless, many developments within a rich research
landscape make monolithic visions of national history appear increasingly problematic.

Continuing and changing spaces

Chinese historiography is part of a rapidly changing academic environment. During the past few decades, the Chinese university system has
experienced expansions and reforms that in terms of scale do not stand
far behind the transformations of the early twentieth century. The government has invested heavily in widening the academic sector, which
had been a rather barren landscape in the aftermath of the Cultural

[233] See, for example, J. Hou (2000). A summary of further recent debates is provided by
F. He and P. Yu (2005).
[234] See S. Zhao (2004), Chapter 6; and Spakowski (2005).
[235] Moreover, in quite a number of publications the concept of the Chinese nation and
civilization are treated as quite synonymous with one another. In the case of Chinese
history this is an easier step compared with, for example, world regions such as Europe
or the Middle East. Here the imagined topographies of national and civilizational
discourses were usually rather dissonant.

Revolution.[236] Particularly since the mid-1990s, the pace of growth has been staggering, with the number of enrolled students climbing from about 860,000 in 1978 to 30 million students in institutions of higher learning in 2010.[237] Much of the impetus behind this development is the buildup of mass education with the projected goal of granting about 40 percent of a generation access to college education by 2020. In line with the guiding principles of "Dengism," such steps to strengthen the national education system have been closely related to internationalization efforts. For example, while about 350,000 Chinese students went abroad between 1978 and 2000, during the first decade of the twenty-first century the number has risen to 1 million.[238] Parallel to broadening the university sector, the government decided to help to build new centers of academic excellence. For example, several institutions of higher learning were selected as "international-level universities" and are now endowed with special funding opportunities in order to make them globally more competitive.[239]

The main thrust of China's academic policies has been aimed at the natural and applied sciences but the social sciences and humanities have also been greatly affected by them. For instance, the rising tides of intellectual migration, coupled with the growing proportion of students returning to China, has started altering the personal experience base of many scholars. In 2005, a survey of thirty-seven world history institutes at Chinese universities revealed that about 42 percent of their faculty received at least parts of their training abroad,[240] mainly in Western countries. In addition to intensifying academic mobility levels, efforts have been stepped up to include segments of Chinese universities in transnational academic structures. For instance, the department of history at Fudan University in Shanghai recently joined a transnational consortium in the field of global studies, which entails student and faculty exchanges.[241] Worth mentioning also is the plethora of cooperations between graduate programs in history in China and other countries.[242] Furthermore, after the opening of

---

[236] G. Yan (2009).
[237] See Kirby (2008). The sharp growth of faculty positions has already had an impact on research. The number of publications produced at Chinese universities and research centers is already the second-highest in the world, after the United States.
[238] "Chinese students studying abroad exceed 1.39 million," People's Daily (March 26, 2009).
[239] Guthrie (2006).   [240] See J. Xia and L. Wan (2006).
[241] See www.uni-leipzig.de/gesi/emgs.
[242] See, for example, the exchange program for graduate students in transnational and world history between Beijing University and Purdue University, USA: http://baokao.

foreign universities in China was permitted in 2003, several foreign or Sino-foreign institutions of higher learning have opened on Chinese soil.[243] In addition, an increasing number of Chinese historians have come to participate in research networks forming both at a global and an East Asian, level and contribute to transnationalizing the modalities of scholarly cooperation.[244] Promising developments in the field of world history, where scholars from the Chinese mainland have played an important role, include the founding of the Asian Association of World Historians at Nankai University in Tianjin in 2008, which held its inaugural conference a year later in Osaka.[245]

While the number of scholars with a transnational education background is rising across wide segments of the Chinese university sector, the possibilities for international collaboration are still rather unevenly distributed among Chinese scholars. In the past, this situation has raised some concerns that the gap between a thin veneer of global players and the main body of historians in China would continue to grow wider.[246] Yet at least at research-oriented universities, the growing availability of research and travel funds as well as the rising mobility of faculty and students is likely to reduce the disparities between globally connected academic players and scholars whose action radius does not transcend China's borders. If current trends continue, these disparities are unlikely to be categorically different from patterns in countries such as Germany and the United States.

The ranks of Chinese scholars maintaining close ties with universities abroad are an important social force behind the flows of concepts, ideas, and individuals across China's borders.[247] Certainly, the growth of

---

china-b.com/lxrz/20090210/7812_1.html; the graduate exchange program between Zhongshan University and Waseda University, Japan: http://history.sysu.edu.cn/bencandy.php?fid=22andid=196l; and the dual bachelor degree program with York University in Canada, which among other fields also entails history: http://baokao.china-b.com/lxrz/20090210/7812_1.html.

[243] The University of Nottingham Ningbo was the first Sino-foreign university in China with approval from the Chinese Ministry of Education. See www.nottingham.edu.cn.

[244] For a discussion of some East Asian examples such as the "Global History and Maritime Asia" project see Akita (2008).

[245] See www.let.osaka-u.ac.jp/seiyousi/AAWH/index.htm. In addition, the National University of Singapore has become a very influential center of activity fostering inter-Asian exchanges and research conceptualizing Asian regions in global and regional contexts. For an overview of university-level research institutes at the National University of Singapore see www.nus.edu.sg/research/university.php.

[246] Problematizing this gap, for example: Leutner (2003).

[247] See, for example, Cheek (2007).

internationally collaborative research has not necessarily led to a trans-nationalization of historical paradigms: in some cases it even reified nation-centered perspectives of the past. Developments of this kind could, for example, be observed in the international historical reconciliation efforts surrounding the memory of the Second World War and Japanese imperialism.[248] Decidedly national perspectives also prevail in the trilateral textbook commissions between China, Japan, and South Korea that have existed since the early 1980s. A first joint textbook was published in all three languages in 2005[249] but the responsibility for writing single chapters remained in the hands of national commissions. This setup contributed to a book which is still divided rather clearly into nationally specific viewpoints and hence does not move very far towards border-crossing perspectives.[250]

As a general trend, however, the growing connections between Chinese and other universities have resonated well with some changes in historiographical cultures in the People's Republic. While it would be too simplistic to assume that some ill-defined "international influence" unilaterally transformed Chinese historical scholarship, its growing methodological diversification certainly needs to be seen in conjunction with the increasing international connectedness of academic life. During the past two decades, historiography in China has become a very pluralistic field, with many different scholarly groups pursuing research interests that may run outside the currents of the disciplinary mainstream. Going beyond that, numerous subfields and academic interest groups have started establishing their own modes of trans-national cooperation.

For example, while nation-centered perspectives remain dominant within the Chinese historians' community, there has also been a rising interest in investigating East Asia as a historical region. Some studies leave strictly international perspectives behind and move towards the study of transregional entanglements, for example by exploring the Eastern Sea rim as an interactive space. Parts of this literature outline possibilities for further investigating zones of interaction that cannot possibly be grasped from nation-centered perspectives.[251] Also the discussion of premodern economic or cultural patterns of interaction in East Asia has witnessed a surge of new methodological

---

[248] See, for example, Q. Ren, L. Hu, and Y. Wang (2004). For additional examples see Spakowski (2008).
[249] Dongya sanguo jinxiandaishi gongtong bianxie weiyuanhui (2005).
[250] See Spakowski (2008).
[251] For a methodological discussion see Z. Ge (2010). See also R. Wang and L. Song (1999); Y. Shi and L. Hu (2005).

approaches.[252] In recent years, the same has been true for topographies of interactions within East Asia during the past two centuries, some of which have been tackled under the aegis of concepts such as "modernization."[253] Moreover, one can observe growing research interests in the history of forms of regional consciousness in premodern East Asia as well as in later forms of East Asian, Pan-Asian, or related identities.[254]

In some cases, the rising interest in regional and transregional dynamics has been closely entangled with a quest to historicize and, by implication, problematize the nation-state as the main frame of historical interaction. As a more general tendency, there has been a growing presence of approaches seeking to critically reconsider categories such as "China" and replace them with more complex, often translocal modes of analysis. For example, works such as Kenneth Pomeranz's *The Great Divergence* have been translated into Chinese and generated significant levels of intellectual interest within academic circles, which is not to say that they did not also meet strong intellectual opposition.[255] Some influential scholars have even come to argue that Chinese world historiography still too readily accepts political boundaries as its main units of analysis.[256] Furthermore, a few prominent theorists like Wang Hui suggested that it was necessary to study more closely the overlapping spaces of global and regional interaction, which led to the advent of nationalism in East Asia.[257] After all, in his sizable history of modern Chinese thought, Wang sought to retrieve connotations of China from narrow national interpretations, for example by paying due attention to the complex and overlapping historical nexuses within Asia and beyond.[258] Indeed, some studies have begun tracing the complex networks and entanglements behind the spread of nationalism and national historiography in China as well as in other countries.[259]

---

[252] For example, F. Chen (2009); and G. Chen (2006). About the history of book printing and publishing in the Yangtze Delta and its implication for cultural contacts in East Asia see Fudan daxue lishixi chuban bowuguan (2009).

[253] For a discussion see S. Kwok (2004), particularly pp. 56–58.

[254] For example, W. Li (2005); and F. Chen (2007).

[255] A great debate was also instigated by the translation of A. Frank (1998). About both works see Chapter 2. The reception of both works in China is discussed in H. Guo (2002); and B. Liu (2000).

[256] For example G. Pan (2000). On the rising interest in regional diversity within China see J. Wang (2001).

[257] H. Wang (2002). See also Z. Wang (2001).   [258] H. Wang (2004–2007).

[259] S. Peng (1992). On Japanese influences on Liang Qichao's thoughts of enlightening China: K. Zheng (2001). On the network of influences between Europe, Japan, and China on the idea of local self-government see D. Huang (2002).

Other disciplinary developments have likewise fostered the growth of translocal scholarship in China, and more projects have come to address the complex outside connections of single Chinese provinces and regions.[260] Not unlike in Germany and the United States, the idea of coherent national narratives has been at least implicitly challenged by new forms of social and cultural history.[261] To a certain extent, in China new approaches in these fields have been influenced by internationally circulating methodological theories;[262] at the same time, there have been attempts to adapt social historical concepts to the specific cultures and structures of historiography in China.[263] In any case, several more recent currents of social and cultural historiography have sought to uncover facets of the past, which had been rendered subaltern in ordinary national historical tropes. For instance, a number of social historians started paying more attention to topics ranging from gender issues to marginal communities such as Africans in Macao.[264] While much of the new social historical work was confined to China, some research projects began exploring spaces across and beyond national communities. For example, in the study of overseas Chinese communities there has been a noticeable trend to relate facets of Chinese and foreign history more closely to each other. Some studies have focused on themes such as the lasting ties between Chinese emigrants and their home communities, which impacted single regions in China in very different ways.[265] Other transnational topics, which have been pursued in the historiography of overseas Chinese, range from continuities of local lineage patterns among emigrant workers to the study of Chinese merchant networks in Southeast Asia.[266]

Also a wide spectrum of other fields has witnessed new kinds of approaches venturing into alternative conceptions of space. For example, some scholars have investigated the history of Chinese neologisms around the turn of the twentieth century under the guiding concept of a transnationally oriented cultural history of politics.[267] On a more general level, there have been increasing levels of research activity on the linguistic

[260] For example on the Yangtze Delta region: Fudan daxue lishixi (2009). Also accentuating the translocal connections of the lower Yangtze region during the late Ming dynasty: S. Fan (2003).
[261] See Leutner (2004), particularly pp.72ff.; and N. Yang (2001).
[262] For instance, on the impact of postmodernism on historiography, which at least fostered certain types of cultural history see Q. Wang (1999b); and Y. Zhang (1998).
[263] For example, S. Zhao and Q. Ding (2001).
[264] See, for example, S. Zhao (2002). Critically examining modern critiques of footbinding: N. Yang (2002). About Africans in Macao: K. Tang and H. Peng (2005).
[265] See, for example, G. Ma (2000).   [266] See L. Zeng (2003); and H. Liu (2000).
[267] X. Huang (2009).

exchanges that greatly transformed the Chinese, Japanese, and other languages, particularly during the late nineteenth and early twentieth centuries.[268] In addition, at least some scholarship on the history of international relations has become more open towards problems such as the impact of transnationally circulating discourses and worldviews on decision-making circles.[269] Similar tendencies can also be observed in the study of international law, intergovernmental organizations and, more generally, research on the global flows of politically relevant ideas and discourses.[270] It is a noteworthy trend that some research in these fields is now shifting away from the West or Japan as the main arenas for transnational or global historical perspectives. For example, one study that investigated the modernization rhetoric in parts of Asia during the 1920s arrived at the conclusion that the Chinese term for "modernization" (*xiandaihua*) may have been imported from the Turkish language.[271] In addition, segments of comparative historical research in China are also no longer primarily based on structural comparisons of allegedly independent national units. Rather, there is now a trend to consider the impact of translocal influences and the entanglements of all compared units within wider, global contexts.

Likewise, within world history as a distinct research and teaching field, social and cultural historical topics have grown at the expense of political history.[272] In the eyes of some official representatives of the field, these and other developments have started to greatly diversify the landscapes of world history in China.[273] Such rather rapid disciplinary changes within a transforming academic community and society beg the question about the future directions of world historical scholarship in China. Discussions on these and related topics have already begun, and they have taken rather interesting directions.

Newly positioning historiography at a global level?

In recent years, many voices in China have called for world history to leave its well-trodden tracks and enter new territories that ultimately may prove to be relevant for the future.[274] For example, there have been

---

[268] For example, G. Shen (2008); and G. Jin and Q. Liu (2009). In the United States, this research field has been prominently advanced by L. Liu (1995).

[269] See L. Xu (2001). For a detailed account of the development of Chinese studies on the history of Sino-German interactions see K. Xu, J. Xu, and Y. Chen (2006).

[270] For example, investigating facets of international law from transnational perspectives: X. Ling (2009).

[271] B. Lin and Z. Dong (1998).   [272] See L. Xu (2010).

[273] Compare P. Yu (2006); D. Jiang (2000); and P. He (2000).

[274] For example, A. Li (2001); and X. Xiang, F. Song, J. Wang, and H. Li (1999).

suggestions that, in the future, at least some world historical research should be structured around the study of key problems rather than certain periods or world regions.[275] Furthermore, there is a sense that Chinese world historiography needs to continue to closely follow scholarship in the West but no longer remain fixated upon it.[276] Still, many scholars and institution builders have come to argue that, in the face of a rapidly changing world, Chinese world historical scholarship will need to broaden its ties with universities in other parts of the globe.[277] Visions of this kind frequently entail the idea that China ought to build up more academic expertise in different parts of the world outside areas such as Western Europe, North America, and East Asia. For a long time, this "Golden Triangle" has dominated levels of global awareness in China, which were institutionally represented at its universities.[278] In a certain way, the idea of connecting with world regions outside of the West may be understood as a continuation of the decentering efforts during the Mao period. At the same time, however, today's guiding principles are no longer closely related to the declared aim of an alliance of underdeveloped societies against an exploitative Global North.

The idea of reaching out to the world is often quite openly tied to the rising international power status of China. Publication titles like *World History in Our Country Needs to Reach a New Level in the New Century* are an indication of the future-oriented climate within which some of the ideas about new directions for this branch of research are being developed.[279] But they also serve as a reminder that despite the diversification of theories and acclaimed internationalization of scholarship, national identities remain a strong element within the landscapes of world historical research in China. In fact, both are often seen as two sides of the same coin: analogous to the debates on modernization and the future of the country, many leading representatives of world history argue that China needs to further accentuate a specific approach to world history through – not in spite of – its growing entanglements with the world.[280] Seen in this context, the suggestion that Chinese historiography should more carefully scrutinize Western theories in terms of

[275] For example, P. Liu (2004).
[276] For example, Z. Lin and Y. Liang (2000); and H. Liu (1999). Looking at allegedly successful and unsuccessful experiences of modernization: C. Qian and J. Liu (1999).
[277] See, for example, Z. Yi (2000); M. Yi (2001); and Z. Cui (1996). Advocating more expertise in foreign history and more exchanges with different countries: C. Zhang (1994); and P. Yu (1994).
[278] Suggesting that single universities should cluster expertise in one particular world region: S. Qi (2000); Y. Wu (2003); and H. Zhang (2002).
[279] J. Hou (2000).
[280] For example, F. He (2004); S. Qi (2000); and Y. Wu (2003).

their applicability to local perspectives is often at least tacitly related to the idea of the primacy of national interests in a changing global environment.[281]

There are thus some reasons to perceive the growing demand for decidedly Chinese outlooks on world history as the beginnings of new visions of history, which are nationally grounded but at the same time not free from global aspirations.[282] Nevertheless, for now attempts to develop specifically Chinese forms of world history are primarily directed at the various facets of Eurocentrism, which have become woven deeply into the fabrics of China's intellectual worlds. In that sense the search for supposedly Chinese visions is largely driven by the sense of a loss of epistemological agency. Indeed, in China there has been a considerable trend to problematize the century-long practice of closely orienting scholarship towards outside societies. Some influential scholars in China have gone further than that and even started to distance themselves quite clearly from the idea of a conceptual rapprochement with scholars in the West.[283] Unfortunately, many critiques of the hegemonic roles of Anglophone and other theories tend to operate with rather stereotyped visions of the "West" and its intellectual landscapes. For example, in academic publications one frequently encounters the idea that linear and universal theories of modernization still rule triumphantly in academic circles in the Atlantic world. The significant academic counter-movements to Western-centrism in much of American and European scholarship during the past few decades are often not taken sufficiently into account.[284] Hence parts of the recent epistemological critiques in China are more directed against a constructed, imagined, and internalized West than deeply engaged with present scholarship in the Atlantic world and elsewhere.

What the alternative, a distinctively Chinese perspective of world history, might look like remains often ill-defined. As discussed, a fair number of articles present Marxist perspectives as one of the main elements distinguishing world historical research in the People's Republic from scholarship in most other parts of the world.[285] Yet the idea of Marxism as the main angle of potential Chinese perspectives is still often presented in a very principled, even dogmatic, manner. Only a fraction of this literature seeks to actively engage with neo-Marxist approaches from

---

[281] For example, G. Zhang (2000).   [282] For a related discussion see Karl (2005).

[283] D. Liu (2001).

[284] Several examples of Chinese scholars discussing Western theories of modernity (in English translation) can be found in the special issue of *Chinese Studies in History*, 43–1 (2009) on "Modernization Theory in/of China," edited by Q. Wang.

[285] For example, Y. Zhang and S. Hu (1999); L. Kong (2002); and S. Li (2001).

China, the United States, Latin America, or elsewhere. This is a missed opportunity since rejuvenated Marxist outlooks on world history would have synergy potentials with many developments in other fields such as social and cultural history.[286] Actually, as a general trend, Marxist and Leninist interpretations have come to stand somewhat apart from the dynamic environments of research in the social sciences and humanities in China. Since the acclamation of Marxist approaches to world history remains particularly guarded by the government, they have not been subject to many controversial debates.

This may also be one of the main reasons why most of the literature postulating decidedly Chinese outlooks of world history has not turned to intensively discuss the Chinese model as it has recently evolved. For instance, critiques emerging from intellectual movements such as the New Left, which point to a progressive erosion of Marxist objectives and communitarian values from the Chinese system, have not played a prominent role in the literature revolving around the idea of a Chinese voice in world history. Yet this would be important if the assertion of locally specific approaches to global and world historical thinking is to be based on the claim of an alternative, lived social, cultural, and political experience in the offing. A closer rapprochement between the theoretical literature on topics such as Chinese modernity and Chinese approaches to world history could potentially lead to very important topics ranging from new, historically informed critiques of hegemony to alternative visions of world order. Qian Chengdan is heading in such a direction:

First, it goes without saying that modernization is the dominant theme in contemporary China ... A new scientific framework of modern world history under the guidance of modernization would possibly help build a modern world history with contemporary Chinese characteristics, and hence make this framework a major component in the discourse. For the longest time, China's world history has been borrowing frameworks from outside sources. But it has reached a fairly mature period and can now experiment with its own framework.[287]

Ultimately the question of specifically Chinese outlooks on world history will be heavily influenced by political developments in the future. For example, much will depend on whether China will carry on developing its global roles based on the primacy of national coherence, or whether a kaleidoscopic pattern of subnational or transnational economic structures, cultural flows, and modes of identity will continue to

---

[286] For example, calling for a dialogue with neo-Marxist currents in the West ranging from Jameson to Giddens: H. Sun (2002).
[287] C. Qian (2009), p. 17.

evolve and impact its social as well as academic life.[288] For the near future, it would certainly mean a great loss for world historical research in China if the quest to decenter Western discourses or globally dominant perspectives is translated into greater pressure for scholars to conform to a supposedly rather mono-tonal or overly harmonious choir of Chinese voices. During the past few decades, this did not tend to be the case, allowing for a greater pluralization of research approaches in world history and other areas of inquiry. However, this is not to say that there are no politically defined limits to transnational perspectives – for example, it would hardly be possible to publish transnational histories of the ethnic groups in China's western territories in ways that would potentially challenge territorial definitions of the country.[289]

Yet despite restrictions of this kind, new forms of social history, cultural history, and other methodological approaches have increased the presence of conceptions of space that do not fit easily into the framework of the nation-state. For example, on a subnational level, it has now become at least easier for subaltern groups in China to articulate their viewpoints in the style of a history from below movement.[290] The same has been true for the rising importance of hitherto unusual areas of research and topics ranging from environmental history to the study of translingual contacts. Likewise, scholarly activities that are decidedly in favor of alternative transnational visions have become more frequent and, in some cases, more concerted with one another. For example, this has been the case with several critical regionalism projects in which scholars from different countries and regions of East Asia started to debate minority, social, and other issues. Not rarely, they do so in ways that decidedly depart from strictly national frameworks of analysis and are oriented after translocal civil society efforts.[291]

Nevertheless, these and other pluralizing facets of transnational and world historical research should not be taken as the main currents running through the historiographical landscapes of China. As this chapter has shown, commitments to patriotism, methodological nationalism, and linear notions of history have continued to play central roles within Chinese academic circles over the past two decades. There have

---

[288] On the idea of overlapping regionalisms across East Asia see X. Chen (2005). About different identity patterns, including the idea of multiple Chinas, see Leibold (2006).

[289] At the same time, one now encounters more frequently postulates and suggestions to grant minorities a more prominent place in national historical narratives. For example see E. Feng (2009).

[290] Compare Duara (2009), particularly p. 64.

[291] See, for example, www.culstudies.com; and www.arenaonline.org. For more information see Spakowski (2008). See also Yuzo and G. Sun (2001).

been different attempts to explain why efforts to deconstruct conceptual worlds such as progressivism or methodological nationalism have not reached the same degree of influence within the social sciences and the humanities in China. For example, some scholars such as Thomas Metzger suggested that the current gravitational centers of approaches, outlooks, and methodological predilections need to be seen against the background of long Chinese intellectual traditions. According to him, these are characterized by a strong epistemological optimism centered on the belief in the betterment of the human condition through self-effort.[292] Heading in different directions, some scholars stressed specific intellectual mentalities and commitments to modernization efforts that the twentieth century's legacy of nation-building processes had forged within the Chinese academic community.[293] Others pointed to factors such as government influence, the prominence of nationalism in mainland Chinese universities,[294] or the rather broad levels of support for the evolving political and economic model across wide sectors of Chinese society, including much of the intellectual realm.[295]

Yet while searching to contextualize dominant historiographical trends in China, the question of why Chinese academic culture has not experienced similar patterns of epistemological change as in several Western societies ought not be taken as a guiding principle. Such an approach would be in danger of defining the scholarly changes in academic communities such as the United States as a standard against which other developments ought to be measured. In fact, taken to the extreme, such a position would be conceptually closely related to positing the Western experience as the normative model of a wider epistemological evolution. This would certainly mean overlooking the highly diverse, locally specific factors that continue to season transnational and world historical writing in the United States just as in other parts of the world. Disregarding these would also imply ignoring such crucial questions as the power gaps between different academic systems around the world.

This brings us back to the problems discussed in the initial parts of this book. There are many reasons to assume that the growing entanglements among university systems will not lead to a global assimilation

[292] Metzger (2005).   [293] See, for example, Duara (1995).
[294] See C. Cheung and S. Kwok (1998).
[295] For example, applications for party membership have risen sharply. For instance, in 2001 an estimated 28 percent of graduate students in China were party members, and one-third of all undergraduates applied for membership. The overall number of party members among students had risen by 1,000 percent during the previous decade. See Wright (2007).

of academic approaches. Rather, it is at least a possibility that in the future differences may be even more blatantly accentuated, constructed, and articulated. While it is certainly significant to develop plural perspectives and centers of enunciation in global history and related areas of inquiry, it is equally important to gain visions of future scholarship that actively work against the idea of political polarization rather than being shaped by it.

Epilogue: Global history in a plural world

Kaleidoscopic patterns

An entire cascade of further case studies could have added many facets to our picture of global history as a wider academic trend. For instance, it would certainly have been interesting to investigate more closely the scholarly communities in India where world historical thinking can be related to a myriad of contexts, ranging from political struggles over national identity to the rather complicated relationship between the local historians' guild and postcolonial theories in Western societies. Significant insights could also have been gained by looking more closely at various other academic realms in places ranging from Japan in the East to Argentina in the West, and from Australia in the South to Russia in the North.[1] In each instance, transnational and world historical scholarship has certainly been characterized by complex interplays between global entanglements and local specificities. The latter includes factors ranging from particular sociocultural and political conditions to distinct academic structures, funding systems, forms of historical memory, and modes of global consciousness.

As this brief sketch of the possibilities for further detailed research suggests, one could easily get lost in an endless search for specificities and variations in those branches of historiography that are often subsumed under the expression "global history." Of primary importance, however, is the fact that global historical scholarship is far from identical all over the world, and it hasn't become so even though many research communities around the globe are transnationally connected and internally fragmented. As a consequence, the complex sceneries of global historical research must be taken into consideration when reflecting upon the status quo and future possibilities of this research

[1] Going further than that, it would have been possible to devote entire case studies to scholarship in transnationally entangled language realms such as the Francophone or the Sinophone worlds. See the Introduction for a more detailed discussion of this possibility.

trend. This is even more important since the growing significance of border-crossing historiography did not disseminate from the West; nor did it take place in isolated national, regional, or otherwise defined academic traditions.

A brief, summarizing look at research in the United States, Germany, and China and its surrounding sociopolitical contexts confirms the idea that the centers of gravity and main trajectories of global historical scholarship remain locally specific, at least in significant regards. In the United States, the developments leading to a growing interest in transnational and global historical scholarship need to be at least partly understood from the context of the significant social and institutional transformations that the country's higher education system has experienced during the past half century. These changes did not take place in an isolated academic world; rather, they were closely related to various political developments, which on the surface were only loosely related to each other. Firstly, after the Second World War the geopolitically motivated expansion of non-Western area expertise as well as the spread of mass college education contributed to the fact that during the following decades increasing numbers of students from hitherto marginalized social, cultural, and ethnic backgrounds gained access to the world of higher education. Secondly, starting from the 1960s, the political struggles over inclusivity during the civil rights movement then contributed to an increasing diversification of the student and faculty body at research universities.

Together with other factors such as institutional reforms, developments of this kind fed into growing levels of criticism voiced against the privileged perspectives from which much of national and world historical scholarship was written. Particularly since the 1970s, new groups of historians have helped to complexify and deconstruct assumptions by shedding more light on the history of women, African Americans, and other groups that had played only a rather subordinate role in many important currents of US national scholarship. At the same time, rising numbers of scholars based in area studies and history departments went openly against the strong influence of Eurocentric visions of world history and assumptions about the uniqueness of Western civilization. Such counter-currents to established forms of national and world historical scholarship did not emerge from a clearly identifiable nucleus but rather could be felt in many branches of historical scholarship ranging from economic history to cultural history, and from gender studies to colonial history. Particularly from the late 1980s and 1990s onwards, border-crossing research grew rapidly within this changing opinion climate, and it did so across vast segments of the rather diverse research environments of historiography in the United States. A growing number of scholars now had their training in the history of two or more world regions, and in their own work they explored the spaces, transformations, and interactions below, across, and beyond them. In a dynamic research environment, the growing presence of the neologism "global history" has been only one among many manifestations of a trend which was largely characterized by the quest for conceptions of space that would overcome different, hitherto dominant forms of nation- and Western-centric visions.

In Germany, the expansions of the university sector during the 1960s also granted new social groups increasing access to universities, but the proportion of intellectual migrants among the faculty body remained very low compared to the United States. Furthermore, despite the traumatic global implications for Germany during the first half of the twentieth century and its multilevel global connections during its second half, the country's academic system has long continued to marginalize non-Western and transcultural history. Up until the present day, only a small, albeit now growing, fraction of scholars based in German history departments primarily focus on transcontinental or non-European themes. In fact, the distribution of regional expertise at German history departments has not changed profoundly since the 1920s. Yet it was not so much the continuation of pre-war nationalism but rather the effort of coming to terms with the dark sides of the German past in the spirit of a postwar westward orientation which was the main force keeping historical scholarship in Germany within rather nationally and Europe-oriented confinements. For example, the generational break of the 1960s and 1970s and the rise of social history was largely centered on the quest to gain newly critical outlooks on the national past, which would take the root causes of the Nazi rule duly into the picture. A subsequent opening of the German historians' community towards transnational and global historical themes during the late 1980s did not turn into a powerful current as the reunification shifted the agenda back to national problems.

Still, especially since the late 1990s, new forms of global and transnational historical research have started to become stronger and more visible within the guildhalls of German historians. Supported by Germany's well-endowed foundations, a growing number of interdisciplinary research centers and academic networks created greater opportunities for cooperation between historians and the area studies. As a consequence, a growing proportion of graduate students in the field of history now has at least a partial background in the area studies. Not uninfluenced by Anglophone scholarship, there have also been surging levels of interest in finding new ways to relate the history of Europe, or parts thereof, and other parts of the world to each other – ways which would no longer mainly define Europe as the center of historical agency. While trans-continental research has been growing in various fields, single research areas were particularly active in cutting important inroads for border-crossing historical scholarship into Germany's historiographical environments. Among those were, for example, the history of migration and colonial history. These fields were also relevant for more public debates on issues such as the atrocities committed under German colonial rule or the question of multiculturalism in the Federal Republic. In many regards, the growing support for transnational and transcontinental research in Germany needs to be seen in the context of the country's wider transformations during the past twenty years. In addition to changing global political environments, changes such as the visible pluralization of German society through migration suggest that historical scholarship needs to add new geographies of awareness to its portfolio.

In contrast to the German case, at Chinese universities foreign and world history enjoyed a significant institutional presence throughout much of the twentieth century. However, the fact that on average about a third of Chinese historians have been based at world history institutes should not lead one to the erroneous conclusion that historical research tended to cover the entire globe evenly and unequivocally. Most world historical scholarship actually focused on some select regions, which varied slightly, depending on China's political regimes as well as their overall contexts. While from the very inceptions of historiography at modern national universities significant resources were dedicated to the study of Western Europe, North America, and Japan, it was particularly during the first half of the Mao period when research capacity on Russia and the Soviet Union was being added. During most time periods, only scant attention was being paid to other parts of the world ranging from Latin America to South Asia. Another remarkable continuity from the first half of the twentieth century to the present has been the rather strict separation between the historiography of China and scholarship on other parts of the world. For many decades, both scholarly communities were only loosely entangled with one another, with many important world historical texts even completely omitting the Chinese past from the picture. In many regards, such institutional divisions reflect some modes of global consciousness underlying the Chinese nation-building project, which remained fixated upon a changing array of reference societies.

Particularly during the past one or two decades, a time in which Chinese society and academia underwent rapid transformations, there have been more concerted efforts to alter the institutional framework of historiography in China. In addition to slowly adding research capacity on other parts of the non-Western world, there have been more concerted efforts to overcome the divide between national history and world history. In this context, the term "global history" (*quanqiu lishi*) has come to be used rather prominently and frequently. Among other projects, quite a few scholars now explore the connections, tensions, and interactions between single Chinese regions and other parts of the world. Moreover, a wide variety of fields ranging from social and cultural history to environmental history have experienced increasing levels of research activity that transgresses national and continental boundaries. While particularly since the 1980s foreign scholarship has been rather influential in Chinese academic circles, some important debates surrounding the field of global and world history have taken remarkably different directions from the trajectories of scholarship in large parts of the Atlantic world. For example, modified versions of modernization theory have played a remarkably influential role in Chinese world historical scholarship. They have done so for a variety of reasons which range from the personal experience base of Chinese scholars to doubts about the idea of revolutions as the key to progress. Moreover, many influential Chinese scholars see globalization and nation-building as complementary processes, and in a following step have come to advocate nationally specific outlooks of world history. However, the latter still remain rather undefined, particularly since historical scholarship has been rather slow to enter the academic debates on what has often come to be referred to as the "Chinese model" of the past thirty years.

One should not jump to the conclusion that the examples discussed in this book typify some more general academic tendencies in entire parts of the world. For instance, it would be erroneous to understand the Chinese scenario as an example of a wider research trend outside of the West. Nevertheless, it is certainly possible to sketch some general contexts that frame the research environments of global historical scholarship in the United States, Germany, and China. Today's university-based historiography is intellectually entangled enough to enable us to observe some common conceptual transformations in different parts of the world. For example, in many world regions, conceptions of space which were long foundational to much of modern academic historiography have become increasingly problematized by members of the professional historians' community. While there have been important earlier forms of criticism, it was particularly during the second half of the Cold War – and increasingly so since the early 1990s – that challenges of Eurocentric master narratives have become more conspicuous in the public spheres of academic historiography. In a related process, many countries witnessed growing efforts to critically rethink the frames of national history and venture into hitherto underexplored spaces of the past.

As the first chapter has shown in some detail, the search for alternative mental maps has grown stronger in the study of history, at least in significant parts of the world. It has done so for a variety of reasons, many of which are related to changing geopolitical and -economic realities that are often subsumed under the slogan of an emerging multipolar world. For example, the study of history has been impacted by changing scopes of regional awareness, which can be observed across all three case studies in this book. In different ways, to varying degrees and along specific timelines, global and world historical research in the United States, Germany, and China has become more regionally diversified over the past few decades. For instance, whereas non-Western and transcontinental history has started to gain a stronger foothold in Germany, Chinese universities are now in the process of investing more research capacity in the study of areas outside of Europe, the United States, and other reference societies on which their scholarship had primarily focused for a long time.

Developments of this kind might be taken as an indication that in recent years the hierarchies in the conceptual worlds of academic historiography have been subject to significant transformations. Indeed, it will likely become far more untenable for historical research and education in the West to marginalize the experiences of other parts of the world. At the same time, it is quite likely that global and world historical scholarship in many parts of the world ranging from Latin America to East Asia can become more decentered in the sense that there will be an increasing search for alternatives to the dual emphasis on the indigenous and the Western pasts. In the coming decades, many countries may well add more capacity to the study of hitherto neglected parts of the world, which in turn will also open up opportunities for new forms of translocal scholarship. Put in a somewhat dramatizing language, after most of the non-Western world became rather provincial in the global structures and cultures of historiography during the nineteenth and much of the twentieth centuries, we may now witness a certain relativization of the West as a historical trope and a source of scholarly production.

While there are indications for academic trends of this kind, we are certainly still very far away from a world in which everybody is becoming equally provincial and, by implication, equally connected. It is important to remind ourselves again that unevenness and gaps in influence remain a key feature of the global academic landscapes in our present world.

Whereas overt forms of Eurocentrism such as the flat logics of Hegelian master narratives have been on the retreat during the past few years, many imbalances continue to characterize the global environments of academic scholarship. Despite all changes, Western academic dominance continues to be expressed by mechanisms such as the widespread culture of disregarding intellectual positions from other parts of the world. Furthermore, issues ranging from the strong global influence of Anglophone scholarship to the discrepancy of funding structures all point to enormous problem zones, which require new topographies of disciplinary communication. Quite obviously, for global and transnational research to proceed further, it would be beneficial to intensify debates within forums that assemble a plurality of scholarly experiences and hence are able to gain new critical perspectives of the cultures and structures of historiography as an international professional realm.

New structures and modalities

The global prototype of universities as it emerged during the nineteenth and twentieth centuries may not be fully equipped to support at least some of the intellectual tasks and disciplinary dialogues that global and transnational historians may choose to entertain in the future. After all, in what is often referred to as "the Humboldtian model," universities were first and foremost local communities, firmly grounded within specific nation-states. During earlier time periods, some systems of higher learning had been characterized by networks of migration and exchange in more immediate ways. Examples include the system of European universities between the High Middle Ages and the Early Modern Period, or the institutions that were frequented by the social milieu of scholar-officials during many Chinese dynasties. By contrast, the structures of today's universities provide only comparatively few incentives and opportunities to engage in more sustained academic dialogues, particularly beyond national or macro-regional boundaries. Certainly, intellectual migrations, research fellowships, and other mechanisms ensure rather steady flows of scholars across national and continental boundaries. Nevertheless, especially in the field of history and some neighboring disciplines most collaborative efforts between international groups of scholars are usually confined to single conferences and conventions. The proceedings of such events are often edited volumes, which in many cases offer important single studies produced by scholars from a variety of backgrounds. At the same time, however, the single chapters of such editions are rarely the results of sustained collaborative efforts or dialogues – which is why they are sometimes rather sarcastically referred to as "bookbinder syntheses."

In the future, new academic structures will need to co-evolve together with a field which reaches beyond the mental maps that have dominated historical scholarship in the past.[2] After all, such topics as colonialism, imperialism, or the mechanisms of dominance and marginalization can only be tackled in a timely, multilateral manner if the institutional fundaments and sociologies of knowledge underlying global history are modified. Ideally it would be the task of this coming generation of global historians to make itself obsolete in the sense that it creates the very structures on which more multilateral and less nation-centered visions of the past could be developed. This cannot and ought not occur as a planned process; rather, new landscapes of scholarly collaboration can only grow through a multitude of emerging projects and experiments with new kinds of academic work modes.

Certainly, also during the past century and even earlier there have been efforts to create lasting cross-regional dialogues and university associations.[3] However, due to several developments it was only in recent times that alternative forms of collaboration have become at least more than utopian visions of a distant future. For example, professional exchanges among historians have reached historically unprecedented degrees in an age in which documents can be transmitted electronically and academic discussion sites draw an increasing number of subscribers and participants.[4] The rapidly growing number of primary and secondary sources now available online facilitates the work of scholars whose mobility is limited for financial, political, or personal reasons.[5] In these and other regards, the revolutions in the communications technology sector, particularly the advent of the internet and email, have had an impact on academic work in general and historiography in particular, which still warrants further

---

[2] Compare Wallerstein (1996), particularly pp. 94–105.

[3] For example, about the world congress of historians in 1898 see Iriye (2002), p. 14; about efforts to build an international association of universities dedicated to peace and justice during the 1950s and 1960s see Bungert (2010). On the failures of efforts to build a global community of historians during the 1950s and 1960s and UNESCO's attempt to create a commonly recognized history of humankind during the same time period see, for example, Manning (2008b) and Moore (1997).

[4] For the field of world history see, for example, H-World (www.h-net.org/~world) as well as the German site "Geschichte Transnational" (http://geschichte-transnational.clio-online.net).

[5] See, for example, Darnton (2009).

research and intellectual reflection.[6] Not less significant for scholars in today's world are changes in the international transportation sector, particularly the reduction of airfares relative to income levels in many parts of the world. Compared to a generation ago, the number of international meetings and transnational projects has risen significantly.

Such developments allow for significant changes in the institutional structures underlying academic collaboration in general and global historical research in particular. For instance, transnational working groups and study programs may still be exceptions within a general pattern, but at least they have become more frequently and clearly visible during the past few decades. Even in the case of historiography, a field that has been far more based on locally confined individual work than other academic disciplines, the list of possible examples is long. Worth mentioning are, for instance, the growth of international global scholarly networks in which participants collaborate over a period of several years.[7] Fields like global labor history have seen a large number of international research projects involving scholars from different parts of the world.[8] Furthermore, projects such as the Flying University based in Korea,[9] or the Global Economic History Network[10] are examples of efforts to transform the mental maps of history in conjunction with the underlying structures of scholarship. Important has also been the rising number of transnational graduate programs in which students are enrolled in networks or consortiums of universities and receive their education at different participating locations.[11] As a consequence, one can expect the number of historians who have been trained in different parts of the world to continue growing in the future.

Yet observing such a trend should not make us fall for any kind of developmental enthusiasm or even technological determinism:

[6] Some brief observations pertaining global history can, for example, be found in Barros (2004), especially pp. 33ff.
[7] On examples of economic and cultural historians who have come together in studies using new spatial approaches see Hopkins (2002b), pp. 4ff.
[8] Van der Linden (2006).
[9] www.h-net.org/announce/show.cgi?ID=174403.
[10] The network is organized by several universities and has set up various international conferences as well as other scholarly exchanges. See www.lse.ac.uk/collections/economicHistory/GEHN.htm. Another example is the Global Price and Incomes Group. In order to facilitate the exchange of data and provide forums for international debates, the International Economic History Association has started to debate the idea of promoting internet hubs that would connect scholars working on a specific theme with each other. See van Zanden.
[11] See, for example, the Erasmus Mundus program in the field of global studies (with a high proportion of global history) which is sponsored by the European Union: www.uni-leipzig.de/gesi/emgs.

increasing connectivity does not necessarily translate into much more equally distributed inclusivity. The rising possibilities for academic linkages offer many opportunities but, at the same time, they also lead to significant dangers and new problem zones.[12] For example, through the growth of major international academic hubs in East Asia and other parts of the world, the global academic system is likely to become less centered on the North Atlantic world. But like the realm of global politics and economics,[13] an emerging multipolar order in academia does not mean that a more balanced system is in the offing. There is a possibility that new hierarchies of knowledge or competing forms of cultural imperialism will replicate the patterns of marginalization and exclusion in new forms and at different levels. While some areas are increasingly interconnected, others, such as parts of Latin America, Central Asia, or sub-Saharan Africa, may even sink deeper into oblivion in the sense of being disconnected from dynamic patterns of global scholarship.

Despite their increasing international connections, historians are still far from producing a scholarly community which closes opportunity gaps between the peripheries and the centers of our global academic landscapes. On a very elementary level, differences in funding structures and political constraints still provide the vast majority of scholars in various parts of the world with highly divergent resources, travel opportunities, and access to scholarship. Such inequalities exist not only between wealthy and impoverished countries but also within single societies. For example, in China, only a small, albeit growing number of historians have the necessary foreign language skills and access to financial resources that would allow them to actively participate in international dialogues and cross-national projects. Here – as in many other cases – one can observe a certain gap between a globally connected elite of scholars and a larger group of academics whose active work experience does not transcend certain national or regional boundaries.[14]

In other words, the internationally mobile, renowned representatives of the profession who tend to frequent global conferences may only be a rather thin veneer on the entire profession. There is at least some danger that the globally connected parts of the academic realm will become an increasingly solipsistic community, a self-referential scholarly network

---

[12] For academic networks in general see Charle, Schriewer, and Wagner (2004).

[13] This statement should not be taken as a position on the question whether the structural transformations in the academic sector take the same directions as geopolitical or -economic changes or whether they follow a different logic.

[14] Compare Leutner (2003).

that is losing touch with academic communities operating more locally. While the perspective of the detached "globalist" is neither thinkable nor desirable, it would nevertheless be equally naive or presumptuous to posit scholars from different societies as representatives of entire academic systems or even world regions. In the future, many historians may increasingly have to face the question of for whom do they write, in what public spheres do they operate, and as a representative of what do they speak about global history.

Problems of this kind point to the question of whether particular languages have acquired a hegemonic position in even more acute ways. The running joke at the Hebrew University in Jerusalem that God wouldn't have gotten tenure since he didn't publish his book in English[15] illustrates the current pressure on national languages within many academic systems rather well. Yet the underlying problems, which this funny story alludes to, are certainly far from amusing since they point to challenging questions. Do, for example, increasing levels of worldwide scholarly connections inevitably lead to the global dominance of English and, perhaps, a few additional languages? This is particularly important for an academic field which, for better or for worse, has long taken its societal roles and political responsibilities very seriously. In the future, global history will need to further debate the practical, political, and ethical dimensions of communication on a global level. Potential positions that have already been articulated range from emancipating the English language as an academic lingua franca from its native-speaking contexts to experiments with multilingual settings or new translation technologies.

Yet while we should not naively regard the deepening of transnational academic contacts as a panacea, it is almost inconceivable that we should further debate the problems surrounding the hierarchies in the worldwide sociologies of knowledge without expanding current forms of transnational academic cooperation and developing new dialogue forums.[16] After all, if we take the quest for multiperspectivity and professional self-reflexivity seriously, it can hardly suffice to raise challenging questions regarding the field of historiography while leaving

---

[15] My thanks go to Diego Olstein for sharing this joke in a presentation during the Harvard/Duke conference "Global History, Globally" in 2008.

[16] Concerned thinkers have addressed these hierarchies from a variety of angles and through a wide spectrum of terminological options. Important concepts are, for example, the ideas of a "world systemic geoculture," "coloniality of power," "subalterneity," "hegemony," or, more plainly, the "theft of history." See, for example, Wallerstein (1997); Mignolo (2000); Chakrabarty (2000); Mudimb (1988); and Goody (2007).

intact the transnational influence gaps and national divisions that long discouraged a spirit of shared concern between different academic systems.[17] New interaction platforms for historians from around the world will likely foster kinds of critical exchanges which have the potential to go beyond debates between extremes such as the flat logics of Western-centrism on the one side and the negating worlds of revanchism and nativism on the other side. Rather, it will be crucial to find new ways of situating scholarship across and between polar opposites of this kind. One of the great potentials of the global trend in historiography is that it can grant more disciplinary weight and influence to approaches which negotiate between global and local perspectives while at the same time allowing both to critically enrich each other.[18]

Given problems and potentials of this kind, one may observe that the academic world has become smaller due to intensifying global interconnections, yet at the same time it has also become bigger because locally seasoned viewpoints may become more present in academic theorizing. In any case, the mere fact that university-based historiography and *homo academicus* as a professional type can be found in most countries around the world is to a significant degree the result of a history of Western dominance; at the same time, it carries a potential for critical global debates that has never been fully actualized. In most academic circles around the world, alternatives to Eurocentrism can be more forcefully developed by working through the structures of this global professional system rather than seeking to return to allegedly unbroken epistemological traditions.[19] More dialogical and interactive structures of historical scholarship will certainly present new intellectual opportunities and possibilities for cross-fertilization between different academic communities. After all, as the case studies have shown, rather different paradigms, scopes of interest, and methodological predilections form the main currents of global historical scholarship in different parts of the world.

In addition, the sustained growth of new transnational structures of academic interactions can open up new opportunities for scholars to accept public responsibilities beyond local or national communities. Within a field that in an institutional and conceptual sense was often primarily framed by the nation-state, such transnational scopes of

---

[17] Much of the literature on cosmopolitanism focuses primarily on networks and tends to disregard the structural power relations within which thinkers and agents from different parts of the world are inevitably embedded. Compare Glick-Schiller (2005), p. 441.

[18] Examples of related (and yet differing) suggestions and visions are Kocka (2002); Bhabha (1988); Habermas (2000), pp. 183–93; and Mignolo (2002).

[19] Heading in a similar direction: Goonatilake (1999).

responsibility were often less emphasized. Intensifying degrees of transnational academic cooperation could contribute "to make global processes visible and accountable to ordinary citizens who might otherwise
be confined to national political arenas"[20] as well as to other objectives
that are often related to the notion of a global civil society in the offing.
Certainly, globally operating academic institutions and projects would
help to fill a relative void of institutions that focus primarily on themes
and problems of global concern. After all, in Chris Bayly's words, "we
are still immobilized in an age of internationalism. We are not yet citizens
of a global cosmopolis."[21]

The present situation is full of developments in which a stronger
interference of globally concerned and transnationally connected historians would be desirable. A branch of historiography, which is globally
aware but at the same time remains locally seasoned, can come to play a
crucial role, not only within the humanities and social sciences but also
within a whole cascade of local and translocal, national and transnational
public realms. For instance, global and transnational historical scholarship has still a lot to contribute to a plethora of issues and problems
related to the idea of global governance. More interventions on themes
and topics ranging from worldwide environmental and economic risks to
the question of legitimacy and civil society may help close the gap
between historiography on the one side and political theory as well as
some additional fields on the other side, which arguably has widened
over the past decades.[22] Moreover, it would be important to confront the
forms of global discourses that are prevalent at intergovernmental institutions such as the United Nations or, for that matter, multinational
corporations, with historically informed perspectives.[23]

In addition, the role of academic historiography in identity politics is
again becoming a crucial issue at a time when, in many world regions,
new forms of political polarization supported by tropes of national or
civilizational belonging are no longer an unlikely scenario.[24] Within
a general situation in which exclusivist identities have often grown at
the expense of contextual ones, even types of world historical accounts,

[20] Batliwala and Brown (2006). Generally on the concept of a global civil society see
Keane (2003). Needless to say, in most academic systems the government remains an
important funding source. But governmental involvement is not excluded from most
current definitions of civil society. About the idea of a global public science see Chase-
Dunn (2005).

[21] Bayly (2005), p. 28.

[22] Suggesting that historical sociology be more inspired by developments within the field of
global history: Knöbl (2007).

[23] Compare Wigen and Lewis (2007).   [24] See, for example, Megill (2008).

which purportedly foster certain cultural stereotypes and forms of national prejudice, have been on the rise in different societies all over the globe.[25] In an arguably related development, textbook controversies have now repeatedly taken rather vehement forms in many regions,[26] indicating that forms of historical memory are becoming more divisive than dialogical in character.[27] Furthermore, it may well be the case that, in future debates about the history of colonialism, even more intense public, political, and academic exchanges will be widened, both in a topical and a geographical sense.[28] After all, in many countries a significant part of the general population shares a sense of having been unjustly marginalized by the West during the past few hundred years. In addition, public debates on highly politicized and, in many cases, polarizing issues ranging from the concept of human rights to the idea of development would greatly benefit from more historically informed, globally concerned, and locally sensitive academic insights.[29]

Yet public interventions of this kind will only be one aspect of global and transnational historical work in the future. Much of the potential of the global historical trend lies more strictly within the confines of academic expertise. Since the developments underlying the growing presence of border-crossing scholarship are tied to large intellectual and structural transformations within and beyond the field, it is highly unlikely that the global trend in historiography will prove to be another fad in an academic setting that is certainly not free from fashions and intellectual bubbles. Terms such as "global history" or "translocal" history may eventually no longer be used but it hardly seems possible that historiography will revert back to a state in which many of its spatial categories remained largely unchallenged. Needless to say, it would be equally naive to assume that this trend will monopolize historiography as an academic discipline. Still, conceptual developments in locally and globally oriented research may increasingly be entangled with each other. In that sense, global and local histories should not be involved in a zero-sum game relationship but should rather complement each other. Only along such lines can it be conceivable to think both globally and historically.

---

[25] Discussing several cases in different parts of the world: Appleby (2002); about right-wing and fundamentalist Christian world histories in the US, see Bentley (2005). On Pan-Islamic and Pan-Asian tropes in the Middle East see Lockman (2004).

[26] See, for example, Nozaki and Selden (2009); Vickers and Jones (2005); and Popp (2009).

[27] Generally on the topic: Margailt (2004).   [28] A point made by Maier (2000).

[29] On the issue of human rights see, for example, Sen (1997); Angle (2002); and Arjomand (2004).

Bibliography

Abu-Lughod, Janet L. 1989. *Before European Hegemony: The World System A.D. 1250–1350.* New York: Oxford University Press.

Acemoglu, Daron, Simon Johnson, and James A. Robinson. 2002. "Reversal of Fortune: Geography and Institutions in the Making of Modern World Income Distribution." *The Quarterly Journal of Economics* 117-4: 1231–94.

Ackermann, Andreas. 1997. "Ethnologische Migrationsforschung – ein Überblick." *Kea. Zeitschrift für Kulturwissenschaften* 10: 1–28.

Adas, Michael. 2004. "Contested Hegemony: The Great War and the Afro-Asian Assault on the Civilizing Mission Ideology." *Journal of World History* 15-1: 31–64.

Adorno, Rolena. 1986. *Guámán Poma: Writing and Resistance in Colonial Peru.* Austin: University of Texas Press.

Ahmad, Aijaz. 1992. *In Theory: Classes, Nations, Literatures.* London/New York: Verso.

Ajayi, Ade and Jacob Festus. 1994. "National History in the Context of Decolonization. The Nigerian Example." In *Conceptions of National History: Proceedings of Nobel Symposium 78*, edited by Erik Lönnroth, Karl Molin and Björk Ragnar, 65–78. Berlin/New York: Walter de Gruyter.

Akita, Shigeru, ed. 2002. *Gentlemanly Capitalism, Imperialism, and Global History.* Basingstoke: Palgrave Macmillan.

——— 2008. "Creating Global History from Asian Perspectives." In *Global Practice in World History: Advances Worldwide*, edited by Patrick Manning, 57–68. Princeton: Wiener.

Akita, Shigeru and Nicholas White, eds. 2010. *The International Order of Asia in the 1930s and 1950s.* Farnham: Ashgate.

Al-Azmeh, Aziz. 2002. "The Coherence of the West." In *Western Historical Thinking: An Intercultural Debate*, edited by Jörn Rüsen, 58–64. New York: Berghahn Books.

Alber, Jens. 1989. "Nationalsozialismus und Modernisierung." *Kölner Zeitschrift für Soziologie und Sozialpsychologie* 41: 346–65.

Allardyce, Gilbert. 1982. "The Rise and Fall of the Western Civilization Course." *American Historical Review* 87: 695–725.

Allen, Robert C., Tommy Bengtsson, and Martin Dribe, eds. 2005. *Living Standards in the Past: New Perspectives on Well-Being in Asia and Europe.* Oxford/New York: Oxford University Press.

Altbach, Philip G. 2007. *Tradition and Transition: The International Imperative in Higher Education*. Rotterdam: Sense Publishers.

Altrichter, Helmut, ed. 2006. *GegenErinnerung: Geschichte als politisches Argument im Transformationsprozess Ost-, Ostmittel- und Südosteuropas*. Munich: Oldenbourg.

American Historical Review Forum. 2007. "Entangled Empires in the Atlantic World." *American Historical Review* 112-3: 710–99.

Amin, Ash. 2002. "Spatialities of Globalisation." *Environment and Planning A* 34-3: 385–99.

Amin, Samir. 1989. *Eurocentrism*. New York: Monthly Review Press.

Amin, Shahid. 1984. "Gandhi as Mahatma: Gorakhpur District, Eastern UP, 1921–22." In *Subaltern Studies 3: Writings on South Asian History and Society*, edited by Ranajit Guha, 1–61. Delhi: Oxford University Press.

Anderson, Benedict, ed. 1991. *Imagined Communities: Reflections on the Origin and Spread of Nationalism*. London/New York: Verso.

Angle, Stephen. 2002. *Human Rights and Chinese Thought: A Cross-Cultural Inquiry*. Cambridge University Press.

Apffel-Marglin, Frédérique and Stephen A. Marglin. 1996. *Decolonizing Knowledge: From Development to Dialogue*. New York: Oxford University Press.

Appadurai, Arjun. 1988. "How to Make a National Cuisine: Cookbooks in Contemporary India." *Comparative Studies in Society and History* 30-1: 3–24.
  1996. *Modernity at Large: Cultural Dimensions of Globalization*. Minneapolis: University of Minnesota Press.

Appiah, Kwame A. 1991. "Is the Post- in Postmodernism the Post- in Postcolonial?" *Critical Inquiry* 17-2: 336–57.
  1997. "Cosmopolitan Patriots." *Critical Inquiry* 23-3: 617–39.

Applebaum, Richard and William I. Robinson, eds. 2005. *Critical Globalization Studies*. New York: Routledge.

Appleby, Joyce O., Lynn Hunt, and Margaret C. Jacob. 1995. *Telling the Truth About History*. New York: W. W. Norton.

Appleby, Scott. 2002. "History in the Fundamentalist Imagination." *Journal of American History* 89-2: 498–511.

Arendt, Hannah. 1951. *The Origins of Totalitarianism*. New York: Harcourt, Brace & Co.

Arjomand, Said Amir. 2004. "Islam, Political Change and Globalization." *Thesis Eleven* 76: 9–28.

Arrighi, Giovanni, Po-Keung Hui, Ho-Fung Hung, and Mark Selden. 2003. "Historical Capitalism, East and West." In *The Resurgence of East Asia: 500, 150 and 50 Years Perspectives*, edited by Giovanni Arrighi, Takeshi Hamashita, and Mark Selden, 259–333. London/New York: Routledge.

Assmann, Aleida and Ute Frevert. 1999. *Geschichtsvergessenheit – Geschichtsversessenheit: Vom Ungang mit deutschen Vergangenheiten nach 1945*. Stuttgart: Deutsche Verlags-Anstalt.

Augstein, Rudolf, Karl Dietrich Bracher, and Martin Broszat, eds. 1987. *Historikerstreit: Die Dokumentation der Kontroverse um die Einzigartigkeit der nationalsozialistischen Judenvernichtung*. Munich: R. Piper.

Averkorn, Raphaela, ed. 1994. *Bericht über die 39. Versammlung deutscher Historiker in Hannover: 23. bis 26. September 1992.* Stuttgart: Ernst Klett.

Aydin, Cemil. 2007. *The Politics of Anti-Westernism in Asia: Visions of World Order in Pan-Islamic and Pan-Asian Thought.* New York: Columbia University Press.

Bade, Klaus J. and Michael Bommes. 2004. "Einleitung: Integrationspotentiale in modernen europäischen Wohlfahrtsstaaten – der Fall Deutschland." In *Migrationsreport 2004*, edited by Klaus J. Bade, Michael Bommes, and Rainer Münz, 11–42. Frankfurt: Campus.

Bade, Klaus J. and Jochen Oltmer. 2004. *Normalfall Migration: Deutschland im 19. und 20. Jahrhundert.* Bonn: BPB.

Baechler, Jean. 2002. *Esquisse d'une histoire universelle.* Paris: Fayard.

Bailyn, Bernard. 2005. *Atlantic History: Concept and Contours.* Cambridge, MA: Harvard University Press.

Bairoch, Paul. 1997. *Victoires et déboires. Histoire économique et sociale du monde de XVIe siècle à nos jours.* Vol. III. Paris: Gallimard.

 2000. "The Constituent Economic Principles of Globalization in Historical Perspective: Myths and Realities." *International Sociology* 15-2: 197–214.

Banning, Garrett. 2001. "China Faces the Debates: The Contradictions of Globalization." *Asian Survey* 41-3 (May/June): 409–27.

Baran, Paul. 1957. *The Political Economy of Growth.* New York: Monthly Review Press.

Barraclough, Geoffrey. 1957. *History in a Changing World.* Oxford: Blackwell.

Barros, Carlos. 2004. "The Return of History." In *History Under Debate: International Reflection on the Discipline*, edited by Carlos Barros and Lawrence J. McCrank, 3–42. New York: Haworth.

Barth, Boris. 2000. "Internationale Geschichte und europäische Expansion: Die Imperialismen des 19. Jahrhunderts." In *Internationale Geschichte: Themen – Ergebnisse – Aussichten*, edited by Wilfried Loth and Jürgen Osterhammel, 309–27. Munich: Oldenbourg.

Barth, Boris and Jürgen Osterhammel, eds. 2005. *Zivilisierungsmissionen: Imperiale Weltverbesserung seit dem 18. Jahrhundert.* Constance: UVK Verlagsgesellschaft.

Basedau, Matthias and Patrick Koellner. "Area Studies and Comparative Area Studies: Opportunities and Challenges for the GIGA German Institute of Global and Area Studies." GIGA German Institute of Global and Area Studies. http://www.giga-hamburg.de/dlcounter/download.php?d=/content/forumregional/pdf/acas_mbpk_0610.pdf.

Bassin, Mark. 1999. *Imperial Visions: Nationalist Imagination and Geographical Expansion in the Russian Far East 1840–1865.* Cambridge/New York: Cambridge University Press.

Bastedo, Michael N. 2005. "Curriculum in Higher Education: The Historical Roots of Contemporary Issues." In *American Higher Education in the Twenty-First Century: Social, Political, and Economic Challenges*, edited by Philip G. Altbach, Robert Berdahl, and Patricia Gumport, 462–85. Baltimore: Johns Hopkins University Press.

Batliwala, Srilatha and L. David Brown. 2006. "Introduction: Why Transnational Civil Society Matters." In *Transnational Civil Society: An Introduction*, edited by Srilatha Batliwala and L. David Brown, 1–14. Bloomfield, CT: Kumarian Press.

Bauböck, Rainer. 2003. "Towards a Political Theory of Migrant Transnationalism." *International Migration Review* 37-3: 700–23.

Bauerkämper, Arnd. 2003. "Geschichtsschreibung als Projektion: Die Revision der 'Whig Interpretation of History' und die Kritik am Paradigma vom 'deutschen Sonderweg' seit den 1970er Jahren." In *Historikerdialoge: Geschichte, Mythos und Gedächtnis im deutsch-englischen kulturellen Austausch*, edited by Stefan Berger, 383–483. Göttingen: Vandenhoeck & Ruprecht.

Bayly, Christopher A. 1997. "Modern Indian Historiography." In *Companion to Historiography*, edited by Michael Bentley, 663–76. London/New York: Taylor & Francis.

2004a. Introduction to *The Birth of the Modern World, 1780–1914: Global Connections and Comparisons*, by Christopher A. Bayly, 1–22. Malden, MA: Blackwell.

2004b. *The Birth of the Modern World, 1780–1914: Global Connections and Comparisons*. Malden, MA: Blackwell.

2004c. "Writing World History." *History Today* 54-2: 36–40.

2005. "From Archaic Globalization to International Networks, circa 1600–2000." In *Interactions: Transregional Perspectives on World History*, edited by Jerry H. Bentley, Renate Bridenthal, and Anand A. Yang, 14–29. Honolulu: University of Hawai'i Press.

Beaujard, Philippe, Laurent Berger, and Philippe Norel, eds. 2009. *Histoire globale, mondialisations et capitalisme*. Paris: La Découverte.

Beck, Ulrich. 1998. *Was ist Globalisierung?: Irrtümer des Globalismus, Antworten auf Globalisierung*. Frankfurt: Suhrkamp.

Beckert, Sven. 2007. "Featured Review: *A Nation Among Nations. America's Place in World History* by Thomas Bender." *American Historical Review* 112-4: 1123–25.

2004. "Emancipation and Empire: Reconstructing the Worldwide Web of Cotton Production in the Age of the American Civil War." *American Historical Review* 109-5: 1405–38.

Bell, Daniel. 2008. *China's New Confucianism: Politics and Everyday Life in a Changing Society*. Princeton University Press.

Bello, Walden F. 2002. *Deglobalization: Ideas for a New Economy*. London: Zed Books.

Bender, Thomas. 1997. "Politics, Intellect, and the American University, 1945–1995." *Dædalus* 126-1: 1–38.

2000. *La Pietra Report: A Report to the Profession*. New York: The Organization of American Historians/New York University Project on Internationalizing the Study of American History.

ed. 2002. *Rethinking American History in a Global Age*. Berkeley: University of California Press.

2006. *A Nation Among Nations: America's Place in the World*. New York: Hill & Wang.

Bentley, Jerry H. 1996a. "Cross-Cultural Interaction and Periodization in World History." *American Historical Review* 101-3: 749–70.

1996b. *Shapes of World History in Twentieth-Century Scholarship.* Vol. XIV of *Essays on Global and Comparative History.* Washington, DC: American Historical Association.

1999. "Sea and Ocean Basins as Frameworks of Historical Analysis." *Geographical Review* 89-2: 215–24.

2003. "World History and Grand Narrative." In *Writing World History, 1800–2000,* edited by Eckhart Fuchs and Benedikt Stuchtey, 47–66. Oxford University Press.

2005. "Myths, Wagers, and Some Moral Implications of World History." *Journal of World History* 16-1: 51–82.

2006. "The Construction of Textbooks on World History." *Comparativ* 16-1: 49–65.

Bentley, Jerry H., Renate Bridenthal and Kären Wigen, eds. 2007. *Seascapes: Maritime Histories, Littoral Cultures, and Transoceanic Exchanges.* Honolulu: University of Hawai'i Press.

Bentley, Jerry H. and Herbert F. Ziegler. 2002. *Traditions and Encounters: A Global Perspective on the Past.* 2 vols. Columbus: McGraw-Hill.

Bentley, Jerry H., Herbert F. Ziegler, and Heather E. Streets. 2009. *Traditions and Encounters: A Brief Global History.* New York: McGraw-Hill.

Berg, Nicolas. 2003. *Der Holocaust und die westdeutschen Historiker: Erforschung und Erinnerung.* Göttingen: Wallstein.

Bergenthum, Hartmut. 2002. "Weltgeschichten im Wilheminischen Deutschland." *Comparativ* 12-3: 49–50.

2004. *Weltgeschichten im Zeitalter der Weltpolitik: Zur populären Geschichtsschreibung im Wilhelminischen Deutschland.* Munich: Meidenbauer.

Berger, Stefan. 1997. *The Search for Normality: National Identity and Historical Consciousness in Germany since 1800.* New York: Berghahn Books.

2002. "Was bleibt von der Geschichtswissenschaft der DDR?" *Zeitschrift für Geschichtswissenschaft* 50: 1016–34.

2007a. "Comparative History." In *Writing the Nation: A Global Perspective,* edited by Stefan Berger, 161–80. Basingstoke: Palgrave Macmillan.

2007b. "Introduction: Towards a Global History of National Historiographies." In *Writing the Nation: A Global Perspective,* edited by Stefan Berger, 1–29. Basingstoke: Palgrave Macmillan.

ed. 2007c. *Writing the Nation: A Global Perspective.* Basingstoke: Palgrave Macmillan.

Berger, Stefan, Mark Donovan, and Kevin Passmore. 1999. *Writing National Histories: Western Europe Since 1800.* London/New York: Routledge.

Bergmann, Sven and Regina Römhild, eds. 2003. *global heimat: Ethnographische Recherchen im transnationalen Frankfurt.* Frankfurt: Kulturanthropologie Notizen.

Berman, Nina. 1996. *Orientalismus, Kolonialismus und Moderne: Zum Bild des Orients in der deutschsprachigen Literatur um 1900.* Stuttgart: M & P.

Bernabé, Jean, Patrick Chamoiseau, and Raphael Confiant. 1993. *Éloge de la créolité.* Paris: Gallimard.

Bernecker, Walther L. and Thomas Fischer. 1995. "Entwicklung und Scheitern der Dependenztheorien in Lateinamerika." *Periplus* 5: 98–118.

Betterly, Jack. 2000. "Teaching Global History: Context, Not Chronicle; Passion, Not Pedantry." *The History Teacher* 33-2: 213–19.

Bhabha, Homi K. 1988. "The Commitment to Theory." *New Formations* 5: 5–23.

1994a. *The Location of Culture.* London/New York: Routledge.

1994b. "Of Mimicry and Man: The Ambivalence of Colonial Discourse." In *The Location of Culture*, by Homi K. Bhabha, 121–31. New York/London: Routledge.

Bindman, David. 2002. *Ape to Apollo: Aesthetics and the Idea of Race in the 18th Century.* London: Reaktion Books.

Black, Jeremy. 2005. *Introduction to Global Military History: 1775 to the Present.* New York/London: Routledge.

Blackbourn, David. 2004. "Das Kaiserreich transnational. Eine Skizze." In *Das Kaiserreich Transnational: Deutschland in der Welt, 1871–1914,* edited by Sebastian Conrad and Jürgen Osterhammel, 302–324. Göttingen: Vandenhoeck & Ruprecht.

Blackbourn, David and Geoff Eley. 1980. *Mythen deutscher Geschichtsschreibung: Die gescheiterte Revolution von 1848.* Frankfurt/Berlin: Ullstein.

Blaut, James M. 1993. *The Colonizer's Model of the World: Geographical Diffusionism and Eurocentric History.* New York: Guilford Press.

Bley, Helmut. 1999. "Weltgeschichte und Eurozentrismus im 20. Jahrhundert. Ein deutscher Sonderweg?" In *Intentionen – Wirklichkeiten. 42. Historikertag in Frankfurt am Main: 8. bis 11. September 1988,* edited by Marie-Luise Recker, Doris Eizenhöfer, and Stefan Kamp, 24–5. Munich: Oldenbourg.

2000. "Afrikanische Geschichte im Kontext von Weltgeschichte: Konsequenzen für die Lehrpraxis." In *Afrikanische Geschichte und Weltgeschichte: Regionale und universale Themen in Forschung und Lehre,* edited by Axel Harneit-Sievers, 38–48. Berlin: Das Arabische Buch.

Bloch, Marc. 1974. *Apologie pour l'histoire ou métier d'historien.* Paris: Colin.

Blom, Ida. 2001. "Gender as an Analytical Tool in Global History." In *Making Sense of Global History,* edited by Sølvi Sogner, 71–86. Oslo: Universitetsforlaget.

Boahen, A. Adu. 1987. *African Perspectives on Colonialism.* Baltimore: Johns Hopkins University Press.

Bodley, John H. 2002. *The Power of Scale: A Global History Approach.* Armonk, NY: M. E. Sharpe.

Boli, John and George Thomas, eds. 1999. *Constructing World Culture. International Nongovernmental Organizations Since 1875.* Stanford University Press.

Bonnelli, Victoria and Lynn Hunt, eds. 1999. *Beyond the Cultural Turn: New Directions in the Study of Society and Culture.* Berkeley: University of California Press.

Bonnet, Alastair. 2000. "Makers of the West: National Identity and Occidentalism in the Work of Fukuzawa Yukichi and Ziya Gökalp." *Scottish Geographical Journal* 118-3: 165–82.

Bordo, Michael D., Alan M. Taylor, and Jeffrey G. Williamson, eds. 2003. *Globalization in Historical Perspective*. University of Chicago Press.

Bornschier, Volker and Christian Suter. 1996. "Lange Wellen im Weltsystem." In *Theorien der Internationalen Beziehungen*, edited by Volker Rittberger. *Politische Vierteljahresschrift* special volume 21: 175–97.

Borstelmann, Thomas. 2002. *The Cold War and the Color Line: American Race Relations in the Global Arena*. Cambridge, MA: Harvard University Press.

Bosbach, Franz and Hermann-Joseph Hiery, eds. 1999. *Imperium, Empire, Reich: Ein Konzept politischer Herrschaft im deutschbritischen Vergleich*. Munich: Saur.

Bose, Sugata. 2006. *A Hundred Horizons: The Indian Ocean in the Age of Global Empire*. Cambridge, MA: Harvard University Press.

Bouchard, Gérard. 2001. *Genèse des nations et cultures du nouveau monde: Essai d'histoire comparée*. Montreal: Boréa.

Bourdieu, Pierre. 1988. *Homo Academicus*. Frankfurt: Suhrkamp.

2002. "Les Conditions sociales de la circulation internationale des idées." *Actes de la recherche en sciences socials* 145: 3–8.

Brady, Anne-Marie. 2008. *Marketing Dictatorship: Propaganda and Thought Work in Contemporary China*. Lanham, MD: Rowman & Littlefield.

Brahm, Felix and Jochen Meissner. 2004. "'Aussereuropa' im Spiegel allgemeiner Vorlesungsverzeichnisse: Konjunkturen der Beschäftigung mit Afrika und Lateinamerika an ausgewählten Hochschulstandorten, 1925–1960." In *Verräumlichung, Vergleich, Generationalität: Dimensionen der Wissenschaftsgeschichte*, edited by Matthias Middell, Ulrike Thoms, and Frank Uekoetter, 70–94. Leipzig: Akademische Verlagsanstalt.

Brenner, Michael. 2004. "Abschied von der Universalgeschichte: Ein Plädoyer für die Diversifizierung der Geschichtswissenschaft." *Geschichte und Gesellschaft* 30: 118–25.

Brewer, Anthony. 1980. *Marxist Theories of Imperialism: A Critical Survey*. London/Boston: Routledge.

Bright, Charles and Michael Geyer. 2002. "Where in the World Is America? The History of the United States in the Global Age." In *Rethinking American History in a Global Age*, edited by Thomas Bender, 63–99. Berkeley: University of California Press.

2005. "Regimes of World Order: Global Integration and the Production of Difference in Twentieth-Century World History." In *Interactions: Transregional Perspectives on World History*, edited by Jerry H. Bentley, Renate Bridenthal, and Anand A. Yang, 202–38. Honolulu: University of Hawai'i Press.

Brody, David. 1993. "Reconciling the Old Labor History and the New." *Pacific Historical Review* 62: 1–18.

Brownlee, John S. 1997. *Japanese Historians and the National Myths, 1600–1945: The Age of the Gods and Emperor Jinmu*. Vancouver, BC: University of British Columbia.

Brunnbauer, Ulf, ed. 2004. *(Re)Writing History: Historiography in Southeast Europe after Socialism*. Münster: Lit Verlag.

Bruns, Claudia, ed. 2009. *Bilder der "eigenen" Geschichte im Spiegel des kolonialen "Anderen" – Transnationale Perspektiven um 1900* (= *Comparativ* 19-5). Leipzig: Leipziger Universitätsverlag.

Budde, Gunilla, Sebastian Conrad and Oliver Janz. eds. 2006. *Transnationale Geschichte: Themen, Tendenzen und Theorien.* Göttingen: Vandenhoeck & Ruprecht.

Bühler, Heinrich. 2003. *Der Namaaufstand gegen die deutsche Kolonialherrschaft in Namibia von 1904–1913.* Frankfurt: IKO-Verlag für Interkulturelle Kommunikation.

Bulliet, Richard T. 2004. *The Earth and Its Peoples: A Global History.* Boston: Houghton Mifflin.

Bungert, Heike. 2010. "Globaler Informationsaustausch und globale Zusammenarbeit: Die International Association of Universities, 1950–1968." *Jahrbuch für Universitätsgeschichte* 13: 177–91.

Burbank, Jane and Frederick Cooper. 2010. *Empires in World History: Power and the Politics of Difference.* Princeton: Princeton University Press.

Burton, Antoinette. 1994. "Rules of Thumb: British History and 'Imperial Culture' in Nineteenth- and Twentieth-Century Britain." *Women's History Review* 3: 483–500.

Calhoun, Craig. 1999. "Nationalism and the Contradictions of Modernity." *Berkeley Journal of Sociology* 42-1: 1–30.

Campt, Tina. 2004. "Schwarze Deutsche Gegenerinnerung: Der Black Atlantic als gegenhistoriografische Praxis." In *Der Black Atlantic,* edited by Tina Campt and Paul Gilroy, 159–77. Berlin: Haus der Kulturen der Welt Verlag.

Canaday, Margot. 2009. "Thinking Sex in the Transnational Turn. An Introduction." *American Historical Review* 114-5: 1250–7.

Cañizares-Esguerra, Jorge. 2007. "Entangled Histories: Borderland Historiographies in New Clothes?" *American Historical Review* 112-3: 787–99.

Cao, Tianyu. 2003. *Xiandaihua, quanqiuhua yu zhongguo daolu* [Modernization, Globalization and China's Path]. Beijing: Shehui kexue wenxian chubanshe.

Caplan, Jane. 1997. "The Historiography of National Socialism." In *Companion to Historiography,* edited by Michael Bentley, 545–90. New York/London: Routledge.

Cardoso, Fernando H. 1977. "The Consumption of Dependency Theory in the United States." *Latin American Research Review* 12-3: 7–24.

Cartier, Carolyn. 1999. "Cosmopolitics and the Maritime World City." *Geographical Review* 89-2: 278–89.

Cartier, Michael. 1998. "Asian Studies in Europe: From Orientalism to Asian Studies." In *Asian Studies in the Age of Globalization,* edited by Tai-Hwan Kwon and Myungk-Seok Oh, 19–33. Seoul: Seoul National University Press.

Castells, Manuel. 1996. *The Rise of the Network Society.* Malden, MA: Blackwell.

Césaire, Aimé. 1955. *Discours sur le colonialisme.* Paris: Présence africaine.

1972. *Discourse on Colonialism.* New York: Monthly Review Press.

Çetinkaya, Handan. 2000. "Türkische Selbstorganisationen in Deutschland: Neuer Pragmatismus nach der ideologischen Selbstzerfleischung." In *Einwanderer-Netzwerke und ihre Integrationsqualität in Deutschland und Israel*, edited by Dietrich Thränhardt and Uwe Hunger, 83–110. Münster: Lit Verlag.

Chakrabarty, Dipesh. 1992. "Postcoloniality and the Artifice of History: Who Speaks for 'Indian' Pasts." *Representations* 37: 1–26.

  2000. *Provincializing Europe: Postcolonial Thought and Historical Difference*. Princeton University Press.

  2006. "A Global and Multicultural 'Discipline' of History?" *History and Theory* 45-1: 101–9.

Chan, Wai-keung. 2007. "Contending Memories of the Nation: National History Education in China, 1937–1945." In *The Politics of Historical Production in Late Qing and Republican China*, edited by Tze-ki Hon and Robert J. Culp, 169–209. Leiden: Brill.

Chanda, Nayan. 2007. *Bound Together: How Traders, Preachers, Adventurers, and Warriors Shaped Globalization*. New Haven: Yale University Press.

Charle, Christophe. 1996. *Les Intellectuels en Europe au XIXe siècle: Essai d'histoire comparée*. Paris: Éditions du Seuil.

  2001. *La Crise des sociétés impériales. Allemagne, France, Grande-Bretagne, 1900–1940: Essai d'histoire sociale comparée*. Paris: Éditions du Seuil.

Charle, Christophe, Jürgen Schriewer, and Peter Wagner, eds. 2004. *Transnational Intellectual Networks: Forms of Academic Knowledge and the Search for Cultural Identities*. Frankfurt/New York: Campus.

Chartier, Roger. 1989. "Le Monde comme representation." *Annales E.S.C.* 44-6: 1505–20.

Chase-Dunn, Christopher. 2005. "Global Public Social Science." *The American Sociologist* 36-3-4: 121–32.

Chatterjee, Kumkum. 2005. "The King of Controversy. History and Nation-Making in Late Colonial India." *American Historical Review* 110-5: 1454–75.

Chatterjee, Partha. 1993. *The Nation and Its Fragments: Colonial and Postcolonical Histories*. Princeton University Press.

Che, Hualing. 2004. " 'Quanqiushiguan' yu zhongxue lishi jiaocai de bianxie" [Global Historical Views and the Composition of History Materials for Secondary School]. *Lishi jiaoxue* [History Teaching] 6: 55–8.

Cheddadi, Abdesselam. 2005. "Reconnaissance d'Ibn Khaldun." *Esprit* 11: 132–47.

Cheek, Timothy. 2007. "The New Chinese Intellectual: Globalized, Disoriented, Reoriented." In *China's Transformations: The Stories Beyond the Headlines*, edited by Lionel M. Jensen and Timothy B. Weston, 265–84. Lanham, MD: Rowman & Littlefield.

Chen, Fenglin. 2007. "Dongya quyu yishi de yuanliu fazhan jiqi xiandai yiyi" [The Origin and Development of East Asian Regional Consciousness and Its Modern Significance]. *Shijie lishi* [World History] 3: 66–75.

  2009. "Dui dongya jingjiquan de lishi kaocha" [Historical Investigations of East Asian Economic Cycles]. *Shijie lishi* [World History] 3: 38–50.

Chen, Guodong. 2006. *Dongya haiyu yiqian nian: lishi shang de haiyang zhongguo yu duiwai maoyi* [One Thousand Years of East Asia Seas: Maritime China and Foreign Trade in History]. Jinan: Shandong huabao chubanshe.

Chen Lai. 2009. *Tradition and Modernity: A Humanist View.* Leiden: Brill.

Chen, Qineng, ed. 1991. *Jianguo yilai shijieshi yanjiu gaishu* [An Introduction to World Historical Research After the Founding of the PRC]. Beijing: Shehui kexue wenxian chubanshe.

Chen, Xiangming. 2005. *As Borders Bend: Transnational Spaces on the Pacific Rim.* Lanham, MD: Rowman & Littlefield.

Chen, Xiaolü, ed. 2004. *Shiwu shiji yilai shijie zhuyao fada guojia fazhan licheng* [The Courses of Development of the Major Developed Countries Since the Fifteenth Century]. Chongqing: Chongqing chubanshe.

Chen, Xiaomei. 1995. *Occidentalism: A Theory of Counter-Discourse in Post-Mao China.* New York: Oxford University Press.

Chen, Zhihua. 1979. "Shijieshi yanjiu yu sige xiandaihua" [World History and the Four Modernizations]. *Shijie lishi* [World History] 5: 3–8.

Chen, Zhiqiang. 2003. "Lishi yanjiu biange da qushi xia de shijieshi chonggou" [The Reconstruction of World History and the Great Trends in the Changes of Historical Research]. *Lishi yanjiu* [Historical Research] 1: 129–39.

Cheng, Anne. 1993. "Ch'un ch'iu, Kung yang, Ku liang and Tso chuan." In *Early Chinese Texts: A Bibliographical Guide*, edited by Michael Loewe, 67–76. Berkeley: Institute of East Asian Studies.

Cheng, Meibao. 2009/2010. "Globalization, Global History, and Chinese History." *Chinese Studies in History* 43–2: 51–6.

Chester, Charles S. 2006. *Conservation across Borders: Biodiversity in an Interdependent World.* Washington: Island Press.

Cheung, Chau-Kiu and Kwok Siu-Tong. 1998. "Social Studies and Ideological Beliefs in Mainland China and Hong Kong." *Social Psychology of Education* 2: 217–36.

Chidester, David. 2000. *Christianity: A Global History.* London: Allen Lane.

Chomsky, Noam, Ira Katznelson, R. C. Lewontin, David Montgomery, Laura Nader, Richard Ohmann, Ray Siever, Immanuel Wallerstein, and Howard Zinn. 1997. *The Cold War and the University: Towards an Intellectual History of the Postwar Years.* New York: New Press.

Choueri, Y. M. 2000. *Arab Nationalism: A History: Nation and State in the Arab World.* Oxford: Blackwell.

Chow, Kai-wing. 2005. *Publishing, Culture, and Power in Early Modern China.* Stanford University Press.

Christian, David. 2005. "Scales." In *Palgrave Advances in World Histories*, edited by Marnie Hughes-Warrington, 64–89. Basingstoke: Palgrave Macmillan.

Clark, Robert P. 1997. *The Global Imperative: An Interpretive History of the Spread of Humankind.* Boulder, CO: Westview Press.

Clavin, Patricia. 2005. "Defining Transnationalism." *Contemporary European History* 14-4: 421–39.

Clinton, Michael. 2005. "Reflections about Peace History and Peace Historians." *Peace and Change* 30-1: 55–6.

Codell, Julie F. and Dianne S. MacLeod, eds. 1998. *Orientalism Transposed: The Impact of the Colonies on British Culture*. Aldershot: Ashgate.

Cohen, Deborah and Maura O'Connor, eds. 2004. *Comparison and History: European in Cross-national Perspective*. New York: Routledge.

Cohen, Paul. 2002. "Remembering and Forgetting National Humiliation in Twentieth-Century China." *Twentieth-Century China* 27-2: 1–39.

2003."Reflections on a Watershed Date: The 1949 Divide in Chinese History." In *Twentieth-Century China: New Approaches*, edited by Jeffrey N. Wasserstrom, 27–36. London/New York: Routledge.

Conkin, Paul. 1995. *Gone with the Ivy: A Biography of Vanderbilt University*. Knoxville: University of Tennessee Press.

Connelly, Matthew. 2008. *Fatal Misconception: The Struggle to Control World Population*. Cambridge, MA: Belknap Press of Harvard University Press.

Conrad, Christoph and Sebastian Conrad, eds. 2002a. *Die Nation Schreiben: Geschichtswissenschaft im internationalen Vergleich*. Göttingen: Vandenhoeck & Ruprecht.

2002b. "Wie vergleicht man Historiographien?" In *Die Nation Schreiben: Geschichtswissenschaft im internationalen Vergleich*, edited by Christoph Conrad and Sebastian Conrad, 11–46. Göttingen: Vandenhoeck & Ruprecht.

Conrad, Christoph and Martina Kessel, eds. 1994. *Geschichte schreiben in der Postmoderne: Beiträge zur aktuellen Diskussion*. Stuttgart: Philipp Reclam.

1998. "Blickwechsel: Moderne, Kultur, Geschichte." In *Kultur und Geschichte: Neue Einblicke in eine alte Beziehung*, edited by Christoph Conrad and Martina Kessel, 9–40. Stuttgart: Philipp Reclam.

Conrad, Sebastian. 1999a. *Auf der Suche nach der verlorenen Nation: Geschichtsschreibung in Westdeutschland und Japan, 1945–1960*. Göttingen: Vandenhoeck & Ruprecht.

1999b. "What Time Is Japan? Problems of Comparative (Intercultural) Historiography." *History and Theory* 38-1: 67–83.

2002. "Doppelte Marginalisierung. Plädoyer für eine transnationale Perspektive auf die deutsche Geschichte." *Geschichte und Gesellschaft* 28: 145–69.

2006. *Globalisierung und Nation im Deutschen Kaiserreich*. Munich: C. H. Beck.

Conrad, Sebastian, Andreas Eckert and Ulrike Freitag, eds. 2007. *Globalgeschichte. Theorien, Ansätze, Themen*. Frankfurt/New York: Campus.

Conrad, Sebastian and Jürgen Osterhammel, eds. 2004. *Das Kaiserreich Transnational: Deutschland in der Welt, 1871–1914*. Göttingen: Vandenhoeck & Ruprecht.

Conrad, Sebastian and Shalini Randeria. 2002a. "Einleitung: Re-Orientierung: Geteilte Geschichte in einer postkolonialen Welt." In *Jenseits des Eurozentrismus: Transnationale und Postkoloniale Ansätze in den Geschichts- und Kulturwissenschaften*, edited by Sebastian Conrad and Shalini Randeria, 9–49. Frankfurt: Campus.

eds. 2002b. *Jenseits des Eurozentrismus: Postkoloniale Perspektiven in den Geschichts- und Kulturwissenschaften*. Frankfurt: Campus.

Conrad, Sebastian and Dominic Sachsenmaier, eds. 2007. *Competing Visions of World Order: Global Moments and Movements, 1880s–1930s.* New York: Palgrave Macmillan.

Conze, Eckart, Ulrich Lappenkuper, and Guido Müller, eds. 2004. *Geschichte der Internationalen Beziehungen: Erneuerung und Erweiterung einer historischen Disziplin.* Cologne: Böhlau.

Cooper, Frederick. 1994. "Conflict and Connection: Rethinking Colonial African History." *The American Historical Review* 99-5: 1516–45.

1997a. "Dialectics of Decolonization. Nationalism and Labor Politics in Postwar French Africa." In *Tensions of Empire: Colonial Cultures in a Bourgeois World*, edited by Frederick Cooper and Ann L. Stoler, 406–35. Berkeley: University of California Press.

1997b. "Modernizing Bureaucrats, Backward Africans, and the Development Concept." In *International Development and the Social Sciences*, edited by Frederick Cooper and Randall Packard, 64–92. Berkeley: University of California Press.

2000. "Africa's Past and Africa's Historians." *Canadian Journal of African Studies* 34-2: 298–336.

2001. "What is the Concept of Globalization Good for?" *African Affairs* 100-339: 189–213.

2005. *Colonialism in Question: Theory, Knowledge, History.* Berkeley: University of California Press.

2007. "Postcolonial Studies and the Study of History." In *Postcolonial Studies and Beyond*, edited by Ania Loomba, Suvir Kaul, Matti Bunzi, Antoinette Burton, and Jed Esty, 401–22. Durham, NC: Duke University Press.

Cooper, Frederick and Ann L. Stoler, eds. 1997. *Tensions of Empire: Colonial Cultures in a Bourgeois World.* Berkeley: University of California Press.

Cox, Robert W. 1996. "A Perspective on Globalization." In *Globalization: Critical Reflections*, edited by James H. Mittelman, 21–30. Boulder, CO: Lynne Rienner Publishers.

Crabbs, Jack. 1984. *The Writing of History in Nineteenth-Century Egypt: A Study in National Transformation.* Detroit: Wayne State University Press.

Crang, Michael and Nigel Thrift. 2000. Introduction to *Thinking Space*, edited by Michael Crang and Nigel Thrift, 1–30. London/New York: Routledge.

Crosby, Alfred W. 1972. *The Columbian Exchange: Biological and Cultural Consequences of 1492.* Westport, CT: Greenwood Press.

2004. *Ecological Imperialism: The Biological Expansion of Europe, 900–1900.* Cambridge/New York: Cambridge University Press.

Crossick, Geoffrey and Heinz-Gerhard Haupt. 1998. *Die Kleinbürger: Eine europäische Sozialgeschichte des 19. Jahrhunderts.* Munich: C. H. Beck.

Crossley, Pamela Kyle. 2008. *What Is Global History?* Cambridge: Polity.

Crozier, Ralph. 1990. "World History in the People's Republic of China." *Journal of World History* 1: 151–69.

Cui, Zhiying. 1996. "Shanghai shi shijieshi xuehui disanjie huiyuan dahui ji 1995 nian nianhui zongshu" [Summary of the Third Plenary Meeting of the

Shanghai World History Association in 1995]. *Shijie lishi* [World History] 5: 126–7.

Cui, Zhiyuan and Roberto Mangabeira Unger. Forthcoming. *China and World.* London: Verso.

Culp, Robert J. 2007. "'Weak and Small Peoples' in a 'Europeanizing World': World History Textbooks and Chinese Intellectuals' Perspectives on Global Modernity." In *The Politics of Historical Production in Late Qing and Republican China*, edited by Tze-ki Hon and Robert J. Culp, 211–47. Leiden: Brill.

Cumings, Bruce. 1998. "Boundary Displacement: Area Studies and International Studies during and after the Cold War." In *Universities and Empire: Money and Politics in the Social Sciences During the Cold War*, edited by Christopher Simpson, 159–88. New York: New Press.

Cunliffe, Barry. 2001. *Facing the Ocean: The Atlantic and Its Peoples, 8000 BC–AD 1500.* Oxford/New York: Oxford University Press.

Cusset, François. 2008. *French Theory: How Foucault, Derrida, Deleuze, and Co. Transformed the Intellectual Life of the United States.* Minneapolis: University of Minnesota Press.

Dabringhaus, Sabine. 2006. *Territorialer Nationalismus in China: Historisch-geographisches Denken, 1900–1949.* Cologne: Böhlau.

Dahlmann, Dietmar. 1986. *Land und Freiheit: Machnovsina und Zapatismo als Beispiele antirevolutionärer Bewegungen.* Stuttgart: Steiner.

Dahrendorf, Ralf. 1958. "Out of Utopia: Toward a Reorientation of Sociological Analysis." *American Journal of Sociology* 64-2: 115–27.

  1965. *Gesellschaft und Demokratie in Deutschland.* Munich: R. Piper.

Dalby, Andrew. 2001. *Dangerous Tastes: The Story of Spices.* Berkeley: University of California Press.

Daniel, Ute. 1993. " 'Kultur' und 'Gesellschaft'. Überlegungen zum Gegenstands-bereich der Sozialgeschichte." *Geschichte und Gesellschaft* 19: 69–99.

Darnton, Robert. 1984. *The Great Cat Massacre: and Other Episodes in French Cultural History.* New York: Basic Books.

  2009. "Google and the Future of Books." *New York Review of Books* 56-2 (February 12): 9–11.

Darwin, John. 2007. *After Tamerlane: The Global History of Empire, 1400–2000.* London: Allen Lane.

Daston, Lorraine. 2000. "Die unerschütterliche Praxis." In *Auf der Suche nach der verlorenen Wahrheit: Zum Grundlagenstreit in der Geschichtswissenschaft*, edited by Rainer Maria Kiesow and Dieter Simon, 13–25. Frankfurt: Campus.

Davies, Sam, Colin J. Davis, David de Vries, Lex Heerma Van Voss, and Lidewij Hesselink, eds. 2000. *Dock Workers: International Explorations in Comparative Labor History, 1790–1970.* 2 vols. Aldershot: Ashgate.

Davis, Nathalie Zemon. 2001. "Global History, Many Stories." In *Eine Welt – Eine Geschichte? 43. Deutscher Historikertag in Aachen: 26. bis 29. September*, edited by Max Kerner, 35–45. Munich: Oldenbourg.

De Freitas Dutra, Eliana. 2007. "The Mirror of History and Images of the Nation: The Invention of a National Identity in Brazil and Its Contrasts with Similar Enterprises in Mexico and Argentina." In *Writing the Nation. A Global Perspective*, edited by Stefan Berger, 84–102. Basingstoke: Palgrave Macmillan.

De Souza, Philip. 2008. *The Ancient World at War: A Global History*. New York/London: Thames & Hudson.

Demandt, Alexander. 2003. *Kleine Weltgeschichte*. Munich: C. H. Beck.

Des Forges, Roger and Xu Luo. 2001. "China's Non-Hegemonic Superpower? The Uses of History Among the *China Can Say No* Writers and Their Critics." *Critical Asian Studies* 33-4: 483–507.

Deutsche Gesellschaft für Asienkunde. 1997. "Die deutschen Asienwissenschaften an der Schwelle zum 21. Jahrhundert. Eine Standortbestimmung." *Asien* 65: 143–9.

Diamond, Jared. 1997. *Guns, Germs, and Steel: The Fates of Human Societies*. New York: W.W. Norton.

2005. *Collapse: How Societies Choose to Fail or Succeed*. New York: Viking.

Dillinger, Johannes. 2008. *Die politische Repräsentation der Landbevölkerung: Neuengland und Europa in der Frühen Neuzeit*. Stuttgart: Steiner.

Diner, Dan. 1987. *Ist der Nationalsozialismus Geschichte? Zu Historisierung und Historikerstreit*. Frankfurt: Fischer Taschenbuch.

2003. *Gedächtniszeiten. Über jüdische und andere Geschichten*. Munich: Beck.

Diouf, Mamadu. 2000. "Des historiens et des histories, pour quoi faire? L'historiographie africaine entre l'État et les communautés." *Canadian Journal of African Studies* 34-2: 337–74.

Dirks, Nicholas B., ed. 1992. *Colonialism and Culture*. Ann Arbor: University of Michigan Press.

Dirlik, Arif. 1978. *Revolution and History: the Origins of Marxist Historiography in China, 1919–1937*. Berkeley: University of California Press.

1994. "The Postcolonial Aura: Third World Criticism in the Age of Global Capitalism." *Critical Inquiry* 20: 328–56.

2000. "Reversals, Ironies, Hegemonies: Notes on the Contemporary Historiography of Modern China." In *History After the Three Worlds: Post-Eurocentric Historiographies*, edited by Arif Dirlik, Vinay Bahl, and Peter Gran, 125–56. Lanham, MD: Rowman & Littlefield.

2002a. "History without a Center? Reflections on Eurocentrism." In *Across Cultural Borders: Historiography in Global Perspective*, edited by Eckhardt Fuchs and Benedikt Stuchtey, 247–84. Lanham, MD: Rowman & Littlefield.

2002b. "Modernity as History: Post-Revolutionary China, Globalization and the Question of Modernity." *Social History* 27-1: 16–39.

Dittmer, Lowell and Samuel S. Kim. 1993. "In Search of a Theory for National Identity." In *China's Quest for National Identity*, edited by Lowell Dittmer and Samuel S. Kim, 1–31. Ithaca, NY: Cornell University Press.

Doering-Manteuffel, Anselm. 1995. "Dimensionen von Amerikanisierung in der deutschen Gesellschaft." *Archiv für Sozialgeschichte* 35: 1–35.

Dong, Fangshuo. 1996. "Xiandaihua de zhuiqiu yu jiazhi zuobiao de xuanze – du Yu Wujin jiaoshou de *xunzhao xin de jiazhi zuobiao*" [The Pursuit of

Modernization and the Choice of Value Standards – Book Review on Prof. Yu Wujin's *Looking for New Value Standards]. Xueshu yuekan* [Academic Monthly] 6: 108–22.

Dongya sanguo jinxiandaishi gongtong bianxie weiyuanhui [Trilateral Textbook Commission for Modern East Asian History]. 2005. *Dongya sanguo de jinxiandaishi* [Contemporary History of the Three Countries of East Asia]. Beijing: Shehui kexue wenxian chubanshe.

Döring, Jörg and Tristan Thielmann. 2008. "Einleitung: Was lesen wir im Raume? Der Spatial Turn und das geheime Wissen der Geographie." In *Spatial Turn: Das Raumparadigma in den Kultur- und Sozialwissenschaften*, edited by Jörg Döring and Tristan Thielmann, 9–45. Bielefeld: Transcript.

Dribins, Leo. 1999. "The Historiography of Latvian Nationalism in the Twentieth Century." In *National History and Identity: Approaches to the Writing of National History in the North-East Baltic Region Nineteenth and Twentieth Centuries*, edited by Michael Branch, 245–55. Helsinki: Finnish Literature Society.

Driver, Felix and David Gilbert, eds. 1999. *Imperial Cities: Landscape, Display and Identity*. Manchester/New York: Manchester University Press.

Du, Zhengsheng. 2002. "Xin shixue zhi lu – jianlun Taiwan wushinianlai de shixue fazhan" [The Path of New Historiography – Examining the Development of Historiography in Taiwan during the Past Fifty Years]. *Xin Shixue* [New Historiography] 13–3: 21–42.

Duara, Prasenjit. 1994. "Transnationalism in the Era of Nation States: China, 1900–1945." *Development and Change* 29-4: 647–70.

1995. *Rescuing History from the Nation: Questioning Narratives of Modern China*. University of Chicago Press.

2000. "Response to Philip Huang's 'Biculturality in Modern Chinese Studies.'" *Modern China* 26-1: 32–7.

2002. "Civilizations and Nations in a Globalizing World." In *Reflections on Multiple Modernities: European, Chinese, and Other Interpretations*, edited by Dominic Sachsenmaier, Jens Riedel, and Shmuel Eisenstadt, 79–99. Leiden: Brill.

2003. *Sovereignty and Authenticity: Manchukuo and the East Asian Modern*. Lanham, MD: Rowman & Littlefield.

ed. 2004. *Decolonization: Perspectives from Now and Then (Rewriting Histories)*. London/New York: Routledge.

2008. "The Global and Regional Constitutions of Nations: The View from East Asia." *Nations and Nationalism* 14-2: 323–45.

2009. *The Global and Regional in China's Nation Formation*. New York/London: Routledge.

Dubois, Laurent M. 2000. "La République métissée: Citizenship, Colonialism, and the Borders of French History." *Cultural Studies* 14-1: 15–34.

2004. *Avengers of the New World: The Story of the Haitian Revolution*. Cambridge, MA: Belknap Press of Harvard University Press.

Duchhardt, Heinz. 1997. "Was ist und zu welchem Ende betreibt man – europäische Geschichte?" In *"Europäische Geschichte" als historiographisches*

Problem, edited by Heinz Duchhardt and Andreas Kunz, 191–204. Mainz: P. von Zabern.

Dudziak, Mary L. 2002. *Cold War Civil Rights: Race and the Image of American Democracy*. Princeton: Princeton University Press.

Durrant, Stephen W. 1995. *The Cloudy Mirror: Tension and Conflict in the Writings of Sima Qian*. Albany: State University of New York.

Dussel, Enrique. 1993. "Eurocentrism and Modernity (Introduction to the Frankfurt Lectures)." *Boundary* 20-3: 65–76.

1998. "Beyond Eurocentrism: The World-System and the Limits of Modernity." In *The Cultures of Globalization*, edited by Fredric Jameson and Masao Miyoshi, 3–38. Durham, NC: Duke University Press.

Eaton, Richard M. 1997. "Comparative History as World History: Religious Conversion in Modern India." *Journal of World History* 8-2: 243–71.

Eckart, Wolfgang. 1997. *Medizin und Kolonialimperialismus: Deutschland 1884–1945*. Paderborn: Schöningh.

Eckert, Andreas. 1999. "Historiker, 'Nation Building' und die Rehabilitierung der afrikanischen Vergangenheit. Aspekte der Geschichtsschreibung in Afrika nach 1945." In *Geschichtsdiskurs*, vol. V: *Globale Konflikte, Erinnerungsarbeit und Neuorientierungen seit 1945*, edited by Wolfgang Küttler, Jörn Rüsen, and Ernst Schulin, 162–87. Frankfurt: Fischer Taschenbuch.

2000. "Weltgeschichte in pragmatischer Absicht? Kommentar zu Helmut Bley." In *Afrikanische Geschichte und Weltgeschichte: Regionale und universale Themen in Forschung und Lehre*, edited by Axel Harneit-Sievers, 49–53. Berlin: Das Arabische Buch.

2002. "Gefangen in der Alten Welt." *Die Zeit*, September 26: 40.

2004a. "Europäische Zeitgeschichte und der Rest der Welt." *Zeithistorische Forschungen – Studies in Contemporary History* 1-3: 416–21.

2004b. "Vom Urknall bis Genua." *Frankfurter Rundschau*, January 8.

2005. "Bitte erklären Sie uns die Welt: Deutschlands Wissenschaft und das aussereuropäische Ausland." *Internationale Politik* 6 (October): 42–9.

2006a. *Kolonialismus*. Frankfurt: S. Fischer.

2006b. "Rezension zu: *Budde, Gunilla; Conrad, Sebastion; Janz, Oliver (Hrsg.): Transnationale Geschichte: Themen, Tendenzen und Theorien. Göttingen 2006.*" *H-Soz-u-Kult* (Oct 16), http://hsozkult.geschichte.hu-berlin.de/rezensionen/2006-4-050.

2009. *Deutscher Kolonialismus*. Munich: C. H. Beck.

Eckert, Andreas and Michael Pesek. 2004. "Bürokratische Ordnung und koloniale Praxis. Herrschaft und Verwaltung in Preussen und Afrika." In *Das Kaiserreich Transnational: Deutschland in der Welt, 1871–1914*, edited by Sebastian Conrad and Jürgen Osterhammel, 87–106. Göttingen: Vandenhoeck & Ruprecht.

Eckert, Andreas and Brigitte Reinwald. 1999. "Das Geisteswissenschaftliche Zentrum Moderner Orient in Berlin." *Periplus: Jahrbuch für Aussereuropäische Geschichte* 9: 151–8.

Eckert, Andreas and Albert Wirz. 2002. "Wir nicht, die anderen auch. Deutschland und der Kolonialismus." In *Jenseits des Eurozentrismus:*

Postkoloniale Perspektiven in den Geschichts- und Kulturwissenschaften, edited by Sebastian Conrad and Shalini Randeria, 372–92. Frankfurt: Campus.

Edelmayer, Friedrich, Peter Feldbauer, and Marja Wakounig, eds. 2002. *Globalgeschichte 1450–1620.* Vienna: Promedia.

Ehmann, Annegret. 2002. "Holocaust in Politik und Bildung." In *Grenzenlose Vorurteile. Antisemitismus, Nationalismus und ethnische Konflikte in verschiedenen Kulturen,* edited by Irmtrud Wojat and Susanne Meinl, 41–68. Frankfurt.

Eisenstadt, Shmuel H. and Wolfgang Schluchter. 1998. "Introduction: Paths to Early Modernities." *Dædalus* 127–3: 1–18.

Eley, Geoff. 1998. "Problems with Culture: German History after the Linguistic Turn." *Central European History* 31: 197–227.

Elman, Benjamin A. 1984. *From Philosophy to Philology: Intellectual and Social Aspects of Change in Late Imperial China.* Cambridge, MA: Harvard University Press.

2001. *From Philosophy to Philology: Intellectual and Social Aspects of Change in Late Imperial China.* 2nd rev. edn. Los Angeles: UCLA Asian Pacific Monograph Series.

Elsenhans, Hartmut. 2001. "Zum Gang der Weltsystemstudien." *Zeitschrift für Weltgeschichte* 2-2: 33–50.

Eltis, David. 1999. "Atlantic History in Global Perspective." *Itinerario* 23-2: 141–61.

Ember, Melvin, Carol R. Ember, and Ian Skoggard, eds. 2005. *Encyclopedia of Diasporas: Immigrant and Refugee Cultures around the World.* New York: Springer.

Engel, Jonathan. 2006. *The Epidemic: A Global History of AIDS.* New York: Smithsonian Books/Collins.

Engel, Ulf and Matthias Middell. 2005. "Bruchzonen der Globalisierung, globale Krisen und Territorialitätsregime-Kategorien einer Globalgeschichtsschreibung." *Comparativ* 5-6: 5–38.

Erdmann, Karl Dietrich. 2005. *Toward a Global Community of Historians: The International Historical Congresses and the International Committee of Historical Sciences 1898–2000.* New York: Berghahn Books.

Ertl, Thomas and Michael Limberger, eds. 2009. *Die Welt 1250–1500.* Vienna: Mandelbaum.

Eschle, Catherine and Bice Maihguashca, eds. 2005. *Critical Theories, International Relations, and the 'Anti-Globalization Movement': The Politics of Global Resistance.* London/New York: Routledge.

Esherick, Joseph W. 2006. "How the Qing Became China." In *Empire to Nation: Historical Perspectives on the Making of the Modern World,* edited by Joseph W. Esherick, Hasan Kayali, and Eric Van Young, 229–59. Lanham, MD: Rowman & Littlefield.

Esherick, Joseph W. and Mary Backus Rankin. 1990. Introduction to *Chinese Local Elites and Patterns of Dominance,* edited by Joseph W. Esherick and Mary Backus Rankin, 1–25. Berkeley: University of California Press.

Espagne, Michel. 2003. "Der theoretische Stand der Kulturtransferforschung." In *Kulturtransfer. Kulturelle Praxis im 16. Jahrhundert,* edited by Wolfgang Schmale, 63–75. Innsbruck: Studien.

Evans, Luther H. 1965. "The Humanities and International Communication." *Publications of the Modern Language Association of America (PMLA)* 80-2: 37–42.

Evans, Richard. 1998. *Fakten und Fiktionen: Über die Grundlagen historischer Erkenntnis.* Frankfurt: Campus.

Fahrmeir, Andreas. 2007. *Citizenship: The Rise and Fall of a Modern Concept.* New Haven: Yale University Press.

Faist, Thomas. 2002. "Transnationalization in International Migration: Implications for the Study of Citizenship and Culture." *Ethnic and Racial Studies* 23-2: 189–222.

Fan, Shuzhi. 2003. *Wanming shi* [A History of the Late Ming]. Shanghai: Fudan daxue chubanshe.

Feierman, Steven. 1993. "African Histories and the Dissolution of World History." In *Africa and the Disciplines: The Contributions of Research in Africa to the Social Sciences and Humanities,* edited by Robert H. Bates, V. Y. Mudimbe, and Jean O'Barr, 167–212. University of Chicago Press.

1999. "Colonizers, Scholars, and the Creation of Invisible Histories." In *Beyond the Cultural Turn: New Directions in the Study of Society and Culture,* edited by Victoria E. Bonnelli and Lynn Hunt, 182–216. Berkeley: University of California Press.

Feldbauer, Peter. 2009. *Die Welt im 16. Jahrhundert.* Vienna: Mandelbaum.

Feldbauer, Peter and Andrea Komolsy. 2003. "Globalgeschichte 1450–1820: Von der Expansions- zur Interaktionsgeschichte." In *Die Welt querdenken: Festschrift für Hans-Heinrich Nolte zum 65. Geburtstag,* edited by Carl-Hans Hauptmeyer, Dariusz Adamczyk, Beate Eschment, and Udo Obal, 59–94. Frankfurt/New York: Peter Lang.

Feldner, Heiko. 2003. "The New Scientificity in Historical Writing Around 1800." In *Writing History: Theory and Practice,* edited by Stefan Berger, Heiko Feldner, and Kevin Passmore, 3–22. London: Arnold.

Feng, Erkang. 2009/2010. "Studies on Qing History: Past, Present, and Problems." *Chinese Studies in History* 43-2: 20–32.

Feng, Gang. 2000. "Guanyu zhongguo jindaishi yanjiu de 'xiandaihua fanshi'" [On the "Paradigm of Modernization" in Contemporary Chinese Historical Research]. *Tianjin shehui kexue* [The Tianjin Social Sciences Journal] 5: 75–8.

Fenske, Hans. 1991. "Ungeduldige Zuschauer. Die Deutschen und die Europäische Expansion, 1815–1880." In *Imperialistische Kontinuität und nationale Ungeduld im 19. Jahrhundert,* edited by Wolfgang Reinhard, 87–123. Frankfurt: Fischer Taschenbuch.

Ferguson, James. 1997. "Anthropology and Its Evil Twin: 'Development' in the Constitution of a Discipline." In *International Development and the Social Sciences: Essays on the History and Politics of Knowledge,* edited by Frederick Cooper and Randall Packard, 150–75. Berkeley: University of California Press.

Ferguson, Niall. 2003. *Empire. The Rise and Demise of the British World Order and the Lessons for Global Power.* London: Penguin.

Fernandez-Armesto, Felipe. 2006. *Pathfinders: A Global History of Exploration.* New York: Oxford University Press.

Ferro, Marc. 1997. *Colonization: A Global History.* London: Routledge.

Fewsmith, Joseph. 2001. *China since Tiananmen: The Politics of Transition.* Cambridge/New York: Cambridge University Press.

Fink, Carole, Philipp Gassert, and Detlef Junker, eds. 1998. *1968: The World Transformed.* Cambridge: Cambridge University Press.

Fischer, Wolfram. 1998. *Expansion – Integration – Globalisierung: Studien zur Geschichte der Weltwirtschaft.* Göttingen: Vandenhoeck & Ruprecht.

Fischer Taschenbuch Verlag. 1965–1981. *Fischer Weltgeschichte.* Frankfurt: Fischer Taschenbuch.

Fischer-Tiné, Harald. 2007. "Global Civil Society and the Forces of Empire: The Salvation Army, British Imperialism and the 'Pre-history' of NGOs (ca. 1880–1920)." In *Competing Visions of World Order: Global Moments and Movements, 1880s–1930s,* edited by Sebastian Conrad and Dominic Sachsenmaier, 29–67. New York: Palgrave Macmillan.

Fitzgerald, Frances. 1979. *America Revised: History Schoolbooks in the Twentieth Century.* Boston: Little Brown.

Fitzpatrick, Matthew. 2005. "Review of Zimmerer, Jürgen; Zeller, Joachim, *Völkermord in Deutsch-Südwestafrika: Der Kolonialkrieg (1904–1908) in Namibia und seine Folgen.*" *H-German* (February), http://www.h-net.org/reviews/showrev.php?id=10206.

2008a. *Liberalism and Imperialism in Germany: Expansionism and Nationalism, 1848–1884.* New York: Berghahn Books.

2008b. "The Pre-History of the Holocaust? The Sonderweg and Historikerstreit Debates and the Abject Colonial Past." *Central European History* 41: 477–503.

Flynn, Dennis O. and Arturo Giráldez. 2004. "Path Dependence, Time Lags and the Birth of Globalization: A Critique of O'Rourke and Williamson." *European Review of Economic History* 8: 81–108.

Fogel, Joshua A., ed. 2000. *The Nanjing Massacre in History and Historiography.* Berkeley: University of California Press.

ed. 2004. *The Role of Japan in Liang Qichao's Introduction of Modern Western Civilization to China.* Berkeley: CA Institute of East Asian Studies.

Frank, Andre G. 1969. *Capitalism and Underdevelopment in Modern Latin America: Historical Studies of Chile and Brazil.* New York: Modern Reader Paperbacks.

1998. *ReOrient: Global Economy in the Asian Age.* Berkeley: University of California Press.

Frank, Thomas. 2004. *What's the Matter with Kansas? How Conservatives Won the Heart of America.* New York: Henry Holt.

Franklin, John Hope. 2005. *Mirror to America: The Autobiography of John Hope Franklin.* New York: Farrar, Straus and Giroux.

Frei, Norbert. 1993. "Wie modern war der Nationalsozialismus?" *Geschichte und Gesellschaft* 19: 365–87.

Freitag, Ulrike. 1997. "The Critique of Orientalism." In *Companion to Historiography,* edited by Michael Bentley, 620–38. London/New York: Taylor & Francis.

1999. "Nationale Selbstvergewisserung und der 'Andere': Arabische Geschichtsschreibung nach 1945." In *Geschichtsdiskurs*, vol. V: *Globale Konflikte, Erinnerungsarbeit und Neuorientierungen seit 1945*, edited by Wolfgang Küttler, Jörn Rüsen, and Ernst Schulin, 142–61. Frankfurt: Fischer Taschenbuch.

2005. "Translokalität als ein Zugang zur Geschichte globaler Verflechtungen." *H-Soz-u-Kult*, hsozkult.geschichte.hu-berlin.de/forum/ 2005–06–001.pdf.

French, John. 2006a. *Globalizing Protest and Policy: Neo-Liberalism, Worker Rights, and the Rise of Alt-Global Politics*. Durham, NC: Duke University Press.

2006b. "Wal-Mart, Retail Supremacy, and the Relevance of Political Economy: The Intermestic Challenge of Contemporary Research (Academic, Agitational, and Constructive)." *Labor: Studies in Working Class History of the Americas* 4-1: 33–40.

Frevert, Ute. 1991. "Klasse und Geschlecht – ein deutscher Sonderweg?" In *Nichts als Unterdrückung? Geschlecht und Klasse in der englischen Sozialgeschichte*, edited by Logie Barrow, Dorothea Schmidt, and Julia Schwarzkopf, 259–70. Münster: Westfälisches Dampfboot.

Frey, Marc. 2007. "Rezension zu: *Klein, Thoralf; Schumacher, Frank (Hrsg.): Kolonialkriege. Militärische Gewalt im Zeichen des Imperialismus. Hamburg 2006*." *H-Soz-u-Kult* (March 16), http://hsozkult.geschichte.hu-berlin.de/ rezensionen/2007–1–179.

Freyer, Hans. 1949. *Weltgeschichte Europas*. 2 vols. Wiesbaden: Dieterich.

1955. *Theorie des gegenwärtigen Zeitalters*. Stuttgart: Deutsche Verlags-Anstalt.

Friedländer, Saul. 1993. *Memory, History, and the Extermination of the Jews of Europe*. Bloomington: Indiana University Press.

Friedrichsmeyer, Sara, Sara Lennox, and Susanne Zantop. 1998. *The Imperialist Imagination: German Colonialism and Its Legacy*. Ann Arbor: University of Michigan Press.

Fuchs, Eckhardt. 2002. "Introduction: Provincializing Europe: Historiography as a Transcultural Concept." In *Across Cultural Borders: Historiography in Global Perspective*, edited by Eckhardt Fuchs and Benedikt Stuchtey, 1–26. Lanham, MD: Rowman & Littlefield.

2005. "Welt- und Globalgeschichte – Ein Blick über den Atlantik." *H-Soz-u-Kult* (March 31), http//hsozkult.geschichte.hu-berlin.de/forum/2005–03– 004.

Fuchs, Eckhardt and Matthias Middell, eds. 2006. *Teaching World History* (= *Comparativ* 16–1). Leipzig: Leipziger Universitätsverlag.

Fuchs, Eckhardt and Benedikt Stuchtey, eds. 2002. *Across Cultural Borders: Historiography in Global Perspective*. Lanham, MD: Rowman & Littlefield.

eds. 2003. *Writing World History, 1800–2000*. Oxford University Press.

Fudan daxue lishixi, ed. 2009. *Jiangnan yu zhongwai jiaoliu – fudan shixue jikan di san ji* [The Yangzi River Delta and China's Foreign Connections – Fudan History Studies Series, vol. III]. Shanghai: Fudan daxue chubanshe.

Fudan daxue lishixi chuban bowuguan, ed. 2009. *Lishishang de zhongguo chuban yu dongya wenhua jiaoliu* [The History of Chinese Publishing and East Asian Cultural Exchanges]. Shanghai: Shanghai baijia chubanshe.

Fuhrmann, Malte. 2006. *Der Traum vom deutschen Orient: Zwei deutsche Kolonien im Osmanischen Reich 1851–1918*. Frankfurt: Campus.

Fulbrook, Mary. 1999. *German National Identity after the Holocaust*. Cambridge: Polity Press.

Furet, François. 1991. *La Révolution, 1770–1880*. Paris: Hachette.

Fürtig, Henner and Gerhard Höpp, eds. 1998. *Wessen Geschichte? Muslimische Erfahrungen historischer Zäsuren im 20. Jahrhundert*. Berlin: Verlag Das Arabische Buch.

Füssel, Karl-Heinz. 2004. *Deutsch-Amerikanischer Kulturaustausch im 20. Jahrhundert: Bildung, Wissenschaft, Politik*. Frankfurt/New York: Campus.

Gabaccia, Donna R. and Franca Iacovetta, eds. 2002. *Women, Gender and Transnational Lives: Italian Workers of the World*. Toronto: University of Toronto Press.

Galtung, Johan. 1999. "World/Global/Universal History and the Present Historiography." *Storia della Storiografia* 35: 141–61.

Galtung, Johan and Sohail Inayatullah, eds. 1997. *Macrohistory and Macrohistorians: Perspectives on Individual, Social, and Civilizational Change*. Westport, CT: Praeger.

Gandhi, Leela. 1998. *Postcolonial Theory: A Critical Introduction*. Edinburgh: Edinburgh University Press.

Gao, Yi. 1997. "French Revolutionary Studies in Today's China." *Canadian Journal of History* 32-3: 437–47.

Garon, Sheldon. 2000. "Luxury Is the Enemy: Mobilizing Savings and Popularizing *Thrift* in Wartime Japan." *Journal of Japanese Studies* 26-1 (Winter): 41–78.

Ge, Zhaoguang. 2010. "Cong 'xiyu' dao 'donghai' – yige xin lishi de xingcheng, fangfa ji wenti" [From the 'Western Regions' to the 'Eastern Sea' – The Genesis of a New History: Methods and Problems]. *Wen shi zhe* [Journal of Literature, History and Philosophy] 1: 18–25.

Geiger, Robert L. 2005. "The Ten Generations of American Higher Education." In *American Higher Education in the Twenty-First Century: Social, Political, and Economic Challenges*, edited by Philip G. Altbach, Robert Berdahl, and Patricia Gumport, 38–70. Baltimore: Johns Hopkins University Press.

Georgi, Viola. 2000. "Wem gehört deutsche Geschichte? Bikulturelle Jugendliche und die Geschichte des Nationalsozialismus." In *"Erziehung nach Auschwitz" in der multikulturellen Gesellschaft. Pädagogische und soziologische Annäherungen*, edited by Bernd Fechler, Gottfried Kößler and Till Liebertz-Groß, 141–62. Weinheim: Juventa.

Gerber, Adrian. 2005. "Transnationale Geschichte 'machen' – Anmerkungen zu einem möglichen Vorgehen." *H-Soz-u-Kult* (April 2), http://hsozkult. geschichte.hu-berlin.de/forum/2005–04–001.pdf.

Gerbig-Fabel, Marco. 2006. "Transnationalität in der Praxis." *Geschichte Transnational* (June 14), http://geschichte-transnational.clio-online.net/ tagungsberichte/id=1150.

Gereffi, Gary and Miguel Korzeniewicz, eds. 1994. *Commodity Chains and Global Capitalism*. Westport, CT: Greenwood Press.

Gerlach, Christian. 2004. "Some Recent Trends in German Holocaust Research." In *New Currents in Holocaust Research*, edited by Jeffrey M. Diefendorf, 285–99. Evanston, IL: North Western University Press.

Gessenharter, Wolfgang. 1994. *Kippt die Republik? Die Neue Rechte und ihre Unterstützung durch Politik und Medien*. Munich: Knaur.

Geulen, Christian. 2004. *Wahlverwandte: Rassendiskurs und Nationalismus im späten 19. Jahrhundert*. Hamburg: Hamburger Edition.

2007. "The Common Grounds of Conflict: Racial Visions of World Order 1880–1940." In *Competing Visions of World Order. Global Moments and Movements, 1880s–1930s*, edited by Sebastian Conrad and Dominic Sachsenmaier, 69–96. New York: Palgrave Macmillan.

Geyer, Martin H. and Johannes Paulmann, eds. 2001. *The Mechanics of Internationalism: Culture, Society, and Politics from the 1840s to the First World War*. Oxford/New York: Oxford University Press.

Geyer, Michael. 1990. "Looking Back at the International Style: Some Reflections on the Current State of German History." *German Studies Review* 13-1: 112–27.

2004. "Deutschland und Japan im Zeitalter der Globalisierung: Überlegungen zu einer komparativen Geschichte jenseits des Modernisierungs-Paradigmas." In *Das Kaiserreich Transnational: Deutschland in der Welt, 1871–1914*, edited by Sebastian Conrad and Jürgen Osterhammel, 68–86. Göttingen: Vandenhoeck & Ruprecht.

2006. "Rezension zu: Budde, Gunille; Conrad, Sebastian; Janz, Oliver (Hrsg.): *Transnationale Geschichte. Themen, Tendenzen und Theorien. Göttingen 2006*." *H-Soz-u-Kult* (October 11), http://hsozkult.geschichte.hu-berlin.de/rezensionen/2006-4-032.

Geyer, Michael and Charles Bright. 1995. "World History in a Global Age." *The American Historical Review* 100-4: 1034–60.

1996. "Global Violence and Nationalizing Wars in Eurasia and America: The Geopolitics of War in the Mid-Nineteenth Century." *Comparative Studies in Society and History* 38-4: 623–53.

Gibbons, Michael, Camille Limoges, Helga Nowotny, Simon Schwartzman, Peter Scott, and Martin Trow. 1994. *The New Production of Knowledge: The Dynamics of Science and Research in Contemporary Societies*. London: Sage Publications.

Giddens, Anthony. 2000. *Runaway World: How Globalization Is Reshaping Our Lives*. New York: Routledge.

Gienow-Hecht, Jessica. 1999. *Transmission Impossible: American Journalism as Cultural Diplomacy in Postwar Germany, 1945–1955*. Baton Rouge: Louisiana State University Press.

Gienow-Hecht, Jessica and Frank Schumacher, eds. 2003. *Culture and International History*. New York: Berghahn Books.

Giere, Jacqueline. 1996. *Die gesellschaftliche Konstruktion des Zigeuners*. Frankfurt: Campus.

Giesen, Bernhard. 1993. *Die Intellektuellen und die Nation: Eine deutsche Achsenzeit*. Frankfurt: Suhrkamp.

Gilroy, Paul. 1993. *The Black Atlantic: Modernity and Double Consciousness.* Cambridge, MA: Harvard University Press.

Glasso, Glenn. 2008. "What Appeared Limitless Plenty: The Rise and Fall of the Nineteenth-Century Atlantic Halibut Fishery." *Environmental History* 13-1: 66–91.

Glick-Schiller, Nina. 2004. "Transnationality." In *A Companion to the Anthropology of Politics*, edited by David Nugent and Joan Vincent, 448–67. Malden, MA: Blackwell.

        2005."Transnational Social Fields and Imperialism: Bringing a Theory of Power to Transnational Studies." *Anthropological Theory* 5-4: 439–61.

Goetz, Walter ed. 1929–1933. *Propyläen-Weltgeschichte. Der Werdegang der Menschheit in Gesellschaft und Staat, Wirtschaft und Geistesleben.* 10 vols. Berlin: Propyläen Verlag.

Goldman, Merle and Andrew J. Nathan. 2000. "Searching for the Appropriate Model for the People's Republic of China." In *Historical Perspectives on Contemporary East Asia*, edited by Merle Goldman and Andrew Gordon, 297–319. Cambridge, MA: Harvard University Press.

Goldthorpe, John H. 1997. "Current Issues in Comparative Macrosociology: A Debate on Methodological Issues." *Comparative Social Research* 16: 1–26.

Gollwitzer, Heinz. 1972–1982. *Geschichte des weltpolitischen Denkens.* 2 vols. Göttingen: Vandenhoeck & Ruprecht.

Gong, Gerrit. 1984. *The Standard of Civilization in the International Society.* Oxford: Clarendon Press.

Goodwin, Neva, Julie A. Nelson, Frank Ackerman, and Thomas Weiskopf. 2008. *Microeconomics in Context.* Armonk, NY: M. E. Sharpe.

Goody, Jack. 1996. *The East in the West.* Cambridge/New York: Cambridge University Press.

        2007. *The Theft of History.* Cambridge/New York: Cambridge University Press.

        2010. *The Eurasian Miracle.* Cambridge/New York: Cambridge University Press.

Goonatilake, Susanta. 1999. *Toward a Global Science: Mining Civilizational Knowledge.* Bloomington: Indiana University Press.

Görtemaker, Manfred. 2002. *Kleine Geschichte der Bundesrepublik Deutschland.* Munich: C. H. Beck.

Gosewinkel, Dieter, Dieter Rucht, Wolfgang van den Daele, and Jürgen Kocka, eds. 2003. *Zivilgesellschaft: National und transnational.* Berlin: Edition Sigma.

Gottlob, Michael. 1997. "Indische Geschichtswissenschaft und Kolonialismus." In *Geschichtsdiskurs*, vol. IV: *Krisenbewusstsein, Katastrophenerfahrungen und Innovationen 1880–1945*, edited by Wolfgang Küttler, Jörn Rüsen, and Ernst Schulin, 314–38. Frankfurt: Fischer Taschenbuch.

Gottlob, Michael, Achim Mittag, and Jörn Rüsen, eds. 1998. *Die Vielfalt der Kulturen.* Frankfurt: Suhrkamp.

Gould, Eliga H. 2007a. "Entangled Atlantic Histories: A Response from the Anglo-American Periphery." *American Historical Review* 112-5: 1415–22.

2007b. "Entangled Histories, Entangled Worlds: The English-Speaking Atlantic as a Spanish Periphery." *American Historical Review* 112-3: 764–86.

Gowilt, Chris. 1995. "True West: The Changing Idea of the West from the 1880s to the 1920s." In *Enduring Western Civilization. The Construct of the Concept of Western Civilization and Its 'Others'*, edited by Sylvia Federici, 37–63. Westport, CT: Praeger.

Grafton, Anthony. 1997. *The Footnote: A Curious History.* Cambridge, MA: Harvard University Press.

2007. *What Was History? The Art of History in Early Modern Europe.* Cambridge/New York: Cambridge University Press.

Graichen, Gisela and Horst Gründer. 2007. *Deutsche Kolonien. Traum und Trauma.* Berlin: Ullstein.

Gran, Peter. 1996. *Beyond Eurocentrism: A New View of Modern World History.* Syracuse University Press.

Grandner, Margarete and Andrea Komlosy, eds. 2004. *Vom Weltgeist beseelt. Globalgeschichte 1700–1815.* Vienna: Promedia.

Gräser, Marcus. 2006. "Weltgeschichte im Nationalstaat. Die transnationale Disposition der amerikanischen Geschichtswissenschaft." *Historische Zeitschrift* 283-2: 355–82.

2009. "World History in a Nation-State: The Transnational Disposition in Historical Writing in the United States." *Journal of American History* 95: 1038–52.

Green, William A. 1998. "Periodizing World History." In *World History: Ideologies, Structures, and Identities*, edited by Philip Pomper, Richard H. Elphik, and Richard T. Vann, 53–68. Malden, MA: Blackwell.

Greenblatt, Stephen. 1995. "Culture." In *Critical Terms for Literary Study*, edited by Frank Lentricchia and Thomas McLaughlin, 225–32. University of Chicago Press.

Greiffenhagen, Martin and Sylvia Greiffenhagen. 1993. *Ein schwieriges Vaterland: Zur politischen Kultur im vereinigten Deutschland.* Munich: List.

Grew, Raymond. 2000. *Food in Global History.* Boulder, CO: Westview Press.

Gries, Peter H. 2004. *China's New Nationalism: Pride, Politics, and Diplomacy.* Berkeley: University of California Press.

2007. "Narratives to Live By: The Century of Humiliation and Chinese National Identity Today." In *China's Transformations: The Stories Beyond the Headlines*, edited by Lionel M. Jensen and Timothy B. Weston, 112–28. Lanham, MD: Rowman & Littlefield.

Gross, Raphael, ed. 2006. *Jüdische Geschichte als Allgemeine Geschichte. Festschrift für Dan Diner zum 60. Geburtstag.* Göttingen: Vandenhoeck & Ruprecht.

Grundy, Kenneth W. 1966. "African Explanations of Underdevelopment: The Theoretical Basis for Political Action." *The Review of Politics* 28-1: 62–75.

Gu, Edward X. 1999. "Cultural Intellectuals and the Politics of Cultural Public Space in Communist China, 1979–1989." *Journal of Asian Studies* 58-2: 389–431.

Guha, Ranajit. 1982a. "On the Historiography of Indian Nationalism." In *Subaltern Studies*, vol. I, edited by Ranajit Guha, 1–8. Delhi: Oxford University Press.

1982b. "The Prose of Counter-Insurgence." In *Subaltern Studies*, vol. II, edited by Ranajit Guha, 45–86. Delhi: Oxford University Press.

Guha, Sumit. 2004. "Speaking Historically: The Changing Voices of Historical Narration in Western India, 1400–1900." *American Historical Review* 109-4: 1084–103.

Guillén, Mauro F. 2001. "Is Globalization Civilizing, Destructive or Feeble? A Critique of Five Key Debates in the Social Science Literature." *Annual Review of Sociology* 27: 235–60.

Gunn, Geoffrey C. 2003. *First Globalization: The Eurasian Exchange 1500–1800*. Lanham, MD: Rowman & Littlefield.

Guo, Huiying. 2002. "Fan 'Ouzhou zhongxin zhuyi' shijie tixi lunzhanli de zhonguo yu shijie" [China and the World in the Debate against 'Eurocentrism' in World System Theory]. *Xin lishi* [New History] 13-3: 241–6.

Guo, Shaotang. 2003. "Wenhua de chongji yu chaoyue: dangdai xianggang shixue" [The Clash of Cultures and the Transcendence of Cultures: Contemporary Historiography in Hongkong]. *Lishi yanjiu* [Historical Research] 1: 120–8.

Guo, Shengming. 1983. *Xifang shixueshi gaiyao* [Outline of the History of Western Historiography]. Shanghai: Shanghai renmin chubanshe.

Guthrie, Doug. 2006. *China and Globalization: The Social, Economic and Political Transformation of Chinese Society*. London: CRC Press.

Guy, R. Kent. 1987. *The Emperor's Four Treasures: Scholars and the State in the Late Ch'ien-lung Era*. Cambridge, MA: Harvard University Press.

Haar, Ingo. 2000. *Historiker im Nationalsozialismus: Deutsche Geschichtswissenschaft und der "Volkstumskampf" im Osten*. Göttingen: Vandenhoeck & Ruprecht.

Habermas, Jürgen. 2000. *The Inclusion of the Other: Studies in Political Theory*. Cambridge, MA: MIT Press.

Haboush, JaHyun Kim. 2005. "Contesting Chinese Time, Nationalizing Temporal Space: Temporal Inscription in Late Choson Korea." In *Time, Temporality, and Imperial Transition: East Asia from Ming to Qing*, edited by Lynn A. Struve, 115–41. Honolulu: Association for Asian Studies and University of Hawai'i Press.

Haddad, Mahmoud. 1994. "The Rise of Arab Nationalism Reconsidered." *International Journal of Middle East Studies* 26-2: 201–22.

Haebich, Anna Elizabeth. 2005. "The Battlefields of Aboriginal History." In *Australia's History. Themes and Debates*, edited by Martyn Lyons and Penny Russell, 1–22. Sydney: University of New South Wales Press.

Hafner-Burton, Emile M. and Kiyoteru Tsutsui. 2005. "Human Rights in a Global World: The Paradox of Empty Promises." *American Journal of Sociology* 110-5: 1373–411.

Hall, Catherine, ed. 2000. *Cultures of Empire: A Reader: Colonizers in Britain and the Empire in the 19th and 20th Centuries*. Manchester/New York: Manchester University Press.

Hall, Marcus. 2005. *Earth Repair: A Transatlantic History of Environmental Restoration*. Charlottesville: University of Virginia Press.

Hamashita, Takeshi. 1988. "The Tribute Trade System and Modern Asia." *Memoirs of the Research Department Toyo Bunko* 46: 7–25.

Harbsmeier, Michael. 1991. "World Histories Before Domestication: The Writing of Universal Histories, Histories of Mankind and World Histories in Late Eighteenth-Century Germany." *Culture and History* 11: 23–59.

Hardt, Michael and Antonio Negri. 2004. *Multitude: War and Democracy in the Age of Empire*. New York: Penguin Press.

2006. *Empire*. Cambridge, MA: Harvard University Press.

Hardy, Grant. 1994. "Can an Ancient Chinese Historian Contribute to Modern Western Theory? The Multiple Narratives of Ssu-ma Ch'ien." *History and Theory* 33-1: 20–38.

Harneit-Sievers, Axel, ed. 2000. *Afrikanische Geschichte und Weltgeschichte: Regionale und universale Themen in Forschung und Lehre*. Berlin: Das Arabische Buch.

2002. *A Place in the World. New Local Historiographies from Africa to South Asia*. Leiden/Boston: Brill.

Hartog, Francois. 1988. *The Mirror of Herodotus: The Representations of the Other in the Writing of History*. Berkeley: University of California Press.

Harvey, John T. and Robert Garnett, eds. 2008. *Future Directions for Heterodox Economics*. Ann Arbor: University of Michigan Press.

Hattendorf, John B., ed. 2007. *The Oxford Encyclopedia of Maritime History*. Oxford/New York: Oxford University Press.

Haupt, Heinz-Gerhard. 2002. "Auf der Suche nach der europäischen Geschichte: Einige Neuerscheinungen." *Archiv für Sozialgeschichte* 42: 544–56.

2004. "Die Geschichte Europas als vergleichende Geschichtsschreibung." *Comparativ* 14-3: 83–97.

2006. "Historische Komparatistik in der internationalen Geschichtsschreibung." In *Transnationale Geschichte: Themen, Tendenzen und Theorien*, edited by Gunilla Budde, Sebastian Conrad, and Oliver Janz, 137–49. Göttingen: Vandenhoeck & Ruprecht.

Haupt, Heinz-Gerhard and Jürgen Kocka, eds. 1996. *Geschichte und Vergleich: Ansätze und Ergebnisse international vergleichender Geschichtsschreibung*. Frankfurt/New York: Campus.

Hausmann, Frank-Rutger. 1998. *"Deutsche Geisteswissenschaft" im Zweiten Weltkrieg. Die "Aktion Riterbusch" (1940–1945)*. Dresden: Dresden University Press.

Hawkins, Michael. 1997. *Social Darwinism in European and American Thought 1860–1945: Nature as Model and Nature as Threat*. Cambridge University Press.

He, Fangchuan. 2000. "Yingjie zhongguo de shijieshi yanjiu xinjiyuan – ershi shiji zhongguo shijieshi yanjiu de huigu yu zhanwang" [Meet the Beginning of a New Era of Chinese World Historical Research – Looking Back at Chinese World Historical Studies during the Twentieth Century and Looking Ahead]. *Shijie lishi* [World History] 4: 74–82.

He, Fangchuan and Yu Pei. 2005. "Shijie lishi yanjiusuo jiansuo sishi zhounian xueshu yantaohui zongshu" [A Summary of the Symposium on the Fortieth Anniversary of the Institute of World History (at the Chinese Academy of Social Sciences)]. *Shijie lishi* [World History] 1: 129–33.

He, Ping. 2000. "Ershi shiji bashi niandai zhongguo shixue fazhan ruogan qushi" [Some Trends in the Development of Chinese Historiography during the 1980s]. *Shixue lilun yanjiu* [Historiography Quarterly] 1: 67–79.

Headley, John M. 2008. *The Europeanization of the World: On the Origins of Human Rights and Democracy.* Princeton University Press.

Hearn, Mark. 2007. "Writing the Nation in Australia: Australian Historians and Narrative Myths of a Nation." In *Writing the Nation. A Global Perspective,* edited by Stefan Berger, 103–25. Basingstoke: Palgrave Macmillan.

Heater, Derek. 1992. *The Idea of European Unity.* New York: St. Martin's Press.

Heil, Johannes. 1999. "Deutsch-jüdische Geschichte, ihre Grenzen, und die Grenzen ihrer Synthesen." *Historische Zeitschrift* 269: 653–80.

Heilbron, Johan, Lars Magnusson, and Björn Wittrock, eds. 1998. *The Rise of the Social Sciences and the Formation of Modernity: Conceptual Change in Context 1750–1850.* Dordrecht: Kluwer Academic Publishers.

Hein, Laura and Mark Selden. 2000. "The Lessons of War, Global Power, and Social Change." In *Censoring History: Citizenship and Memory in Japan, Germany and the United States,* edited by Laura Hein and Mark Selden, 3–52. Armonk, NY: M. E. Sharpe.

Held, David, Anthony McGrew, David Goldblatt, and Jonathan Perraton. 1999. *Global Transformations: Politics, Economics and Culture.* Stanford: Stanford University Press.

Helmolt, Hans, ed. 1899–1907. *Weltgeschichte.* 9 vols. Leipzig: Bibliographisches Institut.

Herbert, Ulrich. 2000. "Extermination Policy: New Answers and Questions About the History of the Holocaust." In *Nationalist Socialist Extermination Policy: Contemporary German Perspectives and Controversies,* edited by Ulrich Herbert, 1–52. New York: Berghahn Books.

   2001. *Geschichte der Ausländerpolitik in Deutschland: Saisonarbeiter – Gastarbeiter – Flüchtlinge.* Munich: Beck.

Herren, Madeleine. 2000. *Hintertüren zur Macht: Internationalismus und modernisierungsorientierte Außenpolitik in Belgien, der Schweiz und den USA.* Munich: Oldenbourg.

Heuss, Alfred. 1960. "Introduction to *Propyläen Weltgeschichte: Eine Universalgeschichte,*" vol. I: *Vorgeschichte – Frühe Hochkulturen,* edited by Alfred Heuss, Golo Mann, and August Nitschke, 11–32. Frankfurt: Propyläen Verlag.

Heuss, Alfred, Golo Mann, and August Nitschke. 1960–1965. *Propyläen Weltgeschichte: Eine Universalgeschichte*: 10 vols. Frankfurt: Propyläen Verlag.

Hevia, James J. 2007. "Remembering the Century of Humiliation: The Yuanming Gardens and Dagu Forts Museum." In *Ruptured Histories: War, Memory, and the Post-Cold War in East Asia,* edited by Sheila M. Jager and Rana Mitter, 192–208. Cambridge, MA: Harvard University Press.

Hiery, Hermann. 1995. *Das deutsche Reich in der Südsee (1900–1921)*. Göttingen: Vandenhoeck & Ruprecht.

Higham, John. 1989. *History: Professional Scholarship in America*. 2nd edn. Baltimore: Johns Hopkins University Press.

Hill, Christopher L. 2008. *National History and the World of Nations: Capital, State, and the Rhetoric of History in Japan, France, and the United States*. Durham, NC: Duke University Press.

Hillenbrand, Carole. 2000. *The Crusades: Islamic Perspectives*. New York: Routledge.

Ho, Engseng. 2004. "Empire Through Diasporic Eyes: A View from the Other Boat." *Comparative Studies in Society and History* 46-2: 210–46.

Hobsbawm, Eric J. 1990. *Nations and Nationalism since 1780: Programme, Myth, Reality*. Cambridge/New York: Cambridge University Press.

1992. *The Invention of Tradition*. Cambridge University Press.

Hoerder, Dirk and Leslie P. Moch, eds. 1996. *European Migrants: Global and Local Perspectives*. Boston: Northeastern University Press.

Hon, Tze-ki. 2007. "Educating the Citizens: Visions of China in Late Qing History Textbooks." In *The Politics of Historical Production in Late Qing and Republican China*, edited by Tze-ki Hon and Robert J. Culp, 79–108. Leiden: Brill.

Hon, Tze-ki and Robert J. Culp, eds. 2007. *The Politics of Historical Production in Late Qing and Republican China*. Leiden: Brill.

Honold, Alexander and Klaus R. Scherpe, eds. 2004. *Mit Deutschland um die Welt. Eine Kulturgeschichte des Fremden in der Kolonialzeit*. Stuttgart: Metzler.

Hopkins, Anthony G., ed. 2002a. *Globalization in World History*. New York: W. W. Norton.

2002b. "Introduction: Globalization – An Agenda for Historians." In *Globalization in World History*, edited by Anthony G. Hopkins, 1–10. London: W. W. Norton.

2006. "Introduction: Interactions Between the Universal and the Local." In *Global History: Interactions between the Universal and the Local*, edited by Anthony G. Hopkins, 1–38. New York: Palgrave Macmillan.

Hoston, Germaine A. 1986. *Marxism and the Crisis of Development in Prewar Japan*. Princeton University Press.

Hou, Jianxin. 2000. "Xin shiji woguo de shijieshi yanjiu yao shang xinshuiping" [In the New Century World Historical Research in Our Country Must Reach a New Level]. *Shijie lishi* [World History] 1, 13-4.

Howe, Stephen. 2001. "The Slow Deaths and Strange Rebirths of Imperial History." *Journal of Imperial and Commonwealth History* 29-2: 131–41.

Hsiung, Ping-chen. 2005. "Moving the World According to a Shifted 'I': World History Texts in Republican China and Post-War Taiwan." *Berliner China Hefte* 27-2: 38–52.

Hsü, Cho-Yun. 1993. "Das Phänomen der Chinesischen Intellektuellen. Konzeptionelle und historische Aspekte." In *Chinesische Intellektuelle im 20. Jahrhundert: Zwischen Tradition und Moderne*, edited by Karl-Heinz Pohl, Gudrun Wacker, and Liu Huiru, 19–26. Hamburg: Institut für Asienkunde.

Hu, Anquan. 2008. "Gaigekaifang chuqi shehui yishi de shanbian yu zhizhengdang de sixiang jianshe" [The Evolution of Social Awareness in Early Stage of Reform and Opening and the Ideological Construction of the Ruling Party]. *Anhui shifan daxue xuebao* [Journal of Anhui Normal University] 6: 626–31.

Hu, Caizhen. 1995. "Ershi shiji shijieshi yanjiu de xin silu – ji 20 shiji shijieshi xueshu taolunhui" [New Ways of Thinking about Twentieth-century World Historical Research – Summary of Symposium on Twentieth-century World History]. *Shijie lishi* [World History] 6: 120–2.

Hu, Fengxiang and Zhang Wenjian. 1991. *Zhongguo jindai shixue sichao yu liupai* [Trends and Schools in Modern Chinese Historiography]. Shanghai: Huadong shifan daxue chubanshe.

Hu, Weixi. 1994. "Chuantong yu xiandaixing – zailun 'qinghua xuepai' de wenhuaguan" [Tradition and Modernity – Again on the Cultural View of the "Qinghua School"]. *Xueshu yuekan* [Academic Monthly] 8: 3–10.

Huang, Annian. 2000. "Lun dangdai shijieshi jiaocai tixi de gaige – jiantan jiaoxue shijian" [Discussing the Reform of the Contemporary World History Materials System. Issues on Historical Teaching]. *Lishi jiaoxue wenti* [History Teaching and Research] 5: 33–41.

Huang, Chun-Chieh. 2007. "The Defining Character of Chinese Historical Thinking." *History and Theory* 46-2: 180–8.

Huang, Donglan. 2006. "Jindai zhongguo de difang zizhi yu mingzhi riben" [Recent Chinese Local Automony and Meiji Japan]. *Lishi yanjiu* [Historical Research] 5: 186–8.

Huang, Hui. 2002. "Overseas Chinese Studies and the Rise of Foreign Cultural Capital in Modern China." *International Sociology* 17-1: 35–55.

Huang, Philip. 1996. *Civil Justice in China: Representation and Practice in the Qing.* Stanford University Press.

    2000. "Biculturality in Modern China and in Chinese Studies." *Modern China* 26-1: 3–31.

Huang, Ruiqi. 1997. "Xiandai yu houxiandai – jidengsi lun xiandaixing" [Modernity and Postmodernism – on Anthony Giddens's Theory of Modernity]. *Dongwu shehuixue bao* 86-6: 281–387.

Huang, Xingtao. 2009. "Xin mingci de zhengzhi wenhua shi – Kang Youwei yu riben xin mingci guanxi zhi yanjiu" [The Cultural Political History of Neologisms – Research on the Relationship between Kang Youwei and Japanese New Terms]. In *Xin shixue*, vol. III: *Wenhuashi yanjiu de zai chufa* [New Historiography, vol. III: A New Perspective of Cultural Historical Studies], edited by Xingtao Huang. Beijing: Zhonghua shuju.

Hübinger, Gangolf, Jürgen Osterhammel, and Erich Pelzer, eds. 1994. *Universalgeschichte und Nationalgeschichten.* Freiburg im Breisgau: Rombach.

Hughes, Christopher. 2006. *Chinese Nationalism in the Global Era.* London: Routledge.

Hughes, Donald. 2001. "Global Dimensions of Environmental History." *Pacific Historical Review* 70-1: 91–101.

Hughes-Warrington, Marnie. 2005. "Shapes." In *Palgrave Advances in World Histories*, edited by Marnie Hughes-Warrington, 112–34. Basingstoke/New York: Palgrave Macmillan.

2009. "Coloring Universal History: Robert Benjamin Lewis's *Light and Truth* (1843) and William Wells Brown's *The Black Man* (1863)." *Journal of World History* 20-1: 99–130.

Hull, Isabel V. 1993. "Military Culture and the Production of 'Final Solutions' in the Colonies: The Example of Wilhelminian Germany." In *The Specter of Genocide: Mass Murder in Historical Perspective*, edited by Robert Gellately and Ben Kiernan, 141–62. New York: Cambridge University Press.

Hunn, Karin. 2004. *"Nächstes Jahr kehren wir zurück ..." Die Geschichte der türkischen Gastarbeiter in der Bundesrepublik*. Göttingen: Wallstein.

Hunt, Lynn, ed. 1989. *The New Cultural History*. Berkeley: University of California Press.

2002. "Where Have All the Theories Gone?" *Perspectives* 40-3: 5–7.

Huntington, Samuel. 1998. *The Clash of Civilization and the Remaking of World Order*. London: Touchstone.

Huters, Theodore. 2005. *Bringing the World Home: Appropriating the West in Late Qing and Early Republican China*. Honolulu: University of Hawai'i Press.

Iggers, Georg G. 1994. "Die Bedeutung des Marxismus für die Geschichtswissenschaft heute." *Comparativ* 4: 123–9.

1996. *Geschichtswissenschaft im 20. Jahrhundert: Ein kritischer Überblick im internationalen Zusammenhang*. Göttingen: Vandenhoeck & Ruprecht.

1997a. *Deutsche Geschichtswissenschaft: eine Kritik der traditionellen Geschichtauffassung von Herder bis zur Gegenwart*. Vienna: Böhlau.

1997b. "Historisches Denken im 19. Jahrhundert. Überlegungen zu einer Synthese." In *Geschichtsdiskurs*, vol. III: *Die Epoche der Historisierung*, edited by Wolfgang Küttler, Jörn Rüsen, and Ernst Schulin, 459–69. Frankfurt: Fischer Taschenbuch.

2002. "What Is Uniquely Western about the Historiography of the West in Contrast to that of China." In *Western Historical Thinking: An Intercultural Debate*, edited by Jörn Rüsen, 101–10. New York: Berghahn Books.

Iggers, Georg G. and James T. Powell, eds. 1990. *Leopold von Ranke and the Shaping of the Historical Discipline*. Syracuse University Press.

Iggers, Georg G., Q. Edward Wang, and Supriya Mukherjee. 2008. *A Global History of Modern Historiography*. Harlow: Pearson Longman.

Inden, Richard. 1986. "Orientalist Constructions of India." *Modern Asian Studies* 20-3: 401–46.

Iriye, Akira. 1989. "The Internationalization of History." *American Historical Review* 94-1: 1–10.

1997. *Cultural Internationalism and World Order*. Baltimore: Johns Hopkins University Press.

2002. *Global Community: The Role of International Organizations in the Making of the Contemporary World*. Berkeley: University of California Press.

2008. "Transnational Moments." Unpublished manuscript. Oxford University.

Iriye, Akira and Pierre-Yves Saunier, eds. 2009. *The Palgrave Dictionary of Transnational History: From the Mid-19th Century to the Present Day.* New York: Palgrave Macmillan.

Jackson, Jean E. and Kay B. Warren. 2005. "Indigenous Movements in Latin America, 1992–2004: Controversies, Ironies, New Directions." *Annual Review of Anthropology* 34: 549–73.

Jäger, Friedrich and Jörn Rüsen. 1992. *Geschichte des Historismus – eine Einführung.* Munich: C. H. Beck.

James, C. L. R. 1938. *The Black Jacobins: Toussaint L'Ouverture and the San Domingo Revolution.* London: Secker & Warburg.

Jameson, Fredric. 1991. *Postmodernism: Or the Logic of Late Capitalism.* Durham, NC: Duke University Press.

Jameson, Fredric and Masao Miyoshi, eds. 1998. *The Cultures of Globalization.* Durham, NC: Duke University Press.

Jarausch, Konrad H. and Michael Geyer. 2003. *Shattered Past: Reconstructing German Histories,* Princeton University Press.

Jarausch, Konrad H. and Matthias Middell, eds. 1994. *Nach dem Erdbeben: (Re-) Konstruktionen ostdeutscher Geschichte und Geschichtswissenschaft.* Leipzig: Leipziger Universitätsverlag.

Jarausch, Konrad H. and Hannes Siegrist, eds. 1997. *Amerikanisierung und Sowjetisierung in Deutschland 1945–1970.* Frankfurt/New York: Campus.

Ji, Shaofu. 1991. *Zhongguo Chuban Jianshi* [A Simple History of Chinese Publishing]. Shanghai: Xuelin chubanshe.

Ji, Xiao-bin. 2005. *Politics and Conservatism in Northern Song China: The Career and Thought of Sima Guang (A.D. 1019–1086).* Hong Kong: Chinese University Press of Hong Kong.

Jiang, Dachun. 2000. "Ershiyi shiji shixue lilun yanjiu duanxiang" [New Thoughts on Historiographical Theory in the Twenty-first Century]. *Shixue lilun yanjiu* [Historiography Quarterly] 1: 10–12.

Jiang, Danlin. 1996. *Dongfang fuxing zhi lu: fei xifang shehui fazhan lilun yu jianshe you zhongguo tese shehuizhuyi* [The Path of the East's Renaissance: Non-Western Theory of Social Development and the Construction of Socialism with Chinese Characteristics]. Guangzhou: Guangdong jiaoyu chubanshe.

Jiang, Yihua and Wu Kequan, eds. 2005. *Ershi shiji zhongguo shehui kexue: lishixue juan* [Twentieth-century Chinese Social Sciences: History Volume]. Shanghai: Shanghai renmin chubanshe.

Jin, Guantao. 1994. "Zhongguo jinxiandai shehui jingji lunli de bianqian: lun shehuizhuyi jingji lunli zai zhongguo de lishi mingyun" [The Change of Modern Chinese Social Economic Ethics: On the Historical Fate of Socialist Economic Ethics in China]. *Yazhou yanjiu* [Asian Studies] 8: 2–50.

Jin, Guantao and Liu Qingfeng. 1993. *Kaifang zhong de bianqian – zailun zhongguo shehui chaowending jiegou* [The Transformation during Opening Processes – Returning to the Question of Chinese Society's Ultrastable Structures]. Hong Kong: Hong Kong University Press.

    2001. "Duoyuan xindaixing jiqi kunhuo" [Multiple Modernities and Its Puzzles]. *Ershiyi shiji* [Twenty-first Century] 66: 18–27.

2009. *Guannianshi yanjiu: zhongguo xiandai zhongyao zhengzhi shuyu de xingcheng* [The Historiography of Ideas: The Formation of Important Chinese Modern Political Terms]. Beijing: Falü chubanshe.

Jin, Yaoji. 1997. "Xianggang yu ershiyi shiji zhongguo wenhua" [Hong Kong and Twenty-first-century Chinese Culture]. *Mingbao yuekan* [Ming Pao Monthly] 1: 18–22.

Jin, Yaoji and Zhou Xian. 2003. "Quanqiuhua yu xiandaihua" [Globalization and Modernization]. *Shehuixue yanjiu* [Sociological Studies] 6: 97–102.

Jones, Alisa. 2005. "Changing the Past to Serve the Present: History Education in Mainland China." In *History Education and National Identity in East Asia*, edited by Edward Vickers and Alisa Jones, 65–100. New York: Routledge.

Jones, Andrew F. 2001. *Yellow Music: Media Culture and Colonial Modernity in the Chinese Jazz Age*. Durham, NC: Duke University Press.

Jones, Dorothy. 2002. *Toward a Just World: The Critical Years in the Search for International Justice*. Chicago: University of Chicago Press.

Jones, Eric. 1981. *The European Miracle: Environment, Economies and Geopolitics in the History of Europe and Asia*. Cambridge: Cambridge University Press.

Jones, Eric L., Lionel Frost, and Colin White. 1993. *Coming Full Circle: An Economic History of the Pacific Rim*. Boulder, CO: Westview Press.

Joyce, John. 1993. "The Globalization of Music: Expanding Spheres of Influence." In *Conceptualizing Global History*, edited by Bruce Mazlish and Ralph Buultjens, 205–24. Boulder, CO: Westview Press.

Kaelble, Hartmut. 1999a. *Der historische Vergleich: Eine Einführung zum 19. und 20. Jahrhundert*. Frankfurt/New York: Campus.

1999b. "Der historische Zivilisationsvergleich." In *Diskurse und Entwicklungspfade: Der Gesellschaftsvergleich in den Geschichts- und Sozialwissenschaften*, edited by Hartmut Kaelble and Jürgen Schriewer, 29–52. Frankfurt/New York: Campus.

2004a. "Social Particularities of Nineteenth- and Twentieth-Century Europe." In *The European Way: European Societies in the 19th and 20th Centuries*, edited by Hartmut Kaelble, 276–317. New York/Oxford: Berghahn Books.

2004b. "Welche Chancen für eine Weltgeschichte?" *Zeithistorische Forschungen/ Studies in Contemporary History*, Online-Edition. www.zeithistorische-forschungen.de/16126041-Kaelble-3-2004.

2005. "Die Debatte über Vergleich und Transfer und was jetzt?" *H-Soz-u-Kult* (February 8), http://hsozkult.geschichte.hu-berlin.de/forum/id=574&type= artikel.

2006a. "Europäische Geschichte aus westeuropäischer Sicht?" In *Transnationale Geschichte: Themen, Tendenzen und Theorien*, edited by Gunilla Budde, Sebastian Conrad, and Oliver Janz, 105–16. Göttingen: Vandenhoeck & Ruprecht.

2006b. "Herausforderungen an die Transfergeschichte." *Comparativ* 16-3: 7–12.

Kaelble, Hartmut, Martin Kirsch, and Alexander Schmidt-Gernig, eds. 2002. *Transnationale Öffentlichkeiten und Identitäten im 20 Jahrhundert*. Frankfurt/ New York: Campus.

Kaelble, Hartmut and Dietmar Rothermund, eds. 2001. *Nichtwestliche Geschichtswissenschaften seit 1945*. Leipzig: Leipziger Universitätverlag.

Kaelble, Hartmut and Jürgen Schriewer, eds. 2003. *Vergleich und Transfer: Komparatistik in den Sozial-, Geschichts- und Kulturwissenschaften*. Frankfurt/New York: Campus.

Kafadar, Cemal. 1996. *Between Two Worlds: The Construction of the Ottoman State*. Berkeley: University of California Press.

Kailitz, Steffen. 2001. *Die politische Deutungskultur im Spiegel des "Historikerstreits"*: *What's Right? What's Left?* Wiesbaden: Westdeutscher Verlag.

Kaiwar, Vasant. 2004. "Towards Orientalism and Nativism: The Impasse of Subaltern Studies." *Historical Materialism* 12-2: 189–247.

Kalberg, Stephen. 1994. *Max Weber's Comparative Historical Sociology*. Cambridge: Westdeutscher Verlag.

Kaldor, Mary. 2003. *Global Civil Society: An Answer to War*. Cambridge: Polity Press.

Karl, Rebecca E. 2002. *Staging the World: Chinese Nationalism at the Turn of the Twentieth Century*. Durham, NC: Duke University Press.

2005. "The Asiatic Mode of Production: National and Imperial Formations." *Historien* 5: 58–75.

Karmel, Solomon M. 2000. "Ethnic Nationalism in Mainland China." In *Asian Nationalism*, edited by Michael Leifer, 38–62. London/New York: Routledge.

Kay, Cristobal. 1989. *Latin American Theories of Development and Underdevelopment*. London/New York: Routledge.

Keane, John. 2003. *Global Civil Society?* Cambridge University Press.

Keck, Margaret F. 1998. *Activists Beyond Borders: Advocacy Networks in International Politics*. Ithaca, NY: Cornell University Press.

Kelly, Robin D. G. 1999. "'But a Local Phase of a World Problem': Black History's Global Vision, 1883–1950." *Journal of American History* 86-3: 1045–77.

Kern, Stephen. 1983. *The Culture of Time and Space: 1880–1918*. Cambridge, MA: Harvard University Press.

Kerner, Max, ed. 2001. *Eine Welt – Eine Geschichte? 43. Deutscher Historikertag in Aachen: 26. bis 29. September*. Munich: Oldenbourg.

Kim, Chun-Shik. 2004. *Deutscher Kulturimperialismus in China. Deutsches Kolonialschulwesen in Kiautschou (China) 1898–1914*. Stuttgart: Steiner.

Kim, Se-Yeon. 1993. *Karl Marx und die nichteuropäischen Gesellschaften: Zur Kritik der eurozentrischen Interpretation der Marxschen Auffassung über die nichteuropäischen Gesellschaften*. Frankfurt: Peter Lang.

Kirby, William C. 2008. "On Chinese, European and American Universities." *Dædalus* 137-3: 139–47.

Kirby, William C. and Niu Dayong, eds. 2007. *Zhongguo yu shijie: guojihua, neihua yu waihua* [China and the World: Internationalization, Internalization, Externalization]. Beijing: Hebei renmin chubanshe.

Kirby, William C., Mechthild Leutner, and Klaus Mühlhahn, eds. 2006. *Global Conjectures: China in Transnational Perspective* (= Berliner China-Hefte, vol. 30). Berlin: Lit.

Klein, Daniel B. and Stern, Charlotta. 2004. "How Politically Diverse Are the Social Sciences and Humanities?" *Ratio Working Papers* 53: 1–20.

Klein, Thoralf and Frank Schumacher, eds. 2006. *Kolonialkriege: Militärische Gewalt im Zeichen des Imperialismus*. Hamburg: Hamburger Edition.

Kleinmann, Hans-Otto. 2001. "Der Atlantische Raum als Problem des europäischen Staatensystems." *Jahrbuch für Geschichte Lateinamerikas* 38: 7–30.

Kleinschmidt, Harald 1991. "Galton's Problem: Bemerkungen zur Theorie der transkulturell vergleichenden Geschichtsforschung." *Zeitschrift für Geschichtswissenschaft* 39-1: 5–22.

1998. *Geschichte der internationalen Beziehungen: Ein systemgeschichtlicher Abriß*. Stuttgart: Reclam.

Klimke, Martin. 2009. *The "Other" Alliance: Global Protest and Student Unrest in West Germany and the U.S., 1962–1972*. Princeton: Princeton University Press.

Knight, Franklin W. and Peggy K. Liss, eds. 1991. *Atlantic Port Cities: Economy, Culture, and Society in the Atlantic World, 1650–1850*. Knoxville: University of Tennessee Press.

Knight, Nick. 1990. "Soviet Philosophy and Mao Zedong's 'Sinification of Marxism.'" *Journal of Contemporary Asia* 20-1: 89–109.

Knöbl, Wolfgang. 2007. *Die Kontingenz der Moderne: Wege in Europa, Asien und Amerika*. Frankfurt/New York: Campus.

Kocka, Jürgen. 1977. *Angestellte zwischen Faschismus und Demokratie: Zur politischen Sozialgeschichte der Angestellten: USA und Deutschland 1890–1914 im Vergleich*. Göttingen: Vandenhoeck & Ruprecht.

1986. "Max Webers Bedeutung für die Geschichtswissenschaft." In *Max Weber, der Historiker*, edited by Jürgen Kocka, 13–27. Göttingen: Vandenhoeck & Ruprecht.

ed. 1988–1989. *Bürgertum im 19. Jahrhundert: Deutschland im europäischen Vergleich*. 3 vols. Munich: Deutscher Taschenbuch Verlag.

1990. "German Identity and Historical Comparison: After the Historikerstreit." In *Reworking the Past: Hitler, the Holocaust and the Historians' Debate*, edited by Peter Baldwin, 279–93. Boston: Beacon Press.

1992. *Die Auswirkungen der deutschen Einigung auf die Geschichts- und Sozialwissenschaften*. Bonn: Friedrich-Ebert-Stiftung.

1997. "Gesellschaftsgeschichte: Profil, Probleme und Perspektiven." In *Historische Familienforschung: Ergebnisse und Kontroversen: Michael Mitterauer zum 60. Geburtstag*, edited by Josef Ehmer, Tamara K. Hareven, and Richard Wall, 57–68. Frankfurt/New York: Campus.

1999. "Asymmetrical Historical Comparison: The Case of the German Sonderweg." *History and Theory* 38-1: 40–50.

2000. "Historische Sozialwissenschaft Heute." In *Perspektiven der Gesellschaftsgeschichte*, edited by Paul Nolte, Manfred Hettling, Frank-Michael Kuhlemann, and Hans-Walter Schmuhl, 5–24. Munich: C. H. Beck.

2002. "Negotiated Universals." In *Reflections on Multiple Modernities: European, Chinese, and Other Approaches*, edited by Dominic Sachsenmaier, Jens Riedel and Shmuel Eisenstadt, 119–28. Leiden: Brill.

2003. "Comparison and Beyond." *History and Theory* 42-1: 39–44.

2005. "Die Grenzen Europas. Ein Essay aus historischer Perspektive." In *Europawissenschaft*, edited by Gunnar Folke Schuppert, Ingolf Pernice, and Ulrich Haltern, 275–88. Baden-Baden: Nomos.

2009. "Die erste Globalisierung." *Frankfurter Allgemeine Zeitung*, February 19.

Kohn, Hans. 1962. *The Age of Nationalism: The First Era of Global History*. New York: Harper.

Kong, Lingdong. 2002. "Maksi de 'shijie lishi' sixiang he jingji quanqiuhua jincheng" [Marx's Thoughts on "World History" and the Processes of Economical Globalization]. *Shixue lilun yanjiu* [Historiography Quarterly] 4: 88–93.

Kossock, Manfred. 1993. "From Universal History to Global History." In *Conceptualizing Global History*, edited by Bruce Mazlish and Ralph Buultjens, 93–112. Boulder, CO: Westview Press.

Kotkin, Joel. 2006. *The City: A Global History*. New York: Modern Library.

Krämer-Lien, Martin. 2004. "Werkstätten der Transformation – Eine Problemskizze zur Arbeitskultur und Entscheidungsgewalt in revolutionären Belegschaften (Char'kov 1917–1927, CSR 1945–1948, Kuba 1959–1962)." *Comparativ* 14-4: 79–104.

Krige, John. 2006. *American Hegemony and the Postwar Reconstruction of Science in Europe*. Cambridge, MA: MIT Press.

Krüger, Gesine. 2005. "The German War Against the Hereros." *Bulletin of the German Historical Institute* 37: 45–9.

Kühl, Stefan. 1997. *Die Internationale der Rassisten: Aufstieg und Niedergang der internationalen Bewegung für Eugenik und Rassenhygiene im 20. Jahrhundert*. Frankfurt/New York: Campus.

Kuhn, Thomas. 1962. *The Structure of Scientific Revolution*. University of Chicago Press.

Kundrus, Birthe. 2003a. *Moderne Imperialisten. Das Kaiserreich im Spiegel seiner Kolonien*. Colgone: Böhlau.

2003b. *Phantasiereiche: Zur Kulturgeschichte des deutschen Kolonialismus*. Frankfurt: Campus.

2004. "Grenzen der Gleichsetzung. Kolonialverbrechen und Vernichtungspolitik." *iz3w* 275: 30–3.

Kuran, Ercüment. 1962. "Ottoman Historiography of the Tanzimat Period." In *Historians of the Middle East*, edited by Bernard Lewis and P. M. Holt, 422–9. London: Oxford University Press.

Kurlansky, Mark. 1997. *Cod: Biography of the Fish that Changed the World*. New York: Walker & Co.

2002. *Salt: A World History*. New York: Walker & Co.

Küttler, Wolfgang. 1992. "Marx's Formationstheorie und die globale Transformation. Grenzen und Chancen an Marx orientierter weltgeschichtlicher Betrachtungsweise." *Comparativ* 1: 105–17.

Küttler, Wolfgang, Jörn Rüsen, and Ernst Schulin, eds. 1993–1999. *Geschichtsdiskurs.* 5 vols. Frankfurt: Fischer Taschenbuch.

Kwok, Siu-Tong. 2003. "Ideologie und Historiographie in den Regionen Chinas im Vergleich." *Zeitschrift für Weltgeschichte* 4-1: 87–102.

2004. "Cultural Migration and Historiography in the Regions of China Since the End of World War II." *Berliner China-Hefte* 26: 53–62.

Kwong, Luke S. K. 2001. "The Rise of the Linear Perspective on History and Time in Late Qing China, c. 1860–1911." *Past & Present* 173-1: 157–90.

Lach, Donald. 1965–1993. *Asia in the Making of Europe.* 4 vols. University of Chicago Press.

Lackner, Michael, Iwo Amelung, and Joachim Kurtz, eds. 2001. *New Terms for New Ideas: Western Knowledge and Lexical Change in Late Imperial China.* Leiden: Brill.

Lackner, Michael and Michael Werner. 1999. *Der cultural turn in den Humanwissenschaften: Area Studies im Auf- oder Abwind des Kulturalismus?* Bad Homburg: Werner-Reimer-Stiftung.

Lal, Vinay. 2002. "The Subaltern School and the Ascendancy of Indian History." In *Turning Points in Historiography: A Cross-Cultural Perspective,* edited by Q. Edward Wang and George Iggers, 237–70. University of Rochester Press.

2003. *The History of History: Politics and Scholarship in Modern India.* New Delhi: Oxford University Press.

Lambert, Peter. 2003. "Friedrich Thimme, G. P. Gooch and the Publication of Documents on the Origins of the First World War: Patriotism, Academic Liberty and a Search for Anglo-German Understanding, 1920–1938." In *Historikerdialoge: Geschichte, Mythos und Gedächtnis im deutsch-britischen kulturellen Austausch 1750–2000,* edited by Stefan Berger, Peter Lambert, and Peter Schumann, 275–308. Göttingen: Vandenhoeck & Ruprecht.

Lamont, Michèle and Laurent Thévenot, eds. 2000. *Rethinking Comparative Cultural Sociology: Repertoires of Evaluation in France and the United States.* Cambridge: Cambridge University Press.

Landes, David S. 1998. *The Wealth and Poverty of Nations: Why Some Are So Rich and Some So Poor.* New York: W. W. Norton.

Lang, Michael. 2006. "Globalization and Its History." *Journal of Modern History* 78: 899–931.

Langewiesche, Dieter. 1995. "Nation, Nationalismus, Nationalstaat. Forschungsstand und Forschungsperspektiven." *Neue Politische Literatur* 40: 190–236.

Latham, David. 2003. *Mandarins of the Future: Modernization Theory in Cold War America.* Baltimore, MD: Johns Hopkins University Press.

Le, Shan, ed. 2004. *Qianliu – dui xiayi minzu zhuyi de pipan yu fansi* [Undercurrents – Critiques and Reflections on Narrow Nationalism]. Shanghai: Huadong shifan daxue chubanshe.

Lee, Benjamin. 1998. "Peoples and Publics." *Public Culture* 10-2: 371–94.

Lefebvre, Henri. 1974. *La Production de l'espace.* Paris: Éditions Anthropos.

Leggewie, Claus, ed. 2004. *Die Türkei und Europa – die Positionen.* Frankfurt: Suhrkamp.

Lehmann, Hartmut, ed. 2006. *Transatlantische Religionsgeschichte: 18. bis 20. Jahrhundert*. Göttingen: Wallstein.

Lehmann, Hartmut and Melten James von Horm. 2003. *Paths of Continuity: Central European Historiography from the 1930s to the 1950s*. New York: Cambridge University Press.

Lehmkuhl, Ursula. 2001. "Diplomatiegeschichte als internationale Kulturgeschichte: Theoretische Ansätze und empirische Forschung zwischen Historischer Kulturwissenschaft und Soziologischem Institutionalismus." *Geschichte und Gesellschaft* 27-3: 394–423.

Leibold, James. 2006. "Competing Narratives of Racial Unity in Republican China: From the Yellow Emperor to Peking Man." *Modern China* 32-2: 181–220.

Lenger, Friedrich. 2009. "Rezension zu: *Osterhammel, Jürgen: Die Verwandlung der Welt: Eine Geschichte des 19. Jahrhunderts. München 2009.*" *H-Soz-u-Kult* (March 13), http://hsozkult.geschichte.hu-berlin.de/rezensionen/2009-1–210.

Lens, Sidney. 1971. *The Forging of the American Empire: From the Revolution to Vietnam: A History of U.S. Imperialism*. New York: Crowell.

Leonard, Jane Kate. 1984. *Wei Yuan and China's Rediscovery of the Maritime World*. Cambridge, MA: Harvard University Council on East Asian Studies.

Lepenies, Wolf, ed. 2003. *Entangled Histories and Negotiated Universals: Centers and Peripheries in a Changing World*. Frankfurt/New York: Campus.

Leutner, Mechthild. 1982. *Geschichtsschreibung zwischen Politik und Wissenschaft: Zur Herausbildung der chinesischen marxistischen Geschichtswissenschaft in den 30er und 40er Jahren*. Wiesbaden: Harrassowitz.

———. 2003. "Die sozialgeschichtliche Wende in China seit den 1980ern: Chinesische und westliche/deutsche Historiographie. Ein Dialog?" *Zeitschrift für Weltgeschichte* 4-2: 103–20.

———. 2004. "Chinese Historiography and (West-) German/Western Historiography: A Dialogue? The Social History Turn in China Since the 1980s." *Berliner China-Hefte* 26: 63–77.

Leutner, Mechthild and Klaus Mühlhahn, eds. 2007. *Kolonialkrieg in China: Die Niederschlagung der Boxerbewegung 1900–1901*. Berlin: Christoph Links.

Levitt, Peggy and Sanjeev Khagram, eds. 2008. *The Transnational Studies Reader: Intersections and Innovations*. London/New York: Routledge.

Lewis, Earl. 1995. "To Turn as a Pivot: Writing African Americans into a History of Overlapping Diasporas." *American Historical Review* 100-3: 765–87.

Lexikonredaktion Brockhaus, ed. 2006. *Weltgeschichte seit der Aufklärung*. Leipzig: Brockhaus.

Li, Anshan. 2001. "Shijieshi yanjiu de guifanhua wenti – jian tanlun zhuzhong zhushi de zuoyong" [The Problem of the Standardization of World Historical Research – Including the Function of Foot-Notes]. *Shixue lilun yanjiu* [Historiography Quarterly] 1: 57–60.

Li, Bozhong. 2001. "Yingguo moshi, jiangnan daolu yu zibenzhuyi mengya" [The British Model, the Yangzi Delta Pathway, and Capitalist Sprouts]. *Lishi yanjiu* [Historical Research] 1: 116–26.

Li, Guojun and Wang Bingzhao. 2000. *Zhongguo jiaoyu zhidu tongshi* [A General History of the Chinese Education System]. Jinan: Shangdong jiaoyu chubanshe.

Li, Huibin. 2003. *Quanqiuhua: zhongguo daolu* [Globalization: Chinese Pathways]. Beijing: Shehui kexue wenxian chubanshe.

Li, Qiang. 1990. "Aisensidate dui xiandaihua lilun ji zhongguo wenhua de zai jiantao" [Eisenstadt's Re-Exploration of Modernization Theory and Chinese Culture]. *Ershiyi shiji* [Twenty-first Century] 1: 60–6.

Li, Shenzhi and He Jiadong. 2000. *Zhongguo de daolu* [The Path of China]. Guangzhou: Nanfan ribao chubanshe.

Li, Shikun. 2001. "Lun shijie lishi lilun yu quanqiuhua" [On Theories of World History and Globalization]. *Beijing daxue xuebao (Zhexue shehui kexue ban)* [Journal of Peking University (Philosophy and Social Sciences)] 2: 5–12.

Li, Shitao, ed. 1999. *Zhishifenzi lichang: jijin yu baoshou zhi jian de dongdang* [The Intellectuals' Standpoints: Conflicts between Radicals and Conservatives]. Changchun: Shidai wenyi chubanshe.

Li, Wen. 2005. *Dongya hezuo de wenhua chengyin* [Cultural Roots for East Asian Cooperation]. Beijing: Shijie zhishi chubanshe.

Li, Xiaodong. 2003. *Quanqiuhua yu wenhua zhenghe* [Globalization and Cultural Integrity]. Changsha: Hunan renmin chubanshe.

Li, Xueqin. 1997. *Zouchu yigu shidai* [Leaving the Doubts about Antiquity]. Shenyang: Changchun chubanshe.

Li, Zehou. 1995. *Gaobie geming: Huiwang ershiyi shiji zhongguo* [Farewell to Revolution: Looking Back at Twentieth-century China]. Hong Kong: Cosmos Books.

2002. "Wenming de tiaotingzhe – quanqiuhua jincheng zhong de zhongguo wenhua dingwei" [The Mediator of Civilizations: The Position of Chinese Culture in the Process of Globalization]. *Mingbao yuekan* [Ming Pao Monthly] 5: 28–9.

Li, Zehou and Liu Zaifu. 1987. *Zhongguo xiandai sixiangshi lun* [History of Contemporary Chinese Thought]. Beijing: Dongfang chubanshe.

Li, Zhizhan. 1994. "Wusi fengxian kaituo jinqu – Shenqie huainian Wu Yujin laoshi" [Selfless Dedication, Pioneering, and Endeavoring – In Memory of Prof. Wu Yujin]. *Shixue lilun yanjiu* [Historiography Quarterly] 1: 35–42.

1996. "Yanjiu ershi shiji shijieshi de ruogan sikao" [Some Thoughts on Research in Twentieth-century World History]. *Shixue lilun yanjiu* [Historiography Quarterly] 3: 5-15.

Li, Zhizhan, Gao Mingzhen, and Tang Xizhong, eds. 1991. *Cong fensan dao zhengti de shijieshi* [From a Scattered to a Holistic World History]. Changsha: Hunan chubanshe.

Liang, Qichao. 1902a. *Xin Shixue* [New Historiography]. Beijing.

1902b. *Xinmin Shuo* [About the New Citizen]. Beijing.

Liao, Guangsheng. 1993. "Xianggang zai Zhongggguo dalu xiandaihua de jiaose" [Hong Kong's Role in the Modernization of the Mainland]. *Yazhou yanjiu* [Asian Studies] 2.

Lieberman, Victor. 2003. *Strange Parallels: Southeast Asia in Global Context, c. 800–1830.* Cambridge University Press.

Lim, Hyunsoo. 2001. "Emerging New Religiosity: Modernity Disputes on Korean Religious Culture – Rethinking the Concept of Time: Modern Historical Consciousness and Historiography in Korean Society." *Korea Journal* 41-1: 44–68.

Lin, Beidian and Dong Zhenghua. 1998. "Xiandaihua yanjiu zai zhongguo de xingqi yu fazhan" [The Rise and Development of Modernization Research in China]. *Lishi yanjiu* [Historical Research] 5: 150–71.

Lin, Judai. 1952. *Waiguo Jindai Shigang* [An Outline of Foreign Contemporary History]. Beijing: Renmin jiaoyu chubanshe.

Lin, Manhong. 1996. "Dangdai Taiwan de shixue yu shehui" [Current History and Society in Taiwan]. *Jiaoxue yu yanjiu* [Teaching and Research] 18: 69–98.

Lin, Min and Maria Galikowski. 1999. *The Search for Modernity. Chinese Intellectuals and Cultural Discourse in the Post-Mao Era*. New York: Palgrave Macmillan.

Lin, Qiuxie. 2004. "90 niandai zhongguo dalu shehui wenhua zhuanxing de fansi yu tantao" [Reflections and Explorations on the Sociocultural Changes in Mainland China in the Nineties]. *Zhanwang yu tansuo* [Prospect and Exploration] 2-12: 85–104.

Lin, Zhenjiang and Liang Yunxiang, eds. 2000. *Quanqiuhua yu zhongguo, riben* [Globalization and China, Japan]. Beijing: Xinhua chubanshe.

Lincke, Hans-Joachim and Sylvia Paletschek. 2003. "Situation des wissenschaftlichen Nachwuchses im Fach Geschichte: Berufungsaussichten und Karrierestadien von Historikern und Historikerinnen an deutschen Universitäten. Ergebnisse einer Erhebung." *Jahrbuch der Historischen Forschung in der Bundesrepublik Deutschland: Berichtsjahr 2002*, edited by Hans-Martin Hinz, 45–55. Munich: Saur.

Lindquist, Sven. 1999. *Durch das Herz der Finsternis. Ein Afrika-Reisender auf den Spuren des europäischen Völkermords*. Frankfurt/New York: Campus.

Lindström, Naomi. 1991. "Dependency and Autonomy: The Evolution of Concepts in the Study of Latin American Literature." *Ibero-Amerikanisches Archiv* 17-2/3: 109–44.

Linebaugh, Peter and Marcus Rediker. 2000. *The Many-Headed Hydra: Sailors, Slaves, Commoners, and the Hidden History of the Revolutionary Atlantic*. Boston: Beacon Press.

Ling, Xuezhong. 2009. *Cong wanguo gongfa dao gongfa waijiao – wanqing guojifa de chuanru, quanshi yu yingyong* [From International Law to Legal Diplomacy – the Introduction, Interpretation, and Application of International Law during the Late Qing Period]. Shanghai: Shanghai guji chubanshe.

Lingelbach, Gabriele. 2003. *Klio macht Karriere. Die Institutionalisierung der Geschichtswissenschaft in Frankreich und den USA in der zweiten Hälfte des 19. Jahrhunderts*. Göttingen: Vandenhoeck & Ruprecht.

Linke, Angelika. 2006. *Attraktion und Abwehr: Die Amerikanisierung der Alltagskultur in Europa*. Cologne: Böhlau.

Lipschutz, Ronnie D., ed. 2006. *Civil Societies and Social Movements: Domestic, Transnational, Global*. Burlington, VT: Ashgate.

Littrup, Leif. 1989. "World History with Chinese Characteristics." *Culture and History* 5: 39–64.

Liu, Beicheng. 2000. "Chonggou shijie lishi de tiaozhan" [The Challenge of Reconstructing World History]. *Shixue lilun yanjiu* [Historiography Quarterly] 4: 67–9.

Liu, Danian. 1998. "Lishixue de bianqian" [Changes of Historiography]. *Beijing daxue xuebao (Zhexue shehui kexue ban)* [Journal of Peking University (Humanities and Social Sciences)] 4: 32–5.

Liu, Dong. 2001. "Revisiting the Perils of 'Designer Pidgin Scholarship.'" In *Voicing Concerns: Contemporary Chinese Critical Inquiry*, edited by Gloria Davies, 87–108. Lanham, MD: Rowman & Littlefield.

Liu, Hong. 1999. "Yinyu, xiangzheng, houzhimin bianqian – zhongguo yu yinni de xiandaihua lunshuo" [Metaphor, Symbol, Postcolonial Change – Discourse on The Modernization of China and Indonesia]. *Xianggang shehui kexue xuebao* [Hong Kong Journal of Sociology] 15: 169–88.

2000. "Xinjiapo zhonghua zongshanghui yu yazhou huashan wangluo de zhiduhua" [The Singapore Chinese Chamber of Commerce and Industry and the Systemization of Asian Merchant Networks]. *Lishi yanjiu* [Historical Research] 1: 106–18.

Liu, Hsin-ju. 1998. *The Silk Road: Overland Trade and Cultural Interactions in Eurasia*. Washington, DC: American Historical Association.

Liu, Kang. 2004. *Globalization and Cultural Trends in China*. Honolulu: University of Hawai'i Press.

Liu, Longxin. 2001. "Xueke tizhi yu jindai zhongguo shixue de jianli" [The Curriculum System and the Establishment of Modern Chinese Historiography]. In *Ershi shiji de Zhongguo: Xueshu yu shehui-shixue juan* [Scholarship and Society in Twentieth-century China: Section on Historical Studies], edited by Luo Zhitian, 449–585. Jinan: Shangdong jiaoyu chubanshe.

Liu, Lydia H. 1995. *Translingual Practic: Literature, National Culture, and Translated Modernity – China, 1900–1937*. Stanford: Stanford University Press.

1999. *Tokens of Exchange: The Problem of Translation in Global Circulations*. Durham, NC: Duke University Press.

Liu, Peng. 2004. "'Quanqiu lishiguan' yu 'duixiang zhongxin lun' – 'shijie lishi' guannian de hongguan he weiguan tixi" ["Global Historical Perspectives" and "Other-Centered Theories" – World Historical Thinking and Macro- and Micro-Systems"]. *Tianshui shifanxueyuan xuebao* [Journal of Tianshui Normal University] 3: 43–6.

Liu, Qingfeng. 2001. "The Topography of Intellectual Culture in 1990s Mainland China: A Survey." In *Voicing Concerns: Contemporary Chinese Critical Inquiry*, edited by Gloria Davies, 47–70. Lanham, MD: Rowman & Littlefield.

Liu, Xincheng. 1995. "Woguo shijie tongshi biancuan gongzuo de huigu yu sikao" [A Review and Reflection on the Compilation of World History in Our Country]. In *Zhongguo lishixue nianjian 1995* [Annual Assessment of Chinese Historiography – Year 1995], edited by Yanjiao Lin, 8–21. Beijing: Sanlian shudian.

2007. "Lunti: shenme shi quanqiushi?" [What Is Global History?]. *Lishi jiaoxue wenti* [History Teaching and Research] 2: 31–7.

Lockman, Zachary. 2004. *Contending Visions of the Middle East: The History and Politics of Orientalism.* Cambridge/New York: Cambridge University Press.

Lohmann, Hans-Martin, ed. 1994. *Extremismus der Mitte: Vom rechten Verständnis der deutschen Nation.* Frankfurt: Fischer Taschenbuch.

Lombard, Denys and Jean Aubin, eds. 2000. *Asian Merchants and Businessmen in the Indian Ocean and the China Sea.* New Delhi/New York: Oxford University Press.

Lönnroth, Erik, Karl Molin, and Björk Ragnar. eds. 1994. *Conceptions of National History: Proceedings of Nobel Symposium 78.* Berlin/New York: Walter de Gruyter.

Loomba, Ania. 1998. *Postcolonialism/Colonialism.* London: Routledge.

Loomba, Ania, Suvir Kaul, Matti Bunzi, Antoinette Burton, and Jed Esty, eds. 2005. *Postcolonial Studies and Beyond.* Durham, NC: Duke University Press.

Lorenz, Chris. 1999. "Comparative Historiography: Problems and Perspectives." *History and Theory* 38-1: 25–39.

Loth, Wilfried and Jürgen Osterhammel, eds. 2000. *Internationale Geschichte: Themen – Ergebnisse – Aussichten.* Munich: Oldenbourg.

Löw, Martina. 2001. *Raumsoziologie.* Frankfurt: Suhrkamp.

Lowen, Rebecca. 1997. *Creating the Cold War University: The Transformation of Stanford.* Berkeley: University of California Press.

Löwith, Karl. 1953. *Weltgeschichte und Heilsgeschehen: Die theologischen Vorraussetzungen der Geschichtsphilosophie.* Stuttgart: Kohlhammer.

Lucassen, Jan, ed. 2006a. *Global Labor History: A State of the Art.* Bern/New York: Peter Lang.

2006b. "Writing Global Labor History c. 1800–1940: A Historiography of Concepts, Periods and Geographical Scope." In *Global Labor History: A State of the Art,* edited by Jan Lucassen, 39–89. Bern /New York: Peter Lang.

Lucassen, Leo. 2004. "Assimilation in Westeuropa seit der Mitte des 19. Jahrhunderts: Historische und Historiographische Erfahrungen." In *Migrationsreport 2004,* edited by Klaus J. Bade, Michael Bommes and Rainer Münz, 43–66. Frankfurt: Campus.

Luo, Rongqu. 1990. *Cong "xihua" dao xiandaihua-wusi yilai youguan zhongguo de wenhua quxiang he fazhan daolu zhengwen xuan* [From Westernization to Revolution: Selected Essays on the Theories about Chinese Cultural Trends and Development Paths Since the May Fourth Period]. Beijing: Beijing daxue chubanse.

1992. "Dongya jueqi dui xiandaihua lilun de tiaozhan" [Challenges to Modernization Theory from a Rising East Asia]. *Ershiyi shiji* [Twenty-first Century] 12: 146–52.

2004. *Xiandaihua xinlun – shijie yu zhongguo de xiandaihua jincheng* [New Theories of Modernity – Modernization Processes in the World and China]. Beijing: Shangwu yinshuguan.

Luo, Zhitian. 1999. *Quanshi zhuanyi – jindai zhongguo de sixiang, shehui yu xueshu* [The Transformation of Authority: Thoughts, Society, and Scholarship in Modern China]. Wuhan: Hubei renmin chubanshe.

Lüsebrink, Hans-Jürgen. 2005. *Interkulturelle Kommunikation. Interaktion, Fremdwahrnehmung, Kulturtransfer.* Stuttgart: Metzler.

ed. 2006. *Das Europa der Aufklärung und die außereuropäische koloniale Welt.* Göttingen: Wallstein.

Lütt, Jürgen. 1998. "Die Orientalismus-Debatte im Vergleich. Verlauf, Kritik Schwerpunkte im Indischen und Arabischen Kontext." In *Gesellschaften im Vergleich. Forschungen aus Sozial- und Geschichtswissenschaften*, edited by Hartmut Kaelble and Jürgen Schriewer, 511–66. Frankfurt: Peter Lang.

Lyotard, Jean-François. 1989. "Universal History and Cultural Differences." In *The Lyotard Reader*, edited by Andrew E. Benjamin and Jean-François Lyotard, 314–23. Oxford: Blackwell.

Ma, Guoqing. 2000. "Quanqiuhua: wenhua de shengchan yu wenhua rentong – zuqun, defang shehui yu kuaguo wenhuaquan" [Globalization: The Production of Culture and Cultural Identities – Ethnicity, Local Society and Transnational Cultural Realms]. *Beijing daxue xuebao (Zhexue shehui kexue ban)* [Journal of Peking University (Humanities and Social Sciences)] 4: 152–61.

MacFarquahar, Roderick and Michael Schoenhals. 2006. *Mao's Last Revolution.* Cambridge, MA: Belknap Press of Harvard University Press.

Magdoff, Harry. 1969. *The Age of Imperialism: The Economics of U.S. Foreign Policy.* New York: Monthly Review Press.

Mai, Manfred. 2006. *Weltgeschichte.* Frankfurt: DTV.

Maier, Charles S. 1988. *The Unmasterable Past: History, Holocaust, and German National Identity.* Cambridge, MA: Harvard University Press.

2000. "Consigning the Twentieth Century to History. Alternative Narratives for the Modern Era." *American Historical Review* 105-3: 807–31.

2006a. *Among Empires. American Ascendancy and Its Predecessors.* Cambridge, MA: Harvard University Press.

2006b. "Transformations of Territoriality, 1600–2000." In *Transnationale Geschichte: Themen, Tendenzen und Theorien*, edited by Gunilla Budde, Sebastian Conrad, and Oliver Janz, 32–55. Göttingen: Vandenhoeck & Ruprecht.

2009. "Nation and Nation State." In *The Palgrave Dictionary of Transnational History: From the Mid-19th Century to the Present Day*, edited by Akira Iriye and Pierre-Yves Saunier, 743–50. New York: Palgrave Macmillan.

Maitland, Stobart. 1999. "Fifty Years of European Co-operation on History Textbooks: The Role and Contribution of the Council of Europe." *Internationale Schulbuchforschung* 21: 147–61.

Malik, Iftikhar H. 2004. *Islam and Modernity, Muslims in Europe and the United States.* London: Pluto Press.

Malinowski, Stephan. 2007. "Der Holocaust als 'kolonialer Genozid'? Europäische Kolonialgewalt und nationalsozialistischer Vernichtungskrieg." *Geschichte und Gesellschaft* 33: 439–66.

Mallon, Florencia. 1994. "The Promise and Dilemma of Subaltern Studies: Perspectives from Latin American History." *American Historical Review* 99-5: 1491–515.

Mann, Charles C. 2005. *1491: New Revelations of the Americas Before Columbus.* New York: Knopf.

Mann, Golo. 1960. "Schlussbetrachtung." In *Propyläen Weltgeschichte: Eine Universalgeschichte*, vol. X: *Die Welt von Heute*, edited by Alfred Heuss, Golo Mann, and August Nitschke, 610–28. Frankfurt: Propyläen Verlag.

Mann, Michael. 2009. "Telekommunikation in Britisch-Indien (ca. 1850–1930). Ein globalgeschichtliches Paradigma." *Comparativ* 19-6: 86–112.

Manning, Patrick. 1996. "The Problem of Interactions in World History." *American Historical Review* 101-3: 771–82.

    2003. *Navigating World History: Historians Create a Global Past.* New York: Palgrave Macmillan.

    ed. 2008a. *Global Practice in World History: Advances Worldwide.* Princeton: Markus Wiener Publishers.

    2008b. "World History Network." In *Global Practice in World History: Advances Worldwide*, edited by Patrick Manning, 167–77. Princeton: Markus Wiener Publishers.

Mao, Zedong. 1969. *Xin minzhuzhuyi lun* [About the New Democracy]. Beijing: Renmin chubanshe.

Marcuse, Harold. 1998. "The Revival of Holocaust Awareness in West Germany, Israel, and the United States." In *1968: The World Transformed*, edited by Carole Fink, Philipp Gassert, and Detlef Junker, 421–38. Cambridge/New York: Cambridge University Press.

    2001. "Generational Cohorts and the Shaping of Popular Attitudes towards the Holocaust." In *Remembering for the Future: The Holocaust in an Age of Genocide*, vol. III, edited by John Roth and Elizabeth Maxwell, 652–63. London: Palgrave Macmillan.

Margailt, Avishai. 2004. *The Ethics of Memory.* Cambridge, MA: Harvard University Press.

Markovits, Claude. 2000. *The Global World of Indian Merchants, 1759–1947: Traders of Sind from Bukhara to Panama.* Cambridge/New York: Cambridge University Press.

Martin, Dorothea L. 1990. *The Making of a Sino-Marxist View: Perceptions and Interpretations of World History in the People's Republic of China.* Armonk, NY: M. E. Sharpe.

Martin, Helmut. 1999. "Vorwort." In *Chinawissenschaften – Deutschsprachige Entwicklungen: Geschichte, Personen, Perspektiven*, edited by Helmut Martin and Christiane Hammer, 1–8. Hamburg: Institut für Asienkunde.

Masuda, Wataru. 2005. *Japan and China: Mutual Representations in the Modern Era.* New York: Palgrave Macmillan.

Matory, J. Lorand. 2005. *Black Atlantic Religion: Tradition, Transnationalism, and Matriarchy in the Afro-Brazilian Candomblé.* Princeton University Press.

Matthes, Joachim, ed. 1998. *Zwischen den Kulturen? Die Sozialwissenschaften vor dem Problem des Kulturvergleichs.* Göttingen: Otto Schwartz.

Mazlish, Bruce. 1993. Introduction to *Conceptualizing Global History*, edited by Bruce Mazlish and Ralph Buultjens, 1–26. Boulder, CO: Westview Press.

1998a. "Comparing Global History to World History." *Journal of Interdisciplinary History* 28-3: 385–95.

1998b. *The Uncertain Sciences*. New Heaven: Yale University Press.

2005. "Terms." In *Palgrave Advances in World Histories*, edited by Marnie Hughes-Warrington, 18–43. Basingstoke: Palgrave Macmillan.

2006. *The New Global History*. New York/London: Routledge.

Mazlish, Bruce and Ralph Buultjens, eds. 1993. *Conceptualizing Global History*. Boulder, CO: Westview Press.

Mazlish, Bruce and Alfred D. Chandler, eds. 2005. *Leviathans: Multinational Corporations and the New Global History*. Cambridge/New York: Cambridge University Press.

Mazlish, Bruce and Akira Iriye. 2005. Introduction to *The Global History Reader*, edited by Bruce Mazlish and Akira Iriye, 1–15. New York/London: Routledge.

Mazower, Mark. 2009. *No Enchanted Place. The End of Empire and the Ideological Origins of the United Nations*. Princeton University Press.

Mazumdar, Sucheta. 1998. *Sugar and Society in China: Peasants, Technology and the World Market*. Cambridge, MA/London: Harvard University Press.

2009. "Locating China, Positioning America: Politics of the Civilizational Model of World History." In *From Orientalism to Postcolonialism. Asia, Europe and the Lineages of Difference*, edited by Sucheta Mazumdar, Vasant Kaiwar, and Thierry Labica, 43–81. London/New York: Routledge.

Mazur, Mary G. 2007. "Discontinuous Continuity: The Beginnings of a New Synthesis of 'General History' in 20th Century China." In *The Politics of Historical Production in Late Qing and Republican China*, edited by Tze-ki Hon and Robert J. Culp, 109–42. Leiden: Brill.

McGerr, Michael. 1991. "The Price of the New Transnational History." *American Historical Review* 96-4: 1056–67.

McKeown, Adam. 2004. "Global Migration, 1846–1940." *Journal of World History* 15-2: 155–89.

2008. *Melancholy Order: Asian Migration and the Globalization of Borders, 1834–1929*. New York: Columbia University Press.

McNeill, John R. 2000. *Something New Under the Sun: An Environmental History of the Twentieth-Century World*. New York: W. W. Norton.

2003. "Observations on the Nature and Culture of Environmental History." *History and Theory* 42-4: 5–43.

McNeill, William H. 1963. *The Rise of the West: A History of the Human Community*. University of Chicago Press.

1976. *Plagues and Peoples*. New York: Anchor Books.

1990. "The Rise of the West after Twenty-Five Years." *Journal of World History* 1-1: 1–21.

1992. "The Human Condition: An Ecological and Historical View." In *The Global Condition: Conquerors, Catastrophes, and Community*, edited by William H. McNeill, 67–132. Princeton University Press.

1995. "The Changing Shape of World History." *History and Theory* 34-2: 8–26.

2005. *The Pursuit of Truth: A Historian's Memoir.* Lexington: University Press of Kentucky.

McNeill, William H. and John R. McNeill. 2003. *The Human Web: A Bird's Eye View of World History.* New York: W. W. Norton.

Medick, Hans. 1984. "'Missionare im Ruderboot'? Ethnologische Sichtweisen als Herausforderung an die Sozialgeschichte." *Geschichte und Gesellschaft* 10: 295–314.

1994. "Mikro-Historie." In *Sozialgeschichte, Alltagsgeschichte, Mikro-Historie: Eine Diskussion,* edited by Winfried Schulze, 40–53. Göttingen: Vandenhoeck & Ruprecht.

Megill, Allan. 2008. "Historical Identity, Representation, Allegiance." In *Narrating the Nation: Representation in History, Media, and the Arts,* edited by Stefan Berger, Linas Eriksonas, and Andrew Mycok, 19–34. New York: Berghahn Books.

Mehl, Margaret. 1998. *History and the State in Nineteenth Century Japan.* New York: St. Martin's Press.

Meier, Christian. 1989. "Die Welt der Geschichte und die Provinz des Historikers." *Geschichte und Gesellschaft* 15: 147–63.

2002. *Von Athen bis Auschwitz: Betrachtungen zur Lage der Geschichte.* Munich: C. H. Beck.

Meisner, Maurice. 1967. *Li Ta-Chao and the Origins of Chinese Marxism.* Cambridge, MA: Harvard University Press.

Mendras, Henri. 1997. *L'Europe des Européens: Sociologie de l'Europe Occidentale.* Paris: Gallimard.

Meng, Xiangcai. 1985. "Liang Qichao." In *Zhongguo shixuejia pingzhuan,* vol. III, edited by Chen Qingquan and Bai Shouyi, 1190–216. Zhengzhou: Zhongzhou guji chubanshe.

Menzel, Ulrich. 1994. *Geschichte der Entwicklungstheorie: Einführung und systematische Bibliogaphie.* 2nd edn. Hamburg: Deutsches Übersee-Institut.

Mergel, Thomas. 2002. "Überlegungen zu einer Kulturgeschichte der Politik." *Geschichte und Gesellschaft* 28: 574–606.

Mergel, Thomas and Thomas Welskopp, eds. 1997. *Geschichte zwischen Kultur und Gesellschaft: Beiträge zur Theoriedebatte.* Munich: C. H. Beck.

Metzger, Thomas A. 2005. *A Cloud across the Pacific: Essays on the Clash Between Chinese and Western Political Theories Today.* Hong Kong: Chinese University Press.

Middell, Matthias. 1992. "Universalgeschichte heute: Einige Bemerkungen zu einem vernachlässigten Thema." *Comparativ* 1: 131–45.

1997. "Doktorandenausbildung in Form interdisziplinärer Promotionskollegs." In *Studienreform Geschichte – kreativ,* edited by Wolfgang Schmale, 381–97. Bochum: Dieter Winkler.

1999. *Historische Zeitschriften im internationalen Vergleich.* Leipzig: Akademische Verlagsanstalt.

2000. "Kulturtransfer und historische Komparatisktik: Thesen zu ihrem Verhältnis." *Comparativ* 10-1: 7–41.

2002a. "Europäische Geschichte oder global history – master narratives oder Fragmentierung? Fragen an die Leittexte der Zukunft." In *Die historische*

Meistererzählung: Deutungslinien der deutschen Nationalgeschichte nach 1945, edited by Konrad H. Jarausch and Martin Sabrow, 214–52. Göttingen: Vandenhoeck & Ruprecht.

2002b. *Weltgeschichtsschreibung im 20. Jahrhundert* (= *Comparativ* 12–3). Leipzig: Leipziger Universitätsverlag.

2003. "Francophonia as a World Region." *European Review of History* 10-2: 203–20.

2004. *Die Karl-Lamprecht-Gesellschaft Leipzig e.v 1991–2001.* Leipzig: Leipziger Universitätsverlag.

2005a. "Universalgeschichte, Weltgeschichte, Globalgeschichte, Geschichte der Globalisierung – Ein Streit um Worte." In *Globalisierung und Globalgeschichte,* edited by Margarete Grandner, Dietmar Rothermund, and Wolfgang Schwentker, 60–82. Vienna: Mandelbaum.

2005b. *Weltgeschichtsschreibung im Zeitalter der Verfachlichung und Globalisierung: Das Leipziger Institut für Kultur- und Universalgeschichte 1880–1990.* 3 vols. Leipzig: Akademische Verlagsanstalt.

ed. 2006. "Transnationale Geschichte als transnationales Projekt: Zur Einführung in die Diskussion." *Historical Social Research* 31-2: 110–17.

2008. "Der Spatial Turn und das Interesse an der Globalisierung der Geschichtswissenschaft." In *Spatial Turn: Das Raumparadigma in den Kultur- und Sozialwissenschaften,* edited by Jörg Döring and Tristan Thielmann, 103–23. Bielefeld: Transcript.

Middell, Matthias and Katja Naumann. 2006. "Institutionalisierung der Lehre in Welt- und Globalgeschichte in Deutschland und den USA – Ein Vergleich." *Comparativ* 16–1: 78–121.

Middell, Matthias and Ulrike Sommer, eds. 2004. *Historische West- und Ostforschung in Zentraleuropa zwischen dem Ersten und dem Zweiten Weltkrieg – Verflechtung und Vergleich.* Leipzig: Akademische Verlagsanstalt.

Mignolo, Walter D. 1993. "Colonial and Postcolonial Discourse: Cultural Critique of Academic Colonialism." *Latin American Research Review* 28-3: 120–34.

2000. *Global Histories/Local Designs: Coloniality, Subaltern Knowledges, and Border Thinking.* Princeton University Press.

2002. "The Many Faces of Cosmo-Polis: Border Thinking and Critical Cosmopolitanism." In *Cosmopolitanism,* edited by Carol Breckenridge, Sheldon Pollock, Homi K. Bhabha, and Dipesh Chakrabarty, 157–88. Durham, NC: Duke University Press.

2005. *The Idea of Latin America.* Malden, MA: Blackwell.

Millet, Nicola. 2006. "The Historiography of Nationalism and National Identity in Latin America." *Nations and Nationalism* 12-2: 201–21.

Milza, Pierre. 1998. "De l'international au transnational." In *Axes et méthodes de l'histoire politique (colloque, Paris, 5–7 décembre 1996),* edited by Serge Bernstein and Pierre Milza, 231–9. Paris: Presses universitaires de France.

Mintz, Sidney W. 1985. *Sweetness and Power: The Place of Sugar in Modern History.* New York: Viking.

Mirsepassi, Ali. 2000. *Intellectual Discourse and the Politics of Modernization: Negotiating Modernity in Iran.* Cambridge, MA: Cambridge University Press.

Miskeé, Ahmed Baba. 1981. *Lettre ouverte aux élites du Tiers-Monde*. Paris: Sycomore.

Mitter, Rana. 2004. *A Bitter Revolution: China's Struggle with the Modern World*. New York/Oxford: Oxford University Press.

Mitterauer, Michael. 2003. *Warum Europa? Mittelalterliche Grundlagen eines Sonderwegs*. Munich: C. H. Beck.

Modelski, George. 1972. *Principles of World Politics*. New York: Free Press.

Modelski, George, Robert A. Denemark, Jonathan Friedman, and Barry K. Gills, eds. 2000. *World System History: The Social Science of Long-term Change*. London/New York: Routledge.

Mohanty, Chandra Talpade. 1988. "Under Western Eyes: Feminist Scholarship and Colonial Discourses." *Feminist Review* 30-1: 61–88.

Mollin, Gerhard T. 2000. "Internationale Beziehungen als Gegenstand der deutschen Neuzeit-Historiographie seit dem 18. Jahrhundert. Eine Traditionskritik in Grundzügen und Beispielen." In *Internationale Geschichte: Themen – Ergebnisse – Aussichten*, edited by Wilfried Loth and Jürgen Osterhammel, 3–30. Munich: Oldenbourg.

Moll-Murata, Christine. 2001. *Die chinesische Regionalbeschreibung. Entwicklung und Funktion einer Quellengattung, dargestellt am Beispiel der Präfekturbeschreibungen von Hangzhou*. Wiesbaden: Harrassowitz.

Momigliano, Arnaldo. 1990. *The Classical Foundations of Modern Historiography*. Berkeley: University of California Press.

Mommsen, Wolfgang. 1969. *Das Zeitalter des Imperialismus*. Frankfurt: Fischer Bücherei.

1977. *Imperialismustheorien: ein Überblick über die neueren Imperialismus-interpretationen*. Göttingen: Vandenhoeck & Ruprecht.

1984. *Max Weber and German Politics, 1890–1920*. University of Chicago Press.

1989. "Ansprache des Vorsitzenden des Verbandes der Historiker Deutschlands." In *Bericht über die 37. Versammlung deutscher Historiker in Bamberg: 12. bis 16. Oktober 1988*, edited by Peter Schumann, 35–7. Stuttgart: Ernst Klett.

1994a. "Europa und die außereuropäische Welt." *Historische Zeitschrift* 258: 661–95.

1994b. "Europa und die außereuopäische Welt." In *Bericht über die 39. Versammlung deutscher Historiker in Hannover: 23. bis 26. September 1992*, edited by Raphaela Averkorn. Stuttgart: Ernst Klett.

Moore, Barrington. 1966. *Social Origins of Dictatorship and Democracy: Lord and Peasant in the Making of the Modern World*. Boston: Beacon Press.

Moore, Robert I. 1997. "World History." In *Companion to Historiography*, edited by Michael Bentley, 918–36. New York/London: Routledge.

Moore-Gilbert, Bart. 1997. *Postcolonial Theory: Contexts, Practices, Politics*. London: Verso.

Morawska, Eva. 2003. "Disciplinary Agendas and Analytical Strategies of Research on Immigration and Transnationalism: Challenges of Interdisciplinary Knowledge." *International Migration Review* 37-3: 611–40.

Morris-Suzuki, Tessa. 1993. *Reinventing Japan: Time, Space, Nation*. Armonk, NY: Palgrave Macmillan.

Moses, John A. 1975. *The Politics of Illusion.* London: Serif.

Motte, Jan, Rainer Ohliger and Anne von Oswald, eds. 1999. *50 Jahre Bundesrepublik – 50 Jahre Erinnerung: Nachkriegsgeschichte als Migrationsgeschichte.* Frankfurt: Campus.

Mudimb, Valentin Y. 1988. *The Invention of Africa: Gnosis, Philosophy, and the Order of Knowledge.* Bloomington: Indiana University Press.

Mühlhahn, Klaus. 1997. *Herrschaft und Widerstand in der "Musterkolonie Kiautschou": Interaktionen zwischen China und Deutschland 1897 bis 1914.* Munich: Oldenbourg.

1999. "Race, Culture and the Colonial Laboratory. Rethinking Colonialism." *Asien Afrika Lateinamerika* 27: 443–59.

2009. *Criminal Justice in China: A History.* Cambridge, MA: Harvard University Press.

Muhs, Rudolf, Johannes Paulmann, and Willibald Steinmetz, eds. 1998. *Aneignung und Abwehr: Interkultureller Transfer zwischen Deutschland und Großbritannien.* Bodenheim: Philo.

Müller, Guido. 2005. *Europäische Gesellschaftsbeziehungen nach dem Ersten Weltkrieg: Das Deutsch-Französische Studienkomitee und der Europäische Kulturbund.* Munich: Oldenbourg.

Müller, Michael G. 2004. "Wo und wann war Europa? Überlegungen zu einem Konzept von europäischer Geschichte." *Comparativ* 14-3: 72–82.

Mungello, David E. 1977. *Leibniz and Confucianism: The Search for Accord.* Honolulu: University of Hawai'i Press.

1999. *The Great Encounter of China and the West, 1500–1800.* Lanham, MD: Rowman & Littlefield.

Münz, Rainer *et al.* 2007. *Wie schnell wächst die Zahl der Menschen? Weltbevölkerung und weltweite Migration.* Frankfurt: Fischer.

Münz, Rainer, Wolfgang Seifert and Ralf Ulrich, eds. 1999. *Zuwanderung nach Deutschland. Strukturen, Wirkungen. Perspektiven.* 2nd edn. Frankfurt: Campus.

Murphy, Craig N. 1994. *International Organization and Industrial Change: Global Governance Since 1850.* New York: Oxford University Press.

Murthy, Viren. 2006. "Modernity against Modernity: Wang Hui's Critical History of Chinese Thought." *Modern Intellectual History* 3-1: 137–65.

Naffrisi, M. R. 1998. "Reframing Orientalism: Weber and Islam." *Economy and Society* 27-1: 97–118.

Nagano, Yoshiko. 2004. "Philippine Historiography and Colonial Discourse: Eight Selected Essays on Postcolonial Studies in the Philippines (An Introduction to the Japanese Translation)." In *Philippine Historiography and Colonial Discourse,* edited by Yoshiko Nagano, 357–85. Tokyo: Mekong Publishing Co.

Nandy, Ashis. 1983. *Intimate Enemy: Loss and Recovery of Self Under Colonialism.* Delhi: Oxford University Press.

Naumann, Katja. 2007. "Von 'Western Civilization' zu 'World History' – Europa und die Welt in der historischen Lehre in den USA." In *Dimensionen der Kultur- und Gesellschaftsgeschichte,* edited by Matthias Middell, 102–21. Leipzig: Leipziger Universitätsverlag.

Naylor, Simon. 2005. "Introduction: Historical Geographies of Science – Places, Contexts, Cartographies." *British Journal of History of Science* 38-136: 1–12.

Nehru, Jawaharlal. 1939. *Glimpses of World History: Being Further Letters to His Daughter, Written in Prison, and Containing a Rambling Account of History for Young People.* London: Lindsay Drummond Limited.

Nettelbeck, Joachim. 2005. "Durchgangszimmer gesucht. Forscher brauchen Räume: Ein Plädoyer für das Fach der Regionalwissenschaften." *Frankfurter Allgemeine Zeitung*, February 22.

Ng, On-cho. 1993. "A Tension in Ch'ing Thought: 'Historicism' in Seventeenth- and Eighteenth-Century Chinese Thought." *Journal of the History of Ideas* 54-4: 561–83.

Ng, On-cho and Q. Edward Wang. 2005. *Mirroring the Past: The Writing and Use of History in Imperial China.* Honolulu: University of Hawai'i Press.

Niethammer, Lutz. 1993. "Die postmoderne Herausforderung. Geschichte als Gedächtnis im Zeitalter der Wissenschaft." In *Geschichtsdiskurs*, vol. I: *Grundlagen und Methoden der Historiographiegeschichte*, edited by Wolfgang Küttler, Jörn Rüsen, and Ernst Schulin, 31–49. Frankfurt: Fischer Taschenbuch.

Nippel, Wilfried. 2003. "Stolperstein für Neugierige." *Die Zeit*, September 10.

Nolte, Ernst. 1986. "Vergangenheit, die nicht vergehen will." *Frankfurter Allgemeine Zeitung*, June 6.

Nolte, Hans-Heinrich. 1985. *Weltsystem und Geschichte.* Göttingen: Muster-Schmidt.

1994. "Zur Rezeption des Weltsystem-Konzepts in Deutschland." *Comparativ* 5: 91–100.

2000. "Eurasien." *Zeitschrift für Geschichte* 1: 35–8.

2005a. "Das Weltsystem-Konzept – Debatte und Forschung." In *Globalisierung und Globalgeschichte*, edited by Margarete Grandner, Dietmar Rothermund, and Wolfgang Schwentker, 115–38. Vienna: Mandelbaum.

2005b. *Weltgeschichte: Imperien, Religionen und Systeme, 15–19. Jahrhundert.* Vienna: Böhlau.

"Der Verein für die Geschichte des Weltsystems." Verein für Geschichte des Weltsystems e.V. www.vgws.org/Texte/nolte-verein.html.

Nolte, Paul. 1999. "Die Historiker der Bundesrepublik: Rückblick auf eine 'lange Generation.'" *Merkur* 53-5: 413–32.

Novick, Peter. 1988. *That Noble Dream. The Objectivity Question and the American Historical Profession.* New York: Cambridge University Press.

Nozaki, Yoshiko and Mark Selden. 2009. "Japanese Textbook Controversies, Nationalism, and Historical Memory: Intra- and Inter-national Conflicts." *Japan Focus* 25-4, www.japanfocus.org/-Mark-Selden/3173.

Nussbaum, Felicity A., ed. 2003. *The Global Eighteenth Century.* Baltimore, MD: Johns Hopkins University Press.

O'Brien, Karen. 1997. *Narratives of Enlightenment. Cosmopolitan History from Voltaire to Gibbon.* Cambridge University Press.

O'Brien, Patrick K. 1992. "The Foundations of European Industrialization: From the Perspective of the World." In *Economic Effects of the European*

Expansion, 1492–1824, edited by José Casas Pardo, 463–502. Stuttgart: In Kommission bei F. Steiner.

2000. "The Status and Future of Universal History." In *Making Sense of Global History: The 19th International Congress of the Historical Sciences*, edited by Sogner Solvi, 15–33. Oslo: Universitetsforlaget.

2003. "The Deconstruction of Myths and Reconstruction of Metanarratives in Global Histories of Material Progress." In *Writing World History, 1800–2000*, edited by Eckhart Fuchs and Benedikt Stuchtey, 67–90. Oxford University Press.

2006. "Historiographical Traditions and Modern Imperatives for the Restoration of Global History." *Journal of Global History* 1-1: 3–39.

O'Hanlon, Rosalind. 1998. "Recovering the Subject: Subaltern Studies and the Histories of Resistance in Colonial South Asia." *Modern Asian Studies* 22-1: 189–224.

O'Rourke, Kevin H. and Jeffrey G. Williamson. 1999. *Globalization and History: The Evolution of a Nineteenth Century Atlantic Economy.* Cambridge, MA: MIT Press.

2002. "When Did Globalization Begin?" *European Review of Economic History* 6-1: 23–50.

Oberkrome, Willi. 1993. *Volksgeschichte: Methodische Innovation und völkische Ideologisierung in der deutschen Geschichtswissenschaft 1918–1945.* Göttingen: Vandenhoeck & Ruprecht.

Oexle, Otto Gerhard. 2004. "Historische Kulturwissenschaft Heute." In *Interkultureller Transfer und nationaler Eigensinn: Europäische und anglo-amerikanische Traditionen der Kulturwissenschaften*, edited by Rebekka Habermas and Rebekka von Mallinckrodt, 25–52. Göttingen: Wallstein.

Ogle, Vanessa. 2004. "Historikertag 2004: Transnationale Geschichte." *H-Soz-u-Kult* (October 29), http://hsozkult.geschichte.hu-berlin.de/forum/id=539&type=diskussionen.

Oldstone, Michael B. A. 1998. *Viruses, Plagues, and History.* Oxford/New York: Oxford University Press.

Oltmer, Jochen. 2004. *Migration und Politik in der Weimarer Republik.* Göttingen: Vandenhoeck & Ruprecht.

Ong, Aihwa. 1999. *Flexible Citizenship: The Cultural Logics of Transnationality.* Durham, NC: Duke University Press.

Opitz, Peter J. 2002. *Die Vereinten Nationen: Geschichte, Struktur, Perspektiven.* Munich: Bayerische Landeszentrale für Politische Bildungsarbeit.

Orleans, Leo A. 1988. *Chinese Students in America: Policies, Issues, and Numbers.* Washington, DC: National Academy Press.

Osiander, Anja and Ole Döring. 1999. *Zur Modernisierung der Ostasienforschung, Konzepte, Strukturen, Empfehlungen.* Hamburg: Institut für Asienkunde.

Osterhammel, Jürgen. 1994a. "Neue Welten in der europäischen Geschichtsschreibung (ca. 1500–1800)." In *Geschichtsdiskurs*, vol. II: *Anfänge modernen historischen Denkens*, edited by Wolfgang Küttler, Jörn Rüsen, and Ernst Schulin, 202–15. Frankfurt: Fischer Taschenbuch.

1994b. "Raumerfassung und Universalgeschichte im 20. Jahrhundert." In *Universalgeschichte und Nationalgeschichten*, edited by Gangolf Hübinger, Jürgen Osterhammel, and Erich Pelzer, 51–72. Freiburg: Rombach.

1995a. "Jenseits der Orthodoxie. Imperium, Raum, Herrschaft und Kultur als Dimensionen von Imperialismustheorie." *Periplus: Jahrbuch für Aussereuropäische Geschichte* 5: 119–31.

1995b. *Kolonialismus: Geschichte, Formen, Folgen*. Munich: C. H. Beck.

1996a. "Sozialgeschichte im Zivilisationsvergleich." *Geschichte und Gesellschaft* 22: 143–64.

1996b. "Transkulturell vergleichende Geschichtswissenschaft." In *Geschichte und Vergleich: Ansätze und Ergebnisse international vergleichender Geschichtsschreibung*, edited by Heinz-Gerhard Haupt and Jürgen Kocka, 271–313. Frankfurt/New York: Campus.

1997a. "Edward Said und die 'Orientalismus'-Debatte. Ein Rückblick." *Asien Afrika Amerika* 25: 597–607.

1997b. "Vorbemerkung: Westliches Wissen und die Geschichte nicht-europäischer Zivilisationen." In *Geschichtsdiskurs*, vol. IV: *Krisenbewußtsein, Katastrophenerfahrungen und Innovationen 1880–1945*, edited by Wolfgang Küttler, Jörn Rüsen, and Ernst Schulin, 307–13. Frankfurt: Fischer Taschenbuch.

1998a. *Die Entzauberung Asiens: Europa und die asiatischen Reiche im 18. Jahrhundert*. Munich: C. H. Beck.

1998b. "'Höherer Wahnsinn': Universalhistorische Denkstile im 20. Jahrhundert." In *Dimensionen der Historik. Geschichtstheorie, Wissenschaftsgeschichte und Geschichtskultur heute. Jörn Rüsen zum 60. Geburtstag*, edited by Horst-Walter Blanke, Friedrich Jaeger, and Thomas Sandkühler, 277–86. Cologne: Böhlau.

2000a. "Internationale Geschichte, Globalisierung und die Pluralität der Kulturen." In *Internationale Geschichte: Themen – Ergebnisse – Aussichten*, edited by Wilfried Loth and Jürgen Osterhammel, 387–408. Munich: Oldenbourg.

2000b. "Raumbeziehungen, Internationale Geschichte, Geopolitik und historische Geographie." In *Internationale Geschichte. Themen – Ergebnisse – Aussichten*, edited by Wilfried Loth and Jürgen Osterhammel, 287–308. Munich: Oldenbourg.

2000c. "Transfer und Migration von Ideen. China und der Westen im 19. und 20. Jahrhundert." In *Das Eigene und das Fremde: Festschrift für Urs Bitterli*, edited by Urs Faes and Béatrice Ziegler, 97–115. Zürich: NNZ.

2001a. "Der europäische Nationalstaat des 20. Jahrhunderts. Eine globalhistorische Annäherung." In *Geschichtswissenschaft jenseits des Nationalstaats: Studien zu Beziehungsgeschichte und Zivilisationsvergleich*, edited by Jürgen Osterhammel, 322–41. Göttingen: Vandenhoeck & Ruprecht.

ed. 2001b. *Geschichtswissenschaft jenseits des Nationalstaats: Studien zu Beziehungsgeschichte und Zivilisationsvergleich*. Göttingen: Vandenhoeck & Ruprecht.

2001c. "On the Spatial Ordering of 'Asia Orientale.'" In *Firenze, il Giappone e l'Asia Orientale: atti del convegno international di studi, Firenze, 25–27 marzo, 1999*, edited by Adriano Boscaro and Maurizio Bossi, 3–15. Florence: Olschki.

2001d. "Transnationale Gesellschaftsgeschichte: Erweiterung oder Alternative?" *Geschichte und Gesellschaft* 27: 464–79.

2002. "Gesellschaftsgeschichtliche Parameter chinesischer Modernität." *Geschichte und Gesellschaft* 28-1: 71–108.

2003. "Transferanalyse und Vergleich im Fernverhältnis." In *Vergleich und Transfer: Komparatistik in den Sozial-, Geschichts- und Kulturwissenschaften*, edited by Hartmut Kaelble and Jürgen Schriewer, 439–66. Frankfurt/New York: Campus.

2004. "Europamodelle und imperiale Kontexte." *Journal of Modern European History* 2-2: 157–81.

2005. "'Weltgeschichte': Ein Propädeutikum." *Geschichte in Wissenschaft und Unterricht* 9: 452–79.

2009. *Die Verwandlung der Welt: Eine Geschichte des 19. Jahrhunderts*. Munich: C. H. Beck.

Osterhammel, Jürgen and Wolfgang Mommsen, eds. 1986. *Imperialism and After: Continuities and Discontinuties*. London: Allen & Unwin.

Osterhammel, Jürgen and Niels P. Petersson. 2003. *Geschichte der Globalisierung: Dimensionen – Prozesse – Epochen*. Munich: C. H. Beck.

Otto, Bishop of Freysing. 1966. *The Two Cities: A Chronicle of Universal History to the Year 1146 A.D.* New York: Octagon Books.

Ou, Zhijian. 2003. "Lishi jiaokeshu yu minzu guojia xingxiang de yingzao: Liu Yizheng *Lidai shilüe* ququ nake tongshi *zhina tongshi* de neirong" [History Textbooks and the Construction of the Image of the Nation-State: The Selective Appropriation of Naka Michiyo's Shina tsushi in Liu Yizheng's *Lidai shilüe*]. In *Qingzhu Biao Xiaoxuan jiaoshou bashi huadan: wenshi lunji* [Celebrating Professor Biao Xiaoxuan's Eightieth Birthday: A Collection of Essays], edited by Dongqing shuwu tongxue hui, 71–96. Nanjing: Jiangsu guji chubanshe.

Packenham, Robert A. 1992. *The Dependency Movement. Scholarship and Politics in Development Studies*. Cambridge, MA: Harvard University Press.

Pai, Hyung-il. 2000. *Constructing "Korean" Origins: A Critical Review of Archeology, Historiography, and Racial Myth in Korean State-Formation Theories*. Cambridge, MA: Harvard University Press.

Palat, Ravi Arvind. 2000. "Fragmented Visions: Excavating the Future of the Area Studies in a Post-American World." In *Beyond the Area Studies Wars: Toward a New International Studies*, edited by Neil L. Waters, 64–108. Hanover, NH: Middlebury College Press.

Palmer, Robert R. 1959. *The Age of Democratic Revolution*. Princeton University Press.

Palti, Elías José. 2001. "The Nation as a Problem: Historians and the 'National Question.'" *History and Theory* 40-3: 324–6.

Pan, Guang. 2000. "Guanyu xinshiji zhongguo shijieshi xueke fazhan de jidian kanfa" [Some Thoughts on the Development of World Historical Studies in China in the New Century]. *Shijie lishi* [World History] 1: 5–6.

Pan, Runhan and Lin Chengjie. 2000. *Shijie jindaishi* [Modern World History]. Beijing: Beijing daxue chubanshe.

Pang, Pu. 2000. "Quanqiuhua yu hua quanqiu" [Globalization and Transforming the Globe]. *Ershiyi shiji* [Twenty-first Century] 61: 76–9.

Park, You-me and Rjeswari Sunder Rajan. 2000. "Postcolonial Feminism/ Postcoloniality and Feminism." In *A Companion to Postcolonial Studies*, edited by Sangeeta Ray and Henry Schwarz, 53–71. Oxford: Blackwell.

Patel, Kiran Klaus. 2003. "Transatlantische Perspektiven transnationaler Geschichte." *Geschichte und Gesellschaft* 29: 625–47.

    2004. "Überlegungen zu einer transnationalen Geschichte." *Zeitschrift für Geschichtswissenschaft* 52: 626–45.

Paulmann, Johannes. 1998. "Internationaler Vergleich und interkultureller Transfer: Zwei Forschungsansätze zur europäischen Geschichte des 18. bis 20. Jahrhunderts." *Historische Zeitschrift* 267: 649–85.

Paxton, Pamela, Melanie M. Hughes, and Jennifer L. Green. 2006. "The International Women's Movement and Women's Political Representation, 1893–2003." *American Sociological Review* 71-6: 893–920.

Peng, Shuzhi. 1992. *Dongfang minzu zhuyi sichao* [Reflections on Nationalism in the East]. Xian: Xibei daxue chubanshe.

Perdue, Peter C. 2005. *China Marches West: The Qing Conquest of Central Eurasia.* Cambridge, MA: Belknap Press of Harvard University Press.

Pernau, Margrit. 2004. "Global History – Wegbereiter für einen neuen Kolonialismus?" *H-Soz-u-Kult* (December 17), http://hsozkult.geschichte. huberlin.de/forum/id=572&type=artikel.

Peukert, Detlev. 1987. *Die Weimarer Republik: Krisenjahre der klassischen Moderne.* Frankfurt: Suhrkamp.

Pietschmann, Horst. 1999. "Geschichte der europäischen Expansion – Geschichte des atlantischen Raumes – Globalgeschichte." In *Überseegeschichte: Beiträge der jüngeren Forschung*, edited by Thomas Beck, Horst Gründer, Horst Pietschmann, and Roderich Ptack, 21–39. Stuttgart: Steiner.

Pigulla, Andreas. 1996. *China in der deutschen Weltgeschichtsschreibung vom 18. bis zum 20. Jahrhundert.* Wiesbaden: Harrassowitz.

Pilz, Erich. 1991. *Gesellschaftsgeschichte und Theoriebildung in der marxistischen Historiographie. Zur Entwicklung der Diskussion um die Han-Gesellschaft.* Vienna: Austrian Academy of Science Press.

Pinch, W. R. 1999. "Same Difference in India and Europe." *History and Theory* 38-3: 389–407.

Pingel, Falk. 2000. *The European Home: Representations of Twentieth Century Europe in History Textbooks.* Strasbourg: Council of Europe.

Pletsch, Carl E. 1981. "The Three Worlds, or the Division of Social Scientific Labor, ca. 1950–1975." *Comparative Studies in Society and History* 23-4: 565–90.

Pohl, Karl-Heinz and Anselm Müller, eds. 2002. *Chinese Ethics in a Global Context.* Leiden: Brill.

Pollock, Sheldon. 1993. "Deep Orientalism? Notes on Sanskrit and Power Beyond the Raj." In *Orientalism and the Postcolonial Predicament: Perspectives on South Asia*, edited by Carol A. Breckenridge and Peter van der Veer, 76–133. Philadelphia: University of Pennsylvania Press.

2002. "Ex Oriente Nox. Indologie im nationalsozialistischen Staat." In *Jenseits des Eurozentrismus. Postkoloniale Perspektiven in den Geschichts- und Kulturwissenschaften*, edited by Sebastian Conrad and Shalini Randeria, 335–71. Frankfurt: Campus.

Pomeranz, Kenneth. 2001. *The Great Divergence: China, Europe, and the Making of the Modern World Economy*. Princeton University Press.

2002. "Political Economy and Ecology on the Eve of Industrialization: Europe, China, and the Global Conjecture." *American Historical Review* 107-2: 425–46.

2008a. "Chinese Development in Long-Run Perspective." *Proceedings of the American Philosophical Society* 152-1: 83–102.

2008b. "Scale, Scope, and Scholarship: Regional Practices and Global Economic History." Paper presented at the Harvard/Duke conference *Global History, Globally*, Cambridge, MA, February 8–9.

Pomper, Philip. 1995. "World History and Its Critics." *History and Theory* 34-2: 1–7.

1998. "Introduction: The Theory and Practice of World History." In *World History: Ideologies, Structures, and Identities*, edited by Philip Pomper, Richard H. Elphik, and Richard T. Vann, 1–17. Malden, MA: Blackwell.

2005. "The History and Theory of Empires." *History and Theory, Theme Issue* 44: 1–27.

Pomper, Philip, Richard H. Elphik, and Richard T. Vann, eds. 1998. *World History: Ideologies, Structures, and Identities*. Malden, MA: Blackwell.

Popp, Susanne. 2009. "National Textbook Controversies in a Globalizing World." In *History Teaching in the Crossfire of Political Interest*, edited by Luigi Cajani, Elisabeth Erdmann, Alexander S. Khodnev, Susanne Popp, Nicole Tutiaux-Guillon, and George Wrangham, 109–22. Schwalbach: Wochenschau Verlag.

Popp, Susanne and Johanna Forster, eds. 2003. *Curriculum Weltgeschichte. Interdisziplinäre Zugänge zu einem global orientierten Geschichtsunterricht*. Schwalbach: Wochenschau.

Porter, Theodore M. and Dorothy Ross, eds. 2003. *The Modern Social Sciences*. Vol 7 of *The Cambridge History of Science*. Cambridge University Press.

Powell, Eve M. Troutt. 2003. *A Different Shade of Colonialism: Egypt, Great Britain, and the Mastery of the Sudan*. Berkeley: University of California Press.

Prakash, Gyan. 1990. "Writing Post-Orientalist Histories of the Third World. Perspectives from Indian Historiography." *Comparative Studies in Society and History* 32-2: 383–408.

1994. "Subaltern Studies as Postcolonial Criticism." *American Historical Review* 99-5: 1475–90.

Pu, Changgen. 2002. "Quanqiuhua yu zhongguo yingdui" [Globalization and Chinese Responses]. *Yazhou yanjiu* [Asian Studies] 44: 7–23.

Puhle, Hans-Jürgen, ed. 1991. *Bürger in der Gesellschaft der Neuzeit*. Göttingen: Vandenhoeck & Ruprecht.

2006. "Area Studies im Wandel. Zur Organisation von Regionalforschung in Deutschland." Center for North American Studies. http://web.uni-frankfurt.de/zenaf/contac/AreaStudies.pdf.

Qi, Shirong. 1994. "Shi tan wo guo shijieshi xueke de fazhan lishi ji qianjing" [Exploring the Past Trajectories and Prospects of World Historical Scholarship in Our Country]. *Lishi Yanjiu* [Historical Research] 1: 155–68.

2000. "Youguan shijie xueke jianshe de liangge wenti" [Two Problems of Establishing the Discipline of World History]. *Shijie lishi* [World History] 4: 71–3.

2006–2007. *Shijieshi* [World History]. 4 vols. Beijing: Gaodeng jiaoyu chubanshe.

Qian, Chengdan. 2003. "Yi Xiandaihua wei zhuti guojian shijie jinxiandaishi xin de xueke tixi" [Creating a New Theoretical System for Modern and Contemporary World History around the Theme of Modernization]. *Shijie Lishi* [World History] 3: 2–11.

2009. "Constructing a New Disciplinary Framework of Modern World History Around the Theme of Modernization." *Chinese Studies in History* 42-3: 7–24.

Qian, Chengdan and Liu Jinyuan, eds. 1994. *Huanqiu toushi: xiandaihua de mitu* [The Road to Modernization Went Astray: A Global Perspective]. Hangzhou: Zhejiang renmin chubanshe.

Qian, Chengdan, Yu Yang, and Xiaolü Chen. 1997. *Shijie xiandaihua jincheng* [The Process of World Modernization]. Nanjing: Nanjing daxue chubanshe.

Quirin, Michael. 1996. "Scholarship, Value, and Hermeneutics in Kaozheng: Some Reflections on Cui Shu (1740–1816) and the Confucian Classics." *History and Theory* 35-4: 34–53.

Radkau, Joachim. 2008. *Nature and Power: A Global History of the Environment*. New York: Cambridge University Press.

Radkau, Verena, Eduard Fuchs, and Thomas Lutz, eds. 2004. *Genozide und staatliche Gewaltverbrechen im 20. Jahrhundert*. Innsbruck: Studien.

Randeria, Shalini. 1999. "Geteilte Geschichte und verwobene Moderne." In *Zukunftsentwürfe: Ideen für eine Kultur der Veränderung*, edited by Jörn Rüsen, Hanna Leitgeb, and Norbert Jegelka, 87–96. Frankfurt/New York: Campus.

Ranft, Andreas and Markus Meumann, eds. 2003. *Traditionen – Visionen. 44. Deutscher Historikertag in Halle an der Saale: Vom 10. bis 13. September 2002*. Munich: Oldenbourg.

Raphael, Lutz. 1990. "Historikerkontroversen im Spannungsfeld zwischen Berufshabitus, Fächerkonkurrenz und sozialen Deutungsmustern." *Historische Zeitschrift* 251: 325–63.

1999. "Die 'Neue Geschichte' – Umbrüche und Wege der Geschichtsschreibung in internationaler Perspektive (1880–1940)." In *Geschichtsdiskurs*, vol. IV: *Krisenbewusstsein, Katastrophenerfahrungen und Innovationen 1880–1945*, edited by Wolfgang Küttler, Jörn Rüsen, and Ernst Schulin, 51–89. Frankfurt: Fischer Taschenbuch.

2000. "Nationalzentrierte Sozialgeschichte in programmatischer Absicht: Die Zeitschrift 'Geschichte und Gesellschaft. Zeitschrift für Historische Sozialwissenschaft' in den ersten 25 Jahren ihres Bestehens." *Geschichte und Gesellschaft* 26-1: 5–37.

2003. *Geschichtswissenschaft im Zeitalter der Extreme: Theorien, Methoden, Tendenzen von 1900 bis zur Gegenwart.* Munich: C. H. Beck.

Raymond, Grew. 2006. "Expanding Worlds of World History." *Journal of Modern History* 78: 878–98.

Redding, S. 1990. *Gordon. The Spirit of Chinese Capitalism.* Berlin/New York: W. de Gruyter.

Reid, Donald M. 1990. *Cairo University and the Making of Modern Egypt.* Cambridge University Press.

Reinhard, Wolfgang. 1983–1990. *Geschichte der europäischen Expansion.* 4 vols. Stuttgart: W. Kohlhammer.

1996a. *Kleine Geschichte des Kolonialismus.* Stuttgart: Kröner.

ed. 1996b. *Power Elites and State Building.* New York: Oxford University Press.

1997. *Parasit oder Partner? Europäische Wirtschaft und Neue Welt, 1500–1800.* Münster: Lit.

2001. "Was ist europäische politische Kultur? Versuch zur Begründung einer politischen historischen Anthropologie." *Geschichte und Gesellschaft* 27-4: 593–616.

2005. *La Vieille Europe et les nouveaux mondes: Pour une histoire des relations atlantiques.* Ostfildern: Thorbecke.

Reitermeier, Arnd and Gerhard Fouquet, eds. 2005. *Kommunikation und Raum: 45. Deutscher Historikertag in Kiel vom 14. bis 17. September 2004.* Neumünster: Wachholz.

Ren, Bingqiang. 2004. "Jiushi niandai yilai zhongguo de minzu zhuyi sichao – jian piping Wang Xiaodong de minzu zhuyiguan" [Chinese Nationalist Thought Since the 1990s – and a Critique of Wang Xiaodong's Idea of Nationalism]. In *Qianliu – dui xiayi minzu zhuyi de pipan yu fansi* [Undercurrents – Critiques of Reflections on Narrow Nationalism], edited by Le Shan, 9–32. Shanghai: Huadong shifan daxue chubanshe.

Ren, Qiang, Hu Lijuan and Wang Yanfeng, eds. 2004. *Zhongguo yu riben de tazhe renshi –zhongri xuezhe de gongtong tantao* [The Mutual Recognition of the Other Between China and Japan – Shared Discussions Between Chinese and Japanese Scholars]. Beijing: Shehui kexue wenxian chubanshe.

Revel, Jaccques. 1996. *Jeux d'échelles: La micro-analyse à l'expérience.* Paris: Seuil.

Reynolds, David. 2000. *One World Divisible: A Global History since 1945.* New York: W. W. Norton.

Ricardo, David. 1817. *On the Principles of Political Economy and Taxation.* London: John Murray.

Richard H. Grove. 1998. "Global Impact of the 1789–93 El Niño." *Nature* 393: 318–19.

Riekenberg, Michael, ed. 2005. *Geschichts- und Politikunterricht zeitgemäß? Fragen und Bemerkungen aus der Sicht der Regionalwissenschaften.* Leipzig: Leipziger Universitätsverlag.

Riley, James C. 2001. *Rising Life Expectancy: A Global History.* Cambridge University Press.

Ritter, Gerhard. 1954. "Das Problem des Militarismus in Deutschland." *Historische Zeitschrift* 177: 21–48.

Rittersberger-Tiliç, Helga. 1998. *Vom Gastarbeiter zum Deutschler: Die Rückkehrergemeinschaft in einer türkischen Kleinstadt,* Potsdam: Verlag Perspektiven.

Ritzer, George. 2004. *The Globalization of Nothing.* Thousand Oaks, CA: Pine Forge Press.

Robertson, Roland. 1995. "Glocalization: Time-Space and Homogeneity-Heterogeneity." In *Global Modernities,* edited by Mike Featherstone, Scott Lash and Roland Robertson, 25–44. London: SAGE.

Robin, Ron. 2001. *Making the Cold War Enemy: Culture and Politics in the Military-Intellectual Complex.* Princeton University Press.

Robinson, Chase F. 2003. *Islamic Historiography.* Cambridge University Press.

Ross, Dorothy. 1991. *The Origins of American Social Science.* Cambridge/New York: Cambridge University Press.

Rothermund, Dietmar. 1996. *The Global Impact of the Great Depression, 1929–1939.* New York/London: Routledge.

   2003. "Indien und der Rest der Welt: Möglichkeiten und Grenzen der Aussereuropäischen Geschichte in Deutschland." *Neue Politische Literatur* 1: 5–14.

   2005. "Globalgeschichte und Geschichte der Globalisierung." In *Globalisierung und Globalgeschichte,* edited by Margarete Grandner, Dietmar Rothermund, and Wofgang Schwentker, 12–35. Vienna: Mandelbaum.

Rothermund, Dietmar and Susanne Weigelin-Schwiedrzik, eds. 2004. *Der Indische Ozean: Das Afro-asiatische Mittelmeer als Kultur- und Wirtschaftsraum.* Vienna: Promedia.

Ruan, Wei. 2001. *Wenming de Biaoxian* [Performances of Civilizations]. Beijing: Jingxiao che Xinhua shudian.

Rueschemeyer, Dietrich. 1991. "Different Methods – Contradictory Results? Research on Development and Democracy." In *Issues and Alternatives in Comparative Social Research,* edited by Charles Ragin, 9–38. Leiden: Brill.

Ruppenthal, Jens. 2007. *Kolonialismus als "Wissenschaft und Technik": Das Hamburgische Kolonialinstitut 1908 bis 1919.* Stuttgart: Steiner.

Rürup, Reinhard. 1984. *Deutschland im 19. Jahrhundert, 1815–1871.* Göttingen: Vandenhoeck & Ruprecht.

Rüsen, Jörn. 1996. "Some Theoretical Approaches to Intercultural Comparative Historiography." *History and Theory* 35-4: 5–22.

   1998. "Theoretische Zugänge zum interkulturellen Vergleich historischen Denkens." In *Die Vielfalt der Kulturen,* edited by Jörn Rüsen, Michael Gottlob, and Achim Mitag, 37–73. Frankfurt: Suhrkamp.

   ed. 2002. *Western Historical Thinking: An Intercultural Debate.* New York: Berghahn Books.

   2004. "How to Overcome Ethnocentrism: Approaches to a Culture of Recognition by History in the Twenty-First Century." *History and Theory* 43-4: 118–29.

Sabrow, Martin. 2004. "Von der Moralisierung zur Historisierung. Überlegungen zur deutschen Geschichtskultur." *Mittelweg* 36: 72–88.

Sachse, Carola. 1997. "Frauenforschung zum Nationalsozialismus." *Mittelweg* 36-6: 24–42.

Sachsenmaier, Dominic. 2001. "The Cultural Transmission from China to Europe (China in Western Chronologies)." In *Handbook of Oriental Studies*, edited by Nicolas Standaert, 879–905. Leiden: Brill.

    2003. "Politische Kulturen in China und Deutschland nach dem Ersten Weltkrieg – Gedanken zu einer globalhistorischen Perspektive." *Zeitschrift für Weltgeschichte* 4-2: 87–102.

    2004. "Die Angst vor dem Weltdorf. Globale und Interkulturelle Forschungen – Neue Ansätze." *WZB: Mitteilungen* 105: 14–18.

    2005a. Conference Report: "German and Chinese Historiography in Dialogue." *Berliner China-Hefte: Beiträge zur Geschichte und Gesellschaft Chinas.*

    2005b. "Global History, Global Debates." *H-Soz-u-Kult* (March 3), http:// hsozkult.geschichte.hu-berlin.de/forum/2005–03–001.

    2006. "Searching for Alternatives to Western Modernity. Cross-Cultural Approaches in the Aftermath of World War I." *Journal of Modern European History* 4-2: 241–59.

    2007a. "Alternative Visions of World Order in the Aftermath of World War I – Global Perspectives on Chinese Approaches." In *Competing Visions of World Order: Global Moments and Movements, 1880s–1930s*, edited by Sebastian Conrad and Dominic Sachsenmaier, 151–80. New York: Palgrave Macmillan.

    2007b. "Chinese Debates on Modernization and the West after the Great War." In *Decentering American History*, edited by Jessica Gienow-Hecht, 109–31. New York: Berghahn Books.

    2007c. "World History as Ecumenical History?" *Journal of World History* 18-4: 433–62.

    2009a. "Little Red Book." In *The Palgrave Dictionary of Transnational History: From the Mid-19th Century to the Present Day*, edited by Akira Iriye and Pierre-Yves Saunier, 686–87. New York: Palgrave Macmillan.

    2009b. "Recent Trends in European History – The World Beyond Europe and Alternative Historical Spaces." *Journal of Modern European History* 7-1: 5–25.

    2009c. "Underdevelopment." In *The Palgrave Dictionary of Transnational History: From the Mid-19th Century to the Present Day*, edited by Akira Iriye and Pierre-Yves Saunier, 1062–5. New York: Palgrave Macmillan.

Sachsenmaier, Dominic, Jens Riedel, and Shmuel Eisenstadt, eds. 2009. *Duoyuan xiandaihua de fansi. Ouzhou, Zhongguo ji qitade chanshi* [Reflections on Multiple Modernities: European, Chinese, and Other Interpretations]. Translated by Guo Shaotang (Cantonese: Kwok Siu-Tong). Hong Kong: Chinese University of Hong Kong Press.

    eds. 2002. *Reflections on Multiple Modernities: European, Chinese, and Other Approaches.* Leiden: Brill.

Said, Edward W. 1979. *Orientalism.* New York: Vintage Books.

Sanders, Thomas. 1998. "Soviet Historiography." In *A Global Encyclopedia of Historical Writing*, 2 vols., edited by D. R. Woolf, 854–6. New York: Garland Publishing.

Sarkar, Sumit. 1997. "The Many Worlds of Indian History." In *Writing Social History*, edited by Sumit Sarkar, 1–49. New York/Delhi: Oxford University Press.

Sarrazin, Thilo. 2010. *Deutschland schafft sich ab. Wie wir unser Land aufs Spiel setzen.* Munich: DVA.

Sassen, Saskia. 1998. *Globalization and Its Discontents: Essays on the New Mobility of People and Money.* New York: New Press.

Sato, Masayuki. 1991a. "Comparative Ideas and Chronology." *History and Theory* 30-3: 275–301.

1991b. "Historiographical Encounters: The Chinese and Western Traditions in Turn-of-the-Century Japan." *Storia della Storiografia* 19: 13–21.

Saunier, Pierre-Yves. 2008. "Learning by Doing: Notes about the Making of the Palgrave Dictionary of Transnational History." *Journal of Modern European History* 6-2: 159–80.

Schaebler, Birgit. 2007. "Writing the Nation in the Arab-Speaking World, Nationally and Transnationally." In *Writing the Nation: A Global Perspective*, edited by Stefan Berger, 179–96. Basingstoke: Palgrave Macmillan.

Schaefgen, Annette. 2006. *Schwieriges Erinnern. Zur Rezeption des Genozids an den Armeniern.* Berlin: Metropol Verlag.

Schäfer, Wolf. 2003. "The New Global History: Toward a Narrative for Pangaea Two." *Erwägen-Wissen-Ethik* 14-1: 75–88.

Schenk, Benjamin Frithjof. 2002. "Mental Maps: Die Konstruktion von geographischen Räumen in Europa seit der Aufklärung." *Geschichte und Gesellschaft* 28: 493–514.

Schleier, Hans. 1993. "Karl Lamprechts Universalgeschichtskonzeption im Umfeld seiner Zeit." In *Karl Lamprecht weiterdenken: Universal- und Kulturgeschichte heute*, edited by Gerald Diesener, 145–55. Leipzig: Leipziger Universitätsverlag.

1997. "Geschichte der internationalen Geschichtswissenschaft im 20. Jahrhundert: Darstellungen – Probleme – Perspektiven." In *Geschichtsdiskurs*, vol. III: *Die Epoche der Historisierung*, edited by Wolfgang Küttler, Jörn Rüsen, and Ernst Schulin, 164–83. Frankfurt: Fischer Taschenbuch.

2003. *Geschichte der deutschen Kulturgeschichtsschreibung*, vol. I: *Vom Ende des 18. bis Ende des 19. Jahrhunderts.* Waltrop: Harmut Spenner.

Schluchter, Wofgang. 1981. *The Rise of Western Rationalism: Max Weber's Developmental History.* Berkeley: University of California Press.

Schlumbohm, Jürgen, ed. 1998. *Mikrogeschichte-Makrogeschichte. Komplementär oder inkommensurabel?* Göttingen: Wallstein.

Schmale, Wolfgang, ed. 1991. *Bericht über die 38. Versammlung deutscher Historiker in Bochum: 26. bis 29. September 1990.* Stuttgart: Ernst Klett.

1997. *Scheitert Europa an seinem Mythendefizit?* Bochum: Winkler.

ed. 1998. "Europäische Geschichte als historische Disziplin. Überlegungen zu einer Europäistik." *Zeitschrift für Geschichtswissenschaft* 46-5: 389–405.

Schnapper, Dominique. 1999. "From the Nation-state to the Transnational World: On the Meaning and Usefulness of Diaspora as a Concept." *Diaspora* 8-3: 225–54.

Schneider, Axel. 1996. "Between Dao and History: Two Chinese Historians in Search of a Modern Identity for China." *History and Theory* 35-4: 54–73.

1997. *Wahrheit und Geschichte: Zwei Chinesische Historiker auf der Suche nach einer modernen Identität für China*. Wiesbaden: Harrassowitz.

2001. "Bridging the Gap: Attempts at Constructing a 'New' Historical-Cultural Identity in the People's Republic of China." *East Asian History* 22: 129–43.

Schneider, Ute. 2004. "Von Juden und Türken. Zum gegenwärtigen Diskurs über Religion, kollektive Identität und Modernisierung." *Zeitschrift für Geschichtswissenschaft* 5: 426–40.

Schölch, Alexander. 1982. "Ägypten und Japan in der zweiten Hälfte des 19. Jahrhunderts. Ein entwicklungsgeschichtlicher Vergleich." *Geschichte, Wissenschaft und Unterrricht* 33: 333–46.

Scholte, Jan Aart. 2000. *Globalization: A Critical Introduction*. New York: Palgrave Macmillan, 2000.

Schönwälder, Karen. 2001. *Einwanderung und ethnische Pluralität: Politische Entscheidungen und öffentliche Debatten in Großbritannien und der Bundesrepublik von den 1950er bis zu den 1970er Jahren*. Essen: Klartext.

Schramm, Gottfried. 2004. *Fünf Wegscheiden der Weltgeschichte*. Göttingen: Vandenhoeck & Ruprecht.

Schubert, Gunter. 2001. "Nationalism and National Identity in Contemporary China." *Issues & Studies* 37-5: 127–56.

Schulin, Ernst, ed. 1974. *Universalgeschichte*. Cologne: Kiepenheuer und Witsch.

1988. "Universalgeschichte und Nationalgeschichte bei Leopold von Ranke." In *Leopold von Ranke und die Moderne Geschichtswissenschaft*, edited by Wolfgang J. Mommsen, 37–71. Stuttgart: Klett-Cotta.

2002. "German and American Historiography in the Nineteenth and Twentieth Centuries." In *An Interrupted Past: German Refugee Historians in the United States After 1933*, edited by Hartmut Lehmann and James Sheehan, 8–31. New York: Cambridge University Press.

Schulte Barbara, ed. 2006. *Transfer lokalisiert: Konzepte, Akteure, Kontexte* (= *Comparativ* 16–3). Leipzig: Leipziger Universitätsverlag.

Schulz, Gerhard. 2004. *Geschichte im Zeitalter der Globalisierung*. Berlin/New York: De Gruyter.

Schulze, Winfried. 1989. *Deutsche Geschichtswissenschaft nach 1945* (= *Historische Zeitschrift, Beiheft 10*). Munich: Oldenbourg.

1990. "Der Wandel des Allgemeinen: Der Weg der deutschen Historiker nach 1945 zur Kategorie des Sozialen." In *Teil und Ganzes. Theorie der Geschichte. Beiträge zur Historik*, vol. IV, edited by Karl Acham and Winfried Schulze, 193–216. Munich: Deutscher Taschenbuch Verlag.

Schulze, Winfried and Otto Gerhard Oexle, eds. 2000. *Deutsche Historiker im Nationalsozialismus*. Frankfurt: Fischer Taschenbuch.

Schumann, Peter. 1989. *Bericht über die 37. Versammlung deutscher Historiker in Bamberg: 12. bis 16. Oktober 1988*. Stuttgart: Ernst Klett.

Schütte, Hans-Wilm. 2004. *Die Asienwissenschaften in Deutschland: Geschichte, Stand und Perspektiven*. Hamburg: Institut für Asienkunde.

2006. "Die Geburt des Instituts für Asienkunde." In *50 Jahre Institut für Asienkunde*, edited by Hans-Wilm, Schütte, 15–86. Hamburg: Institut für Asienkunde.

Schwarz, Benjamin I. 1985. *The World of Thought in Ancient China*. Cambridge, MA: Harvard University Press.

1996. "History in Chinese Culture. Some Comparative Reflections." *History and Theory* 35-4: 23–33.

Schwentker, Wolfgang. 1997. "Zwischen Weltaneignung und Selbstdeutungszwang, Entwicklungstendenzen der Geschichtswissenschaft in Japan 1860–1945." In *Geschichtsdiskurs*, vol. IV: *Krisenbewußtsein, Katastrophenerfahrungen und Innovationen 1880–1945*, edited by Wolfgang Küttler, Jörn Rüsen, and Ernst Schulin, 339–45. Frankfurt: Fischer Taschenbuch.

2005. "Globalisierung und Geschichtswissenschaft. Themen, Methoden und Kritik der Globalgeschichte." In *Globalisierung und Globalgeschichte*, edited by Margarete Grandner, Dietmar Rothermund, and Wolfgang Schwentker, 36–59. Vienna: Mandelbaum.

Scott, John C. 2006. "The Mission of the University: Medieval to Postmodern Transformations." *Journal of Higher Education* 77-1: 1–39.

Seager, Richard H., ed. 1993. *The Dawn of Religious Pluralism: Voices from the World's Parliament of Religions, 1893*. La Salle, IL: Open Court.

Searle, John R. 1994. "Rationality and Realism. What Is at Stake?" In *The Research University at a Time of Discontent*, edited by Jonathan Cole, Elinor Barber, and Stephen Graubard, 55–83. Baltimore: Johns Hopkins University Press.

Seeman, Erik R. and Jorge Cañizares-Esguerra, eds. 2007. *The Atlantic in Global History, 1500–2000*. Upper Saddle River, NJ: Pearson Prentice Hall.

Seigel, Micol. 2005. "Beyond Compare: Comparative Method After the Transnational Turn." *Radical History Review* 91: 62–90.

Sen, Amartya K. 1997. "Human Rights and Asian Values." *The New Republic*, July 14–21.

2005. *The Argumentative Indian: Writings on Indian History, Culture, and Identity*. London: Penguin.

Senghor, Léopold S. 1997. "Negritude: A Humanism of the Twentieth Century." In *Perspectives on Africa: A Reader in Culture, History, and Representation*, edited by Roy R. Grinker and Christopher B. Steiner, 629–36. Cambridge, MA: Blackwell.

Service, Robert. 2007. *Comrades! A History of World Communism*. Cambridge, MA: Harvard University Press.

Shen, Guowei. 2008. "Hanyu de jindai xin ciyu yu zhongri cihui jiaoliu – jianlun xiandai hanyu cihui tixi de xingcheng" [New Words in Contemporary

Chinese and Relations between Chinese and Japanese Words – Discussing the Formation of the Modern Chinese Vocabulary System]. *Nankai yuyan xuekan* [Nankai Linguistics] 1: 72–88.

Shi, Tianjian. 2000. "Cultural Values and Democracy in the People's Republic of China." *China Quarterly* 162: 540–59.

Shi, Yuanhua and Hu Lizhong, eds. 2005. *Dongya hanwenhuaquan yu zhongguo guanxi* [The Relationship between the East Asian Han-Cultural Realm and China]. Beijing: Zhongguo shehui kexue chubanshe.

Shin, Yong-ha. 2000. *Modern Korean History and Nationalism.* Seoul: Jimoondang.

Shirk, Susan L. 1993. *The Political Logic of Economic Reform in China.* Berkeley: University of California Press.

Shore, Chris. 1999. "Inventing Homo Europaeus: The Cultural Politics of European Integration." *Ethnologia Europaea* 29-2: 59–61.

2000. *Building Europe: The Cultural Politics of European Integration.* London: Routledge.

Shteppa, Konstantin F. 1962. *Russian Historians and the Soviet State.* New Brunswick, NJ: Rutgers University Press.

Sigal, Pete. 2009. "Latin America and the Challenge of Globalizing the History of Sexuality." *American Historical Review* 114-5: 1340–52.

Siljak, Ana. 1999. "Christianity, Science and Progress in Sergei M. Soloviev's *History of Russia.*" In *The Historiography of Imperial Russia: The Profession and Writing of History in a Multinational State,* edited by Thomas Sanders, 215–38. Armonk, NY: M. E. Sharpe.

Skocpol, Theda. 1979. *States and Social Revolutions: A Comparative Analysis of France, Russia, and China.* New York: Cambridge University Press.

Sluga, Glenda. 2006. *The Nation, Psychology, and International Politics, 1870–1919.* Basingstoke: Palgrave Macmillan.

Smith, Adam. 1904. *The Wealth of Nations.* 5th edn. London: Methuen & Co.

Smith, Bonnie G. ed. 2000. *Global Feminism Since 1945.* London/New York: Routledge.

ed. 2004–2005. *Women's History in Global Perspective.* 3 vols. Urbana: University of Illinois Press.

Smith, Dennis. 1991. *The Rise of Historical Sociology.* Cambridge: Polity Press.

Smith, Woodruff. 1986. *The Ideological Origins of Nazi Imperialism.* New York: Oxford University Press.

Sogner, Sølvi, ed. 2001. *Making Sense of Global History.* Oslo: Universitetsforlaget.

Soja, Edward W. 1989. *Postmodern Geographies: The Reassertion of Space in Critical Social Theory.* London/New York: Verso.

2003. "Writing the City Spatially." *City: Analysis of Urban Trends, Culture, Theory Policy, Action* 7-3: 269–81.

Spakowski, Nicola. 1999. *Helden, Monumente, Traditionen. Nationale Identität und historisches Bewußtsein in der VR China.* Hamburg: Lit.

2005. "Between Normative and Individualizing Didactics: Suzhi Jiaoyu as a New Term in Chinese Theories of History Teaching." In *Historical Truth, Historical Criticism, and Ideology. Chinese Historiography and Historical Culture from a New Comparative Perspective*, edited by Helwig Schmidt-Glintzer, Achim Mittag, and Jörn Rüsen, 465–81. Leiden: Brill.

2008. "Regionalismus und historische Identität – Transnationale Dialoge zur Geschichte Nord/Ost/Asiens seit den 1990er Jahren." In *Asianismen seit dem 19. Jahrhundert* (= *Comparativ* 18–6), edited by Marc Frey and Nicola Spakowski, 69–87. Leipzig: Leipziger Universitätsverlag.

Speitkamp, Winfried. 2005. *Deutsche Kolonialgeschichte*. Stuttgart: P. Reclam.

Spence, Jonathan D. 2003. "The Whole World in Their Hands." *New York Review of Books* 50-15 (October 9).

Spengler, Oswald. 1918. *Der Untergang des Abendlandes*. Munich: Braumüller.

Spiliotis, Susanne-Sophia. 2001. "Wo findet Gesellschaft statt? Oder das Konzept der Transterritorialitat." *Geschichte und Gesellschaft* 27: 480–8.

Spivak, Gayatri C. 1998. "Can the Subaltern Speak?" In *Marxism and Interpretation of Culture*, edited by Cary Nelson and Lawrence Grossberg, 271–313. Urbana: University of Illinois Press.

Stavrianos, Leften Stavros. 1966. *The World Since 1500: A Global History*. Englewood Cliffs, NJ: Prentice-Hall.

1970. *The World to 1500: A Global History*. Englewood Cliffs, NJ: Prentice-Hall.

Stavrianos, Leften Stavros, Loretta Kreider Andres, George I. Blanksten, Roger F. Hackett, Ella C. Leppert, Paul L. Murphy, and Lacey Baldwin Smith. 1962. *A Global History of Man*. Boston: Allyn and Bacon.

Stearns, Peter N. 2006. *Gender in World History*. 2nd edn. New York: Routledge.

Steinert, Johannes-Dieter. 1995. *Migration und Politik. Westdeutschland-Europa-Übersee 1945–1961*. Osnabrück: Secolo.

Stewart, Charles, ed. 2007. *Creolization: History, Ethnography, Theory*. Walnut Creek, CA: Left Coast Press.

Stoianovich, Traian. 1976. *French Historical Method: The Annales Paradigm*. Ithaca, NY: Cornell University Press.

Stoler, Ann L. 1995. *Race and the Education of Desire: Foucault's History of Sexuality and the Colonial Order of Things*. Durham, NC: Duke University Press.

Stone, Bailey. 1994. *The Genesis of the French Revolution: A Global-Historical Interpretation*. New York: Cambridge University Press.

Stuchtey, Benedikt, ed. 2005. *Science Across European Empires, 1800–1950*. Oxford/New York: Oxford University Press.

Stuchtey, Benedikt and Eckhardt Fuchs, eds. 2003. *Writing World History, 1800–2000*. Oxford: Oxford University Press.

Stürmer, Michael. 1983. *Das ruhelose Reich: Deutschland, 1866–1918*. Berlin: Siedler.

Su, Xiaokang and Wang Luoxiang. 1991. *Deathsong of the River: A Reader's Guide to the Chinese TV Series Heshang*. Ithaca, NY: Cornell University Press.

Subrahmanyam, Sanjay. 1997. "Connected Histories. Notes towards a Reconfiguration of Early Modern Eurasia." *Modern Asian Studies* 31-3: 735–62.

Sugihara, Kaoru. 1996. "The European Miracle and the East Asian Miracle: Towards a New Global Economic History." *Osaka University Economic Review* 12: 27–48.

2003. "The East Asian Path of Economic Development: A Long-Term Perspective." In *The Resurgence of East Asia: 500, 150 and 50 Years Perspectives*, edited by Giovanni Arrighi, Takeshi Hamashita and Mark Selden, 78–123. London/New York: Routledge.

Sullivan, Lawrence. 1993. "The Controversy over 'Feudal Despotism': Politics and Historiography in China, 1978 – 82." In *Using the Past to Serve the Present: Historiography and Politics in Contemporary China*, edited by Jonathan Unger, 174–204. Armonk, NY: M. E. Sharpe.

Sun, Bingying. 1984. *Ouzhou jindai shixueshi* [Modern European Historiography]. Changsha: Hunan renmin chubanshe.

Sun, Guangde. 1994. *Wan Qing chuantong yu xihua de zhenglun* [Debates over Tradition and Westernization in the Late Qing Period]. Taipei: The Commercial Press.

Sun, Hui. 2002. "Dangqian zhongguo makesi zhuyi zhexue yanjiu de jiben qushi" [Basic Trends in Current Chinese Marxist Philosophical Research]. *Zhongguo shehui kexue* [Social Science in China] 3: 117–26.

Sun, Jiang, ed. 2004. *Shijian, jiyi, xushu – xin shehuishi* [Events, Memories, and Narration – The New Social History]. Hangzhou: Zhejiang renmin chubanshe.

Sun, Yanjie and Wang Xuedian. 2000. *Gu Jiegang he tade dizimen* [Gu Jiegang and His Disciples]. Jinan: Shandong huabao chubanshe.

Sun, Zhaiwei. 2005. *Chengqing lishi – nanjing da tusha yanjiu yu sikao* [Clarify History: Research and Reflections on the Nanjing Massacre]. Nanjing: Jiangsu renmin chubanshe.

Sutcliffe, Bob. 2004. "World Inequality and Globalization." *Oxford Review of Economic Policy* 20-1: 15–37.

Sweet, James H. 2003. *Recreating Africa: Culture, Kinship, and Religion in the Afro-Portuguese World, 1441–1770*. Chapel Hill, NC: University of North Carolina Press.

Taher, Mohamed. ed. 1997. *Medieval Muslim Historiography* (= *Encyclopedic Survey of Islamic Culture* vol. 5). New Delhi: Anmol Publications.

Tan, Seng and Amitav Acharya, eds. 2008. *Bandung Revisited: The Legacy of the 1955 Asian-African Conference for International Order*. Singapore: NUS Press, 2008.

Tanaka, Stefan. 2004. 1993. *Japan's Orient. Rendering Past into History*. Berkeley: University of California Press.

New Times in Modern Japan. Princeton: Princeton University Press.

Tang, Kaijian and Peng Hui. 2005. "Shiliu dao shijiu shiji Aomen 'heiren' laiyuan kaoshu" [Research on the Origins of Macao's 'Blacks' Between the Sixteenth and the Nineteenth Centuries]. *Shijie lishi* [World History] 5: 77–83.

Tang, Xiaobing. 1996. *Global Space and the Nationalist Discourse of Modernity: The Historical Thinking of Liang Qichao*. Stanford: Stanford University Press.

Tang, Yijie. 2001. "Some Reflections on New Confucianism in Mainland Chinese Culture of the 1990s." In *Voicing Concerns: Contemporary Chinese Critical Inquiry*, edited by Gloria Davies, 123–34. Lanham, MD: Rowman & Littlefield.

2002. "Wenhua jiaoliu shi renlei wenming jinbu de licheng bei" [Cultural Relations Are the Landmarks of Progress of Human Civilization]. *Zhongxi wenhua yanjiu* [Study of Sino-Western Culture] 1: 74–83.

Tao, Dongfeng. 1996. "Guanyu jiushi niandai zhongguo wenhua yu zhishifenzi wenti de sikao" [Reflections on the Problem of Chinese Culture and Intellectuals during the 1990s]. *Zhongguo yanjiu* [China Studies] 3.

1999. "Cong huhuan xiandaihua dao fansi xiandaixing" [From Calling for Modernization to Reconsidering Modernity]. Ershiyi shiji [Twenty-first Century] 53: 15–22.

Tavakoli-Targhi, Mohamad. 2001. *Refashioning Iran: Orientalism, Occidentalism, and Historiography.* Basingstoke: Palgrave Macmillan.

Taylor, Charles. 1989. *Sources of the Self. The Making of Modern Identity.* Cambridge, MA: Harvard University Press.

Taylor, Victor E. and Charles E. Winquist. 2001. *Encyclopedia of Postmodernism.* London: Routledge.

Tenbruck, Friedrich. 1989. "Gesellschaftsgeschichte oder Weltgeschichte?" *Kölner Zeitschrift für Soziologie und Sozialforschung* 41: 417–39.

Tenfelde, Klaus, ed. 1986. *Arbeiter und Arbeiterbewegung im Vergleich: Berichte zur internationalen historischen Forschung.* Munich: Oldenbourg.

Tenfelde, Klaus and Hans-Ulrich Wehler, eds. 1994. *Wege zur Geschichte des Bürgertums.* Göttingen: Vandenhoeck & Ruprecht.

Thaden, Edward C. 1999. *The Rise of Historicism in Russia.* New York: Peter Lang.

Ther, Philipp. 2004. "Imperial Instead of National History: Positioning Modern German History on the Map of European Empires." In *Imperial Rule,* edited by Alexei Miller and Alfred J. Rieber, 47–69. Budapest/New York: Central European University Press.

Therborn, Goran. 2000. "Globalizations: Dimensions, Historical Waves, Regional Effects, Normative Governance." *International Sociology* 15-2: 151–79.

Thomas, Paul. 1994. *Alien Politics. Marxist State Theory Retrieved.* London/New York: Routledge.

Thorne, Susan. 1997. "The Conversion of Englishmen and the Conversion of the World Inseparable." In *Tensions of Empire: Colonial Cultures in a Bourgeois World,* edited by Frederick Cooper and Ann L. Stoler, 238–62. Berkeley: University of California Press.

Thornton, John. 1998. *Africa and Africans in the Making of the Atlantic World, 1400–1800.* 2nd edn. Cambridge/New York: Cambridge University Press.

Thränhardt, Dietrich. 1995. *Geschichte der Bundesrepublik Deutschland.* Frankfurt: Suhrkamp.

2000. "Einwandererkulturen und soziales Kapital." In *Einwanderer-Netzwerke und ihre Integrationsqualität in Deutschland und Israel,* edited by Dietrich Thränhardt and Uwe Hunger, 15-52. Münster: LIT.

Thränhardt, Dietrich and Uwe Hunger, eds. 2004. *Migration im Spannungsfeld von Globalisierung und Nationalstaat.* Wiesbaden: Westdeutscher Verlag.

Tilly, Charles. 1984. *Big Structures, Large Processes, Huge Comparisons.* New York: Russell Sage Foundation.

Todorova, Maria. 1997. *Imagining the Balkans.* New York: Oxford University Press.

Topik, Steven, Carlos Marichal, and Zephyr L. Frank, eds. 2006. *From Silver to Cocaine: Latin American Commodity Chains and the Building of the World Economy, 1500–2000*. Durham, NC: Duke University Press.

Townsend, Robert B. 2001. "The State of the History Department: A Report on the 1999 Department Survey." *Perspectives on History* 39–8 (November).

2008. "The Status of Women and Minority in the History Profession, 2008." *Perspectives on History* 46–6 (September).

Toynbee, Arnold. 1934–1961. *A Study of History*. 12 vols. New York: Oxford University Press.

Tracy, James, ed. 1990. *The Rise of Merchant Empires: Long Distance Trade in the Early Modern World, 1350–1750*. Cambridge/New York: Cambridge University Press.

Tsai, Weiping. 2006. "Having It All: Patriotism and Gracious Living in Shenbao's Tobacco Advertisements, 1919–1937." In *Creating Chinese Modernity. Knowledge and Everyday Life, 1900–1940*, edited by Peter Zarrow, 117–46. New York: Peter Lang.

Tu, Wei-ming. 1991. "Cultural China: The Periphery as the Center." *Dædalus* 120-2: 1–32.

ed. 1994. *The Living Tree: The Changing Meaning of Being Chinese Today*. Stanford: Stanford University Press.

ed. 1996. *Confucian Traditions in East Asian Modernity: Moral Education and Economic Culture in Japan and the Four Mini-dragons*. Cambridge, MA: Harvard University Press.

2002. "Mutual Learning as an Agenda for Social Development." In *Reflections on Multiple Modernities. European, Chinese, and Other Interpretations*, edited by Dominic Sachsenmaier, Jens Riedel, and Shumel N. Eisenstadt, 129–38. Leiden: Brill.

Tyrell, Ian. 1991. "American Exceptionalism in an Age of International History." *American Historical Review* 96-4: 1031–55.

2007. *Transnational Nation: United States History in Global Perspective since 1989*. New York: Houndmills.

Van der Linden, Marcel. 2006. "The 'Globalization' of Labour and Working Class History and Its Consequences." In *Global Labor History: A State of the Art*, edited by Jan Lucassen, 13–36. Bern/New York: Peter Lang.

2008. *Workers of the World: Essays towards a Global Labor History*. Leiden: Brill.

Van Kley, Edwin. 1971. "Europe's 'Discovery' of China and the Writing of World History." *American Historical Review* 76-2: 358–85.

Van Laak, Dirk. 1999. *Weiße Elefanten: Anspruch und Scheitern technischer Großprojekte im 20. Jahrhundert*. Stuttgart: Deutsche Verlags-Anhalt.

2004a. *Imperiale Infrastruktur: Deutsche Planungen für die Erschliessung Afrikas, 1860–1960*. Paderborn: Schöningh.

2004b. "Kolonien als 'Laboratorien der Moderne'?" In *Das Kaiserreich Transnational: Deutschland in der Welt, 1871–1914*, edited by Sebastian Conrad and Jürgen Osterhammel, 257–79. Göttingen: Vandenhoeck & Ruprecht.

2005. *Über alles in der Welt: Deutscher Imperialismus im 19. und 20. Jahrhundert*. Munich: C. H. Beck.

Van Zanden, Jan. "On Global Economic History: A Personal View on an Agenda for Future Research." International Institute for Social History. www.iisg.nl/research/jvz-research.pdf.

Veit-Brause, Irmline. 1990. "Paradigms, Schools, Traditions – Conceptualizing Shifts and Changes in the History of Historiography." *Storia della storiografia* 17: 50–65.

Vickers, Edward and Alisa Jones, eds. 2005. *History Education and National Identity in East Asia.* New York/London: Routledge.

Vittinghoff, Natascha. 2004. "Networks of News: Power, Language and Transnational Dimensions of the Chinese Press, 1850–1949." *The China Review* 4-1: 1–10.

Vogt, Joseph. 1961. *Wege zum Historischen Universum: Von Ranke bis Toynbee.* Stuttgart: Kohlhammer.

Völkel, Markus. 2006. *Geschichtsschreibung: Eine Einführung in globaler Perspektive.* Cologne: Böhlau.

Vom Bruch, Rüdiger. 1982. *Weltpolitik als Kulturmission: Auswärtige Kulturpolitik und Bildungsbürgertum in Deutschland am Vorabend des Ersten Weltkrieges.* Paderborn: Schöningh.

Von Albertini, Rudolf. 1976. *Europäische Kolonialherrschaft 1880–1940.* Zürich: Atlantis.

Von Laue, Theodore. 1987. *The World Revolution of Westernization: The Twentieth Century in Global Perspective.* New York: Oxford University Press.

Von Pflugk-Harttung, Julius, ed. 1907–1910. *Ullstein Weltgeschichte.* 6 vols. Berlin: Ullstein.

Wagner, Fritz. 1965. *Der Historiker und die Weltgeschichte.* Freiburg: Karl Alber.

Wagner, Peter. 1990. *Sozialwissenschaften und Staat: Frankreich, Italien, Deutschland 1870–1980.* Frankfurt: Campus.

Wakeman, Frederic. 1985. *The Great Enterprise: The Manchu Reconstruction of Imperial Order in 17th century China.* 2 vols. Berkeley: University of California Press, 1985.

Waley-Cohen, Joanna. 1999. *The Sextants of Beijing: Global Currents in Chinese History.* New York: W. W. Norton.

Wallerstein, Immanuel, ed. 1996. *Open the Social Sciences: Report of the Gulbenkian Commission on the Restructuring of the Social Sciences.* Stanford University Press.

   1993. "1968, Revolution in the World System." In *Geopolitics and Geoculture: Essays on the Changing World-system,* edited by Immanuel Wallerstein, 65–83. Cambridge University Press.

   1997. "Eurocentrism and Its Avatars: The Dilemmas of Social Science." *New Left Review* 226 (November–December): 93–107.

Walters, Jonathan S. 1998. *Finding Buddhists in Global History.* Washington, DC: American Historical Association, 1998.

Wang, Ban. 2004. *Illuminations from the Past: Trauma, Memory, and History in Modern China.* Stanford University Press.

Wang, Chaohua. 2003. "Introduction: Minds of the Nineties." In *One China, Many Paths,* edited by Chaohua Wang, 9–45. London: Verso.

Wang, Gungwu. 1975. "Juxtaposing Past and Present in China Today." *China Quarterly* 61: 1–24.

ed. 1997. *Global History and Migrations*. Boulder, CO: Westview Press.

Wang, Hui. 1994. "Chuantong yu xiandaixing" [Tradition and Modernity]. *Xueshu yuekan* [Academic Monthly] 6: 9–11.

1998. "Dangdai zhongguo de sixiang zhuangkuang yu xiandaixing wenti" [The State of Contemporary Chinese Thought and the Problem of Modernity]. *Wenyi zhengming* [Debates on Literature and Art] 6: 7–26.

1999. "Guanyu xiandaixing wenti dawen" [Big Questions on the Problem of Modernity]. *Tianya* [Far Corners of the Earth] 1: 18–34.

2000a. "Dangdai zhongguo de sixiang zhuangkuang yu xiandaixing wenti" [The State of Contemporary Chinese Thought and the Question of Modernity]. *Taiwan shehui yanjiu jikan* [Taiwan: A Radical Quarterly in Social Studies] 37: 1–44.

2000b. *Si huo chong wen* [Warming Up the Extinct Fire]. Beijing: Renmin wenxue chubanshe.

2002. "'Modernity' and 'Asia' in the Study of Chinese History." In *Across Cultural Borders: Historiography in Global Perspective*, edited by Eckhardt Fuchs and Benedikt Stuchtey, 309–34. Lanham, MD: Rowman & Littlefield.

2003. "The New Criticism." In *One China, Many Paths*, edited by Wang Chaohua, 55–86. London: Verso.

2004–2007. *Zhongguo xiandai sixiang de xingqi* [The Rise of Modern Chinese Thought]. 4 vols. Beijing: Sanlian shudian.

Wang, Hui and Theodore Huters. 2003. *China's New Order. Society, Politics, and Economy in Transition*. Cambridge, MA: Harvard University Press.

Wang, Jiafeng. 2009. "Some Reflection on Modernization Theory and Globalization Theory." *Chinese Studies in History* 43-1: 72–98.

Wang, Jing. 1996. *High Culture Fever: Politics, Aesthetics, and Ideology in Deng's China*. Berkeley: University of California Press.

2001. "The State Question in Chinese Popular Cultural Studies." *Inter-Asia Cultural Studies* 2-1: 35–52.

Wang, Lincong. 2002. "Lüelun 'quanqiu lishiguan'" [Outlining "Global Perspectives of History"]. *Shixue lilun yanjiu* [Historiography Quarterly] 3: 100–9.

Wang, Lixi. 2003. "Houzhimin lilun yu jidujiao zai hua chuanjiaoshi yanjiu" [Postcolonial Theory and the Study of Christian Missions in Modern China]. *Shixue lilun yanjiu* [Historiography Quarterly] 1: 31–7.

Wang, Q. Edward. 1991. "Western Historiography in the People's Republic of China [1949 to the Present]." *Storia della Storiografia* 19: 23–46.

1995. "Time Perception in Ancient Chinese Historiography." *Storia della Storiografia* 28: 69–85.

1999a. "History, Space, and Ethnicity: The Chinese Worldview." *Journal of World History* 10-2: 285–305.

1999b. "Ruhe kandai houxiandaihuazhuyi dui shixue de tiaozhan" [How to View the Postmodern Challenge to Historiography]. *Xin Shixue* [New Historiography] 10-2.

2000a. "Between Marxism and Nationalism: Chinese Historiography and the Soviet Influence, 1949–1963." *Journal of Contemporary China* 9-23: 95–111.

2000b. "Historical Writings in 20th Century China: Methodological Innovation and Ideological Influence." In *An Assessment of 20th Century Historiography: Professionalism, Methodologies, Writings*, edited by Rolf Torstendahl, 43–69. Stockholm: The Royal Academy of Letters, History and Antiquities.

2001. *Inventing China through History: The May Fourth Approach to Historiography*. Albany: SUNY Press.

2002. *Taiwan shixue wushi nian: chuancheng, fangfa, quxiang* [Taiwanese Historiography During the Past Fifty Years: Heritage, Methodologies, Trends]. Taipei: Rye Field Publications.

2003a. "Encountering the World: China and Its Other(s) in Historical Narratives, 1949–89." *Journal of World History* 14-3: 327–58.

2003b. "The Rise of Modern Historical Consciousness: A Cross-Cultural Comparison of Eighteenth-Century East Asia and Europe." *Journal of Ecumenical Studies* 40-1/2: 74–95.

2003c. "Zhongguo jindai 'xin shixue' de riben beijing – qingmo de 'lishi geming' he riben de 'wenming shixue'" [Modern Chinese Historiography and Its Japanese Backgrounds: The 'Historiographical Revolution' of the Late Qing and the 'Civilizational History' in Meiji Japan]. *Taida lishi xuebao* [Bulletin of the Department of History of National Taiwan University] 32: 191–236.

2007a. "Between Myth and History: The Construction of a National Past in Modern East Asia." In *Writing the Nation: A Global Perspective*, edited by Stefan Berger, 126–54. New York: Palgrave Macmillan.

2007b. "Is There a Chinese Mode of Historical Thinking? A Cross-Cultural Analysis." *History and Theory* 46-2: 201–19.

2009. "Modernization Theory in/of China." *Chinese Studies in History* 43-1: 3–6.

2009/2010. "Qingshi (Qing History): Why a New Dynastic History?" *Chinese Studies in History* 43-2: 3–5.

2010a. "Globalization, Global History, and Local Identity in 'Greater China.'" *History Compass* 8-4: 320–9.

2010b. "'Rise of the Great Powers' = Rise of China? Challenges of the Advancement of Global History in the People's Republic of China." *Journal of Contemporary China* 19-64: 273–89.

Wang, Rige and Song Li. 1999. "Haiyang siwei: renshi zhongguo lishi de xin shijiao – ping Yang Guozhen zhubian *haiyang yu zhongguo congshu*" [Conceptualizing the Maritime Sphere: New Perspectives on Studying Chinese History – Assessing the Series Book *The Sea and China*, edited by Yang Guozhen]. *Lishi yanjiu* [Historical Research] 6: 170–9.

Wang, Xiaodong. 1996. "Zhongguo de minzuzhuyi he zhongguo de weilai" [China's Nationalism and China's Future]. *Mingbao yuekan* [Ming Pao Monthly] 9: 12.

Wang, Xudong and Li Junxiang. 2003. "Yi xiandaihua wei zhuxian lüelun zhongguo jindaishi yanjiu" [A Short Depiction of Research in Modern Chinese History, Using the Concept of Modernization as the Main Thread]. *Shixue lilun yanjiu* [Historiography Quarterly] 3: 38–46.

Wang, Zhongfu. 1999. "Lishi rentong yu minzu rentong" [Historical Identity and People's Identity]. *Zhongguo wenhua yanjiu* [Chinese Culture Research] 3: 10–16.

Washbrook, David. 1997. "From Comparative Sociology to Global History: Britain and India in the Pre-History of Modernity." *Journal of the Economic and Social History of the Orient* 40-4: 410–43.

Watts, Sheldon. 1999. *Epidemics and History: Disease, Power and Imperialism.* New Haven: Yale University Press.

Wegmann, Heiko. "Kolonialvergangenheit und deutsche Öffentlichkeit." www.freiburg-postkolonial.de.

Wehler, Hans-Ulrich. 1969. *Bismarck und der Imperialismus.* Cologne: Kiepenheuer & Witsch.

1987–2008. *Deutsche Gesellschaftsgeschichte.* 4 vols. Munich: C. H. Beck.

1991. "Selbstverständnis und Zukunft der westdeutschen Geschichtswissenschaft." In *Geschichtswissenschaft vor 2000: Perspektiven der Historiographiegeschichte, Geschichtstheorie, Sozial- und Kulturgeschichte. Festschrift für Georg G. Iggers zum 65. Geburtstag,* edited by Konrad H Jarausch, Jörn Rüsen, and Hans Schleier, 68–81. Hagen: Rottmann.

2001. *Historisches Denken am Ende des 20. Jahrhunderts. 1945–2000.* Göttingen: Wallstein.

2002. "Das Türkenproblem." *Die Zeit* 38.

2006. "Transnationale Geschichte – der neue Königsweg historischer Forschung?" In *Transnationale Geschichte: Themen, Tendenzen und Theorien,* edited by Gunilla Budde, Sebastian Conrad, and Oliver Janz, 161–74. Göttingen: Vandenhoeck & Ruprecht.

Wei, Yuan. 1844–52. *Haiguo tuzhi* [Illustrated Treatise on the Maritime Countries]. Yangzhou: Guweitang.

Wei, Zemin. 2002. " 'Makesizhuyi zhongguohua de quanqiuxing yihan" [The Global Meaning of the 'Sinification of Marxism']. *Gongdang wenti yanjiu* 28–12: 90–91.

Weidner, Marscha Smith, ed. 2001. *Cultural Intersections in Later Chinese Buddhism.* Honolulu: University of Hawai'i Press.

Weigelin-Schwiedrzik, Susanne. 1993. "Party Historiography." In *Using the Past to Serve the Present: Historiography and Politics in Contemporary China,* edited by Jonathan Unger, 151–73. Armonk, NY: M. E. Sharpe.

1996. "On 'Shi' and 'Lun': Towards a Typology of Historiography in the PRC." *History and Theory* 35-4: 74–94.

2005. "History and Truth in Marxist Historiography." In *Historical Truth, Historical Criticism, and Ideology: Chinese Historiography and Historical Culture from a New Comparative Perspective,* edited by Helwig Schmidt-Glintzer, Achim Mittag, and Jörn Rüsen, 421–64. Leiden: Brill.

Weinberg, Gerald L. 1995. *A World at Arms: A Global History of World War II.* New York: Cambridge University Press.

Weisbrod, Bernd. 1990. "Der englische 'Sonderweg' in der neueren Geschichte." *Geschichte und Gesellschaft* 16: 233–52.

Weitz, Eric. 2003. *A Century of Genocide: Utopias of Race and Nation.* Princeton University Press, 2003.

2008. "From the Vienna to the Paris System: International Politics and the Entangled Histories of Human Rights, Forced Deportations, and Civilizing Missions." *American Historical Review* 113-5: 1313–43.

Weller, Robert P. 2006. *Discovering Nature: Globalization and Environmental Culture in China and Taiwan.* Cambridge University Press.

Welskopp, Thomas. 1994. *Arbeit und Macht im Hüttenwerk: Arbeits- und industrielle Beziehungen in der deutschen und amerikanischen Eisen- und Stahlindustrie von den 1860er Jahren bis zu den 1930er Jahren.* Bonn: Dietz.

2002. "Identität ex negativo. Der 'deutsche Sonderweg' als Metaerzählung in der bundesdeutschen Geschichtswissenschaft der siebziger und achtziger Jahre." In *Die historische Meistererzählung: Deutungslinien der deutschen Nationalgeschichte nach 1945*, edited by Konrad H. Jarausch and Martin Sabrow, 109–39. Göttingen: Vandenhoeck & Ruprecht.

Wendt, Reinhard. 2004. "Außereuropäische Geschichte am Historischen Institut der Fern-Universität Hagen." *Periplus: Jahrbuch für Aussereuropäische Geschichte* 14: 246–50.

2007. *Vom Kolonialismus zur Globalisierung. Europa und die Welt seit 1500.* Paderborn: Schöningh.

Werner, Michael. 1995. "Maßstab und Untersuchungsebene. Zu einem Grundproblem der vergleichenden Kulturtransferforschung." In *Nationale Grenzen und internationaler Austausch*, edited by Lothar Jordan and Bernd Kortländer, 20–33. Tübingen: Niemeyer.

Werner, Michael and Bénédicte Zimmermann, eds. 2004. *De la comparaison à l'histoire croisée.* Paris: Seuil.

2006. "Beyond Comparison: Histoire Croisée and the Challenge of Reflexivity." *History and Theory* 45-1: 30–50.

Weston, Timothy B. 2004. *The Power of Position: Beijing University, Intellectuals, and Chinese Political Culture, 1898–1929.* Berkeley: University of California Press.

Whitley, Richard. 1999. *Divergent Capitalisms: The Social Structuring and Change of Business Systems.* Oxford/New York: Oxford University Press.

Wiesner-Hanks, Merry. 2001. *Gender in History.* Malden, MA: Blackwell.

2007. "World History and the History of Women, Gender, and *Sexuality*." *Journal of World History* 18-1: 829–65.

Wigen, Kären E. 2005. "Cartographies of Connection. Ocean Maps as Metaphors for Interarea History." In *Interactions: Transregional Perspectives on World History*, edited by Jerry H. Bentley, Renate Bridenthal, and Anand A. Yang. Honolulu: University of Hawai'i Press: 150–66.

Wigen, Kären E. and Martin W. Lewis. 1997. *The Myth of Continents: A Critique of Metageography.* Berkeley: University of California Press.

1999. "A Maritime Response to the Crisis in Area Studies." *Geographical Review* 89-2: 161–8.

Wigger, Iris. 2007. *Die "Schwarze Schmach am Rhein": Rassische Diskriminierung zwischen Geschlecht, Rasse, Nation und Klasse.* Münster: Westfälisches Dampfboot.

Wilder, Gary. 2004. "Race, Reason, Impasse: Césaire, Fanon, and the Legacy of Emancipation." *Radical History Review* 90: 31–61.

  2005. *The French Imperial Nation-State. Négritude and Colonial Humanism Between the Two World Wars.* University of Chicago Press.

Willner, Mark. 2006. *Let's Review Global History and Geography.* 4th edn. Hauppauge, NY: Barron's Educational Series.

Wills, John E., Jr. 2002. *1688: A Global History.* New York: W. W. Norton.

Wilpert, Czarina. 1992. "The Use of Social Networks in Turkish Migration to Germany." In *International Migration Systems. A Global Approach,* edited by Mary Kritz, Lin Lean Lim and Hania Zlotnik, 177–89. Oxford: Clarendon.

Wimmer, Andreas and Nina Glick-Schiller. 2002. "Methodological Nationalism and Beyond: Nation-State Building, Migration, and the Social Sciences." *Global Networks* 2-4: 301–34.

Winkler, Heinrich August. 2000. *Der lange Weg nach Westen.* 2 vols. Munich: C. H. Beck.

  2002. "Ehehindernisse – Gegen einen EU-Beitritt der Türkei." *Süddeutsche Zeitung,* November 23.

  2004. "Aus Geschichte lernen. Zum Verhältnis von Historie und Politik in Deutschland nach 1945." *Die Zeit,* March 30.

Winnacker, Ernst-Ludwig. 2005. "Die Exzellenzinitiative: Hoffnung auf den grossen Wurf." *Forschung* 30-2: 2–3.

Wirz, Albert. 2001. "Für eine transnationale Gesellschaftsgeschichte." *Geschichte und Gesellschaft* 27: 489–98.

Wissenschaftsrat, ed. 1999. *Stellungnahme zu den Geisteswissenschaftlichen Auslandsinstituten.* Cologne: Wissenschaftsrat.

  ed. 2006. *Empfehlungen zu den Regionalstudien (area studies) in den Hochschulen und ausseruniversitären Forschungseinrichtungen.* Mainz: Wissenschaftsrat.

Wittrock, Björn. 2000. "Modernity: One, None, or Many? European Origins and Modernity as a Global Condition." *Dædalus* 129-1: 31–60.

Wolf, Eric R. 1982. *Europe and the People Without History.* Berkeley: University of California Press.

Wolfe, Patrick. 1997. "History and Imperialism: A Century of Theory, from Marx to Postcolonialism." *American Historical Review* 102-2: 388–420.

Wolff, Larry. 1994. *Inventing Eastern Europe: The Map of Civilization on the Mind of the Enlightenment.* Stanford University Press.

Woll, Allen. 1982. *A Functional Past: The Uses of History in Nineteenth Century Chile.* Baton Rouge: Louisiana State University Press.

Wong, R. Bin. 1997. *China Transformed: Historical Change and the Limits of the European Experience.* Ithaca, NY: Cornell University Press.

Woodside, Alexander. 2006. *Lost Modernities: China, Vietnam, Korea and the Hazards of World History.* Cambridge, MA: Harvard University Press.

Woolf, Daniel R. ed. 1998. *A Global Encyclopedia of Historical Writing.* 2 vols. New York: Garland Publishing.

2005. "Historiography." In *New Dictionary of the History of Ideas*, edited by Maryanne C. Horowitz, 35–85. New York: Charles Scribner's Sons.

2011. *A Global History of History: The Making of Clio's Empire from Antiquity to the Present*. Cambridge University Press.

Wright, David. 2000. "Yan Fu and the Tasks of the Translator." In *New Terms for New Ideas: Western Knowledge and Lexical Change in Late Imperial China*, edited by Michael Lackner, Iwo Amelung, and Joachim Kurtz, 235–56. Leiden: Brill.

Wright, Gwendolyn. 1991. *The Politics of Design in French Colonial Urbanism*. University of Chicago Press.

Wright, Theresa. 2007. "Disincentives for Democratic Change in China." *AsiaPacific Issues* 82: 2–8.

Wu, Yin. 2003. "Shijieshi de xueke dingwei yu fazhan fangxiang – zai 'xinshiji shijieshi xueke jianshe' xueshu yantaohui shang de jianghua" [The Position and Developmental Directions of World Historical Scholarship – Speech on the Symposium 'Establishing World Historical Sciences for the New Century']. *Shijie lishi* [World History] 1: 6–7.

Wu, Yujin. 1995. *Wu Yujin xueshu lunzhu zixuanji* [Personally Selected Academic Works by Wu Yujin]. Beijing: Shoudu shifan daxue chubanshe.

Wu, Yujin and Qi Shirong, eds. 1994. *Shijie shi* [World History]. 3 vols. Beijing: Gaodeng jiaoyu chubanshe.

Wu, Zhiliang. 2002. "Aomen lishi yanjiu shuping – jiantan zhongguo yu xifang de guandian yu fangfa zhi goutong" [Review of Historical Studies on Macao – Considering Exchanges of Perspectives and Methods between China and the West]. *Shixue lilun yanjiu* [Historiography Quarterly] 1: 43–54.

Xia, Jiguo and Wan Lanjuan. 2006. "Teaching World History at Chinese Universities – A Survey." *Comparativ* 16-1: 66–77.

Xiang, Xiang, Song Faqing, Wang Jiafeng and Li Hongtu. 1999a. "Ershi shiji zhongguo de shijieshi yanjiu" [World Historical Research in Twentieth-century China] (Part I). *Xueshu yuekan* [Academic Monthly] 7: 93–6.

1999b. "Ershi shiji zhongguo de shijieshi yanjiu" [World Historical Research in Twentieth-century China] (Part II). *Xueshu yuekan* [Academic Monthly] 8: 99–109.

Xiao, Gongqin. 1995. "Wuxu bianfa de zai fanxing – jianlun zaoqi zhengzhi jijin zhuyi de wenhua genyua" [A Reconsideration of the Wuxu Movement: Discussing the Cultural Origins of Early Political Radicalism]. *Zhanlüe yu guanli* [Strategy and Management] 4: 11–20.

Xie, Xialing. 1994. "Shehui kexue yanjiu guannian bixu gexin" [The Perspectives of Social Scientific Research Must Be Reformed]. *Xueshu yuekan* [Academic Monthly] 4: 4–6.

Xiong, Yuezhi. 1994. *Xixue Dongjian yu wan Qing shehui* [The Dissemination of Western Knowledge and Late Qing Society]. Shanghai: Shanghai renmin chubanshe.

1996. "*Haiguo Tuzhi* zhengyin xishu kaoshi" [An Investigation of Western Writings referred to in Haiguo Tuzhi]. *Zhonghua wenshi luncong* [Journal of Chinese Literature and History] 55: 235–58.

Xu, Ben. 1998. "From Modernity to 'Chineseness': The Rise of Nativist Cultural Theory in Post-1989 China." *Positions* 6-1: 203–37.
 1999. *Disenchanted Democracy: Chinese Criticism after 1989*. Ann Arbor: University of Michigan Press.
Xu, Jilin. 1997. "Fan Xifangzhuyi bu dengyu xiandai minzuzhuyi" [Anti-Westernism Is Not Modern Ethnic Nationalism]. *Mingbao yuekan* [Ming Pao Monthly] 3: 22–6.
 1999. *Ling yizhong qimeng* [Another Type of Enlightenment]. Guangzhou: Huacheng chubanshe.
 2000. "The Fate of an Enlightenment – Twenty Years in the Chinese Intellectual Sphere (1978–98)." *East Asian History* 20: 169–86.
 2004. "Zhongguo de minzu zhuyi: yige juda er kongdong de fuhao" [China's Nationalism – a Huge and Hollow Signifier]. In *Qianliu – dui xiayi minzu zhuyi de pipan yu fansi* [Undercurrents – Critiques and Reflections on Narrow Nationalism], edited by Le Shan, 40–8. Shanghai: Huadong shifan daxue chubanshe.
Xu, Jilin and Chen Dakai. 1995. "Zhongguo xiandaihua de qidong leixing yu fanying xingzhi" [The Initializing Patterns and Reacting Natures of Chinese Modernization]. In *Zhongguo xiandaihua shi 1800–1949* [History of Modernization in China, 1800–1949], edited by Jilin Xu and Chen Dakai, 1–5. Shanghai: Sanlian shudian.
Xu, Kai, Xu Jian, and Chen Yuliang. 2006. "Zhongde guanxi shi yanjiu" [Research on the History of Sino-German Relations, 1996–2005]. *Chinese History and Society/Berliner China-Hefte*: 121–38.
Xu, Lan. 2001. "Jiushi niandai woguo xiandai guoji guanxishi yanjiu zongshu" [A Summary on Research During the 1990s on the History of China's Modern International Relations]. *Shixue lilun yanjiu* [Historiography Quarterly] 2: 144–51.
 2004. "Cong 'xiouzhongxin shiguan' dao 'wenming xingtai shiguan' he 'quanqiu shiguan.'" [From 'Western Europe-centrism' to 'Perspectives Focusing on Cultural Conditions' and 'Global Perspectives']. *Lishi yanjiu* [Historical Research] 4: 24–7.
Xu, Luo. 2002. *Searching for Life's Meaning: Changes and Tensions in the Worldviews of Chinese Youth in the 1980s*. Ann Arbor, MI: University of Michigan Press.
 2007. "Reconstructing World History in the People's Republic of China Since the 1980s." *Journal of World History* 18-3: 325–50.
 2010. "The Rise of World History Studies in Twentieth-Century China." *History Compass* (August 4), http://historycompass.wordpress.com.
Yan, Guangcai. 2009. "The Construction of the Chinese Academic System: Its History and Present Challenges." *Frontiers of Education in China* 4-3: 323–42.
Yan, Yunxiang. 2002. "Managed Globalization. State Power and Cultural Transition in China." In *Many Globalizations: Cultural Diversity in the Contemporary World*, edited by Peter Berger and Samuel Huntington, 19–47. New York & Oxford: Oxford University Press.
Yang, Nianqun, ed. 2001. *Kongjian, jiyi, shehui zhuanxing – 'xin shehuishi' yanjiu lunwen jingxuan ji* [Space, Memory and Social Changes: Selected Research

Essays on the 'New Social History']. Shanghai: Shanghai renmin chubanshe.

2002. "'Guoduqi' lishi de lingyimian" [The Other Side of the History of 'Transitional Periods']. *Dushu* [Reading] 6: 128–35.

Yao, Daxue. 2002. "Xiandaihua shiye zhong de quanqiuhua" [Globalization in the Perspective of Modernization]. *Shixue lilun yanjiu* [Historiography Quarterly] 1: 36–42.

Ye, Weili. 2001. *Seeking Modernity in China's Name: Chinese Students in the United States, 1900–1927.* Stanford University Press.

Yeh, Haiyan. 2003. "Rujia zhexue de dangdai xingtai jiqi kenengxing yanjiu: yi Liu Shuxian yu Tu Weiming wei li" [The Modern Form of Confucian Philosophy and Studies on the Possible: The Examples of Liu Shuxian and Tu Wei-ming]. *Zhexue yu wenhua* [Universitas: Monthly Review of Philosophy and Culture] 30-5: 19–39.

Yeh, Wen-hsin. 1990. *The Alienated Academy. Culture and Politics in Republican China, 1911–1937.* Cambridge, MA: Harvard University Press.

Yi, Mu. 2001. "Shijie wenhua de duoyuan yitihua bulü" [Paths Towards a Pluralistic Integration of World Culture]. *Shixue lilun yanjiu* [Historiography Quarterly] 2: 158–59.

Yi, Zhaoyin, ed. 2000. *Shijie wenhua lishi* [History of World Culture]. Shanghai: Huadong shifan daxue chubanshe.

Yin, Da, ed. 1985. *Zhongguo shixue fazhanshi* [The History of the Development of Chinese Historiography]. Zhengzhou: Zhongzhou guji chubanshe.

Young, John W. and John Kent. 2004. *International Relations since 1945: A Global History.* New York: Oxford University Press.

Young, Robert J. C. 1990. *White Mythologies: Writing History and the West.* London/New York: Routledge.

2001. *Postcolonialism: An Historical Introduction.* Oxford/Malden, MA: Blackwell.

Yu, Heping, ed. 2001. *Zhongguo xiandaihua licheng* [The Journey of Chinese Modernization]. 3 vols. Nanjing: Jiangsu renmin chubanshe.

Yu, Pei. 1994. "Zhuanxing zhong de lishi kexue" [Historical Scholarship in Transition]. *Shijie Lishi* [World History] 5: 11–18.

2000. "Meiyou lilun jiu meiyou lishi kexue – ershi shiji wo guo shixue lilun yanjiu de huigu he sikao" [If There Is No Theory, There Is No Historical Scholarship – Reviews and Reflections on Research in Historical Theory in Twentieth-century China]. *Shixue lilun yanjiu* [Historiography Quarterly] 3: 5–20.

2001. "Quanqiuhua yu 'quanqiu lishiguan'" [Globalization and Global Conceptions of History]. *Shixue jikan* [Collected Papers of History Studies] 2: 1–12.

2003. "Dui dangdai zhongguo shijieshi yanjiu lilun tixi he huayu xitong de sikao" [Reflections on the Theoretical Systems and Chinese Networks in Contemporary Chinese World Historical Research]. *Institute of World History.* worldhistory.cass.cn/index/xueshujiangtan/xsjt_txt/20030627001.htm.

2004. "Hongyang zhongguo shijjieshi yanjiu de minzu jingshen" [Uphold the National Spirit in World Historical Research]. *Shijie lishi* [World History] 5: 4–12.

2006. *Shijieshi yanjiu* [World History Studies]. Fuzhou: Fujian renmin chubanshe.

2007a. "Quanqiushiguan he zhongguo shixue duanxiang." [Global Historical Perspectives and Detailed Visions of Chinese Historiography]. In *Quanqiuhua he quanqiushi* [Globalization and Global History], edited by Pei Yu, 1–10. Beijing: Shehui kexue wenxian chubanshe.

ed. 2007b. *Quanqiuhua he quanqiushi* [Globalization and Global History]. Beijing: Shehui kexue wenxian chubanshe.

2009. "Global History and National Historical Memory." *Chinese Studies in History* 42-3: 25–44.

Yu, Wujin. 2002. "'Quanqiuhua' wenti de zhexue fansi" [Philosophical Reconsiderations of the Problems of Globalization]. *Xueshu yuekan* [Academic Monthly] 5 (2002): 11–31.

Yuan, Weishi. 1996. "Jiusi yisheng de zhongguo xiandaihua" [The Nine Deaths and One Life of Chinese Modernization]. *Yazhou Yanjiu* [Asia Studies] 18.

Yue, Qingping. 2003. "Nuli tuozhan shehuishi yanjiu de shendu he guangdu – zhongguo shehuishi disici yantaohui shuping" [Eagerly Driving Forward the Deepening and Broadening of Social Historical Research – Report on the Fourth Conference of Chinese Social History]. *Zhongguo yanjiu dongtai* 1: 3–9.

Yuzo, Mizoguchi and Sun Ge. 2001. "Guanyu 'zhizhi gongtongti'" [On a 'Knowledge Community']. *Kaifang Shidai* [Open Times] 11: 5–22.

Zanasi, Margherita. 2006. *Saving the Nation: Economic Modernity in Republican China*. University of Chicago Press.

Zantop, Susanne. 1999. *Kolonialphantasien im vorkolonialen Deutschland, 1770–1870*. Berlin: E. Schmidt.

Zeller, Joachim. 2000. *Kolonialdenkmäler und Geschichtsbewusstsein. Eine Untersuchung der kolonialdeutschen Erinnerungskultur*. Frankfurt: IKO-Verlag für Interkulturelle Kommunikation.

Zeng, Ling. 2003. "Huanan haiwai yimin yu zongzu shehui zai jian – yi xinjiapo panjiacun wei yanjiu gean." [Maritime Migrants from Southern China and the Rebuilding of Lineage Society: A Case Study on the Pan Family Village in Singapore]. *Shijie lishi* [World History] 6: 77–84.

Zhang, Binfeng. 2001. "Zhongguo gudai jiujing youmeiyou luoji – dui zhongguo gudai luoji yanjiu de yizhong xin shenshi" [Whether There Was Logic in Ancient China – A New Examination of the Study of Logic in Ancient China]. *Zhexue yu wenhua* [Universitas: Monthly Review of Philosophy and Culture] 28-4: 359–80.

Zhang, Chunnian. 1994. "Zhongguo shixue ying zouxiang shijie" [Chinese Historiography Should Walk towards the World]. *Shijie lishi* [World History] 5: 113–14.

Zhang, Fa, Wang Yichuan, and Zhang Yiwu. 1994. "Cong 'xiandaixing' dao 'zhonghuaxing'– xin zhishi de tanxun" [From "Modernity" to "Chineseness": Exploring New Types of Knowledge]. *Wenyi zhengming* [Debates on Literature and Art] 2: 10–20.

Zhang, Guangzhi. 2000. "Ershiyi shiji zhongguo de xifang shixue lilun yanjiu zhuyi" [Paying Attention to Research on Western Historiographical Theory in Twenty-first-century China]. *Shixue lilun yanjiu* [Historiography Quarterly] 4: 59–62.

Zhang, Haipeng. 2002. "2000 nian zhongguo jindaishi yanjiu xueshu dongtai gaishu" [Report on Trends in the Scholarship on Modern Chinese History in the Year 2000]. *Jindaishi yanjiu* [Modern Chinese History Studies] 1: 200–44.

Zhang, Hongyi. 1992. "Sishi nian lai shijie xiandaishi yanjiu de lilun fansi" [Theoretical Reconsiderations of Research on the World's Modernization during the Past Forty Years]. *Shixue lilun yanjiu* [Historiography Quarterly] 2: 36–46.

Zhang, Kuan. 1999. "The Predicament of Postcolonial Criticism in China." In *Chinese Thought in a Global Context: A Dialogue between Western and Chinese Philosophical Approaches*, edited by Karl-Heinz Pohl, 58–70. Leiden: Brill.

Zhang, Longxi. 1998. *Mighty Opposites: From Dichotomies to Differences in the Comparative Study of China*. Stanford: Stanford University Press.

Zhang, Ming and Li Shitao, eds. 1999. *Zhishifenzi lichang* [The Standpoint of Intellectuals]. 3 vols. Changchun: Shidai wenyi chubanshe.

Zhang, Shuli. 2001. "Circumscribing the Cartographies of Formosa: Motherhood, Motherland, and Modernities." *Zhongshan renwen xuebao* [Sun Yat-sen Journal of Humanities] 12: 45–63.

Zhang, Weiwei. 2008. "Teaching World History at Nankai: A Noncentric and Holistic Approach." In *Global Practice in World History: Advances Worldwide*, edited by Patrick Manning, 69–80. Princeton: M. Wiener.

Zhang, Xudong. 1997. *Chinese Modernism in the Era of Reforms: Cultural Fever, Avant-Garde Fiction, and the New Chinese Cinema*. Durham, NC: Duke University Press.

    1999. "Hou xiandaizhuyi yu zhongguo xiandaixing" [Postmodernism and Chinese Modernity]. *Dushu* [Reading] 12: 12–20.

Zhang, Yiping. 2001. "Lun shijie lishi zhengti jiqi xingcheng" [On the Holistic Character of World History and Its Formation]. *Beijing daxue xuebao (Zhexue shehui kexue ban)* [Journal of Peking University (Philosophy and Social Sciences)] S1: 56–62.

Zhang, Yiping and Hu Suping. 1999. "Lun makesizhuyi de shijie lishi zhengti guan" [On Holistic Perspectives in Marxist World History]. *Shixue lilun yanjiu* [Historiography Quarterly] 4: 5–13.

Zhang, Yonghua. 1998. "Hou xiandai guannian yu lishixue" [Postmodern Ideas and Historiography]. *Shixue lilun yanjiu* [Historiography Quarterly] 3: 62–71.

Zhang, Yuanxin and He Chuanqi. 2004. "Miaohui zhongguo lantu de xiandaihua lilun tuohuang ren" [Pioneers in Outlining the Blueprint of China's Modernization Theory]. *Jingbao* [The Mirror], 323.

Zhang, Zhilian. 1995. *Cong "tongjian" dao renquan yanjiu* [From Studies on the Comprehensive Mirror to Studies of Human Rights]. Beijing: Sanlian shudian.

Zhao, Mei. 2006. "Chinese Views of America: A Survey." In *Chinese Images of the United States*, edited by Carola McGiffert, 59–76. Washington: CSIS Press.

Zhao, Shiyu. 2002. "Lishi renleixue: faxian lishi shiqi nüxing de lishi jiyi shifou you le keneng?" [Historical Anthropology: Is There a Possibility for Including the History of Women in a Period of Historiographical Development?]. *Lishi yanjiu* [Historical Research] 6: 150–2.

Zhao, Shiyu and Ding Qingping. 2001. "Ershi shiji zhongguo shehuixue yanjiu de huigu yu sikao" [A Review and Reflection on Chinese Social History Studies During the Twentieth Century]. *Lishi yanjiu* [Historical Research] 6: 157–72.

Zhao, Suisheng. 1997. "Chinese Intellectuals' Quest for National Greatness and Nationalistic Writing in the 1990s." *China Quarterly* 152: 725–45.

2004. *A Nation-State by Construction: Dynamics of Modern Chinese Nationalism*. Stanford University Press.

Zhao, Xifang. 2004. "Yizhong zhuyi, sanzhong mingyun – houzhiminzhuyi zai liangan sandi de lilun lüxing" [One ism, Three Destinies – The Theoretical Journeys of Post-Colonialism in Three Places on Both Sides of the Taiwan Straits]. *Jiangsu shehui kexue* [Jiangsu Social Sciences] 4: 106–10.

Zhao, Yong. 2005. "Pipan jingshen de chenlun – zhongguo dangdai wenhua piping bingyin zhi wojian" [The Disintegration of Critical Spirit: On the Pathogeny of Contemporary Chinese Cultural Criticism]. *Wenyi Yanjiu* [Literature and Art Studies] 12: 4–12.

Zhao, Yuan. 2006. *Zhidu, yanlun, xintai – mingqing zhiji shidafu yanjiu* [System, Discourse, and Ways of Thinking: Research on Literati during the Ming Qing Transition Period]. Beijing: Beijing daxue chubanshe.

Zheng, Kuangmin. 2001. *Liang qichao qimeng sixiang de dongxue beijing* [The Eastern Studies Background of Liang Qichao's Enlightenment Thought]. Shanghai: Shanghai shudian chubanshe.

Zheng, Su. 2010. *Claiming Diaspora. Music, Transnationalism, and Cultural Politics in Asian/Chinese America*. New York: Oxford University Press.

Zheng, Yongnian. 1999. *Discovering Chinese Nationalism in China: Modernization, Identity, and International Relations*. Cambridge: Cambridge University Press.

2004. *Globalization and State Transformation in China*. Cambridge University Press.

Zhou, Gucheng. 1949. *Shijie Tongshi* [General World History]. 3 vols. Shanghai: Shangwu yinshuguan.

1961. "Ping meiyou shijie xing de shijieshi" [Analysing World History without a World Character]. *Guangming ribao*, February 7.

Zhou, Huimin. 2000. "Cong xifang jingyan kan Taiwan de 'lishi yishi' " [Looking at Taiwanese 'Historical Consciousness' from Western Experiences]. *Jindai Zhongguo* [Modern China] 136: 81–93.

Zhu, Youhuan, ed. 1992. *Zhongguo jindai xuezhi shiliao* [Historical Materials for the Modern Chinese School System]. Vol. 1 part 3. Shanghai: Huadong shifan daxue chubanshe.

Ziebura, Gilbert. 1990. "Die Rolle der Sozialwissenschaften in der westdeutschen Historiographie der internationalen Beziehungen." *Geschichte und Gesellschaft* 16: 79–103.

Zimmerer, Jürgen. 2003. "Krieg, KZ und Völkermord in Südwestafrika: Der erste deutsche Genozid." In *Völkermord in Deutsch-Südwestafrika: Der Kolonialkrieg (1904–1908) in Namibia und seine Folgen*, edited by Jürgen Zimmerer and Joachim Zeller, 45–63. Berlin: Links.

2004a. "Die Geburt des 'Ostlandes' aus dem Geiste des Kolonialismus. Die nationalsozialistische Eroberungs- und Beherrschungspolitik in (post) kolonialer Perspektive." *Sozial.Geschichte* 19-1: 10–43.

ed. 2004b. *Verschweigen – Erinnern – Bewältigen. Vergangenheitspolitik in globaler Perspektive (= Comparativ 14-5/6)*. Leipzig: Leipziger Universitätsverlag.

Zimmermann, Bruno and Sabine Mönkemöller. 1997. "Graduitertenkollegs: Eine Zwischenbilanz." In *Studienreform Geschichte – kreativ*, edited by Wolfgang Schmale, 351–8. Bochum: Dieter Winkler.

Zinn, Howard. 1980. *A People's History of the United States*. New York: HarperCollins.

Zips, Werner, ed. 2003. *Afrikanische Diaspora: Out of Africa – Into New Worlds*. Münster: Lit.

Zufferey, Nicolas. 1999. "The Development of German Sinology from a French Viewpoint." In *Chinawissenschaften – Deutschsprachige Entwicklungen: Geschichte, Personen, Perspektiven*, edited by Helmut Martin and Christiane Hammer. Hamburg: Institut für Asienkunde.

Zürcher, Erik. 1959. *The Buddhist Conquest of China: The Spread and Adaptation of Buddhism in Early Medieval China*. 2 vols. Leiden: Brill.

Zurndorfer, Harriet T. 1997. "China and 'Modernity': The Uses of the Study of Chinese History in the Past and the Present." *Journal of the Economic and Social History of the Orient* 40-4: 461–85.

Index

For EU product safety concerns, contact us at Calle de José Abascal, 56–1°,
28003 Madrid, Spain or eugpsr@cambridge.org.